THIRTEEN WAYS TO STEAL A BICYCLE

THIRTEEN WAYS
TO STEAL A BICYCLE

THEFT LAW IN THE INFORMATION AGE

Stuart P. Green

HARVARD UNIVERSITY PRESS

Cambridge, Massachusetts, and London, England

2012

Library of Congress Cataloging-in-Publication Data

Green, Stuart P.
  Thirteen ways to steal a bicycle : theft law in the information age / Stuart P. Green.
    p. cm.
  Includes bibliographical references and index.
  ISBN 978-0-674-04731-0
  1. Theft—English-speaking countries. I. Title. II. Title: 13 ways to steal a bicycle.
  K5217.G74 2012
  345'.0262—dc23   2011036613

For Jennifer,
who stole my heart

Contents

Preface

The idea for this book grew out of two seemingly unconnected series of news events of the past decade. In 2002, Doris Kearns Goodwin and Stephen Ambrose, two popular historians whose work I admired, were accused, separately, of committing plagiarism. As a criminal law scholar, I was intrigued by repeated references to their acts as a kind of "theft," and I began to wonder what it might mean to "steal" ideas, words, intellectual property, and other intangibles. Then, in 2005, Hurricane Katrina struck my then–home state of Louisiana, and I watched with bewilderment as New Orleans fell victim to extensive looting. In some cases, these lootings involved opportunistic and predatory conduct that seemed even more blameworthy than ordinary theft. In other cases, the perpetrators were otherwise law-abiding citizens who found themselves in circumstances of necessity, without food, clean water, or medicine; their acts did not seem particularly blameworthy at all. Watching all of this unfold on television, I began to think about both the moral significance of the means by which theft is carried out and the relationship between theft law and the broader economic order.

My reflection on these two otherwise unrelated series of events led me, in turn, to begin thinking more generally about theft's legal and normative foundations. In 2006, I published a book on the moral theory of white collar crime that touched briefly on the concept of stealing, but I realized soon thereafter that there was much more to say on the subject. I wanted to explore the basic conceptual framework of theft law and to assess its continuing applicability in an age in which the economy is increasingly based on the commodification of information and other intangibles, where the means of committing theft and fraud have become increasingly sophisticated, and where the gap between rich and poor continues to grow.

The time for such a study is ripe: It has been a half century since the Model Penal Code sought to rewrite the American law of theft, and nearly as long since enactment of the similarly influential English Theft Act. In the intervening years, criminal law theory has made significant strides. The demands of retributivism in particular have emerged as a central focus of analysis. Yet the law and theory of theft have remained largely stuck in the 1960s. My goal in this book is to bring them into the twenty-first century.

*   *   *

The stealing of bicycles referred to in the title provides an image that recurs throughout the book. More than a million bikes are stolen in the United States every year; many readers will have experienced such thefts firsthand. One can imagine a wide range of different ways in which a bicycle could, at least theoretically, be stolen: most commonly, by means of stealth (larceny), but also by means of force (robbery), deception (fraud or false pretenses), coercion (extortion), breach of trust (embezzlement), and so on. One can also imagine the misappropriation of bike-related services (say, using deception to obtain a ride in a bicycle taxi) and bike-related intangible property (like stealing a trade secret regarding a new bicycle production method). If one adds up all of the different ways of stealing bikes and bike-related property that are mentioned in the book, the total comes out to thirteen. But the precise number is not really so important. The main sense of the title is metaphorical: It is meant to convey the messy complexity that characterizes theft law's moral content, of which this book seeks to make sense.

Acknowledgments

It is often said that the best way to learn a subject is to teach it. In my experience, writing a book works too. In my efforts to learn about the many issues that are explored in what follows, I benefited from the knowledge and expertise of many generous friends and colleagues. Those I managed to keep track of (and my apologies to those I've failed to mention) include Annalise Acorn, Peter Alldridge, Andrew Ashworth, Douglas Baird, Jim Bowers, Mike Cahill, James Chalmers, Markus Dubber, Lindsay Farmer, Marcelo Ferrante, David Gray, Emanuel Gross, Audrey Guinchard, Winifred Holland, Jeremy Horder, Tatjana Hörnle, Kyron Huigens, Sonia Katyal, Wayne Logan, Michelle Madden Dempsey, Sam Mandel, Dan Markel, Emanuel Melissaris, Gerry Moohr, David Ormerod, Iñigo Ortíz de Urbina Gimeno, Eduardo Peñalver, Rosemary Peters, Paul Roberts, Paul Robinson, Ron Scalise, Jennifer Smyre, the late Bill Stuntz, Victor Tadros, Malcolm Thorburn, and Lloyd Weinreb. Thanks also to my Rutgers colleagues, including Dean John Farmer, Vera Bergelson, Adil Haque, Sabrina Safrin, George Thomas, Reid Weisbord, and the erudite John Leubsdorf; to my former colleagues at Louisiana State University, where my work on this book began; and to participants at colloquia at the Universities of Edinburgh and London, Florida State University, Louisiana State University, New York University, Pace University, and Rutgers University. No doubt I misappropriated ideas from all of them.

A few others deserve special mention: Antony Duff and Doug Husak provided their usual generous mix of advice, criticism, encouragement, and inspiration. Alex Steel read and offered comments on each chapter as I wrote them, and shared with me his enthusiasm for and encyclopedic knowledge of theft law. Ken Simons also read the whole manuscript and had numerous insightful suggestions for improvement. Matthew Kugler made major contributions to the empirical study of theft seriousness described in Chapter 1, and stimulated my thinking about empirical desert more generally. Paul Axel-Lute and Phyllis Schultze, two exceptional librarians at Rutgers Law School, responded promptly to countless calls for help. Jordon Steele, at the University of Pennsylvania's Biddle Law Library, guided me helpfully through Penn's Model Penal Code archive. Elizabeth Knoll, my editor at Harvard University Press, encouraged me to write this book when it was no more than a half-baked idea in an email, and continued to offer encouragement throughout.

Various pieces of this book have appeared previously in print. I am grateful to the following publications for their permission to use those materials here: "Plagiarism, Norms, and the Limits of Theft Law: Some Observations on the Use of Criminal Sanctions in Enforcing Intellectual Property Rights," 54 *Hastings Law Journal* 167–242 (2002), in Chapter 4; "Consent and the Grammar of Theft Law," 28 *Cardozo Law Review* 2505–22 (2007), and "Looting, Law, and Lawlessness," 81 *Tulane Law Review* 1129–74 (2007), in Chapter 2; "Theft by Omission," in James Chalmers, Lindsay Farmer, and Fiona Leverick (eds.), *Essays in Criminal Law in Honour of Sir Gerald Gordon* (Edinburgh: Edinburgh University Press, 2010), pp. 158–77, in Chapter 3; "Community Perceptions of Theft Seriousness: A Challenge to Model Penal Code and English Theft Act Consolidation" (with Matthew Kugler), 7 *Journal of Empirical Legal Studies* 511–37 (2010), in Chapter 1; and "Thieving and Receiving: Overcriminalizing the Possession of Stolen Property," 14 *New Criminal Law Review* 35–54 (2011), in Chapter 3.

*   *   *

My wife, Jennifer Moses, to whom this book is dedicated, is quite simply the best thing that ever happened to me. Our children, Samuel, Rose, and Jonathan, did not really help that much with the book, but I am tremendously proud of each of them nonetheless. I would also like to acknowledge the contributions of Marion and Amir, who provided good company through thousands of hours of work, with only occasional breaks for tummy rubs.

THIRTEEN WAYS TO STEAL A BICYCLE

Introduction

The crime of theft holds a prominent place in our law and in our culture. It claims more victims and causes greater economic injury, and it may well be committed by a larger number of offenders, than any other criminal offense.[1] The act of stealing—of unlawfully treating *tuum* as *meum*—entails one of the most basic wrongs a person can do to another. It seems likely that prohibitions on theft have been with us for as long as people have made laws and laid claim to property; it is hard to imagine any organized society without them.

Yet theft remains an enigma. For all its timelessness, it is striking that what constituted theft in early eighteenth century England is so different from what constitutes theft in the Anglophone world today. Despite the universality of theft, it is puzzling that different legal systems have sought to conceptualize and structure theft law in such apparently disparate ways. And despite theft's obvious status as one of criminal law's core offenses, there remain fundamentally unresolved questions about exactly what should count as stealing and exactly what types of things can be stolen.

This book seeks to give theft law the thoroughgoing normative analysis that it deserves and that, in recent years, it has failed to receive. The need for such a study has never been greater: In the fifty years since promulgation of the Model Penal Code, and forty-five years since enactment of the English Theft Act, the world has changed dramatically. Information and intellectual property have come to play an increasingly significant role in our economy; the means of committing

1

theft and fraud have grown increasingly sophisticated; and the gap between rich and poor has continued to grow. Meanwhile, criminal law theory has evolved, offering insights into the rationale for, and proper scope of, criminalization that simply could not have been foreseen at mid-century.

The offense of theft that emerges from this book constitutes a uniquely complex crime, encompassing a broad range of conduct, and reflecting two competing sources of normative content. On the one hand, it reflects a prelegal, universal, and naturalistic conception that stealing is in some sense morally wrong. On the other hand, it is dependent on a highly legalized, culturally specific, and positivist conception that turns on technical notions of property, ownership, abandonment, and the like. Indeed, theft law is dependent on the law of personal property, intellectual property, contract, and agency in ways that no other criminal offense is.

The theory of theft outlined in the pages that follow takes account of both retributive and consequentialist considerations. It offers original empirical research into how theft is viewed by the general public and seeks to explain the deeper conceptual thinking that might explain such intuitive judgments. It draws on insights found in moral and political philosophy, legal history, law and economics, social psychology, and criminology. It considers how theft is dealt with in a wide range of legal systems and offers a glimpse of how theft law would function in societies with radically different systems of property ownership. And it considers how the terms *theft* and *stealing* function in our legal and moral discourse, paying particular attention to the sometimes blurry line between literal and metaphorical usage, as when we talk about identity theft, theft of trade secrets, the federal Stolen Valor Act, and plagiarism as theft.

Along the way, the book offers solutions to a host of real-world puzzles arising out of cases such as those involving:

- the magistrate judge who failed to look for the owner of a Rolex watch he found on the floor of a supermarket, and instead gave it to his wife as a birthday gift;
- the Internet user who parked his car outside a Seattle coffee shop and, without ever buying anything, regularly accessed the shop's wireless network;

- the Internet activist who received copies of tens of thousands of confidential U.S. State Department documents, gave them to leading media outlets, and published them on his Web site, WikiLeaks;
- the doctors who, without their patient's permission, used his tissue to harvest a fabulously valuable cell line;
- the woman who wrote letters to the movie star Clark Gable demanding child support for a child she falsely claimed she and Gable had conceived, even though she knew they had never had sexual relations;
- office workers who take office supplies home from work for use on non-work–related projects;
- the editor of a technology blog who bought a lost prototype iPhone from a man who had found it in a Silicon Valley bar;
- the bootlegger who, during Prohibition, stole whiskey from another bootlegger;
- the elderly Florida man who was charged under the federal Stolen Valor Act with falsely telling others that he had won a Medal of Honor;
- the would-be john who falsely promised a prostitute he would pay for sex and then failed to do so;
- the Sardinian tourist, vacationing in London, who took a teddy bear that had been left as a memorial to Princess Diana from outside the gates of St. James's Palace;
- the college student who sneaked into a classroom to read an examination in advance of its administration and left after memorizing the questions but without ever physically taking the paper on which the exam was written; and
- the Internet entrepreneur who allegedly stole from several Harvard classmates the idea for a social network Web site, and turned it into Facebook.

The text will show that the resolution of each of these and other puzzling cases almost invariably depends on the resolution of deeper conceptual issues in the theory of theft.

A ROAD MAP

Chapter 1 offers a critique of twentieth century Anglo-American theft law reform. At the beginning of the century, reformers on both sides of the Atlantic had become convinced that the common law of theft was badly in need of revision. A series of judicial decisions, legislative enactments, and so-called historical accidents had created a piecemeal collection of seemingly arbitrary, overly technical, loophole-ridden legal rules. The reformers were determined to scrap the old law of theft and essentially start over. In the Model Penal Code, the English Theft Act 1968, the Canadian Criminal Code, and the law of several Australian statutes, they did away with supposedly archaic distinctions, such as those between larceny, embezzlement, and false pretenses, and replaced them with a streamlined and consolidated offense of theft. They also jettisoned age-old distinctions concerning the types of things that could be stolen and in their place formulated an all-encompassing definition of property that indiscriminately included tangible personal property, real property, services, and intangibles.

I argue that, in making such changes, the theft law reformers threw out the baby with the bathwater. What was lost were not only useless common law arcana but also key moral distinctions concerning the means by which theft is committed and the kinds of property stolen. If criminal law is to satisfy what has been called the principle of fair labeling—the idea that offenses should be divided and labeled so as to reflect widely held distinctions in the nature and magnitude of blame-worthiness—it must take account of what ordinary people actually think about the law. To that end, I present the results of an empirical study designed to measure people's attitudes concerning theft. The study (which asked subjects to distinguish among various scenarios involving the theft of a bicycle) indicates that people do make sharp blameworthiness-based distinctions as to both the means by which theft is committed and the kinds of property stolen.

Chapter 2 begins the ground-up construction of a normative theory of theft law—in effect, an attempt to explain why people in our study might have made the intuitive judgments they did. The focus here is on three basic (and at times overlapping) elements that define the moral content of any crime: harmfulness, intent, and wrongdoing. The harmfulness in theft consists not only of losses to individual property owners, but also to the system of property ownership more generally. Theft differs from lesser property crimes like trespass and unauthorized use in that it requires a more substantial and more permanent deprivation of rights in property, including, crucially, a deprivation of the right of use. The *mens rea* in theft typically consists of an intent to deprive another of property permanently, rather than just to borrow without permission. Crucial here is the requirement that the defendant have the intent to deprive at the same time the property is appropriated; it is this requirement of concurrence that ultimately distinguishes theft from mere breach of contract.

The third, and most complex, moral element in theft is wrongfulness. I begin by distinguishing between what I call theft's primary and secondary wrongs. The primary wrong consists of depriving the owner of property rights. Crucial here is the ability of theft law to distinguish between those takings that are wrongful and those that are not, depending on whether they are committed without consent, unlawfully, fraudulently, or dishonestly. The secondary wrong in theft consists of the means by which the theft is carried out. Here, I examine the moral content of thefts committed by means of force or violence (robbery), coercion (extortion and blackmail), housebreaking (burglary), stealth (larceny), breach of trust (embezzlement), deception (false pretenses and passing a bad check), and what I describe as exploiting the circumstances of an emergency (looting).

Chapter 3 asks why theft is a crime and when it shouldn't be. The chapter begins by considering the myriad ways in which theft law overlaps with the civil law of conversion, trespass to chattel, and fraud. It then turns to the question of criminalization itself, which is best approached not on the basis of a generalized and undifferentiated notion of theft, but rather with respect to specific forms of the offense. The analysis here is divided into five questions that need to be considered: (1) is the form of theft deserving of the kind of censure that criminal sanctions are intended to impose; (2) is there a significant advantage to be gained by having the prosecution of such conduct initiated by the state rather than or in addition to an action initiated by a private party; (3) does the state have a substantial interest in preventing the harm caused by the prohibited conduct; (4) does the criminal law provide an effective means of preventing such harms from occurring; and (5) would the benefits of criminalization outweigh its costs, including not only the costs of prosecution and incarceration but also the costs of chilling otherwise socially beneficial conduct?

This framework is then applied to a collection of potentially problematic, borderline forms of theft and theft-related conduct, which the Model Penal Code treats as functionally equivalent to, and interchangeable with, larceny, but which, I argue, are deserving of more individualized consideration. The chapter considers *de minimis* thefts (including shoplifting and employee thefts), failing to return lost or misdelivered property, receiving stolen property, committing fraud by false promise or passing a bad check, and extortion where the defendant threatens to do an unwanted but lawful act unless paid. I conclude that most of these forms of conduct should either be decriminalized or subject to lesser penalties than other, core theft offenses.

The final chapter considers the difficult question of whether and in what way theft law should apply to various forms of property. I begin with the claim that, for some good or service to count as property for purposes of theft, it must meet two necessary and sufficient conditions: first, it must be commodifiable, meaning that it is capable of being bought and sold; and, second, it must be rivalrous, meaning that consumption of it by one consumer will prevent simultaneous consumption by others. Rivalrousness, in turn, entails that the thief's misappropriation of the owner's property will constitute a zero sum game, loosely defined: the victim/owner must lose all or substantially all of what the thief gains.

Proceeding, roughly, from more to less concrete forms of property, I begin by focusing on those forms of property that pose an issue with respect to commodifiability. These are things that are illegal to buy, sell, or possess (such as contraband drugs and weapons); things that are illegal to buy and sell, but not to possess (such as human beings, body parts and tissue, sex, and possibly animals); and things that are apparently incapable of being bought or sold (such as undeserved credit taken by the plagiarist or by the Stolen Valor Act offender). The focus then shifts to the rivalrous and zero sum dynamics. I first consider the theft of what I call semi-tangibles: electricity, cable television, and Wi-Fi. I then look at theft of services, both private (such as a haircut) and public (such as a concert in the park). Next, I consider the theft of a range of pure intangibles: information, identities, intellectual property (copyright, patent, trademark, and trade secrets), and virtual property (such as Internet domain names and property generated in online computer role playing games). One of the basic questions here is the extent, if any, to which the illegal copying and sharing of copyrighted materials from the Internet should be regarded—as the Department of Justice and movie and music industries have consistently maintained—as stealing. I argue that, while in most cases misappropriation of intangibles fails to reflect the zero sum dynamic that is characteristic of theft, there are circumstances in which infringement of intangibles effects so significant a deprivation of the owner's property rights that it does amount to theft. The final part of the chapter returns to some of the issues of criminalization first dealt with in Chapter 3, this time in the context of problematic forms of property stolen. I argue that simply because some type of property qualifies as commodifiable and rivalrous, and is therefore theoretically subject to theft, does not necessarily mean that its misappropriation should be subject to criminal prosecution.

The book concludes with a brief "how-to" guide to drafting a better theft statute.

ONE

Theft Law Adrift

Of all the reforms in Anglophone criminal law achieved during the twentieth century, few were as radical in form or as widespread in their impact as those involving the offense of theft. At common law, the means by which a theft was committed, as well as the type of property taken, was of great consequence. Starting in the early 1700s, British (and, later, American, Canadian, and Australian) courts and legislatures began drawing sharp distinctions among offenses such as robbery, larceny, embezzlement, false pretenses, extortion, blackmail, fraudulent conversion, cheating, receiving stolen property, and failing to return lost property. Each offense had its own distinct set of elements, applicable defenses, and pertinent range of punishment. In addition, whether a taking was considered a theft at all and how it should be punished often depended on the type of property alleged to be stolen, whether real or personal, tangible or intangible, a good or a service.

By the middle of the twentieth century, however, a consensus developed in each of these jurisdictions that the common law approach to theft was sorely in need of reform. Distinctions among larceny, embezzlement, and false pretenses were said to "serve no useful purpose"; they were "irrational" and "bewilder[ing]," "technical . . . [and] without any substantial basis," the product of "historical accidents."[1] A succession of judicial decisions and legislative enactments had created a dense body of law, full of arcane and inconsistent rules, overlapping offenses, and procedural loopholes. For example, a defendant charged with false pretenses could escape liability by arguing that he had actually committed

8

embezzlement; and a defendant charged with embezzlement could similarly argue that his actual offense was false pretenses. Defendants were also successful in arguing that an allegedly stolen item was not the sort of property that was properly subject to theft in the first place.

To avoid such problems, law reformers in both the United States and England, when devising the 1962 Model Penal Code (MPC) and the Theft Act 1968, respectively, consolidated many of the traditional common law theft offenses into a single "unitary" offense of theft, with a single broad definition of property (typically, "anything of value"), a single scheme of grading (based, roughly, on the value of the thing stolen), and a single pattern of permitted and excluded defenses.

Despite (or perhaps because of) the radical nature of such changes, scholars have had relatively little to say about this reformed law of theft. English, Canadian, and Australian scholars have been content mainly to explicate the workings of the law and to criticize specific provisions. American scholars have been even more reticent. Virtually no one has questioned the basic assumption that the reformed law of theft is, on the whole, an improvement over what preceded it.[2]

It is precisely that assumption I seek to challenge in this chapter. My argument is not for a return to the law of theft in effect at the time of Blackstone or Hale: I agree that the common law of theft had its flaws and needed to be reformed. Rather, my argument is that the reformers followed the wrong path. In rewriting the law of theft, they threw out the good with the bad. In eradicating morally irrelevant concepts such as asportation, breaking bulk, and trespassory caption, along with esoteric legal fictions such as the distinctions between possession, title, and custody, reformers also did away with morally salient distinctions such as those among theft by stealth (larceny), theft by deception (false pretenses), and theft by coercion (extortion). They replaced the common law of theft with a codified law divested of much of its moral content, inconsistent with community intuitions, and potentially unfair to prospective defendants.

THEFT LAW PRIOR TO CONSOLIDATION

To understand what twentieth-century theft law reformers were reacting to, it is helpful to know what constituted theft at common law and how it evolved. The history of common law theft reflects a steady expansion on two axes: (1) the means by which theft could be committed and (2) the types of property that could be stolen.

Expansion in the Means by Which Theft Could Be Committed

The earliest English theft law offenses were larceny and robbery, which, by the 1160s, had emerged as two of the nine original common law felonies (the "L" and "R" of "MR. and MRS. LAMB").[3] Larceny was defined as the trespassory taking and carrying away of the personal property of another with the intent to deprive him of it permanently.[4] Robbery was defined as the felonious and forcible taking from the person of another goods or money of any value by violence or putting in fear.[5]

As originally conceived, both offenses were designed primarily to prevent and punish breaches of the peace rather than to protect property per se. In the traditional view, according to George Fletcher's classic account, "the thief upset the social order . . . by violating the general sense of security and well-being of the community."[6] "It was assumed . . . that the criminality of the deed had to become manifest in a single brief moment of force or stealth."[7] For this reason, the law of larceny applied to "only the most obvious and direct taking by one person of property which was in the possession of another."[8] The most significant limiting factor in this early conception of theft was the requirement that there be a "trespass in the taking."[9] If the wrongdoer already possessed the owner's property when he converted it or if the transgressor obtained property by lying to or misleading the owner, the potential for violence was thought to be less than in cases of larceny or robbery.[10]

Over time, as manufacturing and commerce expanded and the economy evolved, the legal and business communities recognized that theft law needed to do more than simply punish takings that were violent or stealthy. The requirement of manifestness therefore waned, and the focus shifted to the subjective intent of the defendant and to the protection of property rights per se, regardless of how those rights were usurped. Such a shift, which Fletcher dubbed the "metamorphosis" of theft law, was achieved in two basic ways. First, the offense of larceny itself was repeatedly redefined to include a wider and wider range of conduct, effected in part through awkward legal fictions such as that in the *Carrier's Case* of 1473.[11] Second, during the course of a little over a hundred years or so, beginning in the early 1700s, courts, Parliament, and (once America became independent) state legislatures created a new set of offenses, making it criminal to obtain property by means other than just violence and stealth. Eventually, the unlawful taking of property by means of deception, breach of trust, and coercion would come to be treated as crimes as well.

The first new English theft offense to be defined after robbery and larceny was extortion (in the sense of theft by coercion).[12] Its origins can be traced to the notorious Waltham Black Act of 1722 (the same statute that made it a hanging offense to appear armed in a park or warren or to hunt or steal deer with the face blackened or disguised).[13] The act made it a crime to commit theft by threatening physical harm to a victim owner who did not turn over some requested property. Theft by coercion thus differs from robbery in the sense that robbery involves taking property through force, against the will, and without the consent of the victim, whereas extortion involves coercively obtaining the victim's (invalid) consent to take property.

After extortion, the next kind of theft to be criminalized was theft by deception. Several landmark developments contributed to the definition of this type of theft. In 1779, the court in *R. v. Pear* expanded the offense of larceny to include "larceny by trick," which punished the taking of property with the owner's consent when such consent was obtained by deceit.[14] Then, in 1789, the court in *R. v. Young* reinterpreted legislation first enacted in 1757 to create the new offense of obtaining property by false pretenses, making it a crime to use deception to obtain title to "money, goods, wares or merchandizes" from another "with the intent to cheat or defraud."[15] Most American states enacted similar laws.[16] The difference between the two offenses was that a thief who used trickery to secure title, and not simply possession, was guilty of false pretenses, whereas a thief who secured merely possession, but not title, through fraud was guilty of larceny by trick.[17]

The 1780s saw the development of yet another new common law theft offense, again under the rubric of larceny. This was the crime of finding and failing to return lost, mislaid, or misdelivered property. The earlier view had been that lost chattel could not be the subject of larceny, apparently based on the theory that the owner had lost possession, so the taking by the finder could not constitute trespass.[18] One who found lost goods and failed to return them to their owner upon demand had been liable only in tort for trover.[19] By the time of *Wynne's Case* in 1786, however, courts had begun to treat such cases as larceny based on the legal fiction that the owner who lost property retained constructive possession until such possession was assumed by someone else (namely, the finder).[20]

The crime of embezzlement—or obtaining property through breach of trust—was created as a separate offense in 1799 with the passage of the Embezzlement Act, expressly overruling the case of *R. v. Bazeley*, decided earlier that year.[21] Under the new offense, originally a misdemeanor, it became a crime for employees—such as bankers, merchants, attorneys, agents, and trustees—to convert property entrusted to them for their employers by third parties. Once again, American jurisdictions followed a generally similar approach.[22]

The early nineteenth century saw the creation of another three theft-related offenses. An 1827 English statute created a separate felony of receiving stolen property, a crime that had previously been treated, first, under the general umbrella of misprision of felony, and, then, under the label accessory to larceny after the fact, a less serious form of liability than being a principal in the first or second degree.[23] American jurisdictions followed suit.[24] By the 1830s, Scottish courts had created the offense of theft by housebreaking—an aggravated form of the offense consisting of theft preceded by the unlawful entry of a home.[25] (Theft by housebreaking differed from burglary, which had been a crime at early common law and was codified in 1713,[26] in that the gist of burglary is the unlawful entry, whereas the gist of theft by housebreaking is the theft of property.) Finally, an 1843 English statute made it a crime to obtain property by threatening to do the otherwise lawful act of exposing information of an embarrassing nature—essentially, blackmail.[27] This was generally treated, in both England and the United States, as a less serious offense than robbery.[28]

The crucial point in all of this history is that, under the Anglo-American common law of theft, a wide array of theft and theft-related offenses were viewed as more or less distinct crimes, with distinct labels, elements, and defenses. Even punishments varied more than one would expect in an age when all felonies were theoretically treated as capital offenses. Thus, while felonies like robbery and grand larceny were subject to capital punishment, petit larceny (also originally a felony) was subject to forfeiture and whipping.[29] Cheating, in the sense of obtaining property by means of false weights and measures, was a misdemeanor at common law; the false instrument used to commit the crime was subject to seizure.[30] The statutory offense of embezzlement was punishable by transportation not to exceed fourteen years.[31] By the time of the English Larceny Act 1916, the punishment for embezzlement was fourteen years imprisonment, while the punishment for fraudulent conversion was only seven years.[32] The Scottish offense of theft by housebreaking was regarded as an aggravated form of theft and at one time carried the punishment of death.[33] Blackmail was punishable by transportation for life.[34] Finding and failing to return lost property, once it finally began to be treated as larceny, was punishable as such, at least in theory, though rarely in practice.[35] Receiving stolen property was treated as a felony only when the prior theft was felonious; otherwise, it was treated as a misdemeanor.[36]

The point is not that these various laws constituted a rational or coherent scheme for distinguishing different means of stealing—far from it. Instead, the point is simply that English and American courts were quite capable of overruling earlier cases. Moreover, Parliament and state legislatures, certainly by the eighteenth century, were clearly comfortable expanding, revising, reconfiguring, and repealing old law. Such changes in the law had occurred on numerous prior occasions. Yet, in the realm of theft law, the courts and legislatures frequently chose to fashion new offenses, with discrete elements and distinct punishments, rather than simply revise old law. The end product was admittedly a patchwork, full of gaps and overlaps, inconsistencies, and maddening technicalities. But it is simply implausible to assume that such elaborate distinctions bore no connection at all to underlying moral or public policy considerations, particularly when closely analogous distinctions among various forms of theft also appear in most systems of criminal law outside the Anglophone tradition.

Expansion in the Kinds of Thing that Could Be Stolen

In addition to expanding the *means* by which theft could be committed, Anglo-American courts and legislatures also expanded the range of *kinds of thing* that could be stolen.[37] At early common law, the subject of larceny was limited to tangible personal property, such as cash, jewelry, furniture, and other merchandise. Excluded from the protection of theft law by the requirement of asportation were things at two ends of the property continuum: on one end, real property; on the other, intangible property.[38] Thus, it was not larceny to "steal" real property, which was immovable and more or less indestructible and therefore beyond the scope of what theft law was intended to protect.[39] Nor was it larceny to steal intangibles such as choses in action (i.e., a right to receive or recover a debt) or stocks and bonds.

Land could be "taken" only in the sense that a person might come onto it and evict the rightful possessor or obtain title to unoccupied land by adverse possession.[40] The view was that such harms could be addressed by civil remedies. As for things that became personal property after severance from realty—such as lumber, crops, minerals, and fixtures—the common law view held that to convert them to one's own use was not larceny unless the property had been severed before it came into possession of the thief.[41] At that point, the crop or mineral was said to have become personal property.[42]

The rules concerning the theft of animals were particularly complex.[43] *Ferae naturae*—wild animals, fish in an open river, wild birds— could not be stolen on the obvious ground that no one owned them until capture. Some domesticated animals, such as cattle and horses, and wild animals that were confined on private property (such as in a zoo) or had been killed, could be stolen. Indeed, the cattle thief was the object of special opprobrium.[44] Yet domesticated animals of a "base nature"—defined, surprisingly, to include dogs, cats, and monkeys— were not subject to protection by the common law of theft.[45]

The common law reflected a highly physical conception of property capable of being stolen. Writing in 1883, James Fitzjames Stephen noted, "[i]t is obvious that it is physically impossible to misappropriate a right of action against the world at large, though it is possible to infringe and so diminish or destroy its value."[46] Thus, it was not larceny at early common law to steal intangible personal property, such as stocks, bonds, checks, deeds to land, promissory notes, and choses in action. Nor could a prosecutor argue that what was being stolen was the paper and ink with which such instruments were written since these materials were considered merged into the things they represented.

Similarly, it was not theft to misappropriate personal services, such as a ride on a train or a seat at the opera.[47]

Over time, most of these rules changed. Initially, courts simply redefined larceny to include theft of things not previously covered. Later, Parliament enacted specialized statutes with specified penalties. For example, a great number of statutes were enacted to narrow the *ferae naturae* rule, including specialized provisions relating to hunting in forests and parks and the stealing of hawks, falcons, pheasants, and partridges.[48] Similar legislation narrowed the exception for real property and its produce, including a 1601 statute concerning the theft of corn, grain, and fruit and a host of eighteenth century statutes making it a crime to cut and take *fructus industrials,* such as madder roots, turnips, potatoes, carrots, cabbages, parsnips, and a long list of other cultivated vegetables.[49] A similar pattern occurred with respect to intangibles. In 1729, Parliament passed a statute making it a crime to steal the paper on which a chose in action was written (such as a check), thereby effectively overruling a much criticized 1584 decision by Lord Coke.[50] Moreover, as new technologies, such as natural gas and electric power, came into use, theft law once against responded, sometimes by redefining larceny, sometimes by passing specialized statutes, and sometimes by leaving the law essentially unchanged. Indeed, as Jerome Hall put it, "the subject-matters [of larceny] that swing into the light, from statute to statute, amount to a running commentary on the advance of agriculture, the arts, and finance."[51]

Once again, the punishments varied significantly. For example, the 1601 statute that made it, for the first time, a crime to steal corn, grain, and various fruits treated such thefts as misdemeanors rather than as felonies.[52] Yet the Black Act of 1722 made it a hanging offense to steal rabbits, fish, and deer from an enclosed park, garden, or forest.[53] Similarly harsh penalties applied to the theft of cattle, horses, cloth, minerals, and mail from the post office. Such thefts were, for the most part, capital felonies without benefit of clergy until the beginning of the nineteenth century. In the United States, by contrast, theft was rarely treated as a capital offense except when it came to stealing particularly valuable property, such as slaves, horses, and cows.[54]

As before, I do not mean to suggest that the various laws concerning the type of property that could be stolen constituted a rational or coherent scheme for grading punishments—on the contrary. Rather, I am simply suggesting that the common law of theft did make sharp and often consequential distinctions based on the type of property that was being stolen, whether valuable or cheap, real or personal, tangible or intangible, a good or a service, or found in nature or grown on a farm. Furthermore, such distinctions were not merely formalistic or arbitrary but reflected, at some level, genuine differences in legal and social policy.

Criticism of the Common Law of Theft and the Push for Reform

Criticism of the common law of theft and calls for its reform began early in the nineteenth century, even as Parliament, state legislatures, and courts were still formulating new theft offenses. Indeed, all four of what are generally considered the greatest criminal law reform efforts of the nineteenth century—Edward Livingston's proposed Louisiana Criminal Code of 1826,[55] the English Criminal Law Commissioners' law reform effort of 1833 to 1845,[56] Thomas Babington Macaulay's proposed Indian Penal Code of 1837,[57] and the proposed English Criminal Code of 1879 (attributed mainly to James Fitzjames Stephen)[58]—included, to one degree or another, a plan for substantial changes in the law of theft.

Such reform was viewed as an important test of the reformers' new-found interest in avoiding technicalities, achieving intelligibility, educating the public, and reaching a just result. Only two of these codes were ever adopted—the Macaulay code in India (though not until 1860) and the Stephen Code in Canada (in 1892)—yet the idea that the common law of theft was in need of reform became, for virtually all forward-thinking Anglophone reformers during the nineteenth and early twentieth centuries, practically an article of faith.

Stephen's advocacy is particularly noteworthy. In his *History of the Criminal Law of England,* published in 1883, he noted that "[n]o branch of the law is more intricate [than theft], and few are more technical."[59] Various aspects of theft law, he said, were "irrational," "strange," and "bewilder[ing]."[60] The distinction between larceny and embezzlement was "useless."[61] The distinction between false pretenses and larceny by deceit led to "injustice" and, even after partial reform, remained "defect[ive]."[62]

The twofold solution Stephen offered was prescient. First, he said, the definition of theft should be broad enough to

> include under one description all the cognate offenses which at present make up the crime of theft. Its terms would include larceny, embezzlement, false pretenses, larceny by bailees, fraudulent breaches of trust, and offences by factors, agents, and bankers, and thus five or six useless and intricate distinctions between cognate crimes would be abolished.[63]

Second, he proposed that the object of theft should be defined to "include all property whatever, real or personal, in possession or in action."[64] He was confident that his recommendations would "do away with all the technicalities about the kinds of property which are the subject of larceny, and which arise out of the obscure definition of possession."[65]

Criticism of the common law was at least as vociferous in the United States. In the 1892 Supreme Court of Massachusetts case of *Commonwealth v. Ryan*, Justice Holmes wrote that the common law distinctions between larceny and embezzlement were nothing more than "historical accidents in the development of the criminal law."[66] Numerous other commentators over the next fifty years or so would echo Holmes's sentiment.[67] The distinctions among larceny, embezzlement, and false pretenses were said to "serve no useful purpose";[68] they were "technical . . . [and] without any substantial basis."[69] They "made the law unduly complex, and created unnecessary problems in pleading and proof."[70] They were but "useless handicaps from the standpoint of criminal justice."[71] Their "perpetuation [was] a disgrace."[72] The legal fictions surrounding larceny were said to make "a mockery of any contention that our law of theft is based on logic and common sense."[73] They constituted a "public scandal both because the courts are reluctantly compelled to allow dishonesty to go unpunished, and because of the serious waste of judicial time involved in the discussion of futile legal subtleties."[74]

To the extent that criticism of the common law of theft consisted of more than just slogans, it tended to focus on three major points. First, theft law's conceptual apparatus was too complex for prosecutors, judges, juries, and the public at large to understand; it involved esoteric legal concepts like breaking bulk, asportation, trespassory caption, *animus furandi,* and *ferae naturae,* as well as elusive distinctions between possession, title, and custody, and between larceny by trick and false pretenses. Second, its technicalities and loopholes allowed some defendants to unfairly escape conviction by arguing that their conduct fell into the gap between offenses or that rather than committing the form of theft charged, they had actually committed a different form of theft. Third, the distinctions the common law rested on served no legitimate purpose. There was, as Joshua Dressler has put it, "no meaningful difference between the offenses [of larceny, embezzlement, and false pretenses] in terms of the culpability of the actors, their dangerousness, or the seriousness of the harm caused."[75]

THE CONSOLIDATION OF THEFT LAW

Given the widespread perception that the common law of theft was deeply flawed, it is no surprise that it became a primary target of criminal law reformers in the various English-speaking jurisdictions starting at the end of the nineteenth century and continuing well into the twentieth century. It was this process of reform that constitutes what we can think of as a "second metamorphosis" in the Anglo-American law of theft.[76]

Reform Prior to the Model Penal Code and the Theft Act

The first serious attempt to replace the common law of theft with a consolidated theft statute was the Canadian Criminal Code of 1892, which was largely based on the 1879 Code drafted by Stephen for England (though never enacted there) and was also influenced by the work of Canadian jurist George Wheelock Burbidge.[77] Earlier attempts to reform the law of theft had consisted mainly of reducing the common law to statutory reform without significantly modifying its substance.

Like Stephen's Code, the Canadian Code consolidated the common law offenses of larceny, larceny by a bailee, embezzlement, and fraudulent conversion into a newly conceived offense of theft defined broadly in Section 305 to apply to one who "fraudulently and without colour of right takes . . . or converts to his use or to the use of another person, anything, whether animate or inanimate, with intent . . . to deprive, temporarily or absolutely, the owner of it, or a person who has a special property or interest in it, of the thing or of his property or interest in it."[78] Although the Code did away with the distinction between larceny and embezzlement and with concepts such as possession and custody, it maintained separate provisions for extortion, blackmail, false pretenses, receiving stolen property, and fraud.[79] The Code also offered a long list of various forms of property that could be stolen, including "[e]very inanimate thing whatever which is the property of any person, and which either is or may be made movable."[80]

The Canadian scheme of theft has remained essentially intact, save for a modest change in the definition of property that can be stolen and a renumbering of the relevant provisions.[81] In 1977, the Law Reform Commission of Canada issued a working paper, followed by a report in 1979, proposing a broad revision of the law of theft and fraud.[82] The proposed changes would have replaced the terms *fraudulently* and *with intent to deprive* with *dishonestly*, added provisions concerning fraud, and modified the definition of *property*. These revisions were never adopted, however, and the Commission has since been disbanded.

The first American state to make wholesale changes in its law of theft was Massachusetts, in 1899. Apparently under the influence of Justice Holmes's dictum in *Ryan,* the Massachusetts legislature took what must have then seemed the bold step of consolidating the offenses of larceny, embezzlement, and false pretenses under the label *larceny,* and further provided that an indictment for any one of the three offenses "may be supported by proof that the defendant committed" one of the other two.[83]

Ten years later, in 1909, New York followed suit, once again consolidating larceny, embezzlement, and false pretenses under a single label, this time denominated *theft.*[84] Within the next 40 years, another six states—California (1927), Washington (1932), Arizona (1939), Louisiana (1942), Minnesota (1945), and Montana (1947)—each introduced a form of theft consolidation, more or less similar to the Massachusetts and New York schemes.[85] One of the main purposes of such consolidation, as explained in one California case, was to "relieve the courts from difficult questions arising from the contention that the evidence shows the commission of some other of these crimes than the one alleged in the indictment or information, a contention upon which defendants may escape just conviction solely because of the borderline distinction existing between these various crimes."[86]

Of particular interest is the approach to consolidation taken in the Louisiana Criminal Code of 1942, the first fully integrated state criminal code enacted in the United States, and an important forerunner of the MPC.[87] The principal author of the draft code was Dale Bennett, a law professor at Louisiana State University, who would later serve on the MPC's Advisory Board. In two respects, the approach to consolidation taken by Article 67 of the Louisiana Code was more radical than that in the other pre-MPC consolidated theft provisions. First, the Code entirely omitted any reference to larceny, embezzlement, or false pretenses, as well as the concepts of custody, possession, and title.[88] Instead, it simply defined theft as "the misappropriation or taking of anything of value which belongs to another, either without the consent of the other to the misappropriation or taking, or by means of fraudulent conduct, practices, or representations."[89] Second, the Code contained an extraordinarily broad definition of property subject to theft—to wit, "anything of value which belongs to another"—and elsewhere stated that the term

> "[a]nything of value" must be given the broadest possible construction, including any conceivable thing of the slightest value, movable or immovable, corporeal or incorporeal, public or private, and including transportation, telephone and telegraph services, or any other service available for hire. It must be construed in the broad popular sense of the phrase, not necessarily as synonymous with the traditional legal term "property."[90]

At the same time, however, the Louisiana Code took a less radical approach to consolidation than would be taken by the MPC insofar as it continued to treat as separate offenses not only burglary and robbery, but also extortion, unauthorized use of a movable, issuing worthless checks, and illegal possession of stolen things.[91]

Theft Consolidation under the Model Penal Code

Although the MPC was not the first American criminal code to consolidate the law of theft, it was undoubtedly the most influential. The MPC was a product of the American Law Institute (ALI), a law reform group composed of lawyers, judges, and legal academics, founded in

1923 "to promote the clarification and simplification of the law and its better adaptation to social needs, to secure the better administration of justice, and to encourage and carry on scholarly and scientific legal work."[92] Reform of the criminal law was one of the ALI's priorities from the outset.[93] A proposal for drafting a criminal code was originally put forth in 1931, but funding to carry out the project was not forthcoming during the years of the Great Depression. It was therefore not until 1951, following the receipt of a large grant from the Rockefeller Foundation, that work on the MPC project actually began, and it was not until 1962 that the Code was finally published.[94]

The MPC project was manned (there were, as far as can be determined, no women involved) by scores of lawyers, judges, academics, and policymakers—dubbed, variously, *Reporters, Associate Reporters, Special Consultants, Research Associates, members of the Advisory Committee,* and *Advisers.* But law professors were clearly the driving force behind the document, most especially Herbert Wechsler, a professor at Columbia Law School who served as the Code's Chief Reporter, and Louis B. Schwartz, a professor at the University of Pennsylvania Law School who was appointed Co-Reporter for specific crimes. It is Schwartz in particular who deserves much of the credit—or blame, depending on one's view—for drafting the provisions concerning theft.[95]

Article 223

Provisions concerning property crimes were among the very first drafted by the MPC framers. In a 1952 law review article containing his roadmap for reform, Wechsler set out what he regarded as the problem with the common law of theft:

> [H]ow broadly or how narrowly should individual offenses be defined? The piecemeal, *ad hoc* growth of our penal law has made for great proliferation of offenses with the line of demarcation often far too subtle for effective administration. The problem is well illustrated by the property offenses where theft by trespass, conversion and fraud is [sic] still often, if not usually, subdivided into separate crimes. . . . Such unduly close distinctions—unrelated to the criminality of conduct— serve no useful purpose, but can lead to merely technical acquittals that represent a legal failure and breed disrespect for law.[96]

Wechsler's diagnosis was similar to that of a long line of critics going back to Stephen and Holmes.

A first discussion draft concerning property offenses was circulated to the Advisory Group in November 1952.[97] Even at this early point in the process, the move toward consolidation was clear. The draft's self-proclaimed goal was to "eliminate artificial and obsolete distinctions between some forms of theft, e.g., larceny and embezzlement, so that the law should cease to discriminate between things which citizens and prosecutors regarded as the same thing."[98] The drafters were not modest about the virtues of their approach: "[W]e believe," they said, "the theft proposals represent an advance over any existing or proposed codification, in logic and in that kind of common sense that will promote public understanding and respect for the criminal law."[99]

The scheme of consolidation put forth in the very first discussion draft was the most radical one the ALI would consider. Successive drafts over the next two years would become gradually less so. The first discussion draft made no mention at all of the common law theft offenses or of common law concepts such as possession and custody. It said simply, "[w]hoever appropriates property of another without the effective consent of the owner is guilty of theft if he knows that he is not entitled to appropriate or is indifferent on that score. Effective consent excludes consent obtained by deception or coercion."[100] It included within the definition of *appropriation* "infringement of patents, trademarks, copyrights, [and] franchises, [and] the violation of laws regulating competition."[101] And it provisionally treated robbery, kidnapping for ransom, extortion, forgery, and large scale public frauds as forms of aggravated theft.[102]

By the time the next discussion draft dealing with property offenses was circulated a year later, the scheme had undergone significant moderation and was much closer to what would ultimately become Article 223 in the final draft.[103] This time, instead of simply offering an all-embracing definition of theft, the framers enumerated six means of committing theft—by taking or misappropriation, by deception, by intimidation, by failure to pay or account, by finding lost or misdelivered property, and by unlawful temporary deprivation or use—while at the same time specifying that all were to be treated as a "single offense regardless of means employed."[104] They further specified, crucially, that an "accusation of theft may be supported by evidence that it was committed in any manner that would be theft under this Article, despite any particularization in the indictment or other specification regarding the manner of the theft"—a rule that was "subject only to the power of the Court to ensure fair trial by granting a continuance or other appropriate relief where the conduct of the defense would be prejudiced by lack of fair notice or by surprise."[105] The draft also included, as other means of committing theft, theft of labor or services and theft of contraband, even though both are arguably more properly thought of as variations in the type of property stolen. In addition, the draft included special provisions regarding theft within a household (by one spouse from another), it continued to treat robbery as an aggravated form of theft, and it indicated the need for a not-yet-drafted offense of receiving stolen goods.

The final version of Article 223 would include eight means of committing theft: theft by unlawful taking, theft by deception, theft by extortion, theft of lost or mislaid property, receiving stolen property, theft of services, theft by failure to make required disposition of funds received, and unauthorized use of automobiles and other vehicles. Robbery would be moved out of theft entirely and placed in its own separate article, as would the offenses of writing a bad check and burglary.[106]

In consolidating these eight forms of theft, the MPC went significantly beyond the consolidation that had occurred earlier in Canada, Massachusetts, California, New York, and even Louisiana. Earlier efforts at consolidation had been limited to larceny, embezzlement, and false pretenses. The MPC theft provision included, in addition, extortion, failure to return lost property, receiving stolen property, and unauthorized use of property, treating them all as interchangeable. No other code had ever consolidated so extensive a collection of theft offenses.[107]

A second major innovation was to treat all of the traditional common law theft offenses according to a unified grading scheme. Under what would become the final version of Section 223, a theft constituted a felony of the third degree if the amount involved exceeded $500 or if the property stolen was a firearm, automobile, airplane, motorcycle, motorboat, or other motor-propelled vehicle; if the property was not covered by the first provision, it was treated as a misdemeanor unless the amount involved was less than $50, in which case it was a petty misdemeanor.[108]

Finally, the MPC did away with most of the distinctions among different kinds of stolen property. An early draft of March 1953 had contained a laundry list of specific things that would be treated as property subject to theft:

> realty, anything growing on, affixed to or found in land, chattels, money, notes, bills of exchange, checks and other commercial instruments, warehouse receipts, bills of lading and other documents of title, stock certificates, bonds and other securities, tickets, accounts receivable and other transferable contract rights, patents, copyrights, and trademarks, and any other thing of value.[109]

By the time it appeared in Section 223.0(6), the MPC's final definition of property would begin with the phrase "anything of value," omit the explicit reference to patents, copyrights, and trademarks, and include references to "real estate, tangible and intangible personal property, contract rights, choses-in-action and other interests in or claims to wealth, admission or transportation tickets, captured or domestic animals, food and drink, electric or other power."[110] Thus, if read in conjunction with Sections 223.7 and 223.1(1),[111] this section treats theft of tangible goods, theft of intangible goods, and theft of services as equivalent and subject to the same punishment. In doing so, the MPC went well beyond the degree of consolidation that had occurred anywhere else (with the sole arguable exception of Louisiana).

Theory Underlying the MPC

Like other twentieth-century theft law reformers, the authors of the MPC tended to think of the common law distinctions among different forms of theft mostly as accidents of history. As Co-Reporter Schwartz put it, the offenses of obtaining by false pretense, extortion, and receiving stolen property reflected "a record of the history of the advance of criminal law. . . . Each new step was given a new name and became a distinct crime."[112] Understood this way, the process of consolidation consisted of "saying, now let's look at all the ground that has been covered and see if we do not have essentially a single crime, a single crime of acquisition of others' property without a right.[113]

Yet the framers of the MPC were not completely oblivious to the possibility that distinctions between common law offenses reflected more

than simply historical fortuities. As the Commentary to Discussion
Draft No. 1 put it:

> If history were the whole explanation of the existence of distinctive
> theft crimes, there would be little reason to preserve a differentiation
> whose subtleties have in the past caused serious procedural difficulties.
> The case is not so simple. History has its own logic. Our criminal law
> reached larceny first and embezzlement first because of real distinc-
> tions between stranger theft and the peculations of a trusted agent. . . .
> The ordinary trespass-thief was a stranger, an intruder with no sem-
> blance of right even to touch the object. He was easily recognized by
> the very taking, surreptitious or forceful, and so set apart from the law-
> abiding community. No bond of association in joint endeavor linked
> criminal and victim. In contrast, the embezzler stands always in a lawful
> as well as in a putatively unlawful relation to the victim and property.
> He is respectable; we tend to identify with him rather than with the
> bank or insurance company from whom he embezzles.[114]

In the end, however, the framers of the MPC put such concerns aside.
The fact that theft by coercion (extortion) might entail more culpability than receiving stolen property, and, therefore, presumably justify
more severe punishment, was for them irrelevant. The authors of the
MPC subscribed to the idea that crime should be "forbidden" and "prevented," and where not preventable, its perpetrators "treated" and
"rehabilitated," rather than punished.[115] The Code itself never spoke
about assessing "blame" or "culpability" or "desert" (though the Commentary occasionally did). And it certainly made no claim that crimes
treated as equivalent for purposes of punishment should be regarded
as equivalent in terms of blameworthiness. Indeed, the MPC studiously
avoided claims about the moral wrongfulness of crime other than to
say that one of the purposes of its provisions concerning sentencing
was to "safeguard[] offenders against excessive, disproportionate, or
arbitrary punishment."[116] Instead, according to the Commentary, consolidation was viewed solely as a way to "eliminate[] procedural problems arising from . . . a defendant's claim that he did not misappropriate
the property by some other means and from the combination of such a
claim with the procedural rule that a defendant who is charged with
one offense cannot be convicted by proving another."[117]

In implementing their radical vision of consolidation, it appears that Wechsler and Schwartz faced little in the way of dissent.[118] Only two members of the ALI raised even slightly skeptical voices in connection with the MPC's approach to theft consolidation, both in floor proceedings conducted during 1954. One was Emory Niles, a judge on the Baltimore City Court. While he agreed with the idea "that larceny, embezzlement, [and] obtaining by false pretenses, naturally fall together in this consolidation of definitions," he expressed doubt that consolidation should be extended beyond that. In particular, he was concerned about the inclusion of blackmail and extortion. These offenses, he said, "seem . . . to bring in quite separate considerations."[119] The other somewhat skeptical voice belonged to Floyd Thompson, a Chicago criminal defense lawyer and former member of the Illinois Supreme Court. Thompson said that he had "no problem with consolidating the usual things we talk about as theft, like the bailee and embezzlement, and the confidence game, and all that sort of thing. The thing that disturbs me is consolidating into the theft picture this invasion of property rights as they involve immovable property or real estate. . . . I am having an awful struggle with trying to figure that out as theft."[120]

Schwartz was unreceptive to both criticisms. With respect to Thompson's point regarding the inclusion of real estate within the definition of "property," Schwartz said simply that this was not an issue that went to consolidation but rather to the "scope of theft" itself.[121] With respect to Niles's point that extortion should be treated differently than embezzlement and false pretenses, Schwartz contended that the "wrong form of theft" problem was just as serious in the case of extortion as with other theft offenses. Then, in a statement that can be taken to sum up his and the Institute's philosophy of theft consolidation, Schwartz had this to say: "There are a lot of ways of stealing. The basic conception of this draft is that it does not make any difference which way you choose to steal. If you are stealing, you are a thief."[122]

Post-MPC Developments

By any measure, the MPC's influence on American criminal law was profound in terms of state statutory revisions, in the way American lawyers have come to think about the subject, and in the way criminal law is practiced. The influence of the MPC on the American law of theft has been particularly notable.

The MPC's Influence on American Theft Law

During the 1960s and 1970s, well over half the states rewrote their criminal statutes to comply at least in part with its recommendations. The most influential provisions in the MPC are generally thought to be those found in Part I, the General Part, particularly those concerning *mens rea* and the elements of various defenses. Among the provisions in Part II, however, none has had a greater impact than those concerning theft; they were, as Charles McClain and Dan Kahan have put it, perhaps the Special Part's "most signal achievement."[123]

A survey of American criminal codes today, fifty years after the MPC was promulgated, reveals the following:

- Eighteen states have effected a "complete consolidation" of theft law, meaning that all of the traditional species of theft (larceny, embezzlement, false pretenses, extortion, receiving stolen property, failure to return lost property, and unauthorized use) have been consolidated into a single offense of theft.[124] Proof of any one of these crimes will constitute proof of the unified offense, even if another of the theft crimes constituted the formal charge.
- Twenty states and the District of Columbia have enacted what might be called "partial" consolidation, meaning that the three traditional common law crimes of larceny, embezzlement, and false pretenses are consolidated, but at least one other morally relevant kind of theft is left as a separate charge.[125] In eleven of these intermediate consolidation states, the nonconsolidated offense is extortion.[126] In four states and the District of Columbia, the nonconsolidated offenses are extortion and receiving stolen goods.[127] In one state, the nonconsolidated offenses are extortion and theft of lost property.[128] In one other state, the nonconsolidated offense is receiving stolen property.[129] In three additional states, the nonconsolidated offense is unauthorized use.[130]
- The remaining twelve states have adhered to what should be regarded as a nonconsolidated law of theft, meaning that at least one or more of the three central common law theft offenses

remain separate offenses (even though in some cases they have adopted the MPC terminology of theft by deception, theft by unlawful taking or disposition, and the like).[131]

The scheme of theft that exists in American law today is thus radically different from the scheme that had existed in 1900 or even 1960, and the overwhelming inspiration for this change has been the MPC.

Effects of Consolidation in Practice

How has the consolidation of American theft law worked in practice? On one level, it has clearly been a success. Two generations of lawyers and judges in a majority of states have mostly been spared the need to deal with the arcane intricacies of asportation, trespassory caption, custody, possession, breaking bulk, and the like (though prospective lawyers are still expected to be familiar with the common law elements of theft when they sit for the Multistate Bar Exam). As a result of consolidation, American theft law is undoubtedly simpler and more accessible than it was under prior law. What is less clear is how consistent it is with the community's sense of morality and whether it leads to just results.

As previously noted, the most radical change effected by the MPC's theft scheme occurs in Section 223.1(1), which says that an "accusation of theft may be supported by evidence that it was committed in any manner that would be theft under [the relevant law], notwithstanding the specification of a different manner in the indictment or information."[132] Four recent cases from states with consolidated theft statutes illustrate the dramatic practical effect of this provision:

- In the Pennsylvania case of *Commonwealth v. Lewis*, the defendants were charged with robbery and theft by unlawful taking, but not with receiving stolen property.[133] At trial, the evidence showed that the victim had been attacked by several youths who took his wallet. Although there were witnesses to the incident, none was able to identify the assailants. There was evidence, however, that, in the period following the theft, the defendants had possessed the victim's wallet and divided its contents among themselves. At trial, the prosecution argued that, despite the fact that it had failed to prove the theft offenses charged, it should, under

Pennsylvania's consolidation provision, be permitted to obtain a conviction for the uncharged offense of receiving stolen property. On appeal, the court agreed, citing as support the MPC-inspired consolidation provision in the Pennsylvania theft statute and explaining that "[t]his statute means that a specific charge of theft will permit evidence showing another type of theft."[134]

- In the Nebraska case of *State v. Jonusas,* the defendant was charged with theft by deception.[135] The evidence showed that he had acted as a broker between the buyers and sellers of a tavern. The buyers had given him $50,000, which was supposed to be placed in an escrow account. After the deal soured and the buyers asked for their money back, the defendant revealed that he had lost it all in bad investments. At the end of trial, the prosecution conceded that it had been unable to prove the offense alleged, but it asked the jury to convict the defendant of theft by unlawful taking instead. The jury did so. In affirming the conviction, the Nebraska Supreme Court followed the MPC approach, stating that "[t]he consolidation statute . . . provides that the offense of theft may be supported by evidence that it was committed via any manner described in [the consolidated theft statute] regardless of the manner by which the information alleges the theft occurred."[136]

- In the New Jersey case of *State v. Talley,* the defendant was indicted for robbery.[137] The indictment alleged that he had forced his victim, at gunpoint, to surrender the $300 he had in his wallet. In his defense, the defendant testified that he had obained the $300 from the victim not by pointing a gun in his face, but rather by selling him a quantity of herbal tea on the false pretense that it was marijuana. The jury apparently believed the defendant's version of the events, but rather than acquitting him of robbery, it convicted him of false pretenses, a crime with which he had never been charged. On appeal, the New Jersey Supreme Court held that there was nothing wrong with such a verdict, reasoning that under the state's consolidated theft statute, false pretenses and robbery were just two different ways of committing the same offense of theft.[138]

- In the New Hampshire case of *State v. Hill,* the defendant was charged with being an accomplice to Reilly in the theft of services.[139] The evidence showed that the defendant and Reilly had unlawfully taken Reilly's car from a towing service's lot after Reilly had refused to pay for the cost of towing as had been ordered by the police. On appeal, the state conceded that the elements of theft of services could not be satisfied since Reilly had not obtained any services. However, the court allowed the prosecution to proceed under the theory that the defendant had committed theft by unlawful taking or transfer. Citing the MPC-derived consolidation language in New Hampshire's Criminal Code, the court explained that it did not matter whether the means by which the theft that had been proved differed from the means by which the theft that had been charged.[140] Nor, presumably, did it matter that the form of the property shown to be stolen (namely, a good) was different from the form of the property alleged to be stolen (namely, a service), although the court did not address this issue explicitly.

In each of these cases, the evidence supported a different form of theft than that with which the defendant had been charged. Yet, in each case, the court allowed the prosecution to proceed or the conviction to stand. In none of the cases did the court determine that doing so would result in the conduct of the defense being "prejudiced by lack of fair notice or by surprise," and, indeed, such cases are extremely rare. What was important, the courts said, was not the means by which the victim had been deprived of his property or the type of property stolen, but simply the fact that such misappropriation had occurred. In reaching this result, the courts implicitly viewed the traditional distinctions between the common law theft offenses as nothing more than the result of historical accident—arbitrary categories that could easily be swept aside by a streamlined and modernized criminal code. In so doing, each of the courts, like the MPC itself, implicitly assumed that such offenses are morally equivalent (i.e., that depriving another of his property by stealth is no more or less wrongful than doing so by deception, or receiving stolen property, or even, as in *Talley*, by force).

The Effects of Sentencing

As presented above, the tendency of modern Anglo-American law has been to authorize the same punishment or range of punishments for a collection of theft offenses that, under earlier law, would have been subject to varying punishments. The effect has been a flattening in the moral landscape of theft law. One might well wonder, however, whether some of the moral sensitivity that has been lost through legislative consolidation might have been restored by judges on a case-by-case basis at sentencing. For example, is it possible that, even though the statutory punishments for extortion and receiving stolen property are identical, judges might nevertheless have a tendency to sentence one offense more harshly than the other?

The question is reasonable, but there are several reasons for skepticism. The first relates to the use of sentencing guidelines, which largely dictate the terms of sentencing in the United States and, to a lesser extent, in England. Is there evidence that state sentencing guidelines somehow restore moral content lost during consolidation? In an effort to answer this question, I examined sentencing schemes from six states with either complete or intermediate statutory theft consolidation (namely, Maryland, Minnesota, Pennsylvania, Utah, Washington, and Wisconsin).[141] I found that the guidelines largely tracked the consolidated statutory provisions themselves. Indeed, the guidelines in Minnesota explicitly recommend that the offenses of theft by unlawful taking, receiving stolen property, refusing to return lost property, theft by false representation, theft by check, and theft of services, among other offenses, should all be "treated similarly."[142] To the extent that state guidelines do go beyond such statutory provisions, they tend to take account of factors such as the amount of property stolen (by far the most important factor in all of the guidelines I examined) and the kinds of property stolen (theft of firearms, theft of motor vehicles, and theft of livestock all commonly result in enhanced sentences). Less commonly, state guidelines consider factors such as the motivation for the theft (e.g., greed versus the need for basic necessities)[143] and the impact on, and vulnerability of, the victim.[144] The closest thing to an arguable restoration of moral content lost during consolidation was in several jurisdictions whose guidelines recognized an aggravating factor for "abuse of trust" or "misappropriation by fiduciaries."[145] Based on this survey, therefore, the impact of sentencing guidelines in this context seems minimal.

Harder to assess is the extent to which moral content might be restored by individual judges making discretionary sentencing decisions in specific cases. The problem is that little data on the sentencing of specific forms of theft are currently maintained. (Presumably, this is because statutory consolidation has mostly eliminated the need for compiling such data.) The most comprehensive set of data concerning length of sentences imposed in U.S. state courts is that maintained by the Department of Justice's Bureau of Justice Statistics (BJS). The latest available data show that, in 2004, the aggregate median sentence for offenders convicted of robbery was sixty months; for burglary, thirty-six months; fraud, twenty-four months; motor vehicle theft, twenty-four months; and larceny, sixteen months.[146] Such data are of very limited value for present purposes, however. For one thing, they reveal nothing about sentencing for such key offenses as embezzlement, extortion, blackmail, receiving stolen property, and failing to return lost property. Moreover, even with respect to robbery, burglary, and larceny, the data show little that is useful. Information regarding what is undoubtedly the single most important variable in all of the cases—namely, the amount of property stolen—is not included in the data set and thus cannot be controlled. Indeed, the fact that the median sentence for fraud was longer than the median sentence for larceny, even though the empirical findings described later in this chapter indicate that people tend to view larceny as the more serious crime, is probably best explained by the simple fact that fraud is more likely to involve theft of higher value property than larceny. Nor does the BJS report reveal anything about the possibility that some forms of theft may involve a higher level of recidivism, another key factor in determining sentences.[147]

Data obtained directly from individual states also do little or nothing to support the view that sentencing in practice restores moral content removed by consolidation. For example, the Washington State Statistical Summary of Adult Felony Sentencing specifies the percentage of defendants convicted of various forms of theft—identity theft, retail theft, theft of a firearm, theft of livestock, theft of telecommunications, theft of rental or leased property, and theft of a motor vehicle—that have been sentenced to prison and the percentage sentenced to something other than prison.[148] Data from Maryland indicate the average length of sentence for robbery, burglary, felony theft, and misdemeanor theft.[149] And data from Florida indicate what percentage of those convicted of what is referred to as property theft/fraud/damage were sent to state prison, what percentage were put on probation, and what percentage were sentenced to county jail.[150] But none of these reports answers the question posed regarding the restoration of moral content. Without further, extensive study of files in individual cases, one simply cannot conclude that moral content of the sort that concerns us here is routinely being restored by judges at sentencing; the hypothesis remains nothing more than that.

Moreover, even if it could be demonstrated that *judges* were exercising their limited discretion at sentencing to correct for the effects of consolidation, there would remain the problem of *prosecutors* using evidence of one theft offense to convict defendants of a different theft offense. To the extent that such results are regarded as unfair, this is not a problem that can easily be fixed by sentencing guidelines or individualized sentencing decisions.

Finally, even if judges and prosecutors did their utmost to correct for the errors of consolidation, the MPC approach would still be flawed. The principle of fair labeling, discussed below, involves the idea that widely felt moral differences between criminal offenses should be respected and signaled by the law itself. The clearest, most transparent, and most consistent way to do this is through legislation. Even if judges or prosecutors were to correct for the overly broad classification system in some individual cases, the basic problem would remain unresolved.

Proliferation of Specialized Theft Statutes

One additional development in American law that might be regarded as something of a counterweight to consolidation is the proliferation of various subject-specific theft statutes occurring at both the state and federal levels. In 1998, Ronald Gainer counted 232 theft or fraud statutes appearing in the federal criminal code alone, most of which were of fairly recent vintage.[151]

There are at least four varieties of such specialized statutes (though there are certainly overlaps). First are statutes making it a crime to steal specific types of property. For example, California has special provisions for theft of farm animals, avocados, artichokes, dogs, gold dust, amalgam, and quicksilver, among other things.[152] Illinois has a special provision regarding theft of delivery containers and library books.[153] In the federal context, probably the most famous statute of this sort is the National Motor Vehicle Theft Act (Dyer Act), originally enacted in 1919.[154] The prize for the most extensive list of specialized "designer" theft statutes, however, goes to Louisiana, with its hopeless tangle of overlapping provisions making it a crime not only to commit theft and theft of goods, but also theft of animals, livestock, crawfish, alligators, oilfield geological surveys, timber, petroleum products, firearms, motor vehicle fuel, utility services, and anhydrous ammonia.[155] (This hyperproliferation of theft offenses in Louisiana is particularly ironic given the radically stripped-down approach to consolidation contained in the original 1942 Code.) Second are statutes making it a crime to engage in theft or fraud in specific industries or in connection with certain kinds of legal procedures. For example, specialized statutes in federal law make it a crime to engage in theft or fraud related to health care, banking, accounting, and bankruptcy.[156] Third are statutes that make it a crime to steal from specific kinds of victim, such as the federal government, Native American Indian tribes, museums, and employee pension funds.[157] Finally, there are statutes that make it a crime to commit theft or fraud by use of specific kinds of instrumentality, such as the mail, wire communications, computers, or credit cards.[158]

There is no easy explanation for why such specialization occurred more or less simultaneously with consolidation. There is certainly no evidence of any conscious anti-MPC backlash. Rather, the proliferation of specialized theft statutes seems to have been a function of the more general trend toward an ever-growing, ever more complex body of substantive criminal law.[159]

Historically, theft law has always reflected a certain amount of specialization with respect to the types of property that could be stolen and the specific social context within which such stealing occurred. Roman law had a complex classification system involving different procedures and penalties depending on whether the thing stolen was cattle, trees, crops, sacred items in the temple, slaves, or things that were part of an inheritance.[160] Jewish law traditionally treated theft of property used in worship as a more serious offense than theft of secular property.[161] Islamic law treats the stealing of property that is of value only to non-Muslims (such as pork and alcoholic drinks) as a lesser offense than theft of property that is of value to Muslims.[162] And English law long distinguished between thefts based not only on the type of property stolen (e.g., economically valuable animals such as cows and horses versus what were perceived as less valuable animals, such as dogs and cats), but also on the type of victim from whom goods were stolen (e.g., thefts from weaving sheds, spinning mills, and iron works each had their own legal regime).[163]

What, if anything, justifies such an approach? In thinking about such statutes, it is worth considering three basis issues: First, does such specialization reflect any difference in the blameworthiness of the underlying conduct? For example, can an argument be made that, other things being equal, it is more (or less) harmful or wrongful to steal a firearm than it is to steal timber; to steal from the government, a charity, or a pension fund, rather than from a business or individual; or to steal a sacred object rather than a profane one? Such an approach is not necessarily wrong in principle. Surely, a legal system is entitled to give more value to certain kinds of property than others, and hence to regard the theft of certain kinds of thing as more blameworthy. Although one of the requirements for a thing's being susceptible to theft is that it be commodifiable (as I will argue in Chapters 2 and 4), that does not necessarily mean that the degree of a given theft's blameworthiness will always be perfectly correlated with the market value of the thing stolen. Rather, it is perfectly reasonable for a lawmaking body to decide, prospectively, that certain *types* of property are deserving of special protection by the state—whether it is the infamous *Arbeit macht frei* sign that hangs over the entry gate of Auschwitz (stolen in late 2009 and recovered a few days later); a nearly 800-year-old relic of St. Anthony of Padua (stolen from a church in Long Beach, California, in 2011 and also recovered a few days later); or seventeen pounds of priceless moon rocks (stolen from the Houston Space Center by several NASA interns in mid-2002 and recovered later that year).[164]

The second question is whether there are other considerations—involving matters of detection, proof, or deterrence—that might justify specialized treatment for certain kinds of theft. For example, specialized statutes may be justified as a response to the distinctive enforcement concerns that arise in connection with theft and fraud occurring in highly regulated industries like health care, banking, accounting, and bankruptcy. (The mere fact that a given industry has lobbied for special protection, however, is not, of course, a valid justification for specialized legislation.)

Third, there is a significant potential downside to such specificity. Criminal codes with too many specialized theft statutes risk being overly complex and confusing. And where statutes overlap (recall the Louisiana provisions criminalizing theft, theft of goods, theft of animals, and theft of livestock), there is a risk that prosecutors will use the option of redundant charge stacking to obtain unfair leverage over defendants, subjecting them to the threat of multiple (and therefore, likely, disproportionate) punishment.[165]

Consolidation under Theft Act 1968

More or less contemporaneous with the push to consolidate theft law in the United States was the effort to do the same in England and Wales. In 1861 and again in 1916, England had enacted statutes that put the common law of theft into statutory form.[166] But these statutes did little to make the law of theft more coherent or accessible.

In 1959, the Home Secretary, R. A. Butler, asked the Criminal Law Revision Committee (CLRC), the precursor to the Law Commission of England and Wales, "to consider, with a view to providing a simpler and more effective system of law, what alterations in the criminal law are desirable with reference to larceny and kindred offences and to such other acts involving fraud or dishonesty as, in the opinion of the committee, could conveniently be dealt with in legislation giving effect to the committee's recommendations of the law of larceny."[167]

Lord Justice Frederic Sellers was named as chairman of the Committee, which in turn set up a subcommittee to consider the subject. As in the case of the MPC, the driving force behind the subcommittee was its professorial members, most notably, Glanville Williams, of Cambridge, and J. C. Smith, of the University of Nottingham. (Smith would subsequently author a leading treatise on English theft law.) While the Committee was undoubtedly concerned with what it perceived as genuine deficiencies in the law of theft, it also viewed the reform of theft law as a kind of trial run for a more comprehensive codification of the criminal law.[168]

In 1966, after seven years of work, the CLRC presented to Parliament its findings titled *Eighth Report: Theft and Related Offences*, recommending a major statutory overhaul. The draft bill annexed to the report, slightly amended, was the basis of the Theft Bill that was introduced in the House of Lords in December 1967 and ultimately came into effect on January 1, 1969.[169]

Given that the Theft Act 1968 was enacted only five years after the publication of the MPC, and that Glanville Williams had played a role in both efforts (indeed, he seems to have been the only foreigner who played a consulting role on the MPC drafting team), it is puzzling that the MPC received essentially no discussion in the CLRC report. The parallels between the MPC and the Theft Act are nonetheless clear. According to the Committee, "[t]he law on most of the offences proved on examination to be so defective that it was necessary to go back to first principles, to consider what were the essential elements of the offence and to reconstruct the law relating to it accordingly."[170] The Theft Act thus sought to eliminate "unnecessary matter, in particular obsolete and redundant offences and procedural provisions."[171] It represented for theft law what has been called "an almost completely fresh start."[172]

In one respect at least, the Theft Act is more radical in its approach to consolidation than the MPC; but in others, it is substantially less so. The Theft Act's consolidation is more radical in the sense that, unlike the MPC, it completely omits any reference to the common law offenses, instead offering a single definition of theft—to wit, "dishonestly appropriating property belonging to another with the intention of permanently depriving the other of it."[173] On the other hand, the Theft Act is less radical than the MPC in the crucial sense that it maintains separate provisions not only for burglary and robbery (as the MPC also does) but also for false pretenses, blackmail, handling stolen goods, false accounting, and making off without paying (which the MPC does not).[174] The Theft Act makes no explicit reference to theft by finding, though as J. C. Smith noted, with one important exception, the Act is "obviously intended" to preserve the substance of the common law rule.[175] As for the offense of writing bad checks, that is addressed under the Fraud Act 2006 as a potentially more serious offense.[176]

No explanation is offered for maintaining blackmail and handling as separate offenses. Despite the example of the MPC, the decision is presented as if it were obvious (which it may well be). But the CLRC report is quite candid about the struggle its framers went through in deciding how to deal with the theft by deception offenses:

The sub-committee for a considerable time proposed that the general offence of theft should be made to cover the present offence of obtaining by false pretences under 1916 s. 32(1). It might seem appropriate to extend theft in this way in order to make it cover as many ways as possible of getting property dishonestly. But in the end the sub-committee gave up the idea (to the regret of some members), and the full committee agreed. In spite of its attractions, it seemed to the majority of the committee that the scheme would be unsatisfactory. Obtaining by false pretenses is ordinarily thought of as different from theft, because in the former the owner in fact consents to part with his ownership; a bogus beggar is regarded as a rogue but not as a thief, and so are his less petty counterparts. To create a new offence of theft to include conduct which ordinary people would find difficult to regard as theft would be a mistake.[177]

Like the MPC, the Theft Act also did away with the requirement that property actually be taken and carried away. In its place it required merely an *appropriation,* which it defined as "any assumption by a person of the rights of an owner," and then extended the concept to cover a case where *D* (the defendant) has come by the property without stealing it and subsequently assumes "a right to it by keeping or dealing with it as owner."[178]

The Theft Act follows a mostly uniform approach to sentencing. As the CLRC put it in its *Eighth Report,* "[e]xcept in three cases (burglary, criminal deception and taking a motor vehicle or other conveyance without authority) we have provided single maximum penalties for the offences in place of the present widely different penalties depending on various factors—the kind of property involved, the relations between the offender and the owner, [and] the method by which or the place where the offence is committed."[179] The result of all this was a leveling in the punishment of theft, with maximum penalties raised with respect to some theft offenses, and lowered with respect to others.

Finally, the Theft Act offers a consolidated definition of property that, though certainly broader than at common law, is nevertheless narrower than under the MPC. The Theft Act replaces the ad hoc, piecemeal approach that characterized the common law and older statutes with a uniform definition of property, which includes "money and all other property, real or personal, including things in action and other intangible property." But at the same time, it excludes from its scope the theft of services, which is dealt with in a separate provision and subject to a maximum penalty of five years,[180] and offers special rules regarding the theft of land, wild animals, fruits, flowers, foliage, and mushrooms.[181] Finally, like the legislative history of the MPC, the legislative history of the English Theft Act has little or nothing to say about the implications of treating as equivalent for purposes of sentencing theft offenses that may or may not be equivalent in terms of blameworthiness. The sole rationale offered for consolidation was a desire to simplify the arcane complexities of the common law.[182]

The influence of the English Theft Act's approach to consolidation on the development of Anglophone law was arguably even greater than the MPC's. Unlike the MPC, which must be enacted piece by piece in each state, the Theft Act became the law of the land in England and Wales essentially overnight. The introduction of the concept of dishonesty has had a particularly profound influence on how English-speaking lawyers think about theft (as covered in Chapter 2). And it has been the English Theft Act, rather than the MPC, that has provided the more direct model for consolidation in Australia.

Theft Law in Australia and Scotland

As in the United States, but unlike in England and Canada, the criminal law of Australia varies significantly from state to state.[183] This is strikingly true in the case of theft law. On the one hand is New South Wales, Australia's largest state, comprising nearly a third of its population, which continues to adhere to the common law of theft, with some statutory extensions. On the other hand is Victoria, which, starting in 1975, derived its law of theft from the English Theft Act (though Australian judicial interpretation of the Theft Act deviates in some ways from judicial interpretation in England).[184] Meanwhile, Queensland and Western Australia subscribe to a code originally adopted in 1900 (the Griffith Code), which was based on Stephen's codification of common law.[185] Tasmania has a code as well, but it is based on common law. In the mid-1990s, work began on an Australian Model Criminal Code project. One of the first objects of reform was the law of theft.[186] Rather than rewriting the law of theft from scratch, the Code committee drafted what was essentially a modified version of the Theft Act. That model version, in turn, was adopted, with some minor changes in wording, by the Australian Capital Territory (ACT) as well as in federal (Commonwealth) legislation.[187]

As for Scotland, it alone among Anglophone jurisdictions retains not only a common law of theft, but also a common law of murder, rape, assault, and other core offenses. In 2003, in the wake of devolution of sovereignty to the Scottish Executive, an attempt was made, unofficially, by several legal academics—including, interestingly, Edinburgh University Professor Alexander McCall Smith, who would soon thereafter go on to fame and fortune as the author of the *No. 1 Ladies' Detective Agency* books—to draft a new criminal code for Scotland.[188] Section 77 of the draft code broadly defined theft as "steal[ing] another person's property," and defined stealing, in turn, as "appropriating property, without the owner's consent, with the intention of depriving the owner permanently of it or being reckless as to whether or not the owner is deprived permanently of it."[189] Another significant provision in Section 77 stated that "depriving a person of property includes depriving that person of its value."[190] Elsewhere in the Code, the term *property* was defined to include "property of every description, whether moveable or not and whether corporeal or not, and . . . money and electricity."[191] According to the Commentary, "Section 77 restores the definition of theft to what most people would regard as theft. It brings the law more into line with ordinary usage."[192] Despite its broad definition of theft, however, the proposed Code retained separate provisions for piracy, robbery, extortion, fraud, embezzlement, forgery, reset (the Scottish version of receiving stolen property), and making off without payment.[193] The Code went through a fairly extensive process of commentary, but in the end essentially died in committee, and Scotland, for the present, retains its common law of crimes.[194]

* * *

In sum, between approximately 1900 and 1975, Canada, the United States, England and Wales, and Australia saw a radical transformation in the law of theft. The result has been a simpler—but also flatter and more homogenized—law of theft, one denuded of much of its moral content.

Theft Law outside the Anglophone Tradition

Much of the rhetoric of theft law reform supposes that the distinction among the various common law theft offenses was primarily the product of accidents in the history of Anglo-American law. According to the accepted view, English judges and Parliament created a succession of separate theft offenses not because they reflected any "meaningful difference . . . in terms of the culpability of the actors,"[195] but rather because creating such distinctions was an expedient way of circumventing existing limitations in theft law doctrine.

If that was all there was to such offenses, however, one would not expect to see them occurring outside the common law tradition. Curiously, the framers of the MPC and the English Theft Act seem to have made almost no attempt to think comparatively.[196] Had they done so, they would have observed something quite striking: they would have seen that the basic distinctions recognized by English common law—between theft by stealth, theft by deception, theft by coercion, theft by breach of trust, and the like—have also been recognized in numerous other systems of criminal law around the world, including systems with little or no historical or cultural connection to English common law. This suggests the possibility that such distinctions are *not* just the product of arbitrary historical accidents, or even the particular economic history of England in the Industrial Revolution and later, but instead reflect something deeper and more universal.

Consider the case of the *Strafgesetzbuch* (StGB), the German Criminal Code.[197] Section 242 (*Diebstahl*) defines the basic offense of larceny as "tak[ing] chattels belonging to another away from another with the intention of unlawfully appropriating them for himself or a third person." Section 244(1)(3) defines a separate offense of theft by housebreaking. Section 253 (*Erpressung*) makes it a crime to engage in extortion, defined as using force or threat to coerce another to commit an act causing economic detriment to himself or another. Section 257 (*Begünstigung*) makes it a crime to buy or possess stolen goods. Section 263 defines the basic offense of fraud (*Betrug*) as obtaining property by pretending false facts or distorting or suppressing true facts. Section 266 defines the separate offense of embezzlement or abuse of trust (*Untreue*). None of these offenses are interchangeable with respect to charging or proof. In some cases, the StGB also distinguishes thefts based on the type of property stolen. For example, Section 242 is limited to theft of chattels (*bewegliche Sache*). Using deception to obtain goods results in a maximum penalty of five years while using deception to obtain services results in a maximum penalty of one year.[198] There is, in addition, a separate provision for theft of electrical energy (Section 248c).

The Argentine *Código Penal* follows a roughly parallel approach.[199] As Marcelo Ferrante has explained, the Code has "nothing like an umbrella crime type of theft under which every case of misappropriation might fall."[200] Instead, its approach to theft is more like the common law's than the MPC's. Article 162 (*Hurto*) broadly defines the offense of larceny in terms of misappropriating someone else's movable property, but it is invariably construed more narrowly to require that the offender "take away" the stolen thing from its legitimate holder. The maximum penalty is six years. Article 168 (*Extorsión*) makes it a crime to use "intimidation" to obtain property. The maximum penalty is ten years. Article 172 (*Estafa*), defining fraud, or obtaining by deception, has been interpreted by courts and commentators as requiring that the offender use deception to cause "a person mistakenly to believe that there are reasons to transfer property . . . and the deceived person, acting on the basis of her mistaken beliefs, makes the transfer and thus she (or somebody else) gets harmed."[201] Article 173, Section 7 (*defraudación*) defines the offense of embezzlement and is intended to "capture[] the behavior of an agent who bears special duties to act on behalf of another person—particularly on behalf of another person's interests—and, by violating any such duty, set[s] back the property interests she was obliged to advance or protect."[202] The Argentine Code also contains a provision on receiving stolen property, but it is contained in a separate chapter concerning crimes against public administration rather than against property.[203] Once again, the interchangeability of MPC Section 223.1(1) is missing.

Indeed, virtually every criminal code that one looks at from outside the Anglophone world—including those in Austria, Finland, France, Japan, the Netherlands, Nigeria, Spain, and Sweden—contain separate provisions, separate punishments, and no evidentiary interchangeability for offenses that resemble common law offenses like larceny, embezzlement, false pretenses, extortion, and receiving stolen property.[204] Similar patterns can also be found in the law of ancient Rome and in Jewish law.[205]

This is not to say, of course, that what constitutes false pretenses, extortion, or embezzlement in Germany, Argentina, or elsewhere is exactly the same as what constituted these offenses under the

Anglo-American common law of theft. Nor is it to suggest that we would necessarily be better off with a system of theft law modeled on the German, Argentine, French, or Japanese systems; each presumably has its own problems. But it is telling that the framers of the MPC and the Theft Act never sought to make such a comparison. Had they done so, they would have found that, contrary to what Professor Schwartz had to say, in most of the world, it does indeed make a "difference which way you choose to steal."

Scholarly Reaction (or Lack Thereof) to Consolidation

Given the scope and significance of the changes that Anglo-American theft law experienced during the last century, it is surprising how little scholarly commentary the move to consolidation has generated. The literature that did emerge during the twentieth century can be divided, roughly, into three baskets.

The first basket, as noted earlier, includes early law review literature that critiqued the common law of theft and almost invariably called for reform through consolidation. For obvious reasons, this literature mostly ended in mid-century, though there continue to be calls for consolidation in those few jurisdictions, such as Virginia, that remain primarily common law in their approach.[206]

The second basket includes works that are mostly historical. Of particular interest are two major books that employed the common law history of theft law as a vehicle for examining broader theoretical issues in the criminal law. The first is *Theft, Law and Society*, by Jerome Hall, originally published in 1935, and republished in revised form in 1952. Writing from the perspective of sociological jurisprudence (as defined by Cardozo and Pound), Hall sought to show the social and historical bases for a series of changes in the law of theft, beginning in the fifteenth century. For Hall, the development of theft law occurring during the crucial period of the eighteenth century was primarily the product of the rise of the modern commercial economy. Hall also sought to place the modern debate over statutory reform, particularly with respect to offenses like receiving stolen property and automobile theft, within the context of public policy, inquiring into the likely effects of various proposed changes in the law. However, despite his efforts to explain the origins of some of the most puzzling aspects of the common law of theft, as well as his interest in the process of law reform itself, Hall never expressly argued for or against consolidation.

Notwithstanding Hall's position as one of the leading criminal law theorists of the mid-twentieth century, his influence on actual law reform was minimal. He had been a member of the faculty at Louisiana State University only a few years before the draft Louisiana Code of 1942 was enacted, yet he is cited nowhere in the extensive commentary prepared by Dale Bennett and his colleagues. And though Hall was appointed a member of the Council of the ALI at the time it began its work on the MPC, he resigned before the project had progressed very far, presumably as a result of his disagreement with Wechsler and Schwartz concerning the proper approach to criminal law reform.[207] Indeed, given Wechsler's earlier scathing criticism of Hall's embrace of retributivism, it is surprising that Wechsler would have seen Hall appointed to the Council in the first place.[208] Perhaps, given Hall's eminence, Wechsler felt he had no choice. In any event, Hall's role in formulating the MPC, including the theft provisions, was negligible. The man who was not only one of the giants of twentieth-century criminal law theory but also arguably its leading theorist of theft law therefore seems to have played virtually no role in the century's most significant reforms.

Also of major importance is George Fletcher's 1978 book, *Rethinking Criminal Law*, justifiably regarded as one of the twentieth century's most significant works of Anglo-American criminal law theory.[209] For Fletcher, the common law development of theft law was not primarily about historical accidents *or* social and economic development. Fletcher's analysis of theft law is rooted in the internal logic of the law itself. He uses the history of theft law in an ingenious and distinctive way to bring out what he perceives as various deep conceptual patterns in criminal law generally, especially the shift from what he calls the pattern of "manifest" criminality (which connotes some observable harm or social mischief in the offender's act) to "subjective" criminality (which begins with the notion that the core of criminal conduct is the intention to violate a legally protected interest).[210] Fletcher's interest was almost exclusively in the historical development of the common law of theft rather than in its modern, consolidated form. Yet, given his fundamental respect for both the common law history as well as the German tradition of criminal law, it is not surprising that he would express skepticism, if only in passing and somewhat tangentially, about the idea of wholesale consolidation. As Fletcher puts it (referring not to the MPC per se, but rather to the earlier, more basic conceptualization of theft law as a crime against interests in property):

> The curious aspect of this reduction . . . is that it equates all [such] offenses in their gravity. Yet we have reason to believe that the offenses should be differentiated in their seriousness. How else can we explain why larceny dates back to the beginning of recorded legal history, while embezzlement is born of legislative command in the late eighteenth century? How else can we explain the tendency at various stages of history to regard one of the offenses as worthy of greater condemnation?[211]

This is one of numerous penetrating insights contained in Fletcher's book, though it never leads to any specific critique of consolidation or call for revision.

A third basket of theft law scholarship consists primarily of doctrinal works written in common law jurisdictions other than the United States— including books by Winifred Holland (in Canada); by C. R. Williams and M. S. Weinberg (in Australia); and by A. T. H. Smith, Edward Griew, Edward Phillips and colleagues, and J. C. Smith (in England).[212] Although such works are critical of various aspects of contemporary theft law, and occasionally shed light on its deeper normative structure, hardly any question the basic assumption that consolidation is well-founded.[213] (The most notable exception is Alex Steel, who has argued for a "disaggregation" of theft offenses under Australian law.[214])

In the United States, by contrast, there has been nothing more than a trickle of literature on post-consolidation theft law. What little American scholarship there has been has focused almost exclusively on the history of theft at common law.[215] Most striking has been an almost complete lack of any critical assessment of the MPC's scheme of consolidation.

A CRITIQUE OF CONSOLIDATION

The law of theft as it stood at the beginning of the twentieth century undoubtedly contained many unnecessarily complex and essentially useless distinctions. Twentieth-century reformers were right to want to rid the law of them. But in rewriting the law of theft as they did, they went too far. While ridding the law of what was bad, they eliminated much that was good as well. It didn't have to be this way.

Problems with MPC Consolidation from an Internal Perspective

Before offering my challenge to the foundations of the modern, consolidated law of theft, it is appropriate to briefly consider several ways in which the MPC theft scheme is problematic even on its own terms.

To begin with, even if it made sense to use the value of property stolen as the sole criterion for grading thefts, the particular grading scheme that the Code uses would still be far too blunt. The MPC makes theft of property worth less than $50 a petty misdemeanor, theft of goods valued between $50 and $500 a misdemeanor, and theft of property worth more than $500 a third-degree felony.[216] Such a scheme is incapable of making the kinds of distinctions necessary. For example, under the MPC scheme, the thieves who stole Leonardo da Vinci's *Madonna of the Yarnwinder* (valued at $65 million) from Drumlanrig Castle in Scotland in 2003 would be subject to the same range of punishment as a thief who stole a Trek Soho SS bicycle (which retails for $549): a minimum of one to two years and a maximum of five years imprisonment.[217]

Part of the problem is that the MPC has too few grading categories not just for theft but for all crimes.[218] But the problem is exacerbated in the case of theft, where even the most serious cases are never treated as first or second degree felonies. Of course, any punishment scheme that is based on the value of property stolen must have cutoffs at some point. Since the MPC is only a model, states are obviously free to enact inflation-adjusted cutoffs of their own. Still, the idea that two cutoffs alone—one between petty misdemeanors and misdemeanors and a second between misdemeanors and third-degree felonies—could ever be sufficient to capture the kind of moral distinctions we regularly make on the basis of the value of property stolen seems plainly wrong.

A better, though hardly perfect, model is provided by the *Federal Sentencing Guidelines Manual,* which contains sentencing ranges for forty-three of the most frequently prosecuted federal crimes.[219] Each of the offenses is assigned a base offense level from which upward and downward departures are made. The theft offenses found in

Table 1 Federal Sentencing Guidelines—level of punishment as function of value of property stolen

	Loss	Increase in level
(A)	$5,000 or less	No increase
(B)	More than $5,000	Add 2
(C)	More than $10,000	Add 4
(D)	More than $30,000	Add 6
(E)	More than $70,000	Add 8
(F)	More than $120,000	Add 10
(G)	More than $200,000	Add 12
(H)	More than $400,000	Add 14
(I)	More than $1,000,000	Add 16
(J)	More than $2,500,000	Add 18
(K)	More than $7,000,000	Add 20
(L)	More than $20,000,000	Add 22
(M)	More than $50,000,000	Add 24
(N)	More than $100,000,000	Add 26
(O)	More than $200,000,000	Add 28
(P)	More than $400,000,000	Add 30

Section 2B1.1 of the Guidelines have a base offense level of 6. The most significant factor in determining the ultimate punishment is the value of the property stolen. The Guidelines instruct that if the loss exceeds $5,000, the offense level should be increased according to the scale shown in Table 1, which is obviously far more finely graded than that found in the MPC.

In my view, the Sentencing Guidelines—both because they contain more sentencing categories and because those categories track differences in value—offer a more sensible approach to grading theft than that taken by the MPC.

Another internal problem with the Code's approach to theft can be found in Section 223.0(6), which defines the key term *property* as "anything of value, including ... tangible and intangible personal property."[220] The idea of defining property in terms of *property* is not necessarily flawed. One could certainly imagine a provision that said something to the effect that "property [for purposes of theft law] shall include both tangible and intangible property . . . *consistent with a common sense understanding of those terms,*" or "*as those concepts were traditionally*

understood at common law," or *"as they are understood in civil law."*[221]
Though a bit vague, such an approach would nevertheless be meaningful. But the MPC provision does not say any of these things, and
one is left scratching one's head as to how the term *property* is meant to
be understood.

Finally, there is Section 223.7, the Theft of Services provision, which
reflects a category mistake. All of the other nondefinitional provisions
in Section 223 involve variations in the *means* by which theft can be
committed. Section 223.7 is the only provision that involves the *type* of
property that is stolen. To the extent that theft of services presents
unique issues not presented by theft of goods or real property, it should
have been dealt with in Section 223.0, which defines the types of property that can be stolen.

Distinctions Useful and Useless

One of the main goals of consolidation was to rid theft law of concepts
excessively technical and essentially useless. As an example, consider
the following two hypotheticals of the sort that typically appear in bar
exam preparation materials:[222]

- *A* owns a firm that sells and repairs automobiles. *A* entrusts his
  employee D^1 with a car for his use while he is on the job. D^1 takes
  the car and fails to return it, converting it to his own use and
  intending to keep it. What offense has D^1 committed?
- *A* owns a firm that sells and repairs automobiles. *C*, a customer of
  A's, gives his car to D^2, an employee of *A*, for repairs. D^2 then
  converts the car to his own use, intending to keep it. What
  offense has D^2 committed?

The answers are larceny and embezzlement, respectively. Larceny
involves the trespassory taking of property from the possession of
another. Embezzlement consists of appropriating property with which
one has been entrusted. D^1 is said to have been given custody of the
car rather than possession. A person with physical control of property
has custody of it, but the right to use it is substantially restricted by the
person who is in constructive possession of it. Employees often have
mere custody of property they use on behalf of their employer. If D^1
keeps the car and converts it to his own use, then he has violated *A*'s

right to possession; his act is trespassory, and the offense he has committed is therefore larceny. In the second case, by contrast, D^2 has been *given* possession of the car. When he keeps it and converts it to his own use, he cannot commit larceny, because larceny is an offense against possession. Instead, the offense D^2 has committed is embezzlement.

Granted, it makes no sense to treat these cases as involving distinct offenses. From a moral perspective, they are virtually indistinguishable. Both involve a person who is (1) entrusted with the temporary care of another's property and (2) breaches that trust to convert the property, permanently, to his own use.[223] Both are also essentially indistinguishable in terms of deterrence, detection, and proof. To treat one case as larceny and the other as embezzlement, and to subject them to potentially different penalties, makes little sense. To the extent that twentieth-century reformers did away with such meaningless distinctions, they did the right thing. But the fact that it makes no sense to treat *these* two cases as involving distinct offenses does not necessarily mean that there should be no distinction at all between larceny and embezzlement, or between larceny and false pretenses, extortion, and receiving stolen property.[224]

The "Wrong Form of Theft" and "In the Gap" Defenses

Another rationale for consolidation was that the common law of theft allowed too many culpable offenders to escape liability by arguing that (1) the form of theft they had actually committed was different from the form of theft charged, or (2) their conduct fell into a "gap" between offenses. (There are also cases in which the defendant argued that the kind of property he actually stole was different from that alleged in the indictment.[225]) How serious were these problems under pre-consolidation theft law? It is difficult to say. The MPC Commentary offers no statistics, and the anecdotal evidence is thin.

Here is how the wrong form of theft (WFT) defense problem is described in the MPC Commentary:

> An offender who is prosecuted for fraud might escape [conviction] by proving that the victim did not believe the representations made to him but was merely frightened by them. Similarly, one who gives a bad check as a down payment on an automobile which is thereupon

delivered to him on conditional sale may defeat criminal prosecution for obtaining by false pretenses by arguing that the vendor reserved title and that the vendee could therefore only be guilty of larceny, the offense against possession.[226]

As evidence of this problem, the commentary cites a total of five appellate court cases, all federal. On examination, however, none of the cases involves a scenario in which a defendant was charged with one common law theft offense and argued that he had actually committed a different common law theft offense. Instead, all of the cases involve defendants who were charged with a federal offense (mail fraud, wire fraud, bribery, or extortion) and argued that they had actually committed a different offense, whether federal or state. Moreover, none of the cases cited involved larceny, embezzlement, receiving stolen property, failing to return lost property, or the state law offenses of false pretenses or extortion.

I suspect that cases in which defendants have successfully proffered a WFT defense are, in fact, quite rare. My own search turned up only a handful of cases in which this occurred.[227] Moreover, a student author in Nevada actually asked prosecutors whether they had "ever encountered a problem where they charged a defendant under one particular common law theory, like larceny, but the evidence later turned out to support a different theory."[228] All of them stated that they had never seen such a case.

More importantly, even in those apparently rare cases in which the WFT defense has been successful, it is not clear that the defense necessarily led to any injustice. Consider *Norton v. United States,* the only WFT case discussed in any detail by the MPC Commentary.[229] The defendant, Violet Wells Norton, was charged with scheming to defraud the movie star Clark Gable by writing him letters demanding child support for her daughter, Gwendoline. In the letters, Norton falsely claimed that she had conceived the child with Gable while he was in England in September 1922. In fact, Norton knew that she and Gable had never had sexual relations. Therefore, it seems highly unlikely that she intended to deceive him into handing over the money; rather, she was probably intending to coerce him. For this reason, the court of appeals reversed her conviction. It determined that what Norton had actually committed was not false pretenses, but rather blackmail.[230]

It is hardly clear, however, that there was anything unjust about the court's decision in Norton's favor. After all, theft by false pretenses almost certainly *was* the wrong charge. Norton could have been convicted of that offense only if she had intended to deceive Gable himself into believing that she had conceived the child with him. To be sure, Gable was a well-known womanizer. It might well have been possible to deceive him into believing that he had conceived a child with a woman with whom he had actually had relations. It seems less likely, however, that he could have been deceived into believing that he had conceived a child with a woman whom he apparently had never met, particularly when he was not even in the country at the time the encounter was alleged to have occurred. The proper charge, then, *was* blackmail, just as Norton had argued. For her to make that argument and prevail on it does not seem to reflect any particular injustice in the system.

Moreover, even if the WFT defense really was a major problem, there would clearly be ways of fixing it other than allowing evidence of one form of theft to establish proof of an entirely different form. There is no reason, constitutional or otherwise, why prosecutors could not charge two or more offenses in the alternative. Presumably, all of the jurors would have to be convinced that the defendant had committed one particular kind of theft, but it is hard to see why this is a problem. Indeed, this is precisely how the jury system is supposed to function.

Finally, even where a defendant was successful in obtaining an acquittal or reversal on the grounds that she had committed a form of theft different from that charged, there would ordinarily be no procedural bar to her subsequent prosecution for the alternative form of theft. Under *Blockburger v. United States,* successive prosecution following acquittal is barred by the Double Jeopardy Clause only where the two offenses for which the defendant is punished or tried are regarded as the same offense.[231] If two offenses each contain an element not contained in the other, then they are not the same offense, and subsequent prosecution is permitted. In cases such as *Norton,* the same offense test would not be met since extortion contains an element not contained in fraud (namely, coercion or threats), and fraud contains an element not contained in extortion (namely, deception).[232]

And what about the "in the gap" defense? How serious a problem did that pose under common law? Once again, the MPC Commentary offers little guidance. My own research indicates that there

certainly were cases at common law in which defendants were successful in arguing that their dishonest appropriations of property constituted no form of theft at all. A good example is the 1957 English
case of *Moynes v. Coopper,* decided under the Larceny Act 1916.[233] A pay
clerk miscalculated the amount of money Moynes was to receive in his
pay packet. At the time he received the packet, Moynes did not know
there was an excess. He discovered it only later, at which point he
decided to keep the extra money rather than return it. Moynes was
charged with larceny and convicted. On appeal, the court reversed his
conviction, reasoning that he lacked the *animus furandi* necessary to
commit the offense.[234]

Admittedly, such cases present a problem. It was indeed unjust for
the defendant in *Moynes,* who was clearly acting dishonestly, to avoid
conviction. But, once again, the question is whether creating a single
overarching theft offense is the appropriate solution. Coopper's conviction was reversed because there was no concurrence between his
taking possession of the pay packet and his intent to deprive; he formed
that intent only after he already had the packet in his possession.
There was a relatively easy fix for the problem presented: rather than
requiring that the offender necessarily "take" property belonging to
another, it was enough that the law be changed to say that one commits theft if one "exercises unlawful control over" it (as under the
MPC), "converts" it to one's own use (as under the Canadian Criminal
Code), or "assumes rights of the owner" over it (as under the English
Theft Act). It was not necessary to completely rewrite the law of theft
to achieve such a result.

Consolidation and the Principle of Fair Labeling

Regardless of whether the law of theft *could* have been improved
without eradicating basic distinctions in the means by which theft is
committed and the type of property stolen, the question remains
whether theft law *ought* to preserve such distinctions. I believe the
answer is yes, and that the rationale lies in the notion of what has been
called the principle *fair labeling.*

Most scholars agree that society's ability to enforce compliance with
the law lies less in the power to impose sanctions if they stray than it
does in the norms by which people direct their own lives. Generally,

people refrain from committing crimes not because they fear punishment but because they believe crime is morally wrong.[235] Thus, it is important that the law be consistent with moral norms. As Paul Robinson and John Darley have put it:

> The criminal justice system's power to stigmatize depends on the legal codes having moral credibility in the community. The law needs to have earned a reputation for accurately representing what violations do and do not deserve moral condemnation from the community's point of view. This reputation will be undercut if liability and punishment rules deviate from a community's shared intuitions of justice.[236]

Where the criminal law is viewed as offering a reliable statement of what the community regards as wrongful, citizens are more likely to follow its lead in cases that are unclear. When criminal codes deviate from the norms of the community, citizens may be less likely to cooperate with or acquiesce in the system's demands.[237]

It is not merely the case that social norms play a role in shaping the criminal law. The criminal law also plays an important role in informing, shaping, and reinforcing societal norms. Children and adults learn what is wrong in part from what the law says is wrong. When the law deviates too far from existing norms, its instructive function is impaired as well. Maintaining consistency between the law and social norms is important not only in connection with deciding *which* conduct should or should not be criminalized; such consistency is also vital in deciding *how much* to punish. If the legal system imposes more, or less, punishment on some crimes than citizens believe is deserved, the system seems unfair; it loses its credibility and, eventually, its effectiveness.

What is ultimately at stake is what Andrew Ashworth has called the principle of fair labeling, the idea that "widely felt distinctions between kinds of offences and degrees of wrongdoing are respected and signaled by the law, and that offences should be divided and labeled so as to represent fairly the nature and magnitude of the law-breaking."[238] A corollary of this principle, presumably, is that distinctions between kinds of offenses and degrees of wrongdoing that are *not* widely felt should *not* be reflected in the law. As Ashworth puts it, "one of the basic aims of the criminal law is to ensure a proportionate response to law-breaking, thereby assisting the law's educative or declaratory function in sustaining and reinforcing social standards."[239] Where people consistently regard two or more types of conduct as different in terms of blameworthiness, the law ought to reflect those differences. Other things being equal, it ought to punish the more blameworthy act more severely and the less blameworthy act less severely.[240]

All of these considerations would seem to apply in the case of theft.[241] If the law treated some kinds of theft more, or less, harshly than people believed was warranted, the law would be seen as unjust and out of step, and would lose some of its moral authority and effectiveness. The same could be said if the law failed to criminalize some forms of theft that people believed should be criminalized, or criminalized other forms of theft that people thought should be free of criminalization.

This is not to deny the potential for *over*-particularism. As James Chalmers and Fiona Leverick have argued, "[n]ot only does [very specific crime labeling] over-complicate the law, running the risk of needless arguments about the appropriate charge in respect of indisputably criminal conduct, it also runs the risk that novel conduct will not be covered at all because offences have been drawn up with too high a degree of specificity."[242] The challenge for criminal law codifiers is thus to find the optimal level of specificity—one that balances consistency with widespread social norms on the one hand, and administrability on the other.

Testing Community Perceptions of Theft Seriousness Empirically

To determine the extent to which the principle of fair labeling has or has not been respected in the consolidated law of theft, it is necessary to know whether and to what extent moral distinctions between various kinds of theft are in fact widely felt. And the only way to make such a determination is to ask people how they feel. Many studies measuring community perceptions of crime seriousness have included theft offenses among the crimes ranked; however, such studies are of relatively little value for present purposes.

Typical is a study done by Michael O'Connell and Anthony Whelan, testing the perception of crime seriousness among a representative sample of Irish citizens.[243] Among the ten crime scenarios ranked by their subjects, six involve what might be properly viewed as theft or theft-related conduct (the other scenarios involved murder, selling drugs, assault, and underage sex). Ranked in descending order of seriousness, the six acts were as follows:

> The offender, a Garda [police] officer, who discovers a burglary in a shop, steals £30 worth of goods from a store.
> The offender, using physical force, robs a victim of £75. The victim is injured but not sent to a hospital.
> The offender sets up a bogus mail-order company and through it fraudulently obtains £1,500 from a number of private individuals.
> The offender sets up a bogus company and through it, fraudulently obtains £3,000 from a big manufacturer.
> The offender breaks into a person's house and steals property worth £30.
> The offender dishonestly obtains social welfare benefits to the value of £30.

The problem with these rankings, at least for present purposes, is that they fail to keep constant key factors such as the value of property stolen (property values range from £30 to £3,000), the identity of the victims (these include a big company, the state, and private individuals), the identity of the offenders (offenders include a police officer and private individuals), and the means by which the theft was effected (means include violence, deceit, and housebreaking). It is thus impossible to know, for example, whether, other things being equal, stealing property by means of physical force was viewed as more serious than stealing property by means of deceit; whether stealing property from an individual was viewed as more serious than stealing property from a big company; or even whether stealing £3,000 was viewed as more serious than stealing £30.

Other studies, both before and since, have suffered from similar limitations.[244] To improve upon the research, my collaborator, social psychologist Matthew Kugler, and I devised a study to determine the extent to which people's moral intuitions about the blameworthiness of different forms of theft are consistent with the way in which such offenses are treated under a consolidated theft regime. In particular, we wanted to know if, and to what extent, people view various acts of theft as morally distinguishable based on (1) the means by which the act was committed, and (2) the type of property stolen.

Before describing the study, a brief word about the use of experimental methods in such contexts is in order. Experimental philosophy is an emerging area of academic study that seeks to shed light on traditional philosophical problems by gathering information about how people think and talk about such problems and by studying how they behave in practice.[245]

As an example, especially apt for present purposes, consider a recent study by Eric Schwitzgebel entitled "Do Ethicists Steal More Books?"[246] Schwitzgebel examines the claim, made by various philosophers over the years, that explicit reflection about morality promotes morally correct conduct. To test this hypothesis, he asks whether ethics professors, who presumably spend a lot of their time thinking about morality, are more likely to behave ethically. To this end, he examined the rates at which books about ethics are missing from leading academic libraries compared to other philosophy books similar in age and popularity. He found that relatively obscure, contemporary ethics books likely to be borrowed mainly by professors and advanced philosophy students were about 50 percent *more* likely to be missing than non-ethics books and that classic (pre-1900) ethics books were about twice as likely to be missing. He concludes that, "[w]ith respect to their treatment of library books, then, it does not appear that the people reading philosophical ethics behave any better than those reading other sorts of philosophy; indeed, the opposite seems to be the case."[247]

Whether or not Schwitzgebel's methodology is valid (and I admit to considerable skepticism concerning the notion that we can discover anything meaningful about the moral lives of philosophers by looking at which books are missing from their university libraries), the basic idea that intuitions are sometimes worth testing empirically seems correct. If we take seriously the claim that deep, reflective thinking about ethics has the tendency to make one behave more ethically, we ought to be willing to put that claim to the test. (The problem, of course, is figuring out how to do so accurately.) Similarly, if we believe in the notion that criminal liability and punishment rules should aspire to consistency with a community's shared intuitions of justice, we should be prepared to measure what those shared intuitions of justice are. In this case, my pre-study intuition was that there *are* morally salient differences among types of theft depending on the means by which the theft is committed and the type of property stolen. I wanted to know if these intuitions were shared by others.

I should be clear, however, about what I believe is, and is not, the value of studying community attitudes regarding the seriousness of crime. First, I do not mean to suggest that the criminal law should always follow popular opinion, or that people's moral intuitions are necessarily correct.[248] Second, I do not mean to imply that empirical studies of this sort can provide a substitute for serious normative reflection about deontological desert.[249] Third, I acknowledge that giving subjects relatively brief descriptions of fictional crime scenarios and asking them to make blameworthiness judgments is not the only, and perhaps not even the most accurate, way to assess their views regarding the relative seriousness of criminal acts.[250] Fourth, although I do believe that the basic prohibition on theft is probably universal, I make no claim that the sometimes subtle blameworthy distinctions our subjects made regarding the means by which theft is committed and the type of property stolen are also universal.[251] Rather, I view empirical studies regarding community views of crime seriousness as a *supplement* to normative analysis, a way for the analyst (in this case, me) to check the validity of his or her own intuitions, and as a means for assessing the likely effectiveness of offense grading.

Description of the Study

The study included 172 participants.[252] All were first-year Rutgers University–Newark law students, who completed the study during their orientation period prior to the start of classes in the Fall 2008 semester.[253] The test was conducted in an auditorium, with all participants being run at the same time. As study materials were distributed, participants were told that they would be asked to evaluate two sets of stories related to theft offenses. The first set (of twelve scenarios) concerned the theft, by various means, of a $350 bicycle. The scenarios were pasted on index cards that were labeled with random letter combinations. The cards were shuffled to randomize the order of the cards for each participant. Participants were told to read the scenarios, sort them from most to least blameworthy, and record their rankings on an answer sheet. If scenarios were tied by blameworthiness, participants could indicate this by writing their codes on the same line or by making a note to that effect. They then rated each story's blameworthiness on a scale of 1 to 9 and assigned a punishment. The experimenter also informed participants, orally, that the sentence for thefts of this type could range from no punishment or a few days up to 20 years in extreme cases.

The second set of stories concerned the theft of a $50 test preparation tool prepared by the ABC Test Prep Company. The form of the study aid varied. In one scenario it was a physical book; in another, a downloaded electronic file containing the text of the book; in yet another, a seat at a lecture for which the hall had empty seats (thus the illicit attendee did not prevent a paying customer from attending); and, in a final scenario, a seat at a lecture for which the hall did not have any empty seats (potential paying customers were thereby denied admission). These vignettes were presented as paired comparisons. Participants were asked whether one story was more blameworthy than the other. They also rated the scenarios' blameworthiness on a scale of 1 to 9.

Varying the Means by Which Theft Is Committed

As noted, the first set of stories concerned the theft of a $350 bicycle. The owner of the bike, Owen, was described in the instructions as having a good job, a family, and a desire to get in better shape. The thief, Tom, was described as living alone in an apartment, holding a modest job, and being able to meet all of his basic needs. Varying across scenarios were the circumstances under which Tom acquired the bicycle. Subjects were asked to assess the wrongfulness of and assign a penalty to thefts that varied in method. The scenarios given to the subjects (without the identifying labels) were as follows:

Aggravated or armed robbery: While Owen was cleaning his bike in the driveway outside his house, Tom walked up to him, pointed a gun at him, and said, "Give me your bike or I will shoot you." Owen handed Tom the bike and Tom rode it away, intending to keep it.

Simple robbery: While Owen was cleaning his bike in the driveway outside his house, Tom walked up to him, grabbed the bike out of his hands, and rode it away, intending to keep it.

Extortion: While Owen was cleaning his bike in the driveway outside his house, Tom walked up to him and said, "Give me your bike or tomorrow I will burn down your house." Owen handed Tom the bike and Tom rode it away, intending to keep it.

Blackmail: While Owen was cleaning his bike in the driveway outside his house, Tom walked up to him and said, "Unless you give me your bike, I'm going to show your boss these embarrassing pictures of you from college." Owen handed Tom the bike and Tom rode it away, intending to keep it.

Theft by housebreaking/burglary: Owen put his bicycle in the basement of his house and then drove his car to the grocery store. While Owen was away, Tom climbed through a window into the basement, took Owen's bike, and rode it away, intending to keep it.

Larceny: Owen locked his bike with a chain to the front porch by his driveway and then drove his car to the grocery store. While Owen was away, Tom came up to the porch, picked the lock on the bike, and rode it away, intending to keep it.

Embezzlement: Owen's bike needed repairs, so he took it to the bike shop, where Tom works. At the end of the day, Tom took Owen's bike out of the shop and to his own apartment, intending to keep it for himself.

Looting: Owen left town because of an approaching hurricane. The storm was worse than expected: there was general chaos, flooding, and no electricity. Owen's garage door was damaged in the storm and the alarm system had no power. Tom walked into Owen's garage, took his bike, and rode the bike away even though he already had a bike. He planned to sell it for fast cash.

False pretenses: Owen realized that he didn't have enough time to ride his bicycle and decided to sell it. He placed an advertisement in a local newspaper, to which Tom responded. Tom negotiated a price with Owen and said, "I'll bring you the money tomorrow after I'm paid." At the time he said this, Tom had no intention of keeping his promise. Tom rode the bike away, intending to keep it.

Passing a bad check: Owen realized that he didn't have enough time to ride his bicycle and decided to sell it. He placed an advertisement in a local newspaper, to which Tom responded.

Tom negotiated a price with Owen, gave him a check, and rode the bike away, intending to keep it. At the time he gave the check to Owen, Tom knew that he did not have enough money in his account and that the bank would not cover the check.

Failing to return lost or misdelivered property: Owen's bike needed repairs, so he took it to the bike shop, which agreed to have a service deliver it to Owen's house once the repairs were done. Because of a computer glitch, the bike was accidentally delivered to Tom's apartment even though the tag had Owen's proper address. Tom decided to keep the bike and not tell Owen or the delivery service about it.

Receiving stolen property: Tom was walking along a street. The previous day, Owen's bike had been stolen. A person Tom did not know rode Owen's bike up to him and said, "I stole this bike and I'll sell it to you for just $20." Tom bought the bike and rode it away, intending to keep it for himself.

Results

Participants ranked the scenarios in order of blameworthiness and assigned a sentence to each of them. Ties in rank order data were entered as the midpoint of the tied range. For example, if theft by deadly threat was ranked as the most serious offense, it received a 12. If the next two crimes were tied, then each would be given a rank of 10.5 (falling midway between 10 and 11). The next crime would have a rank of 9, and so on.

Participants assigned punishment in terms of days, weeks, and years.[254] There was considerable variation in sentencing across participants. Some participants assigned a maximum sentence of many years; others, just a few weeks. Since our key interest in the study was how severely participants wished to punish each case relative to the other cases, we divided a person's sentence for a given scenario by his or her average sentence. Thus, the sentencing data are proportional in nature. This transformation also makes the sentencing data conform to statistical assumptions of normality.[255]

Data from all measures were remarkably consistent. Table 2 reports all means and standard deviations. For each measure, means that share a subscript are not significantly different from each other.[256] The rank

Table 2 Evaluations of scenarios from set 1

	Rank		Sentence		Blameworthiness	
Receiving stolen property	2.13_g	(1.30)	0.11_h	(0.18)	4.39_f	(2.34)
Failing to return misdelivered property	2.27_g	(1.56)	0.12_h	(0.24)	4.37_f	(2.37)
False pretenses	4.46_f	(1.83)	0.35_g	(0.36)	6.11_e	(2.01)
Passing a bad check	4.71_f	(1.93)	0.40_g	(0.41)	6.30_e	(2.05)
Looting	5.74_e	(2.56)	0.58_f	(0.55)	$6.51_{d,e}$	(2.01)
Embezzlement	5.98_e	(1.95)	0.55_f	(0.47)	$6.88_{c,d}$	(1.78)
Larceny	6.84_d	(1.79)	$0.69_{e,f}$	(0.51)	7.22_c	(1.56)
Blackmail	7.23_d	(3.14)	$0.86_{d,e}$	(0.76)	6.94_c	(2.04)
Simple robbery	8.38_c	(2.11)	1.00_d	(0.78)	7.70_b	(1.39)
Theft by housebreaking	8.53_c	(1.83)	1.24_c	(0.76)	7.73_b	(1.44)
Extortion	9.79_b	(2.25)	1.98_b	(1.22)	8.10_b	(1.41)
Armed robbery	11.86_a	(0.48)	4.10_a	(1.97)	8.95_a	(0.25)

Note: Means (standard deviations in parentheses) for all scenarios from the first set. Higher numbers indicate more blameworthy ranks, longer sentences, and higher blameworthiness scale scores. Means not sharing subscripts are significantly different at the $p < .05$ level.

order data shows a clear pattern. Theft using deadly threat (armed robbery) is considered the most blameworthy by a considerable margin. Extortion by threat of arson is a step below. Breaking into Owen's house and stealing from his basement (theft by housebreaking) is tied in the ranking with grabbing the bike from his hands on the street (simple robbery), though the former receives a slightly more severe sentence. On the next step, we have blackmail and taking the bike from Owen's porch (larceny). Below those are embezzlement (Tom-as-employee stealing the bike from the repair shop) and looting the bike for profit after the storm. Tied below those are the two cases of theft by deception: false pretenses and passing a bad check. Least blameworthy are receiving stolen property and failing to return misdelivered property. Figure 1 shows the rank order data in a bar chart (scale on the right axis).

The sentence data strongly support the rank order data. The sentence for theft by blackmail falls between theft by minimal force and

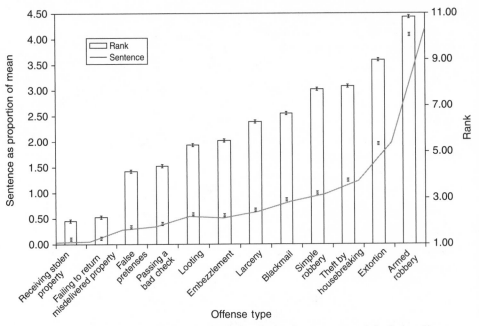

Figure 1 Sentence and rank order ratings for the various means of theft (set 1). *Note:* All error bars are +/- 1 standard error of the mean.

larceny and fails to differ significantly from either, but the significant differences in rank order otherwise replicate perfectly. The mean sentence for theft with minimal force (simple robbery) happens to be 1.00. This means that simple robbery received the average sentence. Theft with deadly threat (armed robbery) has a score of 4.20, meaning it received, on average, 4.2 times that sentence. Because the scale is proportional, it is also possible to say that theft by means of a bad check (.40) received on average 3.33 times as much punishment as retaining misdelivered property (.12); the sentence for extortion (1.98) was nearly twice that for simple robbery (1.00); and passing a bad check (.40), the worst of the fraud offenses, was punished only 40 percent as much as simple robbery, and only 47 percent as much as blackmail (.86). The sentence data are expressed as a line graph in Figure 1 (scale on the left axis). The blameworthiness rating scale data are consistent with both the rank order and sentence data. Differences on the blameworthiness scale are less clear than on the other measures because there was a ceiling effect; some participants considered all methods to be very blameworthy and the distinctions that they drew on other measures were not well reflected on this one.

For the rank order data, there is a clear pattern of five basic "bands" of blameworthiness. The first band consists of aggravated robbery, which was ranked by nearly every subject as significantly more blameworthy and deserving of significantly more punishment than every other theft offense, including simple robbery. To the extent that the MPC and the Theft Act treat robbery *in general* as the most serious theft offense, they are consistent with our assessment of public sentiment. But insofar as they fail to distinguish between aggravated and simple robbery, they are inconsistent with lay intuitions. Such intuitions are more consistent with the law in those states, such as New York, that distinguish between first and second degree robbery.[257]

The second band consists of extortion, which our subjects viewed as significantly more blameworthy than every other theft offense except aggravated robbery, but which the MPC treats as interchangeable with, and equivalent to, offenses such as theft by deception, receiving stolen property, blackmail, and the like. In this area, the MPC seems seriously out of touch with lay intuitions. Under current law, the punishment assigned to extortion is either too lenient or the punishment assigned to these other offenses is too harsh. The MPC and English Theft Act are also both inconsistent with lay intuitions to the extent that they fail to distinguish between theft by threats that are unlawful (extortion) and theft by threats that are not unlawful (blackmail).

After armed robbery and extortion, breaking into Owen's house to steal from his basement (theft by housebreaking/burglary) and grabbing the bike from his hands on the street (simple robbery) rank next, though the former received a slightly more severe sentence. Immediately below these are blackmail and taking the bike from Owen's porch (larceny). It is consistent with the MPC and the Theft Act that burglary was seen as worse than simple larceny; burglary receives elevated sentencing in both codes. It may be that the added component of invasion of the victim's home in the burglary case is seen as an aggravating factor. With respect to the simple robbery scenario, our subjects' attitudes were consistent with the elevated sentencing that occurs in non-MPC jurisdictions.

Below larceny and blackmail are embezzlement and looting the bike for profit after the storm. These results were somewhat surprising. The betrayal of trust involved in embezzlement and the element of exploitation in looting arguably aggravate their seriousness and might have been expected to increase their blameworthiness rating. Neither the MPC nor the Theft Act distinguishes these cases from simple theft.

Fraud proved to be one of the most theoretically interesting case categories. Obtaining the bicycle by falsely promising to pay the seller later or by writing a worthless check was seen as substantially less blameworthy than merely walking off with it (larceny). This could be seen as somewhat counterintuitive since fraud involves the additional wrong of deception. One possible explanation is that participants thought the victim of false pretenses was partly to blame for his plight. As noted earlier, the MPC treats passing a bad check as less serious than most other forms of theft and false pretenses as equivalent; the Fraud Act treats both passing a bad check and false pretenses as potentially more serious than other forms of theft.

Retaining misdelivered property and receiving stolen property fall at the very bottom of the blameworthiness and deserved punishment rankings. In fact, both offenses often received no punishment at all. These are interesting cases in that the actor being judged did not cause the victim's initial loss of property. In one case, Tom received an object in error and only then decided to retain it; in the other, Tom knowingly benefited from the wrongful act of another. To the extent that the participants ranked these acts as less serious than every other form of theft, their judgments were once again inconsistent with both the MPC and the Theft Act.

Varying the Form of Property Subject to Theft

The question of whether theft of intangible property should be regarded as morally equivalent to theft of tangible property has figured in various debates in both popular and academic culture in recent years. Many observers have wondered why people who would never think of walking into a store and shoplifting a CD or DVD nevertheless seem to have little hesitation in illegally downloading music and video from the Internet. The movie and music industries have waged major public relations efforts aimed at convincing people that Internet "piracy" is theft and that "pirates" are thieves. Whatever the success of these efforts, the incidence of unauthorized downloading of material from the Internet remains far higher than the incidence of theft of tangible goods. And what public opinion surveys have been conducted indicate that a majority of people believe that such downloading is less wrongful than theft of tangible property (if wrongful at all).

Although much has been written concerning the theft of intangibles, I am unaware of any previous studies testing people's attitudes concerning the theft of services. While the MPC treats the theft of services as equivalent to the theft of goods, the English Theft Act treats it as a lesser offense. It is therefore worth asking whether the public would regard stealing a ride on a train or a seat at a performance as any more or less wrongful than stealing a tangible object.

The modern trend has been to define the kinds of property subject to theft more broadly than at common law. The MPC defines property subject to theft as "anything of value, including real estate, tangible and intangible personal property, contract rights, choses-in-action and other interests in or claims to wealth, admission or transportation tickets, captured or domestic animals, food and drink, electric or other power."[258] Theft of services is also treated under the broad umbrella of Section 223's definition of theft and is subject to the same punishment as theft of any other form of property.[259] The Theft Act, similarly, defines property subject to theft as "money and all other property, real or personal, including things in action and other intangible property."[260] Theft of services is dealt with separately under Section 11 of the Fraud Act, replacing the former offense of Obtaining Services by Deception under Section 1 of the Theft Act 1978,[261] and subjecting a convicted defendant to a maximum penalty of five years.[262]

For the study at Rutgers, participants were asked to compare four pairs of scenarios that involved the stealing of property in one of four distinct forms. The scenarios presented (again unlabeled) were as follows:

> Physical book: ABC Test Prep offers a test-preparation book for sale at a booth on campus. The book sells for $50. Sally went to the booth, put a copy of the book in her bag, and walked away without paying for it, intending to keep it.
> Electronic book: ABC Test Prep offers a computer file of the test-preparation book that can be downloaded for a fee from its Web

site for $50. Sally figured out a way to download the file from the
Web site without paying for it and did so.

Lecture hall, full: ABC Test Prep offers a test-preparation lecture,
which is held at an auditorium on campus. Seating is by general
admission and costs $50. When all of the seats are filled, ABC
stops selling tickets. Sally walked in an open side door of the
auditorium, sat in a seat, and listened to the entire lecture
without paying for it. The auditorium that day was full. As a
result, ABC could not sell Sally's seat to someone else who
wanted to attend the lecture.

Lecture hall, not full: ABC Test Prep offers a test-preparation
lecture, which is held at an auditorium on campus. Seating is by
general admission and costs $50. When all of the seats are filled,
ABC stops selling tickets. Sally walked in an open side door of
the auditorium, sat in a seat, and listened to the entire lecture
without paying for it. The auditorium that day was not full;
several seats remained empty.

Participants were presented with four paired alternatives. Pair 1 asked
them to compare theft of the physical book (a tangible good) and the
electronic book (an intangible good). We predicted that the theft of
the physical book would elicit more punishment. Pair 2 asked participants to compare the theft of a physical book and illicitly attending a
lecture (a service). We predicted that stealing the book would be seen
as more blameworthy, reflecting the common law distinction between
goods and services. We decided to make it clear that the service had a
limited and depleted supply, saying that the lecture hall was full. This
allowed us to conservatively test the strength of the good/service distinction by holding constant these potentially confounding factors.
Pair 3 tested whether it mattered that the service had been depleted
through theft by comparing the empty seat lecture hall scenario to the
full lecture hall scenario. We predicted that the theft of the depleted
service would be seen as more blameworthy because of the greater
burdens it imposes. Pair 4 compared the intangible (and effectively
undepletable) good of the electronic book to the undepleted service,
the lecture in the hall with empty seats. We predicted that the theft of
the intangible electronic book would be ranked as more blameworthy
than the lecture in the partially empty hall.

Table 3 Percentage of participants choosing each of the blameworthiness alternatives in set 2

Pair 1		Pair 2		Pair 3		Pair 4	
Physical book	56%	Physical book	67%	Lecture, not full	7%	Lecture, not full	14%
Electronic book	3%	Lecture, full hall	10%	Lecture, full hall	55%	Electronic book	57%
No differ- ence	41%	No differ- ence	22%	No differ- ence	38%	No differ- ence	28%

Note: Margin of error +/- 7.58%

These four paired comparisons were presented to participants on a single sheet of paper. They were asked to record whether they found one scenario more blameworthy than the other and, if so, which. They also rated the scenarios' blameworthiness on a scale of 1 to 9.

Results

The data are presented in Table 3. In each pair, the predicted pattern was observed. In pair 1, more people thought stealing the tangible good (physical book) was more blameworthy than stealing the intangible good (electronic book). In pair 2, subjects reported that stealing the tangible book was worse than stealing a service (attendance in the full lecture hall). In pair 3, respondents rated stealing a service worse if the lecture hall was full and the service was depleted. Finally, in pair 4, participants ranked stealing an intangible and an undepletable good (the electronic book) worse than stealing an undepleted service (a seat in the unfilled auditorium).

Each of the four vignettes was used in two comparisons. The blameworthiness scores for each scenario were averaged across these two occasions and the resultant blameworthiness scores are presented in Table 4. Once again, those scenarios with different subscripts are significantly different from each other. As can clearly be seen, the blameworthiness scale data fully supports the choice data in each of the four pairs.

With respect to the types of property stolen, our data once again revealed clear distinctions in blameworthiness that are not reflected under current law. All else being equal, our subjects consistently

Table 4 Average blameworthiness scores for the scenarios in set 2

	Blameworthiness	
Lecture, not full	5.17$_c$	(2.30)
Lecture, full hall	6.01$_b$	(2.17)
Electronic book	6.30$_b$	(2.20)
Physical book	7.65$_a$	(1.71)

Note: Means (standard deviations in parentheses) for all scenarios from the second set. Higher numbers indicate higher blameworthiness scale scores. Means not sharing subscripts are significantly different at the $p < .05$ level.

ranked the theft of tangible goods as more blameworthy than the theft of intangibles, and the theft of intangible goods as more blameworthy than the theft of services. Current law reflects a very different paradigm: under the MPC, theft of tangibles, intangibles, and services are all subject to the same punishment, while the Theft Act subjects theft of tangibles and intangibles to the same punishment and theft of services to a lesser punishment.

In short, the data obtained indicate a significant divergence between lay intuitions and major aspects of the current, consolidated law of theft. Whereas the consolidated law of theft tends to treat most forms of theft as interchangeable and deserving of the same punishment, and tends not to distinguish among the types of property stolen, our study suggests that most people make moral distinctions based on just such factors. The remainder of this book aims, in a sense, to analyze the reasoning by which such intuitions are informed.

TWO

The Gist of Theft

As discussed in the previous chapter, the law of property crimes in Anglophone jurisdictions experienced a radical transformation during the twentieth century—from a loose collection of common law offenses like larceny, embezzlement, false pretenses, and extortion, to what is, in essence, a single, consolidated offense of theft. Such consolidation had the effect of flattening or homogenizing the moral content of theft law so that long-standing and venerable distinctions between offenses were uncritically discarded, sometimes with unforeseen and poorly thought-through consequences.

My claim about this second metamorphosis in theft law needs to be examined in more detail. The question is whether these traditional distinctions among various theft offenses really are worth preserving. How can they be justified in terms of the basic goals of the criminal law? What additional policy considerations, if any, justify turning back the clock on, or at least temporizing the effects of, nearly a century of criminal law reform?

To answer these questions, it will be necessary to develop a theory of theft law practically from scratch. In this chapter, I consider theft law's basic moral character. In the next chapter, the focus will shift to the question of what additional conditions would have to be satisfied to justify specifically criminal sanctions, rather than simply require thieves to return stolen property or pay compensation. The framework developed in these two chapters should also prove helpful in the later consideration of issues such as the extent to which theft law should apply to the misappropriation of intangible property like trade secrets and collections of data (the subject of Chapter 4). This project can be thought of as a kind of "normative reconstruction" of theft law. As the late Neil MacCormick put it, the task of the legal theorist is to dismantle the wide range of legal sources and then

> to reconstruct them in a way that makes them comprehensible because they are now shown as parts of a well ordered though complex whole. This requires explanatory principles establishing criteria of what counts as well ordered and rational. . . . Of course, it is an intellectual process, involving a new imagining and describing of the found order. . . . [T]here has to be some discrimination between the parts that belong in the coherent whole and the mistakes or anomalies that do not fit and ought to be discarded or abandoned or at least revised.[1]

Consistent with the practice of normative reconstruction, the picture of theft law presented in this book is idealized and ahistorical; it corresponds to no specific definition of the offense in any particular jurisdiction (although the points of reference, for the most part, continue to be Anglophone). Instead, an attempt is made to develop a rational and coherent understanding of the underlying norms while acknowledging where such a conception departs from one or more common formulations of the offense.

CONCEPTUAL FRAMEWORK

This section offers a basic framework for evaluating the moral content of theft. It begins by looking at the significance of blameworthiness in the criminal law generally and then turns to the elements of blameworthiness.

The Significance of Blameworthiness

Two basic kinds of reasons explain why the state might be justified in punishing theft (or any other crime), which correspond to two basic theories of punishment: consequentialism and retributivism. Consequentialism seeks to justify punishment on the basis of the good consequences that would flow from it. Retributivism can be understood as a theory that imposes punishment on the offender because he "deserves" it. The hybrid approach to theft law that will be pursued here incorporates elements of both types of theory.

The outlines of consequentialism are familiar. At least four main benefits are said to come from punishment: (1) deterrence of the offender from committing future crimes (specific deterrence), (2) deterrence of others in society from committing future crimes (general deterrence), (3) incapacitation of the offender so that she cannot commit crimes during the term of imprisonment, and (4) rehabilitation of the offender so that she will not commit future crimes. Much of Chapter 3 will focus on the question of general deterrence. Among the issues to be considered there is the extent to which it is possible to gauge penalties for theft so as to steer an even course between under- and overdeterrence.

The focus of retributivism is quite different. Joel Feinberg expressed the core notion:

> It is morally fitting that a person who does wrong should suffer in proportion to his wrongdoing. That a criminal should be punished follows from his guilt, and the severity of the appropriate punishment depends on the depravity of the act. The state of affairs where a wrongdoer suffers punishment is morally better than one where he does not, and is so irrespective of consequences.[2]

Thus, whereas deterrence theory and other forms of consequentialism look forward to the good results that will be obtained from punishing, retributivism looks backward to the wrongdoing already committed. It views punishment as an end in itself, a good that is valued for its own sake.

For present purposes, I shall assume that it is intrinsically wrong for society to punish criminal offenders who are blameless (and also wrong to punish blameworthy offenders more harshly than they deserve). To talk this way is to appeal to a familiar weak or negative form of retributivism. The claim is not that society should punish the blameworthy because they deserve it, but simply that society should *not* punish those who are not blameworthy. In short, I intend to rely on moral desert as a side constraint on whatever other rationale exists for imposing criminal sanctions (such as some version of consequentialism).[3]

The Elements of Blameworthiness

Assuming that punishment for theft (like every other crime) is properly imposed only if the offender is morally blameworthy, the question is how and when such blameworthiness occurs. My primary focus is not on the culpability of individual offenders committing specific acts of theft—crime tokens—but rather on the degree to which particular kinds of conduct—crime types—can be said to entail moral fault. The latter inquiry is a kind of generalization about criminal conduct, similar to the sort of inquiry that a legislature makes (or ought to make) in determining whether a certain kind of conduct justifies criminal penalties, and, if so, what kind and what amount. The question is, in effect, to what extent the sort of defendant who commits theft can be said *on average,* or *typically,* to be at fault. In such an assessment, it is normal to assume that no applicable exculpatory conditions, such as mistake, duress, or justification, apply; and the individual motivations or personal histories of particular defendants who commit such acts are not ordinarily a concern.[4]

Following a methodological approach developed in earlier work,[5] I divide the moral content of criminal offenses into three basic elements: (1) Harmfulness reflects the degree to which a criminal act causes, or risks causing, what Feinberg called a "significant setback to another's interests";[6] (2) *Mens rea,* in the elemental sense in which it will be used here, constitutes the mental state required in the definition of an offense or with which a criminal act is committed, such as intent, knowledge, recklessness, or negligence; and (3) Moral wrongfulness reflects the extent to which the act involves the violation of a freestanding moral norm, rule, right, or duty. For present purposes, I offer no argument that such elements comprise a set of necessary and sufficient conditions for criminalization. Nor do I mean to suggest that these elements do not overlap to some significant degree. Instead, I hope to show merely that all three kinds of elements are relevant to determining whether an actor's conduct should be regarded as blameworthy.

Let me offer a preliminary example of how such distinctions would play out in the context of theft. Imagine a case in which Tom takes a bicycle owned by Owen from his possession with the intent of depriving him of it permanently. To the extent that Tom has caused Owen to lose his property, Tom has caused Owen *harm:* Owen's interests have been set back; he no longer has the bike at his disposal to ride, sell, give away, or hang on his wall. But suppose it turns out that Tom works for the U.S. Marshal's Service and that Owen's bicycle is subject to government seizure under a proper order of forfeiture. In such a case, whatever (intentional) harm Owen has suffered, he has not been *wronged*, since there was no violation of a freestanding norm, rule, right, or duty. Alternatively, suppose that, in taking Owen's bicycle, Tom made a reasonable and good faith mistake in thinking that it was his own. Here, though Tom's act of depriving Owen of his property was once again harmful, it was not done with the *mens rea* required of such an act (namely, intent). For these reasons, Tom's act cannot be viewed as blameworthy.[7] In what follows, I will consider each of these three elements of blameworthiness in turn.

HARMFULNESS AND *MENS REA*

This section offers an analysis of the first two elements of theft's moral content: harmfulness and *mens rea*.

The Harm in Theft

According to the liberal harm principle developed by Mill and later elaborated by Feinberg, the state's moral authority to criminalize extends only to conduct that causes (or risks) serious harm (or possibly offense) to others (or possibly self).[8] For present purposes, I shall assume that this principle plays a key role in defining the proper limits of the criminal law. The issue to consider, then, is the nature of theft-caused harm.

Harms to Interests in Property

The essence of theft and other property offenses is that they involve an offender's (wrongfully) causing harm to another's interests in, and rights to, property. Property, in turn, is best thought of not as a physical thing but as the bundle of rights organized around the idea of securing, for the right of the holder, exclusive use or access to, or control of, a thing.[9] Such control may take various forms, including the right or privilege or power to use the property, to exclude others from using it, and to transfer it, and immunity from having it taken or damaged without one's consent.[10] Tony Honoré divides what he calls the liberal concept of full ownership into a list of components: the right to possess, use, and manage a thing; the right to income from its use by others; the right to sell, give away, consume, modify, or destroy it; the power to transmit it to the beneficiaries of one's estate; and the right to security from expropriation.[11] As discussed in Chapter 4, to say that a thing constitutes property means different things in different legal contexts. I shall argue that the particular kind of property that can be subject to theft reflects two basic requirements: first, it must be commodifiable, meaning that it is capable of being bought and sold; and, second, it must be rivalrous, meaning that consumption of it by one user will prevent simultaneous consumption by others.

Different property crimes affect different sticks in the bundle in different ways. Trespass, joyriding, and unauthorized use of a movable consist of temporarily using another's property without permission—a kind of temporary dispossession, but without any requirement of damage to property. Infringement of intangible and intellectual property can also be conceptualized as a kind of temporary dispossession. Vandalism and criminal damage, on the other hand, typically involve damage to the owner's property, but no dispossession.

The most venerable property crime—theft—has traditionally required a particularly substantial interference with an owner's property rights, including, often, though not always, the right of possession. Theft involves not just a temporary violation of the owner's right to exclude others from using the property, but also a more permanent violation of the owner's right to use it himself. But the line between theft and trespass or unauthorized use is not a bright one: the concepts form a continuum. There is a threshold point at which a trespass becomes so significant that we can say that a stealing has occurred.

Theft is harmful in the narrow sense that it deprives the property owner of a thing that saves him labor, or from which he derives pleasure, or which generates income for him. More generally, such conduct is harmful because it undermines the very reason we have a system of property rights in the first place—namely, to facilitate the creation and preservation of wealth that makes many forms of human endeavor possible. As Andrew Simester and Andrew von Hirsch have put it:

Stealing my old clothes not only sets back the interest, if any, that I have in the clothes; it also undermines the regime by which my property right in the clothes is recognized. That is to say, more than one type of interest is at stake when my clothes are stolen. Apart from my immediate interest in the clothes, both I and others have an interest in the existence of a system for allocating and reallocating property rights in general. Thus, even where a theft does not set back V's personal interests, it sets back the interest we all have in the effective existence of a property law regime.[12]

In this broader sense of harm, what matters is not that the specific action itself undermines the institution of property ownership, but that it is the kind of action that would do so if generally practiced and unpunished.[13]

Assessing the Harms of Theft

To assess the extent to which a given instance of theft causes harm, a number of factors must be considered. The first is the kind of property affected. The misappropriation of tangible goods, for example, will cause kinds of harm that differ from the kinds of harm caused by the misappropriation of services or intangible goods, and this is true even if the property taken in each case has the same market value. Indeed, as Chapter 4 will show, part of what makes the misappropriation of intangible property so vexing is that it does not seem to conform to the basic notion that the owner of property must suffer a permanent violation of the right of use.

The second factor to consider is the value of the property affected. Other things being equal, the higher the value of goods stolen or damaged, the more serious the crime and the higher the possible sentence or fine. English common law traditionally distinguished between grand and petit larceny (the dividing line being twelve pence). The punishment for the former was death while the punishment for the latter was whipping or imprisonment.[14] The rationale was that:

Three half-pence a day was considered sufficient to support a man. To deprive him of twelve pence was to deprive him of sustenance for eight days, at the end of which time he might be expected to die. Twelve pence, therefore, had reference to the destruction of life, for which offense a man is rightfully put to death.[15]

As discussed in Chapter 1, modern legislation such as the Federal Sentencing Guidelines makes much more finely graded distinctions regarding the value of stolen property.

One problem here is caused by the difficulty of interpersonal utility comparisons.[16] Simply put, different people value the same property in different ways, owing in part to the law of diminishing marginal utility, which states that the more of a good one has, the less utility one receives from an additional unit of the good. Consider the case of the luckless Antonio in Vittorio De Sica's heartbreaking film, *The Bicycle Thief.* When his bicycle is stolen, Antonio is unable to keep his job putting up advertising posters around Rome; as a result, he becomes unable to feed himself and his family, and in desperation becomes a bicycle thief himself. The theft of Antonio's bike obviously has a very different impact—is more harmful, I would say—than the theft of a bicycle from, say, the wealthy actor and comedian Robin Williams, who reportedly owns more than fifty.

So what relevance should a given theft's impact on its victim play in assessing its blameworthiness? The criminal law has traditionally been uncomfortable with the idea of distinguishing between criminal acts based on victim impact. Normally, victim impact is relevant only in the case of violent crimes and only at the sentencing rather than liability stage, and even there it is controversial.[17] The problem is that victim impact statements tend to shift the jury's focus in a potentially prejudicial way, from consideration of the *defendant's* conduct to consideration of the *victim's* bona fides.[18] Although the penal consequences are far more serious in capital murder cases, the concern with prejudice in theft cases is nonetheless analogous, and for this reason I would oppose the admission of evidence concerning victim impact in theft cases as well.

Related is the problem presented by the theft of property with sentimental value. For example, I have in my home a small silver Kiddush cup that one of my ancestors brought from Europe during emigration. The cup would not be worth much on the open market, but it has great sentimental value to me. If the cup were stolen, should the criminal law take account of such value? One could potentially find support for such an approach in the work of Margaret Jane Radin, who has distinguished between property that is so "closely related to one's personhood" that its "loss causes pain that cannot be relieved by the object's replacement" (the example she gives is of a wedding ring stolen from a loving wearer), and property that is held "purely instrumentally" (such as fungible cash or the wedding ring when stolen from a jeweler).[19] Whatever the validity of Radin's approach in conceptualizing property generally, however, I believe that the law of theft is ill-equipped to make distinctions based on sentimental value. The problem goes beyond that of potential prejudice arising from victim impact statements. In assessing the sentimental value of property stolen, the prosecutor or court would have to rely almost entirely on the victim's subjective testimony. The argument for excluding evidence of stolen property's sentimental value is thus even stronger than the argument for excluding evidence of the theft's economic impact on the victim.

There is also the question of how the law should respond to the theft of items with a negligible monetary value. Various legal systems have responded in different ways. Maimonides reasoned that, "it is prohibited to steal an object of however small a value. . . . [T]hese acts are forbidden, lest one become accustomed to practicing them."[20] The majority of jurisdictions in the United States and England follow a similar approach.[21] Even in these jurisdictions, however, as Tony Smith has explained, "in particularly unmeritorious prosecutions [e.g., for stealing a dead match or a used bus ticket], it would be open to the judge to dismiss the charges."[22] (I will have more to say about the appropriateness of a *de minimis* exception for theft in Chapter 3.)

Theft also causes harms beyond those caused to specific property owners. Such secondary harms are more diffuse and indirect than the kinds of harm discussed so far. Widespread theft, vandalism, and arson all tend to have a destabilizing effect on neighborhoods and on the economy more generally. Citizens are forced to pay more for goods and services because businesses tend to pass on the costs of security systems, guards, and loss of inventory; insurance rates also tend to rise. More subtly, knowledge that others have been subject to theft can cause one to doubt one's own security of property; it makes people less confident that the investments they have made in creating or acquiring goods will be protected. As Chapter 3 will show, it is the public character of such harm, in part, that justifies its treatment as a crime rather than merely a matter of civil law.

Finally, as discussed in Chapter 1, theft can be committed by a wide range of means. In addition to the harms caused by the deprivation of property rights itself, there is a group of harms associated with the specific means by which such deprivation is achieved. Larceny, false pretenses, extortion, robbery, embezzlement, burglary, robbery, and looting are each associated not only with their own distinctive wrongs (stealth, deception, coercion, breach of trust, invasion of privacy, violence, and exploitation of special vulnerability, respectively), but also with their own distinctive harms. For example, false pretenses and fraud tend to undermine the confidence that people have in markets and commercial dealings; embezzlement damages the trust that people feel in their agents and employees; robbery makes people frightened for their physical safety; burglary weakens the security that people feel in their homes; looting tends to exaggerate the seriousness of natural and human-made emergencies; and so on.

What Constitutes Appropriation?

Exactly what kinds of interference with the bundle of property rights should constitute misappropriation has confounded much of theft law's history. Indeed, it can be understood as the key to the difficult question of what should constitute the *actus reus* of the offense.

The common law offense of larceny required both caption and asportation. Caption occurred when the offender secured dominion or actual physical control of the property, if only for a moment. Under common law, it was not sufficient that the offender merely deprive the victim of possession; the offender also had to gain control over the property. Thus, merely knocking an article from a person's hand was not larceny if the defendant did not thereafter take complete control of it.[23] The second requirement, asportation, consisted of carrying the property away. In addition to gaining dominion over the property, the thief also had to move it from its original position. The entirety of the property had to be moved. Thus, as Wayne LaFave once noted with some bemusement, this requirement was the difference between rotating a doughnut (larceny) and rotating a pie (not larceny), as *all* of the doughnut is moved through rotation while the pie's exact center remains in the same place when rotated.[24]

Thankfully, the modern, consolidated law of theft has done away with the requirements of caption and asportation. The Theft Act 1968 replaced the "taking and carrying away" language of the Larceny Act 1916 with the requirement of "appropriation," defined as "the assumption of the rights of the owner."[25] The Model Penal Code (MPC) said simply that an offender who "takes, or exercise[s] unlawful control over" property is guilty of theft.[26] And the proposed Scottish Criminal Code says (1) that a person commits theft if he steals, (2) that he steals if he deprives another of property, and (3) that he deprives another of property if, *inter alia*, he "depriv[es] that person of its value."[27]

The shift from caption and asportation to appropriation, unlawful control, or deprivation of value represents the culmination of the centuries-long shift from a law of theft focused primarily on preventing violence arising out of dispossessory acts to one focused primarily on protecting property rights. The question remains, however: At what point are an owner's property rights so infringed that the thief can be said to have appropriated or obtained unlawful control over the property? The most common form of appropriation continues to involve the taking of physical possession of *O*'s property. But there are many cases in which *D* appropriates property that either (1) is *already* in his possession or (2) never comes into his possession. For example, imagine that *V* entrusted *D* with possession of his car for some purpose—say, he has rented it to him or given it to him for repairs or as collateral on a loan. If *D* converted the property to his own use or destroyed, or sold it, or gave it away to a third party, he would not have committed larceny at common law (though he might have committed some other theft-related offense such as embezzlement). He would, however, have committed theft under modern theft law. Alternatively, imagine that *D* tricked or coerced *V* into turning over title to real or personal property that was sitting in a bank vault or hanging on a wall in a gallery. Once again, it is doubtful that he would have committed larceny at common law, since no caption was effected. But under modern theft law, *D*'s obtaining of title would be sufficient to constitute appropriation. This is as it should be. If I am right that the primary harm caused by theft is *D*'s permanent assumption of *O*'s right to use the property as he sees fit, then it should not matter when exactly possession was obtained, or indeed whether it was obtained at all. As long as *D* assumes the rights of *O*, that should be sufficient to satisfy the *actus reus*.

Theft, crucially, involves a transfer of property from victim/owner to thief. It cannot occur where the owner steals "from himself." For example, in the English case of *R. v. Turner*, the defendant delivered his car to Brown's garage for repairs and later took it back without paying for Brown's services.[28] Turner was charged with theft not of services but of the car itself, and in a much-criticized decision, his conviction was affirmed.[29] The decision is clearly wrong: though Brown had temporary possession of the car, Turner was still its owner, and Brown was merely a bailee. If it could be proved that Turner never intended to pay the repair bill in the first place, then the proper charge would be theft of services. Otherwise, he would have merely breached the contract he had with Brown.[30]

This (involuntary) transfer from victim to thief can be considered in terms of a common sense (if not strict economic) notion of zero sumness: what is the thief's gain must be the victim's loss.[31] This is not to say that thief and victim must necessarily *value* the stolen asset in the same way. My claim is simply that theft and stealing, as historically, culturally, and morally understood, reflect a particular dynamic that is distinct from that reflected in concepts such as trespass, unauthorized use, and infringement. (As Chapter 4 will show, this claim has important implications in the context of so-called theft of identities, information, intellectual property, and other intangibles.)

This is not to say that it will always be clear in all cases of theft whether the required transfer of even tangible property has occurred. In the English case of *R. v. Morris,* for example, D switched the labels on two articles lying on the shelves of a supermarket with the intention of buying the more expensive article for the price of the less expensive one.[32] Did such switching constitute appropriation? The House of Lords said that the theft was complete as soon as the labels were switched. I am skeptical of this result. Had D actually purchased the higher priced item at the lower price, there is no question that he would have committed theft. But until he actually walked off with the item, and thereby deprived the store of its use, it seems to me that his crime was, at most, attempted theft.

Irreversibility of Appropriation

An additional feature of appropriation merits mention here. Consider a case in which D stole property from V but then had a change of heart and voluntarily returned it. Assume further that V never missed the property while it was gone. Should the law of theft include a defense of abandonment or renunciation, as the law of attempt does in many jurisdictions?

The traditional Anglo-American law of theft admits of no such defense. According to Holmes, all that is necessary for the crime to be committed is for the defendant to take the victim's property from his possession with an intent to deprive him of it permanently; there is no requirement that the owner actually lose possession permanently.[33] Once the appropriation has occurred, it cannot be taken back, even if the thief decides to do so voluntarily. At most, the repentant thief will receive credit at the time of sentencing. The justification for such an approach seems to be a practical one: as Holmes puts it, the law simply "cannot wait until the property has been used up or destroyed in other hands than the owner's . . . in order to make sure that the harm which it seeks to prevent has been done."[34]

This result may seem surprising. If D murders or rapes V, it is impossible ever to fully erase the harm done, even if D fully and voluntarily repents. But if D steals property from V and then voluntarily returns it, the harm done to V is essentially erased. Under Talmudic law, thieves who voluntarily confessed to their crime and returned the stolen property could avoid the fine they otherwise would have incurred.[35] Is such a defense of renunciation worth considering in American law? I believe it is. Allowing a defense of renunciation would create positive incentives for would-be thieves having second thoughts about their intentions, to stop and return stolen property to its rightful owner.

Harmless and Justified Thefts

All of the cases of theft considered so far have involved a fairly clear instance in which O's interests as a property owner are set back by D's act. But the harm in theft is not always so clear. Consider a hypothetical imagined by Andrew Simester and Bob Sullivan involving "V, a misanthropic billionaire, who has inherited and not created any of his wealth":

> He has withdrawn all his money from his investments, trusts, and bank accounts and stacked the cash away in cardboard boxes that litter the floor of his grim mansion. He is determined that no-one shall have any use or pleasure from his wealth and has resolved that when his time is nigh, he will immolate himself and his cash. D is V's selfless

home-carer. Although paid a pittance by V, out of the goodness of her heart she ministers to V's needs beyond any call of duty. From time to time [and unbeknownst to V], she takes cash from one or another of the boxes, never for herself, but to ease the path of friends and acquaintances who are in dire economic straits. There is no profligacy in this: she takes enough, just enough, to stave off the worst consequences of the privations that afflict the people she helps.[36]

In such a case, they say, the victim suffers no "substantive disvalue or setback of human interests." Rather, he has been harmed in a "wholly conventional sense."[37] Nevertheless, they contend, D should surely still be regarded as a thief (though whether she should be prosecuted as such is presumably a different matter).

Simester and Sullivan's conclusion seems to me basically correct, but it needs a bit of elaboration. The first point is that nothing here is unique to theft law: one can almost always find or construct cases in which the harm of a given crime token is elusive or absent. Imagine a case in which V, having been stabbed without justification by D^1 and now comatose, is certain to die from his injuries in another ten minutes. Whether to alleviate V's suffering or because she also desires V's death, assume that D^2 administers a *coup de grâce*, which causes V to die in nine minutes, a bit ahead of schedule. Surely, in such a case D^2 has done everything that is required to be guilty of murder despite the fact that the harm she has caused to V is in some sense conventional. Like all prospective criminal lawmaking, theft law inevitably deals in generalities. Legislatures criminalize because they want to punish and deter certain kinds of acts that *in general* are harmful. There will always be individual cases, whether real or imagined, in which a specific crime token does not cause harm or in which the harm is *de minimis* or merely conventional.

The traditional way to deal with cases in which a defendant's act avoids more harm than it causes is under the necessity defense. The paradigm, discussed in the MPC's Commentary, is that of the hiker, stranded in the wilderness in a snow storm, without shelter or food, who breaks into an empty cabin and consumes canned provisions found therein.[38] It is also easy to imagine cases in which a Robin Hood figure steals excess wealth from the idle rich and gives the proceeds to the desperate poor. Theoretically, cases of this sort would seem to satisfy the elements of the necessity defense, assuming they can also satisfy the normal requirements of imminence, lack of alternatives, and clean hands.

In practice, however, reported cases in which a defendant charged with theft has been successful in asserting a necessity defense are exceedingly rare, at least in modern times—rarer even than reported cases involving more serious crimes such as murder.[39] The case of Jean Valjean in *Les Misérables* is doubly illustrative here. Victor Hugo's story of a man who steals a loaf of bread to feed his starving family is often cited as the paradigmatic example of a crime committed out of necessity. But it is worth recalling that, like almost every other (real-world) modern case in which necessity has been asserted as a defense to charges of theft or trespass, Valjean's (fictional) plea was unsuccessful.

What accounts for this divergence between clear-cut theoretical acceptance and the real-world futility of necessity as a defense to theft? Given that the harm caused by theft is normally less than the harm caused by murder or rape, one would expect theft to have a *higher* success rate for the necessity defense. Yet just the opposite seems to be true.

One possible explanation is that prosecutors are unlikely to bring charges of theft at all when it is clear that the defendant's acts were occasioned by grave distress; defendants would therefore not even have the occasion to assert a necessity defense. Another, more far-reaching explanation is that the case-by-case, seemingly ad hoc nature of the necessity defense tends to cause "anxiety" among decision makers in the criminal justice system by, as John Parry puts it, "undermin[ing] the consistency and predictability that we often view as essential to the rule of law."[40] Third, a defendant is typically foreclosed from asserting a necessity defense if lawmakers previously "anticipated the choice of evils and determined the balance to be struck between the competing values" in a manner that conflict with the defendant's choice.[41] This is arguably the case for all economically motivated thefts (except for rare and dire natural emergencies).

I find this tendency unfortunate. Precisely because the moral content of property crimes (unlike that of crimes like rape and murder) is so dependent on changing social and cultural circumstances, I believe that courts should be more, not less, open to allowing application of the fact-specific necessity defense.[42] One possible solution to this morass would be to draft statutes that specifically contemplate the circumstances in which the defense of necessity will be recognized. In other words, rather than leave the defense of necessity to generalized, broadly worded, anxiety-producing, choice-of-evils provisions, where it is likely to be marginalized, it would be better to include provisions in theft statutes that specifically enumerate the possible circumstances in which the defense of necessity might arise.

Mens Rea in Theft

Having dealt with the first element of moral blameworthiness in theft—namely, harmfulness—I now turn to the second element—the *mens rea,* or mental state, with which theft must be committed.

Intent to Deprive

Under the common law definition of larceny, the appropriation of property had to be committed with *animus furandi,* understood as an intent to permanently deprive another of the possession of property. Under this rule, *D* would be guilty of larceny if he drove away in *V*'s automobile with the intent of keeping it, but not if he intended to keep the vehicle only temporarily and later return it (though, interestingly, it might be contended that *D* did have the intent to deprive *V* permanently of the *gasoline* in the car's tank unless, that is, he actually intended to refill it later). This continues to be the approach taken by the Theft Act and the MPC, with one important modification, discussed below.[43]

The rule requiring permanent deprivation is hardly universal, however. Under Canadian law, theft requires an intent to deprive "temporarily" *or* "absolutely."[44] Scots law and the Indian Penal Code of 1860 follow the same approach.[45] Roman law and some civilian jurisdictions subscribe to the analogous doctrine of *furtum usus* (clandestine taking), under which theft includes the unlawful temporary use of property.[46] Jewish law also regards borrowing without the owner's permission as stealing except in cases where the thing was borrowed in the past and the borrower is certain that the owner will not mind.[47]

In jurisdictions where theft requires an intent to deprive permanently, there is often a separate, lesser offense of dishonest borrowing of moveable property (sometimes limited to automobiles, motorcycles, and motorboats, as in the MPC) and popularly known as joyriding.[48]

The punishment for such offenses is significantly less than for theft, suggesting that they are viewed as involving conduct that is less culpable.

Which approach makes more sense: the traditional Anglo-American approach or the Canadian/Scots/Roman/civilian/Jewish/Indian approach? In my view, the preferred approach is found in the compromise made by the MPC and by the Theft Act, which look to the nature of the property and how long the borrowing lasts. The Theft Act explains:

> [A] person appropriating property belonging to another without meaning the other permanently to lose the thing itself is nevertheless to be regarded as having the intention of permanently depriving the other of it if his intention is to treat the thing as his own to dispose of regardless of the other's rights; and a borrowing or lending of it may amount to so treating it if, but only if, *the borrowing or lending is for a period and in circumstances making it equivalent to an outright taking or disposal*.[49]

The MPC reaches a similar result by defining the word *deprive* in the phrase *purpose to deprive* to mean "withhold property of another permanently *or for so extended a period as to appropriate a major portion of its economic value*."[50]

Thus, imagine that you borrow my car without my permission for the next six months, putting 5,000 miles on it. You not only lessen the value of the car, but also deprive me of its use for a long enough period of time that I will likely need to acquire another. To borrow in this manner is thus to deprive me of a significant part of the good's value.[51] It makes sense to treat such cases as theft despite the fact that you did not intend to deprive me of my car permanently. On the other hand, if you borrow my car without my permission for the afternoon or even for a week, and return it with the gas tank full, that probably should not count as theft. Whether a sufficient deprivation has occurred ultimately depends on the nature of the property taken. For example, if instead of borrowing my car, you borrow the fresh baguette I just brought home from the *boulangerie* and return it to me a week later, completely stale, it makes sense to say that you committed theft. The same would be true if you borrowed my tickets for tonight's Yankees game (assume you didn't actually use them; you just showed them around to your friends and then returned them to me tomorrow, after the game had already been played).

The same principle should apply in the context of so-called wardrobing, in which an offender purchases, uses, and then returns an article of clothing or other commodity, a practice that is said to cost the U.S. retail industry an estimated $16 billion annually.[52] Since the wardrober initially pays for the article of clothing, and has no intent to deprive the store of the item permanently, one might assume that this is not theft. But I would disagree. Because the clothes have been used, they are worth considerably less than before. I would therefore say, following the logic of the Theft Act and the MPC, that the wardrober so substantially diminishes the economic value of the good that we should regard the act as stealing.

Another important question concerning the *mens rea* requirement in theft is whether the traditional requirement of intent to deprive should be replaced by an easier-to-satisfy mental requirement such as recklessness. Most jurisdictions have resisted such a change.[53] Ordinarily, it is not theft to take a thing realizing only that the owner may not, or probably will not, get it back. But if the thing taken may be easily broken or damaged, and if the defendant realized that this was the case, some courts have held that the intent to deprive requirement is met.[54]

Beyond requiring that the property rights of the owner be deprived *intentionally* or *purposely,* theft statutes also typically require that such deprivation or appropriation be done *unlawfully* (in the case of the MPC), *dishonestly* (in the case of the Theft Act and some Australian states), or *fraudulently* (in the case of the Canadian Criminal Code and the codes of other Australian states). Such elements are frequently spoken of as elements *of mens rea.*[55] There is in my view no real harm in doing so, but within the analytical framework that is being developed here, in which *mens rea* is used to refer, narrowly, to a specific mental element with which a prohibited act must be performed, it is more appropriate to deal with such elements in the context of moral wrongfulness, as I'll do later in this chapter.

Difficult questions also arise when a defendant claims a lack of the requisite *mens rea* to commit theft on account of a mistake. Traditionally, the law has viewed mistakes of fact more generously than mistakes of law. In the case of theft, the most common kind of mistake concerns the identity of the property's owner: the thief mistakenly believes that the property is his own or that it is has been abandoned. Such mistakes can be characterized as mistakes of fact just as readily as they can be characterized as mistakes of law, and vice versa.[56] This is a reflection of the peculiar, hybrid prelegal/naturalistic/law-dependent/positivistic form that theft law takes, discussed below.

There are also questions about whether the mistake made by the alleged thief should have to be a reasonable one. The traditional rule is that, for specific intent offenses such as theft (as opposed to general intent crimes such as rape and assault), even an unreasonable mistake will serve to negate the requisite *mens rea*.[57] From within the logic of the criminal law, this rule makes sense: if the defendant made a good faith mistake about whether the property belonged to someone else, then as a factual matter he lacked the intent to steal, and it should not matter whether his mistake was reasonable or unreasonable. From a public policy perspective, however, it may seem perverse to allow a defendant whose mistake was unreasonable to escape conviction entirely. For such cases, it makes sense to consider creating a lesser offense such as reckless or negligent appropriation of property.[58]

Finally, it should be pointed out that *mens rea* is not the same as motive. While the early common law required that the thief act "for the sake of gain," or *lucri causa,* later cases rejected this view.[59] Although avarice or acquisitiveness are common motivations behind theft, thieves may act out of any number of other motives. For example, a thief may, out of a sense of social justice, steal from the rich and give to the poor; he may, out of a sense of concern for the welfare of animals, steal a dog from a research laboratory before it can be operated on; or he may be like the dairy employee who, from a misplaced sense of largesse, gave away a quantity of his employer's cream to a laborer who had helped him load cans of it onto a train.[60] In none of these cases would the lack of bad motive be held to negate intent. Nor, as explained below, would it negate the requirement of dishonesty. In each case, the law would regard the defendant as guilty of theft.

Concurrence of Elements and the Difference between Theft and Breach of Contract

Criminal law has traditionally required that the *actus reus* and *mens rea* of a given offense concur—that the defendant possess the requisite *mens rea* at the same time he performs the *actus reus*. In the case of theft, this requirement leads to an interesting result. Consider two paradigmatic cases:

Case 1: D^1 *falsely* promises to deliver to V a shipment of widgets in return for payment. He takes V's money and then fails to deliver.

Case 2: D^2 *truthfully* promises to deliver to V a shipment of widgets in return for payment. He takes V's money and then fails to deliver.

D^1's conduct constitutes a species of theft known as promissory fraud or false pretenses (though, as described in Chapter 3, such fraud can also be dealt with as a civil wrong). At the time D^1 promised to deliver the widgets, he had no intention of doing so. There was thus a temporal concurrence between his *actus reus* (the taking of V's money) and *mens rea* (his intent to deprive V of his property permanently). Essentially, D^1 used deceit to obtain money from his victim. Case 2, by contrast, involves a mere breach of contract. At the time D^2 promised to deliver the widgets, he intended to do so. It was only later that he changed his mind or was unable to do so; there was thus no theft. The interesting question is why should the law treat D^1's conduct as a crime but not D^2's (if in fact it should). To put it another way, why should D's state of mind at the time he entered into the contract determine whether he has committed theft or breach?

In Case 2, it is necessary to distinguish between breaches of contract that are voluntary or willful and those that are not.[61] Suppose D agrees to supply V with a thousand widgets and is subsequently unable to do so because his business has gone bankrupt, he has become ill, or the raw materials for widgets can no longer be obtained. In each of these cases, D no longer has the means to do what he promised to do. If nothing else, such behavior lacks the voluntariness expected of criminal conduct. Physical inability to perform an action one is obligated to perform has always been a sufficient means for negating the prosecution's case. To convict the unwilling contract breacher of a crime would be to use the criminal courts as a kind of debt collection service and essentially return us to the days of the debtor's prison.[62]

Thus, the real question is, why not treat D^2's breach of contract as a crime in those cases in which his breach *was* voluntary or willful? The question is a difficult one. To respond that D^2's conduct, even when his breach is voluntary, is different from D^1's because the remedy for V in

Case 2 is to sue for breach of contract obviously begs the question. Nor does it help to say that some breaches of contract are efficient, and therefore to be encouraged, since there are plenty of willful breaches that are not efficient, and there are also plenty of *thefts* that might be regarded as efficient, in the sense that property is transferred from a low-value user to a high-value one.[63]

A better answer is that, though D^2's conduct in voluntarily breaching the contract was blameworthy, it was less blameworthy than D^1's conduct in falsely entering into the contract in the first place. D^1's act was more blameworthy than D^2's because D^1 deprived his victim of her already-vested rights in property, while D^2 merely violated V^2's right to a contractual expectation, a not-yet-ripened interest in property.[64] Moreover, even assuming for purposes of discussion that D^1 and D^2 were equally blameworthy, the law might still not want to treat the voluntary breach of a contract as a crime for fear that such a policy would overly chill the environment for the formation of contracts. If people felt that they might face criminal sanctions every time they entered into a contract in good faith and subsequently were unable or unwilling to perform, they might be overdeterred from entering into such contracts to begin with. Such a concern would not occur in cases in which a person entered into a contract with no intention of performing in the first place.

Now consider a third case:

> Case 3: D^3 goes to a service station intending to buy gas. He fills up his tank, then decides not to pay, and drives off without doing so.

From a formal perspective, this case is indistinguishable from Case 2. D^3 entered into a tacit agreement with the service station to take gas in return for payment. Only later did he decide not to honor the agreement. There was no concurrence of the elements between D^3's appropriation and his *mens rea,* and therefore, it might be argued, he did not commit theft.

Yet Case 3 certainly *feels* different from Case 2. In Case 2, it seems more plausible that D really did change his mind between agreeing to deliver and not delivering. In Case 3, by contrast, so little time has elapsed between the time of D's agreement and his breach that one cannot help but be skeptical about his intent to pay when he was initially pumping the gas.

English law offers an intriguing way to deal with such cases of making off without payment. Section 3(1) of the Theft Act 1978 provides that

> a person who, knowing that payment on the spot for any goods supplied or services done is required or expected from him, dishonestly makes off without having paid as required or expected and with intent to avoid payment of the amount due shall be guilty of an offense.[65]

The offense is punishable on summary conviction and subject to a lesser punishment than for theft proper (a maximum of two years or a fine of £5,000).[66]

Is the English scheme defensible? Does Section 3(1) violate the principle that failure to pay a debt should not be a crime? At least two theories suggest that the scheme upholds the principle. One theory rests on the presumption that people who take gas and then drive off without paying always, or almost always, did not intend to pay for it in the first place. Is that presumption well founded? I'm not so sure. One can certainly imagine an offender who implicitly agreed to pay $3.879 per gallon of gas and then changed his mind after realizing that it would cost him $57 to fill the tank. The other approach, applied in the case of *DPP v. Ray,* is to think of the offender's deception as occurring *at some point* during his time at service station.[67] But this approach seems, at best, highly artificial; and in those cases in which the offender really did change his mind only after all of the gas has been pumped, even worse—misleading.

The truth is that there will be some defendants who genuinely do change their minds only after taking the gas (or restaurant meal, or whatever). In such cases, the proper action would be for breach of contract, but the possibility that such an action would be brought seems remote given the costs of litigation and the quantum of likely damages. So the English making off provision can be understood as reflecting a kind of compromise: defendants who promise *falsely* to pay for gas and then fail to do so are treated *less* harshly than they deserve to be, while defendants who promise *truthfully* to pay and then change their minds are treated *more* harshly than *they* deserve to be. Recognizing the difficulty of distinguishing between the two kinds of cases in practice, the statute settles on a middle ground.

THE WRONGS OF THEFT

The previous several sections looked at the various ways in which the concepts of harmfulness and *mens rea* inform the moral content of theft and other property offenses. The following sections turn to the two basic kinds of moral wrong by which such crimes are informed.

The first kind of wrong (which I shall refer to as the *primary wrong*) is that which attends the basic deprivation of property rights itself. The mere fact that D causes harm to V by taking possession of his property, and does so intentionally, is not sufficient to justify criminal penalties. After all, D may have had a perfectly valid legal right to take V's property (as in the case of a contract, tort judgment, eminent domain, or forfeiture proceeding). Some form of moral wrongfulness is also necessary, and that requires some explanation.

The second kind of wrong (referred to as the *secondary wrong*) is that which derives from the *means* by which such stealing is effected. The fact that theft (or trespass or unlawful borrowing) is committed by stealth, deceit, violence, coercion, breach of trust, invasion of privacy, or in circumstances of natural disaster or civil unrest affects not only the kinds of harm caused but also the wrongfulness of the act. As discussed in Chapter 1, it is precisely these distinctions among secondary wrongs that have been blurred—even eradicated—by the consolidation of theft law that occurred during the latter half of the twentieth century.

When I say that theft contains a primary and secondary wrong, however, it should be clear that I am doing so for the limited purpose of analysis. I do not mean to suggest that the wrongs are separable in practice. Theft by deception, force, or coercion is just that: using deception, force, or coercion to obtain property unlawfully. Analytically, it can be broken down into the primary wrong of taking property and the secondary wrongs of using deception, force, or coercion; but that does not mean that the primary and secondary wrongs should be *punished* separately.

I thus disagree with the approach recommended by Paul Robinson, who in arguing for his own proposed criminal code, has offered a property crime provision that is even more stripped down than the MPC's. Under his proposal, theft and other property crime provisions would be replaced by a provision that says simply that one "may not damage, take, use, dispose of, or transfer another's property without the other's consent."[68] The purpose of Robinson's proposal is to eliminate what he calls the unnecessary proliferation of criminal offenses. As he puts it:

> Proliferation . . . occurs where offenses combine prohibitions already contained individually in other offenses. The offense of robbery, for example, simply prohibits a combination of theft and assault. Perhaps such conduct should be graded higher than it would be if punished separately as a theft and an assault. If this is so, then the adjudication code should reflect such a policy. But creation of a robbery offense adds nothing to the law's statement of prohibited conduct; the theft and assault prohibitions already clearly criminalize the conduct described in the robbery offense.[69]

Thus, according to Robinson, rather than prosecuting one who steals money by means of force or violence for robbery, the law should prosecute him for two separate offenses: theft and assault.

As I see it, there are several problems with Robinson's approach. The first and most significant is that to say that robbery is simply the sum of theft and assault is to miss what is distinctive about robbery. Using violence to take another's property is not ultimately reducible to its constitutive elements. Crimes like robbery and burglary reflect a totality of social, moral, and cultural meanings that transcend the mere sum of their elements.[70] Second, it is hardly clear that Robinson's approach would lead to a simplification of criminal law, as claimed. Indeed, things would arguably be *more* complex. Under his approach, rather than proving just one offense—robbery—the prosecution would have to prove two offenses—assault and theft. Third, even if Robinson's approach did make sense for robbery (or burglary, the other offense he considers in this context), it would not work for false pretenses (theft by deception), embezzlement (theft by breach of trust), or blackmail (theft by making a threat to do an otherwise lawful act), since there is no separate offense of deception, breach of trust, or lawful threat-making, respectfully, with which a defendant could be charged.

Theft's Primary Wrong

What exactly does it mean to steal, and in what sense is it morally wrong to do so? Under the deontological approach to morality that I have been pursuing, what makes an act wrongful is some intrinsic violation of a free-standing moral rule or duty rather than the act's consequences. Such wrongdoing is typically directed towards a particular victim or group of victims that is wronged, as opposed to being, in Feinberg's terms, a free-floating evil.[71] The nature and origin of this moral wrong can be described by means of four more or less complementary approaches: a Lockean property rights-based approach, an anthropological approach, a law-dependent approach, and a functional, in-practice approach.

Stealing as a Violation of an Owner's Lockean Rights in Property

To understand what makes stealing wrong, it is helpful to understand why people have a right to own property in the first place. Of course, this is one of the most complex and contested issues in all of political and legal theory. It is far beyond the reach of this study to develop anything like a comprehensive theory of property rights. Instead, I propose to show how one particularly influential theory— John Locke's labor theory of property—might address the question.

Locke's basic theory—much criticized and subject to varying interpretations—goes something like this: we begin from a state of nature in which goods are held in common through a grant from God for the benefit of humanity. And how do these goods become private property? Locke says that every person begins with property rights in his own body and therefore, he says, in his labor. When an individual removes a good from the state of nature and mixes his labor with it, thereby enhancing its value, he converts it into his own private property.[72]

In Locke's hypothetical state, there are enough unclaimed goods so that everyone can appropriate the objects of his labors without infringing on goods appropriated by others. What is referred to as the "enough and as good" condition means that every person can obtain as much as he is willing to work for without competing with others. Locke also introduces a "non-waste" condition which prohibits the accumulation of so much property that some will need to be destroyed without being used. Given this condition, Locke believes, even after the primitive state has ceased to exist, there will, at least in some societies, still be enough and as good left in the common to give those without property the opportunity to gain it.[73]

The question is how does the conversion of goods into private property through the application of one's labor affect rights owed to him by others? "God gave the world to men in common," Locke says.[74] "[B]ut since he gave it them for their benefit and the greatest convenience of life they were capable to draw from it, it cannot be supposed he meant it should always remain common and uncultivated."[75] "He gave it to the use of the industrious and rational—and labor was to be his title to it." "He that had as good left for his improvement as was already taken up needed not complain, ought not to meddle with what was already improved by another's labor; if he did, it is plain he desired the benefit of another's pains which he had no right to."[76] In other words, Locke seems to be saying that once an individual mixes his labor with a good and thereby obtains a right of ownership in it, it follows that others in society have a duty to leave the object alone, and that if they violate this duty, they do the individual a wrong.

Wendy Gordon elaborates on the logic of Locke's approach:

> Imagine that there is a forest of wild apple trees in full fruit, and that someone has collected a few apples from each tree and piled the apples neatly on some moss with the expectation of taking them home to eat. Imagine further that the gatherer has left more than enough fruit on easily-reached boughs to satisfy anyone who might come along, that she has posted a notice on the apples declaring the nature of her investment and interest in them, and that the apples in her pile are no better than any of the apples remaining on the trees. If a stranger came along—someone whose characteristics are no different from what the laborer's were when she began working that morning—and he took her apples, it would be clear he was taking them only to save his labor.[77]

"The apple-taking stranger," Gordon says, "can offer no justification for his act except that he prefers his own welfare over the gatherer's. This will not justify the action, since he commits a fundamental wrong when he uses another solely as a means toward his own welfare. The stranger is treating the laborer not only 'as if [s]he existed for purposes [s]he does not share, but also as if she were less worthy than he.' "[78]

If this disrespect/using-another-solely-as-as-means-toward-one's-own-welfare account of the wrongfulness of theft is correct, then it would seem to offer an explanation for why D wrongs V when he takes that which is owned by V without V's consent. But, of course, it is a very limited explanation. It says nothing about cases in which V claims a right in ownership that does not derive directly from the value-added/labor theory of property as it exists in the Lockean state of nature (which itself is highly controversial). For example, it says little or nothing about why V would still have a right not to have his property stolen by D where V, say, obtained her property through inheritance rather than by working for it, or where D lacked reasonable opportunities to obtain property through lawful means. Recognizing the complexity of these questions and the need to move on to other issues more specific to theft law, however, I leave such theorizing to the scholars of property law.

The Prelegal Norm against Stealing

The previous section considered a possible connection between the rights that people have in their property and the wrongfulness of stealing. The discussion was pitched at a high level of abstraction, it depended on a theory of property rights that was itself highly controversial, and it was severely circumscribed by various hypothetical conditions that arguably make it of only limited relevance in a modern market economy. What follows looks at the problem in somewhat less abstract terms, focusing more directly on the normative structure of the rule against stealing itself.

Commentators have staked out two basic positions on the source of norms that underlie theft law. Some, such as Bentham, have stressed the culturally specific and law-bound character of the norm against stealing.[79] Others, including Hume, have emphasized the universal, prelegal, natural law aspect of the norm against stealing and of property rights more generally.[80] In fact, as I shall argue, the better view is that the norm against stealing does have a prelegal, natural existence, but that the norm is so thoroughly mediated and shaped by the law of property and by other cultural and social forces that we cannot make much practical sense of it without reference to such influences. In other words, the relationship between the law of theft and the moral concept of stealing is properly understood as a reciprocal one—with the former shaped by the latter, and vice versa.

To what extent does the moral norm against stealing exist independently of the legal prohibition on theft? There are a number of reasons to believe that the norm does have a distinctive prelegal, naturalistic character, similar to the norms against murder and rape. This is not to say that the norm against stealing necessarily developed prior in time to the law of theft and property; it seems unlikely, in any event, that such a claim could ever be verified. Nevertheless, there is compelling evidence—from history, anthropology, psychology, and evolutionary theory—to suggest that the norm against stealing has, to some degree, developed independently of the law of theft. The point is not that such evidence could offer a *justification* for the rule against stealing. To argue that would be to commit an obvious naturalistic fallacy. Rather, it is to raise the possibility that the basic idea that stealing is morally wrong is not solely the product of legal rules, and that it does in some sense precede, or arise simultaneously with, such rules.

The first piece of evidence is the simple observation that we tend to think of the rule against stealing at least as much as a moral concept as a legal one. We regard people who steal as bad people and teach our children not to steal at the same time and in the same manner we teach them not to lie or cheat. Stealing is regarded as both sinful and deeply threatening to society. The rule against it appears in both the Noachide Laws and in the Torah, along with other basic, presumably prelegal norms against murder, bearing false witness, and the like.[81]

Second, in every age there are acts regarded as theft by the law that are not regarded as stealing by the person in the street, and, conversely, acts that are not regarded as theft by the law that the person in the street commonly *does* regard as stealing. And, indeed, the law of theft has long been criticized for its inconsistency with extra-legal morality. For example, in eighteenth-century England, as Douglas Hay has explained:

The judicial definition of theft did not coincide . . . with the popular one. A wide variety of practices that were punished by law were considered legitimate by the rural poor: miners taking coals as perks, cottagers taking wood from ancient commons, smugglers and tradesmen evading excise. In all such cases, however, the practices were rigidly defined by custom, and the goods involved were sharply distinguished from other property. Legitimating ideas must be clear to the whole community concerned, and the practices they sanction unambiguously defined. Poaching was such an offence; promiscuous pilfering could not be.[82]

Similarly, as Robert Hughes explains, in the early nineteenth century, "ordinary Australians hardly thought of . . . horse stealing [and] cattle rustling . . . as crimes at all."[83] In the modern day, a similar pattern can be observed in connection with the unauthorized downloading of music, movies, information, and computer programs from the Internet (a topic discussed in detail in Chapter 4.) Despite the widespread legal prohibition on such forms of conduct, there is, as in eighteenth-century England, a significant segment of the public that does not regard them as wrongful. Conversely, we have seen that, until 1757, it was not a crime to obtain title to another's property by fraud (though such conduct could give rise to a civil action). Although evidence of public opinion is hard to come by for this period, it seems quite plausible that such acts were nevertheless viewed as morally equivalent to larceny. Indeed, it is just such gaps between law and morality that help explain why the criminal law has felt ongoing pressure to widen the definition of what constitutes theft.

Third, studies in developmental psychology indicate that even young children develop a sense of ownership and an awareness that it is wrong to take something that belongs to, or at least is in the possession of, another. Lawrence Kohlberg conducted a famous series of studies in which he presented children of different ages with a collection of hypothetical moral dilemmas and asked them to reason through them. One of the dilemmas involved a man, Heinz, whose wife was ailing, and who felt compelled to commit theft to obtain medicine that he could not obtain in any other way. What Kohlberg found, among other things, was that the vast majority of the youngest children interviewed felt that Heinz had done something wrong and should be punished (though they did so in an admittedly simplistic way). It was not until about the age of ten years that the children seemed able to see the complexity of the problem and appreciate the dilemma that Heinz faced and the possibility that his act might have been justified. For current purposes, what is important is that even the youngest children believed that it was wrong to steal even though they were presumably too young to be aware of the law of theft or of property.[84] More recent studies, though in various ways critical of Kohlberg's overall theory of moral development, have not undermined his basic findings in this regard.[85]

Fourth is a collection of anthropological studies of "primitive" societies, such as the Yurok, Hupa, and Karok Indians of Northern California, the Ifugao of Northern Luzon (Philippines), and the Kapauku Papuans of Western New Guinea. According to these studies, each society has possessed only the most rudimentary institutions of government and social organization, and none has had the centralized authority or power to force compliance or levy sanctions on behalf of the society at large. The primitive property rights were de facto, not de jure, as one scholar as put it.[86] Yet each of these cultures has reflected clear rules against stealing and a basic understanding of ownership and possession.[87] As Lawrence Friedman has explained, "the most primitive and basic rules in the criminal justice system were those that protected property rights. . . . Probably all human communities punish theft in one way or another; it is hard to imagine a society that does *not* have a concept of thievery, and some way to punish people who help themselves to things that 'belong' to somebody else."[88]

Finally, studies in evolutionary theory and cognitive psychology suggest that, just as human beings share a language instinct, they may also share what Jeffrey Stake has called a property instinct.[89] According to this view, the fundamental "deep structure" of property reflects various "hard-wired" mental mechanisms which have evolved through the need to deal repeatedly with various issues that arise with respect to limited resources.[90] The scarcity of resources creates competition, which can potentially result in harms to competitors. The costs of competition can be reduced, says Stake, through the adoption of strategies for determining the outcome of conflict while minimizing physical damage. Competitors need to know when to be assertive and when to be deferential with respect to material goods.[91] Persons who miscalculate the appropriate behavior will find themselves trying to obtain what others are prepared to defend fiercely, and those who do not recognize their own rights of possession will lose track of things they could easily have secured. Given the evolutionary advantages they enjoy, it seems reasonable to surmise that most humans alive today are descended from ancestors who were good at determining property rights.[92]

If Stake is correct that human beings have a property instinct of this sort, then it seems quite plausible that such an instinct also underlies the norm against theft.[93] (Of course, this is not to deny the possibility that there might also be an instinct *to* steal, which exists in tension with the instinct to respect property rights.) The basic rule against stealing is in some sense the most basic rule of property: what is mine is mine, what is yours is yours; I will respect your property rights if you respect mine. Stealing turns this relation on its head, treating *tuum* as *meum,* as the Criminal Law Revision Committee put it.[94] The unauthorized taking of one's possessions constitutes a challenge to one's well-being. Human beings (as well as animals[95]) are instinctively prepared to defend their claims of ownership. Indeed, there is evidence that the community will be prepared to intervene on behalf of owners to protect their property from threats by challengers.

How Law Informs the Norm against Stealing

Whereas the previous section offered evidence suggesting that the norm against stealing exists prior to, and independent of, the law, this section will consider the extent to which the law thoroughly infuses and mediates the basic norm. Such a view was endorsed by Bentham, who sought to show that the rule "Thou shalt not steal" cannot be understood without reference to a complex set of rules concerning what it means to have title to a thing and what it means to have that thing taken away.[96] As Bentham put it, "[p]roperty and law are born together, and die together. Before laws were made there was no property; take away laws, and property ceases."[97]

Under this view, the basic norm against stealing acts as a kind of place holder, with the laws of property, contract, and agency providing much of its content. Thus, while people recognize in some intuitive or natural sense that it is wrong to appropriate without permission what belongs to someone else, it is often impossible to make anything like a fully informed moral judgment about the blameworthiness of a given act of alleged theft until highly legalized concepts such as property,

ownership, possession, title, contract, offer, acceptance, appropriation, and fiduciary duty are thoroughly understood.

Consider two cases that illustrate this principle:

- Bennett and LeFave entered into an agreement under which
  LeFave would bring a truck trailer to a location where Bennett
  was staying and Bennett would pay for the trailer in several
  installments, after which he would receive title. Bennett also
  agreed not to move the trailer until the full purchase price had
  been paid. LeFave delivered the trailer as promised, but when
  Bennett moved the trailer in violation of the agreement, LeFave
  reported the trailer as stolen, and Bennett was prosecuted for
  theft. A jury convicted him and he was sentenced to eight years
  in prison.[98] Was the conviction proper?
- Sobiek and a group of friends formed a partnership to invest in
  second mortgages. Sobiek was elected president and gradually
  assumed more and more control of the partnership's funds.
  Eventually, he appropriated most of the partnership's assets
  for his own purposes. He was charged with theft and sought
  dismissal on the grounds that property owned jointly cannot
  be the subject of theft by one of the co-owners.[99] Was he right?

We might agree that, in both cases, what the defendant did was avari-
cious or dishonest or devious. But whether he stole anything is unde-
termined until the underlying applicable civil law of property is
examined.

In *State v. Bennett,* the Idaho Supreme Court reversed the conviction.
The Idaho theft statute required that the offender wrongfully take,
obtain, or withhold property from its owner. The term *owner,* in turn,
was defined as "any person who has a right to possession thereof superior to that of the taker, obtainer, or withholder."[100] Because "the criminal code did not provide guidance on possessory rights," the Court
said, it was "necessary to examine Article 2 of the [Uniform Commercial Code]."[101] After doing so, the court determined that, despite Bennett's violation of the agreement, his possessory rights remained
superior to LeFave's. Therefore, while Bennett might have been liable
to LeFave for breach of contract, he was not guilty of theft.

In *State v. Sobiek,* by contrast, the California appellate court held that
the prosecution should proceed.[102] In so doing, the court rejected the

rule articulated by earlier courts that for a theft to occur, the state must show not only that property belonged to another, but that it belonged wholly to the other. The court said it was "both illogical and unreasonable to hold that a partner cannot steal from his partners merely because he has an undivided interest in the partnership property."[103]

Although one of the admitted virtues of twentieth-century reforms was their tendency to reduce theft law's dependence on arcane and morally irrelevant legal concepts like breaking bulk and trespassory caption, the concept of stealing in the post-consolidation era nevertheless remains very much dependent on law.[104] My point here is not the tautologous one that we need to know what the law is at any given time to make a judgment as to whether the defendant committed the criminal offense of *theft*, but, rather, that we need to know the law to make a judgment as to whether the defendant committed the morally wrongful act of *stealing*.

As explained in Chapter 1, much of what we regard today as theft was not regarded as such only a couple of centuries ago, including misappropriating intangible and immoveable property; stealing dogs and cats; stealing by means of deception; and unauthorized use. (Similarly, until the time of the Napoleonic wars in the early eighteenth century, looting and plunder that occurred in the military context were viewed not as a crime, but as a prerogative, a legitimate form of compensation for otherwise poorly paid soldiers and a bona fide spoil of war to which the victors were entitled.[105])

Given how much more narrowly than modern law the English common law defined the circumstances in which theft could occur, the question arises whether an eighteenth- or nineteenth-century Englishman would also have had a narrower view of what constitutes stealing than his twenty-first-century counterpart. Unfortunately, evidence on such matters is scarce. The relevant social histories give only the barest hints on the topic. For example, as indicated earlier, in early eighteenth-century England, poaching was widely condoned in the communities in which it was practiced. Yet, as Clive Emsley points out, subsequent developments such as the enactment of legislation like the Poaching Prevention Act 1862, which empowered police to stop and search suspects, and the Ground Game Act 1880, which gave tenant farmers inalienable rights over hares and rabbits on their property, had a significant impact on public attitudes towards poaching. In Emsley's words, such legal changes "reduce[ed] sympathy for the poacher and ma[de] him appear more of a 'criminal.' "[106] In that limited respect, at least, we can say that the public of the eighteenth or early nineteenth century did have a narrower conception not only of what constitutes theft but also of what constitutes stealing than in our own time.

Today, developments in the law continue to have a significant impact on what is regarded, from a moral perspective, as stealing. While a significant segment of the population still does not believe that the unauthorized downloading of music and other content from the Internet constitutes stealing, attitudes do seem to be changing. The percentage of people who say that such acts are wrongful has gone up in recent years.[107] It is likely that such changes in attitude are at least partly the result of new legislation and stepped-up enforcement. Whether the unauthorized taking of intangible property like information will ever be viewed as morally equivalent to the unauthorized taking of tangible property like automobiles and jewelry remains to be seen. But it is clear that public attitudes in this area are in transition, in part because of changes in the governing law.

Theft in Unjust Societies

As we have seen, the extent to which a given act of appropriation will be viewed as wrongful depends, to a significant degree, on the precise manner in which a given society delineates its system of property rights.[108] In societies in which property rights are distributed in a manner radically different from how they are distributed in our society, what constitutes theft will also look very different.[109] For example, in a society in which all property was held communally, stealing would undoubtedly mean something quite unlike what it means in a private-ownership society. In a communal society, since everyone by definition would have a right to use all property at all times, the only way to violate another's property rights, presumably, would be to exclude him from use.[110]

This brings us to the problem of theft committed in societies in which property is distributed in a radically unjust manner. Imagine, for example, a society in which, as a result of the social caste into which he has been born, D and others in his class are denied the right to own property.[111] If D unlawfully took property from one who was not part of the discriminated-against class, is there an argument that his act should not be viewed as wrongful? I believe there is.

Claims of property make sense only in a social context in which there is some level of cooperative behavior.[112] Whether it is wrong to violate a given law against theft, and whether it is therefore just to be subjected to criminal penalties for doing so, depends on whether the property regime within which such law functions is itself just.[113] In their extensive dependence on legal rules, property crimes differ significantly from crimes like murder and rape. There are two complementary ways to characterize the difference: one is in terms of the traditional distinction in criminal law between *mala in se* and *mala prohibita*; the other is in terms of Rawls's distinction between natural duties and political obligations.

Crimes have traditionally been said to be *mala in se* if they involve conduct that is wrongful regardless of whether the conduct has been made illegal (murder and rape are good examples), and *mala prohibita* if they involve conduct that is wrong solely, or primarily, in virtue of their being illegal (the best example here are certain regulatory offenses).[114] In fact, however, there is no such thing as a pure *malum in se* or *malum prohibitum* offense. Even those crimes that can most plausibly be considered *mala in se* are to some extent defined by law. Conversely, even conduct that is most clearly *malum prohibitum* has attributes of *malum in se*. The point is that *malum in se* and *malum prohibitum* are better thought of as contrasting qualities along a continuum that, to one degree or another, characterize all criminal offenses, rather than as precise categories into which specific offenses either fit or don't fit. In that sense, theft is properly thought of as being more *malum prohibitum* in its character than highly *mala in se* crimes like murder and rape. That is, the moral wrongfulness of theft is *more dependent* on what the law (of property, contract, or fiduciary duty) prescribes than are crimes like murder and rape, which correspond primarily to norms that are based on morality rather than law.

Another way to think about the distinction is in terms of how Rawls distinguished between crimes based on "natural duties" and crimes based on "political obligation."[115] Under this approach, the moral obligation that *D* breaches when he commits a violent offense against another person is an obligation owed to his fellow human beings, as individuals, rather than to the government or to society generally. The special sanctity of life and of physical and sexual integrity, and therefore the wrongfulness of murder, assault, and rape, are easily recognized without presupposing any developed institutional structure. This is in contrast to crimes arising at least in part out of political obligation, like theft and trespass. As Jim Harris put it:

> The background right [to property] is historically situated. It does not have the same ahistorical status as do rights not to be subjected to unprovoked violence to the person. There are no natural rights to full-blooded ownership of the world's resources.
>
> Good faith implementation of the moral background right may or may not achieve a threshold of justice for a property institution. If it does, the trespassory rules of the institution are, *prima facie,* morally binding. Murder, assault, and rape are always moral wrongs. Theft is morally wrong only when this justice threshold is attained.[116]

And when does a given property institution achieve a threshold of justice? That, of course, is an immensely complex and controversial question, one that lies beyond the scope of this study. For the moment, however, it is safe to assume that the threshold would not be met by a regime under which a whole class of citizens was unjustly forbidden from owning property. In such a society, *D,* as a member of that class, would not be morally blameworthy for stealing property from *V,* at least to the extent that *V* helped create or perpetuate the conditions that caused *D*'s unjust impoverishment.[117] (Note that the question is different from the question of how to deal with cases in which a defendant steals out of necessity, since one can assert a defense of necessity regardless of whether one has systematically been denied the right to own property.)[118]

Characterizing Theft's Primary Wrong in Practice

To this point, I have considered two fundamental features of the law of theft that help shape its moral content: the way in which it draws on prelegal norms concerning stealing and ownership and the way in which such norms are mediated by the law of property and rules regarding the distribution of wealth that apply in a given society. What remains is to describe more precisely the nature of the norm against stealing itself. What exactly makes the appropriation of property a *mis*appropriation? To put it another way, how can appropriations of property that are not wrongful be distinguished from those that are? The question is not easy to answer. For a start, we can consider the various ways that the law of theft itself distinguishes between lawful and unlawful appropriations of property. I have in mind the terms *lack of consent, unlawfulness, fraudulence,* and *dishonesty.*[119]

Lack of Consent.   One possible way to characterize the primary wrong in theft is that the offender must take or use the owner's property *without the owner's consent.* This lack of consent made the taking trespassory at common law. Indeed, the common law elements of larceny often included, in addition to the wrongful taking of another's personal property and an intent to permanently deprive the owner of such property, an express requirement that the owner had failed to give consent.[120] Today, lack of consent rarely appears as an explicit element in theft's *prima facie* case. Instead, the contention that the victim consented to the taking surfaces primarily as an affirmative defense.[121] Nevertheless, if lack of consent did prove to be a key to understanding the wrongfulness of stealing, that would be significant, since it would suggest a parallel between the moral structure of theft and crimes like rape and perhaps assault, which are also informed by lack of consent.

Unfortunately, though lack of consent clearly plays a significant role in defining the moral structure of theft, there is a danger in putting too much weight solely on that concept. For a start, it is clear that lack of consent does not *sufficiently* describe the wrongfulness of stealing, since there are many cases in which property taken without the consent of the owner does not constitute stealing, such as where the taker acts under a claim of right or (if the taker is the government) pursuant to its power of eminent domain, forfeiture, or taxation.

The more difficult question is whether lack of consent should be regarded as a *necessary* condition for stealing. A trio of post-Theft Act cases in England might be thought to raise doubt about this contention. The first is *Lawrence v. Metropolitan Police Commissioner.*[122] Occhi, an Italian who spoke little English, arrived in England and hired Lawrence, the defendant taxi driver, to take him to an address in London. Occhi offered Lawrence enough money to cover the lawful fare, but Lawrence asked for more, and while Occhi held his wallet open, Lawrence helped himself. The defense argued that no theft had been committed because Occhi had consented to Lawrence's taking of the extra money. In rejecting this argument and upholding the conviction, the Law Lords said that, under the Theft Act, lack of consent was "no longer an ingredient of the offense." Rather, it was sufficient that the appropriation be performed "dishonestly."

R. v. Gomez is to the same end.[123] The defendant, an employee at an electrical store, persuaded his unwitting manager to accept two worthless building society checks, known by the defendant to have been stolen, in exchange for goods sold at the shop where they worked. In upholding the conviction, the Lords stated that whether the act was done with the manager's consent was immaterial. Citing *Lawrence,* the Lords said it was "unequivocal []" that "an act may be an appropriation [for purposes of the Theft Act] notwithstanding that it is done with the consent of the owner."

Finally, there is *R. v. Hinks.*[124] The defendant befriended and cared for Dolphin, an elderly man of limited intelligence. As a result of the defendant's manipulation, Dolphin decided to give her legally valid "gifts" constituting a significant amount of his life savings. Once again, the Law Lords upheld the conviction: the fact that the gifts had been given consensually was no basis for reversal under the Theft Act.

Do these cases really establish the proposition that lack of consent should no longer be regarded as a necessary element of theft? To understand why they do not, it is necessary to look more deeply into what is meant by *consent.* The problem is that consent (or lack of it) means different things in different contexts. Thus, those cases that at first seem to have eliminated lack of one form consent as an element of theft may in fact still require lack of consent in a different form.

A good place to begin this inquiry is with the work of Peter Westen, who, though focusing primarily on the offense of rape, has provided insight into how we conceive of consent more generally.[125] Westen describes four basic senses in which to talk about the concept, but for present purposes the key distinction is between factual attitudinal consent, factual expressive consent, and prescriptive consent. *Factual attitudinal consent* reflects the consenter's state of mind at the time she consents; it occurs when the consenter's "all things considered" desire is to acquiesce in the requested conduct. Thus, a person who agrees to have sex or surrender property to avoid threatened physical injury can be said to have consented in the factual attitudinal sense of the term because, all things considered, she prefers to submit rather than to suffer the threatened harm. With *factual expressive consent,* the consenter not only acquiesces mentally to the proposed action, but also makes her acquiescence known to others. Factual attitudinal or expressive consent is involuntary if it is made under the pressure of coercion; it is unknowing if it is obtained through deception; and it is incompetent if it is given by one who is incapable of understanding that to which she consents. Such forms of consent are to be contrasted with *prescriptive consent,* which to be recognized by the law as consent must be made voluntarily, knowingly, and competently.[126]

Westen's framework is helpful for understanding the role that lack of consent plays in defining the moral content of theft crimes. Consider again the three House of Lords decisions discussed above. In each case, an argument can be made that, though the defendant gave his factual expressive consent, he did not give his prescriptive consent: In *Lawrence,* the victim taxi passenger's English was poor, he apparently did not understand how much the taxi fare should have cost, and he was presumably nervous and intimidated; in *Gomez,* the victim employer was deceived by the defendant into believing that the checks were "good as cash"; and in *Hinks,* the victim was of low intelligence and was essentially under the coercive influence of the defendant. Thus, when the Law Lords said in each case that lack of consent was no longer an element of the offense, what they really meant is that lack of *factual expressive* consent is no longer an element of the offense, not that lack of *prescriptive* consent is no longer an element. Had the victims of Lawrence, Gomez, and Hinks not been duped or coerced into giving up the money that they did, the outcome of the cases would surely have been different.

A similar dynamic can be observed in the context of extortion, which is defined in the Hobbs Act as "the obtaining of property from another, *with his consent,* induced by wrongful use of actual or threatened force, violence, or fear."[127] On the face of it, extortion would seem to constitute another, even more obvious, form of theft that does not require lack of consent. But, of course, the kind of consent required is merely factual expressive consent. Valid *prescriptive* consent is still lacking, since it has been given under the force of coercion.

And what about cases in which an owner who suspects that his goods are being stolen purposely exposes them to easy taking, such as by leaving a door open, with the expectation that the police, standing by, will make an arrest? Although generally concluding that such takings are nonconsensual, courts and commentators have struggled to find any principled basis for reaching this conclusion.[128] In one sense, the owner did desire that the offender take, or attempt to take, his goods, since unless the offender did so, there would be no legal basis for apprehending him. But the important point is that, even if the owner did consent to the taking of his goods, he was consenting only to their *temporary* and *limited* taking. He never consented to having his goods taken permanently or completely, which is what would be required to negate the charge of theft.

Based on the foregoing analysis, it seems reasonable to conclude that lack of consent (or, at least, lack of prescriptive consent) is a necessary, though not sufficient, condition for a theft to occur. It thus plays a significant role in defining what makes theft morally wrongful, though an incomplete one. Because there are cases in which an owner might have his property appropriated without his consent that nevertheless do not constitute stealing, we need to think further about what distinguishes morally and legally acceptable appropriations from morally and legally unacceptable ones.

Unlawfulness.   *Unlawfully* is the term used by the MPC and the German *Strafgesetzbuch* (StGB) to describe the kind of appropriation that must be performed for theft to be committed. The MPC says that a person is guilty of theft if he unlawfully takes, or exercises unlawful control over, the moveable property of another (with the intent to deprive him thereof).[129] The StGB says that the *zuzueignen* (appropriation) in theft must be done *rechtswidrig* (unlawfully or illegally).[130] According to the MPC Commentary, the word *unlawful* "implies a lack of consent or authority and specifically the absence of any defense under Section 2.11 [consent], Section 223.1(3) [claim of right], or Article 3 [general principles of justification, including choice of evils]."[131]

Unlawfully seems like an improvement over *without consent* standing alone, at least to the extent that it conveys a sense of both lack of consent *and* lack of other forms of legal authority (such as claim of right or justification). But unlawfully is far from perfect as a description of what makes theft morally wrongful. As indicated earlier, theft reflects both law-based *and* prelegal norms. By describing the wrongfulness of theft in terms of unlawfulness, the law-based aspect of theft is emphasized over its moral aspect.

Imagine that it is 1756 and that *D* has deceived *V* into permanently giving up possession of his horse. At the time, such an act would not have been regarded as criminal, or even necessarily as unlawful. Yet it is hard to imagine that it would not have been viewed as morally wrongful. Conversely, imagine a case today in which *D* downloads without authorization a music file from *V*'s Web site. Such a case would presumably meet the requirements of unlawfulness in that it was performed without consent or claim of right or other legal justification. Yet many people would not regard *D*'s conduct as wrongful. Given the gap between the legal concept of theft and the moral concept of stealing, the notion of unlawfulness thus seems inadequate to capture the sense in which theft can be identified as wrongful.

Fraudulence.   The term *fraudulently* functions, in the (now-repealed) English Larceny Act of 1916, the Canadian Criminal Code, the Queensland and Western Australia Codes, and the French *Code Pénal* in much the same way that *unlawfully* and *dishonestly* function in the MPC and the Theft Act, respectively.[132] Yet the Canadian scholar Winifred Holland has claimed that the term reflects "an element of moral obloquy which is not captured by the [intent to deprive and lack of consent]"[133] As such, *fraudulently* may potentially offer a general means for distinguishing between wrongful and non-wrongful appropriations of property.

Unfortunately, the precise meaning of *fraudulently* is far from clear.[134] Some courts and commentators have thought that it meant nothing more than "without color of right" or "intentional and deliberate."[135] Other authorities have viewed *fraudulently* as the difference between an intent to deprive permanently and an intent to deprive only temporarily.[136] Still others have understood it to mean that the actor was motivated by a desire for personal gain.[137]

For present purposes, the real question is whether there are circumstances in which a defendant might have acted without consent or claim of right and still not have satisfied the requirement of fraudulence. There are two sorts of cases in which such arguments have arisen. The first was in jurisdictions like England under the 1916 Act, which followed the traditional rule that theft requires an intent to deprive permanently. In such cases, a defendant borrowed cash from an employer's till, without authorization or consent, planning to repay it later. Because the actual notes returned were bound to be different from the original ones taken (which would almost certainly have been spent), prosecutors argued that the defendant did in fact have an intent to deprive permanently. In response, the defendants contended that, despite such intent, they did not act fraudulently within the meaning of the Act. Perhaps surprisingly, some courts agreed with the defendants; to prove such a state of mind, they said, it is necessary to show that the defendant intended to "act to the detriment of any person against that person's wishes."[138]

The second kind of argument is made in jurisdictions like Canada, which follow the non-Anglo-American rule that even an intent to deprive only temporarily will suffice to establish theft. In such jurisdictions, a defendant will sometimes argue that, despite his intent to deprive an owner temporarily of his property, he was only playing a prank. In *R. v. Wilkins*, for example, the accused took a police officer's scooter and drove it a short distance while the officer was writing out a parking ticket, intending to play a joke. Once again, the Court of Appeals agreed with the defendant, reversing his conviction for theft on the grounds that the prosecution had failed to prove that he had acted fraudulently. The court said that the intention to perpetrate the joke, "stupid though it was, is incompatible with the *evil intent* which is inherent in the crime of theft."[139]

Such cases signal an attempt on the part of the courts to endow the term *fraudulently* with genuine moral significance. For that, I think they deserve credit. In the final analysis, however, the term is hardly ideal for distinguishing between wrongful and non-wrongful appropriations of property. Among other things, *fraud* traditionally connotes a sense of deceit or duplicity, as opposed to a more general notion of dishonesty.[140] As such, I believe it is too narrow for these purposes.

Perhaps as a result of such concerns, there has been something of a push, in those jurisdictions that still use *fraudulently*, to switch to a different term to distinguish between wrongful and non-wrongful takings. The preferred alternative is usually *dishonesty*. For example, both the Law Reform Commission of Canada and the Model Criminal Code Officers Committee of Australia have recommended that the latter term be substituted for the former, though these changes have not yet been effected in law.[141] Indeed, one of the arguments in favor of such a change is that use of the term *dishonest* "bolsters fundamental values."[142] What exactly *dishonesty* means and whether it really is a preferable term to describe the wrongfulness in theft is a subject to which we now turn.

Dishonesty.   In England and Wales, since the enactment of the Theft Act, dishonesty has come to be seen as the key concept that defines the moral wrongfulness in theft. The concept of dishonesty has also figured increasingly in the social psychology literature.[143] Unfortunately, neither the Theft Act nor the psychology literature ever says what it means to be dishonest. At best, the Theft Act tells us what it means *not* to be dishonest.

This is said to occur in three closely related circumstances. First, according to Section 2(1)(a) of the Act, a person is not dishonest if he appropriates property "in the belief that he has in law the right to deprive the [owner] of it, on behalf of himself or of a third person."[144] Thus, a defendant who takes money from *V* believing that *V* owes it to him would not ordinarily be said to have acted dishonestly. Similarly, the defendant will be held not to have acted dishonestly if he took property in the belief that it had been abandoned. The defense will ordinarily apply when the defendant turns out to have been mistaken about the underlying substantive law. Indeed, such a provision again illustrates the ways in which the moral concept of stealing is dependent on the substantive civil law of property and contract. The second express circumstance in which the defendant will be held not to have acted dishonestly is if she believes that the owner would have consented to the appropriation if he had known about it.[145] This situation is apt to occur where a person buys property from an absent seller, as where a young girl took a bottle of milk from a farm stand, leaving a sum of money in return.[146] And the third circumstance is where the defendant believes that the owner is undiscoverable, as where the offender finds money on a public road and, concluding that it would be too difficult to trace the owner, spends it; the owner subsequently discovers what has had happened and was able to establish title.[147]

Beyond these express provisions describing what dishonesty is *not*, it is harder to say exactly what it *is*. The English courts have struggled mightily with this question, particularly with the extent to which the judge should guide the jury in its determination of whether the defendant has acted dishonestly, and by whose standards they should make such a judgment. (Indeed, the question of who—judge or jury—should decide what constitutes dishonesty, and what standard should apply, has been among the most common targets of those who disapprove of *dishonesty* as a term of art.[148])

For present purposes, the question is whether there are cases in which a defendant, despite his having acted without consent or claim of right, should nevertheless be said to have acted honestly, and therefore not to have stolen. Four cases of this type merit consideration. The first is illustrated by the facts in *R. v. Feely*, in which D "borrowed" money from his employer's safe, without any acknowledgement or IOU, and despite a warning that employees must not do so.[149] D was transferred to another branch office at short notice and the taking was then discovered, without his having had the opportunity to make good on his debt. His explanation was that he intended to repay the sum out of the money his employer owed him, which would have amply covered the deficiency. In reversing the conviction below, the appellate court held that the defendant was entitled to show his intention to repay and his belief that he could do so. In other words, a jury, applying "the current standards of ordinary decent people," could conclude that the defendant was honest, and therefore had not stolen, even though the property had been taken without consent or claim of right.[150]

The second way a defendant acts without consent or claim of right and yet is said to be honest is illustrated by the hypothetical case (given in *R. v. Ghosh*) of a foreign traveler who comes from a country where public transportation is free. On his first day in England, he travels on a bus and gets off without paying. Once again, the court says that the offender's act should be regarded as honest since his is a case to which "no moral obloquy could possibly attach."[151] Here again, no stealing has occurred.

The rule in both cases seems to me correct. Neither involves an intentional violation of the victim's property rights, and neither should properly be called stealing. The fact that the taking was done without consent or claim of right tells only part of the story. Dishonesty connotes some additional moral content. It suggests that the offender lacked integrity or probity. It conveys a moral sense that is independent of the law. To say that a defendant acted honestly or dishonestly is to say something more generally about his character as a person, beyond merely his specific acts.

Now contrast two other hypothetical scenarios suggested by *Ghosh*: In one, Robin Hood takes from the rich and gives to the poor. In the other, a member of an animal rights group takes dogs from a research laboratory to prevent their being used in medical experiments.[152] In both cases, the defendants regard themselves as "morally justified in doing what they do."[153] Nevertheless, it seems to me (as well as to the court in *Ghosh*) that both acts are properly viewed as stealing. Both involve an intentional usurpation of the victims' property rights. Whether or not the defendant's conduct was justified is an issue that is properly viewed as separate from the question of whether he stole.

In short, the term *dishonesty* seems a useful one for distinguishing between those appropriations that should count as stealing and those that should not, particularly when the term is compared to the alternatives. Unlike *unlawfully,* the term *dishonesty* is not based exclusively on law; and unlike *fraudulently,* it does not connote any overly narrow sense of deceit or duplicity. *Dishonesty* connotes a lack of honesty, probity, or integrity; a thievishness.[154] It exists as a free-standing concept of morality. As such, it offers an appropriate label for the wrongful element in stealing.

Other Forms of Dishonest or Wrongful Appropriation of Property. Despite the virtues of the term *dishonesty* as a means to distinguish wrongful from non-wrongful takings of property, there is a potential hazard that deserves mention. The focus so far has been on cases in which a defendant took property without consent or other legal authority and yet, because his act was deemed honest, was said not to have stolen. In such cases, the requirement of dishonesty served as a *limiting* factor. The question I want to consider now is whether there might be cases that involve the converse situation, in which a defendant takes property with both consent and lawful authority, but is nevertheless said to have done an act that is dishonest, and therefore is said to have stolen. That is, might there be cases in which the concept of dishonesty would lead to a *broadening* of what constitutes stealing?

Talmudic law presents a puzzling possibility in this regard. The Talmud uses the same term, *gezel*—translated as *theft*—to refer not only to the taking of property without the owner's consent, but also to the taking of proceeds in gambling.[155]) How can this be? What basis is there for regarding the obtainment of money through gambling as a form of theft, and therefore subject to the usual remedies for theft? As I understand it, there are two possible explanations for such a view.

The first considers the transaction from the perspective of the alleged victim. Under this view, one whose property is taken to satisfy a gambling debt does not truly consent to such taking. This seems to be the view taken by Menachem Elon, who argues that the earnings in such a case "come by means of a game in which the result is a gamble, and there is therefore no unreserved consent and unqualified intent to give up the money in case one loses."[156] This argument is valid inasmuch as property taken without consent does ordinarily constitute theft. But it is nevertheless unsound since it is based on an implausible premise: at least according to a modern understanding, it is inaccurate to say that one who loses property pursuant to a voluntary, informed, and knowing wager does not thereby consent to at least the risk of losing the property.

The second kind of explanation looks at the transaction from the perspective of the alleged thief. This explanation poses a more radical challenge to the conception of stealing so far offered here. According to Maimonides:

> If person[s] play with blocks of wood or stone or bone or the like and stipulate among themselves that the winner of the game receives a certain amount from the other, this is deemed [theft] on the authority of the Scribes, *even though the winner gets his winnings with the consent of the owner.* He is committing robbery, seeing that *he takes another's money for nothing by means of a game or sport.*[157]

Thus, Maimonides concedes that the victim consents to the taking of his property, but he believes the taker has committed theft nonetheless. Maimonides focuses on what he views as the inherent immorality of gambling. He seems to be saying that to obtain money through gambling is, *ipso facto,* to obtain it dishonestly. Whether gambling really is immoral or dishonest, and if so why, is an interesting question, though one that lies beyond the scope of this study.[158] In any event, what is troubling here is the possibility that, under a dishonesty-type approach, the definition of stealing might be expanded to include not just the familiar forms of unlawful takings, but also other kinds of taking that, for one reason or another, are deemed dishonest.

Theft's Secondary Wrongs

So far this chapter has considered the various ways in which theft involves the wrongful act of stealing, or dishonestly depriving another of his property rights. I referred to such stealing as theft's primary wrong. Theft's secondary wrongs involve not the deprivation of property rights per se, but rather the wrongful means by which such deprivation is carried out.

At common law, as described in the previous chapter, whether property was taken by means of, for example, deception rather than stealth could determine not only which particular form of theft was prosecuted, and therefore what the punishment would be, but also whether a crime could be charged at all, since theft by deception did not become a crime until relatively late in English legal history. Under the modern, consolidated law of theft, however, the means by which the misappropriation is effected has lapsed in significance. In the name of criminal law reform and simplification, moral distinctions that persisted through centuries have been discarded. The result, as I have noted, has been a marked flattening of the moral content of theft law and an undermining of the principle of fair labeling. Yet, as the empirical study described in Chapter 1 shows, people continue to make significant moral distinctions based on the means by which a theft is committed. They reject the assumption, implicitly made by the framers of the MPC, that all forms of theft are morally equivalent. Why do people make such differing judgments of blameworthiness depending on the means by which the theft is committed?

The various theft scenarios that were the subject of the empirical study first described in Chapter 1 can help answer this question. Each scenario (with the possible exception of receiving stolen property) reflects the same primary wrong—namely, Tom's dishonestly or unlawfully depriving Owen of property rights in his bicycle. What vary are the distinctive secondary wrongs that attend each case. In the rest of this chapter, I consider the moral content of seven types of stealing: by stealth (as in larceny), by force or violence (as in aggravated and simple robbery), by invasion of privacy (as in theft by housebreaking or burglary), by breach of trust (as in embezzlement), by deception (as in false pretenses and passing a bad check), by coercion (as in blackmail and extortion), and by exploiting emergency circumstances (as in looting). (The next chapter will deal with the offenses of receiving stolen property, finding and failing to return lost or misdelivered property, and *de minimis* thefts, and will revisit the offenses of passing a bad check and blackmail.)

Recall the results of the study: armed robbery was, by a considerable margin, considered the most blameworthy of the theft-related offenses. Extortion was a step below. Theft by housebreaking was tied in the ranking with simple robbery, though the former received a slightly more severe sentence. On the next step were blackmail and larceny. Below that were embezzlement and looting. Tied below those were the two cases of fraud—false pretenses and passing a bad check. Ranked as least blameworthy were receiving stolen property and failing to return misdelivered property.

Before delving further, note that my approach here is intended to be idealized and ahistorical. That is, I am concerned less with the precise way in which such offenses historically *have* been defined than with the way in which such offenses plausibly *could* be defined in a system that was appropriately sensitive to the demands of fair labeling. In doing so, I am thus continuing to adhere to the reconstructive approach to analysis that I described at the outset.

Also, though all of the various forms of stealing described in the empirical study were designed to be mutually exclusive, in the real world, they need not be. For example, V can have his property taken by a combination of coercion and deceit, as where D pretends to be a police officer and threatens to arrest V unless he pays some amount of money.[159] In such a case, charges of false pretenses, extortion, and possibly robbery would all be appropriate (though I don't mean to suggest that it would be just to punish a defendant for all three at once). Similarly, V can have his property taken by a combination of deceit and breach of trust, as where a lawyer converts a client's trust account to his own use. Burglary as well can be committed by a range of different means: through deception (as where an intruder obtains permission to enter the premises through a lie or trick);[160] through threats or violence (as where the intruder points a gun at the head of the homeowner who answers the door and demands entry);[161] and through breach of trust (as where a servant within the house acts in concert with an intruder).[162] Despite the possibility of such overlaps, however, there is no reason not to continue the effort to make conceptual distinctions among various forms of theft.[163]

Theft by Force or Violence (Robbery)

Robbery consists of taking property by means of force or the threat of force. It is the only form of theft that involves aggressive physical contact or the threat of physical contact between offender and victim. There are two paradigms here. The first is reflected in what our study refers to as simple robbery, in which Tom simply grabs the bike from Owen's hands. The case is reminiscent of a famous scene in Gogol's story, "The Overcoat." The luckless Akaky is walking in the dark through a St. Petersburg city square wearing his beloved new overcoat, on his way back home from the Civil Servant's party, when two men with moustaches approach him. As Gogol describes:

> [Akaky] felt dazed and his heart began beating violently against his ribs. "Look, here is my overcoat!" one of the men said in a voice of thunder, grabbing him by the collar. Akaky was about to scream, "Help!" but the other man shook his fist in his face, a fist as big as a Civil Servant's head, and said, "You just give a squeak!" All poor Akaky knew was that they took off his overcoat and gave him a kick which sent him sprawling in the snow. He felt nothing at all anymore.[164]

In neither case—Owen's or Akaky's—is there consent of any sort, attitudinal, expressive, or prescriptive. The property is simply ripped from the victim's hands.

Such cases are to be distinguished from the study's armed robbery scenario in which Tom threatens Owen with a gun unless he surrenders the bike. In that instance, Owen has consented in both the attitudinal and expressive senses of the term, but not, of course, in its prescriptive sense. In deciding to surrender his bicycle, and expressing such consent to Tom, Owen has decided that, all things considered, he would prefer to surrender his bike rather than be shot or otherwise physically harmed. But because Owen was subject to violent threats from Tom, he lacks the voluntariness that true prescriptive consent requires.

There is an interesting question about how the offense of robbery should be classified. As shown in Chapter 1, robbery has generally not been consolidated with the other theft offenses, and it is unclear whether it should even be regarded as a property crime in the first place. The MPC classifies it as such, but there is a more modern trend towards classifying it, along with rape and assault, as a crime against the person.[165] Which choice is made presumably depends on which aspect of the offense is emphasized—whether it is the threat of physical violence or the misappropriation of property.[166] This choice has practical consequences in cases in which the same property is possessed by more than one person. In such cases, the prosecutor must decide whether to charge only one count of robbery or multiple counts.[167]

Robbery was probably the first form of theft to be criminalized. It has a strong claim to being the most morally wrongful and socially harmful form of theft and, indeed, the empirical study described in Chapter 1 indicated that it occupied a class by itself in terms of blameworthiness. Little elaboration is presumably needed to explain why it is morally wrong to inflict unjustified pain or fear on others. Any theory of morality, whether consequentialist or non-consequentialist, will regard such acts as among the most wrongful. The seriousness with which robbery is viewed by the criminal law—Coke called it "amongst the most heinous [of] felonies"[168]—is evidenced by the fact that the penalties for robbery are invariably higher than for other forms of theft. In this, the law of robbery parallels the law of sexual assault, which normally treats forcible rape as a more serious crime than rape by deception or coercion.[169] At the same time, it is worth noting that despite the fear and loathing with which robbery is normally viewed, there are nevertheless cases in which robbing bandits are celebrated as heroes who (whether they intend to or not) serve an important societal function.[170]

The secondary wrong in robbery is so significant that it tends to overshadow the primary wrong of misappropriation. As the MPC Commentary puts it:

> The violent petty thief operating in the streets and alleys of big cities—the "mugger"—is one of the main sources of insecurity and concern in the population at large. There is a special element of terror in this kind of depredation. The ordinary citizen does not feel particularly threatened by surreptitious larceny, embezzlement, or fraud. But there is understandable abhorrence of the robber who accosts on the streets

and who menaces his victims with actual or threatened violence against which there is a general sense of helplessness.[171]

At the same time, it is important not to underestimate the way in which the wrongfulness of robbery is colored by the element of property misappropriation. Consider the most recent legal debacle involving O. J. Simpson.[172] In September 2007, Simpson and several associates burst into a room at a Las Vegas hotel, several of them brandishing guns, and seized various mementos, including many items previously autographed by Simpson. In his subsequent trial, Simpson maintained that he had been conducting a "sting operation" to recover property that, he claimed, had been stolen from him years earlier by a former agent. Assuming for the moment that his factual contention was true, could the fact that Simpson owned the property legitimately serve as a defense to robbery? Interestingly, the law varies. A handful of courts—such as the Nevada court in which Simpson was ultimately convicted—have said that the proper charge was robbery regardless of who owned the property.[173] However, I believe the better view is that the proper charge was not robbery but rather assault, since, assuming Simpson actually did have a right to recover the goods, he would not have been attempting to violate anyone's rights to property.[174]

It is also worth considering how robbery should be distinguished from mere larceny, particularly in cases of pickpocketing. Jewish law takes a subjective approach: if the victim is aware of the physical taking from his person, the act is robbery; if not, the act is considered larceny.[175] Anglo-American law takes a contrasting, objective approach. Simply having physical contact with the victim is not enough to merit charges of robbery, even if the victim is aware of the contact. For there to be a robbery, there must be some objective violence or intimidation.[176]

Unfortunately, the line between robbery and larceny is not always clear. Even relatively light force, such as barging into someone or tugging at a handbag in such a way that the owner's hand is pulled downwards, has been held to constitute force sufficient to constitute robbery.[177] Yet, as Andrew Ashworth has suggested, such cases are troubling. "It is difficult," he says, "to draw the line between sufficient and insufficient force, but if robbery is to continue to be regarded as a serious offense, triable only on indictment and punishable with life imprisonment, surely something more than a bump, a push, or a pull should be required."[178] Indeed, as Ashworth points out, the law surrounding robbery, at least in England, is much less finely graded than that surrounding assault. Because of this, he argues that robbery, in its current form, plainly breaches the principle of fair labeling. He therefore recommends a statutory scheme that would reflect the moral distinction between theft by means of a "mere push" and theft by means of "serious violence."[179]

I assume that Ashworth would prefer something like the approach to robbery taken in the United States. Under the MPC, only those thefts involving the infliction or threat of immediate "serious bodily injury" are treated as robbery and subject to heightened punishment.[180] If the theft involves only minimal force, the MPC treats it as "ordinary theft."[181] Many states have an even more finely graded robbery offense scheme, which distinguishes among offenses such as simple robbery, armed robbery, first degree robbery, second degree robbery, purse snatching, and carjacking.[182] In general, the more aggravated forms of robbery tend to be those in which the offender uses a weapon or inflicts or threatens serious physical injury.

Theft by Coercion (Extortion and Blackmail)

Extortion and blackmail both involve obtaining property from a victim by means of coercing the victim's consent. The coercion invalidates the consent, making the act theft.[183] Making a threat for the purpose of obtaining something other than property, such as sexual favors or political endorsements, is not extortion, though it might constitute the separate offense of criminal coercion.

As I shall use the terms here, *extortion* refers to cases in which the threatened conduct is itself unlawful, while *blackmail* refers to cases in which the threatened conduct, though unwanted, is not unlawful.[184] Thus, in the extortion scenario discussed in Chapter 1, Tom threatens to do the illegal act of burning down Owen's house if he does not hand over the bicycle. In the blackmail scenario, by contrast, Tom threatens to do the otherwise lawful act of showing embarrassing photos of Owen to Owen's boss.[185]

In their assessments, participants ranked the extortion scenario as significantly more blameworthy than the blackmail one. There are several possible explanations for this. One is that the subjects did distinguish between threatened conduct that is lawful and threatened conduct that is not. A second is simply that arson is a more wrongful act than circulating embarrassing photos. A third possibility is that Owen might have been viewed as somehow partly responsible for his plight in the blackmail scenario in a way that he was not in the extortion scenario. Whatever the explanation, our subjects' intuitions differed from current law.

The MPC makes no distinction between stealing by means of threats to do what is unlawful and stealing by means of threats to do what is lawful. It uses the term *theft by extortion* to refer to both kinds of cases and treats them as equal in seriousness to, and interchangeable with, other forms of theft, such as larceny, embezzlement, receiving stolen property, failing to return found property, and the like.[186] The Theft Act also does not distinguish between the two kinds of act. Instead, it uses the term *blackmail* to refer both to threats to do what is lawful and threats to do what is unlawful, and it imposes a higher maximum penalty for both acts than for basic theft.[187]

Ordinarily, what the extortionist threatens the victim with is future economic harm. Extortion of this sort is thus distinguishable from robbery, in which property is obtained through threats of immediate physical harm.[188] In Westen's terminology, the victim of extortion has once again consented in both the attitudinal and expressive senses of the term, but not in its prescriptive sense. *V* has decided that, all things considered, he would prefer to surrender his bike rather than suffer the threatened harm that would result if he did not surrender it. But because Owen was subject to coercion, his conduct lacks the voluntariness that true prescriptive consent requires.

One of the keys to understanding the moral content of both extortion and blackmail is to recognize the role that threats and coercion play in defining such offenses. When *D* threatens *V*, *D* is promising *V* that he will bring about some unwanted state of affairs for *V*. Often, but not always, threats are conditional. In such cases, *V* is given a choice between doing what is demanded or opting instead for the consequences threatened. When *D* threatens *V*, she is promising to make *V worse off* in relation to some relevant baseline position than if *V* does not accept her proposal. This is in contrast to cases in which *D* makes an offer to *V*, and *V* is given an inducement to action. If *V* accepts *D*'s proposal, *V* will be made *better off* in relation to some relevant baseline position.[189]

The essential point for now is that the moral content of extortion (and blackmail) is distinguishable from that of other theft offenses. For example, whereas the victim of extortion is unable to give valid prescriptive consent to the taking of his property because he has been subject to coercion, the victim of false pretenses is unable to give valid consent because he has been subject to deception. Chapter 3 will further examine the kinds of theft by coercion that should or should not be subject to criminal sanctions.

Theft by Housebreaking and Burglary

In the scenario ranked next most blameworthy, Tom climbs through a window into the basement of Owen's house and steals his bike. The scenario loosely tracks the offense of burglary, which consists of breaking into and entering another's dwelling with the intent to commit a theft or other felony therein.[190] Both the MPC and the Theft Act treat burglary as an offense separate from theft.[191] The MPC treats burglary as a felony of the second degree if it is perpetrated at night; otherwise, it is a felony of the third degree (the same as theft).[192] The Theft Act treats burglary as a significantly more serious offense than theft, imposing a maximum term of fourteen years if it involves a dwelling and ten years in other cases (whereas the maximum term for theft is seven years).[193]

Burglary, as the term has traditionally been understood, need not involve a theft at all. In some cases, the burglar will enter with an intent to commit an entirely different crime, such as murder or rape.[194] In other cases, the burglar will be apprehended or will change his mind after entering but before committing the target crime. The scenario presented in the empirical study thus corresponds more precisely to the Scottish offense of theft by housebreaking, an aggravated form of theft that consists of stealing by means of unlawful entry, and I shall therefore use that term here.[195]

Like robbery and extortion, which involve the primary wrong of stealing plus a separate secondary wrong (force and coercion, respectively), theft by housebreaking also involves both a primary and a secondary wrong. Here, the secondary wrong consists of the invasion of the homeowner's privacy and a blow to his sense of security, a fact that was particularly clear at common law where burglary was limited to unauthorized entry into dwelling houses at night. Entry by the intruder presents some physical danger to the homeowner who is at home, though studies suggest that the public widely overestimates the significance of this danger.[196] The more significant wrong is that associated with the homeowner's sense of violation, based on appreciation of the intention of the burglar to invade the home.[197] This becomes clear in interviews with victims of theft by housebreaking. As one study found, "citizens have a sense of outrage on returning to their home and finding it ransacked. They are shocked by the crude violation of their privacy, and they have a sickening feeling that they will never again feel safe in their homes."[198] On the other hand, it is worth noting that particularly daring and skillful burglars—whether real, like the notorious nineteenth-century English cat burglar Charles Peace or fictional, like Cary Grant's John Robie in the film *It Takes a Thief*—are sometimes celebrated in popular culture, especially when it is the wealthy and fashionable from whom they are stealing.

Theft by Stealth (Larceny)

In the larceny scenario, Tom came up to Owen's porch, picked the lock on the bike that was chained there, and rode it away, intending to keep it. These facts would clearly make out a case under the common law definition of larceny—namely, the unlawful taking and carrying away of the personal property of another with the intent to permanently deprive the possessor of the property.[199] Neither the MPC nor the Theft Act has a separate offense of larceny. In the MPC, the closest analogue is the offense of theft by unlawful taking or disposition, which is interchangeable with and subject to the same punishment as false pretenses, extortion, failing to return lost or misdelivered property, and receiving stolen property.[200] The Theft Act, for its part, folds larceny into the general offense of theft.[201]

Unlike extortion, false pretenses, robbery, and embezzlement, larceny (at least in its classical form[202]) typically involves no direct contact between offender and victim. The property is taken without the owner's consent—whether attitudinal, expressive, or prescriptive—because the owner is never given an opportunity to consent. In some sense, then, larceny is best understood as theft *simpliciter*—that is, theft without any wrong beyond the primary wrong of unlawfully depriving the victim of property rights.

There is, however, also another way to think about a possible secondary wrong associated with larceny that reflects, if not its formal elements, then at least its history and the practical circumstances in which it tends to be committed. What I have in mind here is the possibility of thinking of larceny as a kind of "theft by stealth."

Consider the history. The first form of theft to be criminalized was robbery, based on the notion of *trespass vi et armis* (i.e., trespass with force and arms, as opposed to trespass on the case, which is committed without force).[203] This was the most manifest and most threatening form of theft, the one most likely to lead to violence, and the one therefore of greatest immediate concern to the community. It was not until later, via the ancient quasi-criminal writ of trespass, that theft law was expanded to cover other takings of property without the owner's consent, even though no force was used.[204] This form of theft came to be known as larceny, the dominant "motif" of which, as George Fletcher has suggested, was furtive or stealthful conduct.[205] Indeed, the Latin term for theft, *furtum,* is the source of the English word *furtive.*[206] And the term *steal* derives from the same root as *stealth.*[207] There are thus etymological reasons for associating larceny with stealth. Even today, the term larceny is often used to refer to those acts of theft that are committed in secret. This is because acts of theft committed in the open are likely to be treated as some other offense, such as robbery or extortion. To the extent that theft is carried out without the victim's knowledge, then, it is reasonable to ascribe to it the sense of stealth or secrecy.

Of course, engaging in secrecy is not always wrong. When secrecy is put to good ends, we value it: We expect our family, friends, lawyers, and doctors all to keep our secrets. But we condemn secrecy when it is put to bad ends.[208] To the extent that secrecy is put to the wrongful end of depriving another of his right to property, an argument could be made that such taking is aggravated in a way similar to force (in the case of robbery), coercion (in the case of extortion), or invasion of privacy (as in theft by housebreaking). To keep a secret from someone, to hide it, to do something stealthily, is to deprive the person of information he may well have a right to. A person who has property taken from him would ordinarily have a right to know that such taking was occurring; such knowledge would afford him or others in the community an opportunity to put an end to it. On the other hand, having one's property taken openly entails an element of danger and consequent fear that having it taken in secret does not; and many victims, given the choice between the two ways of having their property taken, might well prefer the latter.

Theft by Breach of Trust (Embezzlement)

In the scenario ranked next most serious, Tom obtained Owen's bike by gaining Owen's trust and then violating that trust. Starting in 1799 in England, Tom's act would have constituted embezzlement. To be convicted of embezzlement, the defendant must (1) come into possession of the personal property of another as the result of its being entrusted by or for the owner of the property and (2) thereafter do some act intended to deprive the owner of the property permanently.[209]

What distinguishes embezzlement from other theft offenses is once again the secondary wrong—in this case, a breach of trust.[211] To understand what it means to commit an act like theft through breach of trust, it is necessary to understand what it means to have a relationship of trust. To have such a relationship means to be true or faithful to someone, often in the context of a specific kind of relationship, such as employee-employer or lawyer-client. A breach of trust consists of more than merely the absence of trust.[210] Just as promise-breaking requires that *X* be bound by a promise, a breach of trust presupposes that *X* be bound by some duty of trust. A relationship of trust entails that *X* act in the interest of *Y*. A breach of trust involves the pursuit of alternatives that are in conflict with the principal bond. Thus, in *Henry IV, Part I*, Falstaff is entrusted by Hal to be leader of the infantry in the war against the Percys. Hal meets with him, explains his responsibilities, and gives him the money to recruit and equip his soldiers. Instead of recruiting a capable army, however, Falstaff keeps the funds for himself and recruits less able men from the streets. "If I be not ashamed of my soldiers," he says, "I am a soused gurnet. I have misused the king's press damnably. I have got in exchange of a hundred and fifty soldiers, three hundred and odd pounds."[212] In converting the money given him by the prince to his own purposes, Falstaff has betrayed Hal's trust and thereby committed embezzlement.[213]

Given the formal parallels between embezzlement (theft by breach of trust) and robbery, extortion, and burglary, it may seem surprising that embezzlement was not ranked as more blameworthy than it was and, additionally, that the law has not traditionally treated embezzlement as an aggravated form of theft. One possible explanation is offered by Islamic law, which, interestingly, punishes both theft by stealth and theft by force more severely than theft by breach of trust. As Hisham Ramadam explains, the "zone of harm in embezzlement" is said to be "limited to the creation of a sphere of mistrust between the victim(s) and the offender in addition to the value of the property stolen." In contrast, Ramadan says, larceny and robbery "negatively affect[] the entire sphere of social peace and order. . . . [If they] became common, [they] would promote an environment of guardedness and suspicion which would deter everyday activities, causing financial loss."[214] It is perhaps reasoning like this that also helps explain a distinction made in Jewish law between embezzlement from a public authority and embezzlement from a private individual, with the former being treated as the more serious offense.[215]

Theft by Exploiting the Circumstances of an Emergency (Looting)

In what is presumably the most exotic of all the hypothetical cases presented, Tom deprives Owen of his property in the wake of a hurricane. This hypothetical situation involves an act of looting, which typically requires that the defendant (1) makes an unauthorized entry into a home or business (2) in which normal security of property is not present by virtue of some natural disaster or civil disturbance (and in which potential victims are therefore made more vulnerable) and (3) thereby obtains control over, damages, or removes the property of another.[216] Looting was never a separate crime at common law, under the MPC, or the Theft Act. Looting is, however, a separate crime under the law of a handful of American states, in various nations with a civilian tradition, and under international law.[217]

In my view, looting should be recognized as a distinct form of theft, conceptually on par with embezzlement, extortion, and false pretenses, and characterized by its own set of secondary wrongs.[218] And what are those secondary wrongs? Here it is necessary to distinguish between different kinds of looting arrayed along a continuum.

At one end of the continuum are cases of what we might call "good looting." These are cases in which otherwise law-abiding citizens who, as a result of forces beyond their control—for example, a natural disaster, war, or civil unrest—find themselves and their families hungry, exposed to the elements, perhaps without needed medicines; they are forced to break into a grocery store or pharmacy and take only enough (quite possibly perishable) goods to last until the emergency is likely to end. Such circumstances make the looter's stealing a necessity, and thereby mitigate the wrongfulness of the act.

At the other end of the spectrum is "bad looting." In these cases, urban predators, perhaps already pursuing a life of crime, use the occasion of an emergency to exploit their neighbors at the hour of their greatest vulnerability, carting away goods of types and quantities they could hardly begin to use for themselves, which they plan to sell for a quick profit. Such looters, it would seem, are motivated not by the urge to survive, but by greed and opportunism. Natural disasters like hurricanes and earthquakes often cause great loss and suffering for their victims. The natural and healthy human response to those who are suffering is pity or compassion. As events like those surrounding Hurricane Katrina and September 11 illustrate, many people respond to such suffering heroically.[219] The bad looter has exactly the opposite reaction: at the very moment when morality demands kindness and caring, even self-sacrifice, he responds with selfishness. He preys on and exploits the plight of his fellow human beings when they are most vulnerable.[220] Further, the looter expresses a disregard for the law and an embrace of anarchy. Looting is disturbing because it exposes the apparent fragility of the social contract. Beneath the thin crust of civilization, it has been said, "lurks a savage animal that will emerge under stress circumstances."[221] Bad looting is the product of an inversion of moral norms in which what is normally illicit becomes licit. Lawlessness is not only tolerated, but encouraged. Looting shakes the confidence we feel in our social institutions, and, perhaps more generally, the faith we have in our fellow human beings. In such cases, heightened penalties—higher than for "ordinary" burglary and larceny—seem appropriate.

Between these two poles lies a wide range of conduct that often involves impoverished and alienated citizens living on the edges of society, who are encouraged by powerful group dynamics and the apparent suspension of civil order to steal property from what are often heavily insured businesses owned by anonymous shareholders and managed by executives in far-off cities.

The facts of the looting hypothetical explained that

> Owen left town because of an approaching hurricane. The storm was worse than expected; there was general chaos, flooding, and no electricity. Owen's garage door was damaged in the storm and the alarm system had no power. Tom walked into Owen's garage, took his bike, and rode the bike away even though he already had a bike. He planned to sell it for fast cash.

This description was intended to make out a fairly clear case of bad looting. However, our subjects ranked this case as less blameworthy than robbery, burglary, blackmail, larceny, and embezzlement. This was a surprising result. Perhaps the scenario was more ambiguous than intended. In any event, I believe that such moral indeterminacy demonstrates why looting deserves to be treated as a separate and distinct theft offense, with different degrees of seriousness, rather than merely as a subtype of larceny or burglary.

Theft by Deception (False Pretenses and Passing a Bad Check)

The empirical study included two scenarios that involved theft by deception. In one, Tom accepts the bike from Owen after falsely promising to return the next day with payment. In the other, Tom accepts the bike from Owen after giving Owen a check knowing that he does not have enough money in his account to cover it. The first scenario involved a case of false pretenses, defined at common law as knowingly obtaining title to another's property by means of a lie or misrepresentation.[222] The second scenario involved the offense of passing a bad check. Both cases involve attitudinal and expressive consent, but no prescriptive consent. Owen falsely believed that Tom was or would soon be paying him for the bike, and he acquiesced on the basis of this false belief. Owen was unable to give prescriptive consent because he lacked the relevant knowledge that prescriptive consent requires.

To deceive is to communicate a message with which the communicator, in communicating, intends to mislead—that is, to communicate a message that is intended to cause a person to believe something that is untrue.[223] As in the case of using stealth or coercion to commit a theft, using deception to commit a theft arguably tends to aggravate the underlying (primary) wrong of unlawful misappropriation of property. Indeed, theft by deception—the Hebrew term is *geneivat da'at*, translated literally as "theft of one's mind"—is regarded as among the most serious forms of theft identified in the Talmud.[224]

In light of such authority, the results of the empirical study may seem surprising: the two forms of theft by deception, false pretenses and passing a bad check, were ranked as less blameworthy not only than robbery, blackmail, embezzlement, and looting, but also than the baseline offense of larceny. Indeed, only receiving stolen property and failing to return misdelivered property were ranked lower than theft by deception.

One possible explanation for why the subjects ranked theft by deception so low is that, unlike the victim of robbery and extortion, the victim of false pretenses is viewed as deserving at least some of the blame for the offender's act. As some commentators have suggested, the victim who is duped by a fraudster should have known better and therefore is partially to blame.[225] Such an argument has been made even in the case of Bernie Madoff, the Ponzi-scheming investment advisor who defrauded investors of a sum estimated at $18 billion. As *New York Times* business columnist Joe Nocera put it in his blog:

> [S]houldn't the Madoff victims have to bear at least some responsibility for their own gullibility? Mr. Madoff's supposed results—those steady, positive returns quarter after blessed quarter—is a classic example of the old saw, "when something looks too good to be true, it probably is." What's more, most of the people investing with Mr. Madoff thought they had gotten in on something really special; there was a certain smugness that came with thinking they had a special, secret deal not available to everyone else. Of course, it turned out they were right—they did have a special deal. It just wasn't what they expected.[226]

In truth, it is hard to generalize about theft by deception. Probably no area of theft law is more complex and fragmented. Prior to consolidation, the major common law deception offenses were false pretenses, larceny by trick, false weights and measures, forgery, and, in some limited cases, embezzlement. In the United States, under the influence of the MPC, the traditional offense of false pretenses has been replaced by the offense of theft by deception (interchangeable, of course, with all of the other theft offenses); it consists of purposely obtaining property of another by deception.[227] Passing bad checks is treated as a distinct, lesser offense, separate from theft, and punishable as a misdemeanor.[228] The MPC also maintains separate offenses of forgery, deceptive business practices (similar to the common law offense of false weights and measures), rigging contests, defrauding secured creditors, and fraud in bankruptcy.[229] England and Wales deal with theft by deception quite differently. The Theft Acts of 1968 and 1978 created eight offenses of dishonestly obtaining something by deception.[230] Parliament subsequently enacted the Fraud Act 2006, which superseded the deception offense provisions in the earlier acts and replaced them with a slightly less particularized list of offenses: fraud, fraud by false representations, fraud by failing to disclose information, fraud by abuse of a position of financial trust, and possessing or making articles to commit frauds.[231] Bad checks are addressed under yet another provision as a potentially more serious offense.[232]

The obvious question is why, even in the face of theft consolidation, has the law of theft by deception remained so much more fragmented than that of other forms of theft? The answer is complex. Let me suggest, for a start, at least three factors that play a role in distinguishing theft by deception from most other forms of theft.

First, as a historical matter, courts and legislatures were slow to condemn theft by deception in the same terms as other forms of theft. Stealing by deception was viewed as less threatening to society than stealing by other means. For much of common law history, a rule of *caveat emptor* has applied in this area: buyers of goods who were misled by deceptive sellers were viewed as partly responsible for their plight. As Chief Justice Holt famously asked in *R. v. Jones,* "shall we indict one man for making a fool of another?"[233]

Related to this is the fact that society maintains something of a grudging respect for, or at least fascination with, particularly clever and audacious fraudsters (as it does for skillful cat burglars). A good example is Frank Abagnale, the former con man and check forger turned security consultant, whose story was told in the memoir, film, and Broadway show *Catch Me if You Can.* Another is George C. Parker, who made a handsome living "selling" the Brooklyn Bridge, Statue of Liberty, Grant's Tomb, and other New York landmarks to unwitting tourists and immigrants during the early years of the twentieth century. Despite their dishonesty, one cannot help but admire their skill and nerve.

Second, as a matter of proof, thefts by deception are more likely to blur into legitimate, or at least non-criminal, forms of behavior. Consider again the case in which D enters into a contract with V to deliver a shipment of widgets in return for payment. If V pays what is owed and D fails to deliver the widgets, it's difficult to say whether D has committed theft by deception or if, instead, he has merely breached a contract. As discussed above, D's intentions at the time he entered into the contract must be evident. Given the difficulties of proving the requisite intent in such cases, and the danger of imposing criminal liability where it may not be justified, it is not surprising that such cases have spawned a set of specialized rules.

Third, even in a system that unambiguously condemned theft by deception, it would be difficult to say exactly which forms of deception should count as legally culpable and worthy of criminal penalties and which should not. For example, should fraud encompass any misleading conduct or only lies that are expressed through statements, whether written or oral? Should it include both misleading omissions and affirmative statements? Should it include both misleading statements and misleading opinions? Should it include false promises as well as false statements of fact?

Because such lines are so hard to draw and so context–specific, an elaborate body of law has developed around them. The challenge for the criminal law is to determine which acts of appropriation—whether by deceit, stealth, breach of trust, threat, violence, or otherwise—the law should deal with as crimes, which as civil wrongs, and which as neither.

THREE

Theft as a Crime

Imagine that Tom steals Owen's bicycle and thereby violates some collection of Owen's property rights. Under what circumstances, if any, should the law impose criminal sanctions on Tom rather than simply require him to return the bike or pay some other form of compensation? Although theft has an obvious claim to being an offense within the "core" of criminal law,[1] its criminalization is nevertheless puzzling. Theft proper involves none of the violent assaults on life, limb, or bodily integrity that characterize murder, rape, and battery. What is at stake in theft are rights in property. Is theft really the kind of offense for which society should want to deploy its "heavy artillery"?[2]

The answer is a surprisingly complex one. For almost every act of stealing that is subject to criminal penalties, there is a corresponding remedy in civil law. How should we choose between them? And to what extent will the answer differ depending on the kind of theft involved? This chapter attempts to answer these questions. The crucial point throughout is that, in assessing the arguments for and against criminalization, it is necessary to look beyond the general, undifferentiated concept of theft and toward specific forms of theft. In so arguing, I seek to advance my more general critique of theft consolidation.

ALTERNATIVES TO CRIMINAL SANCTIONS

Before considering the extent to which theft in its various forms should be criminalized, it will be helpful to look at the alternatives. Among the noncriminal approaches to theft considered in this section are civil law actions such as tortious conversion, misappropriation, trespass to chattel, and misrepresentation, and nonlegal approaches such as better security, informal norms, and private institutional remedies.

What Are Criminal Sanctions?

To determine if a given remedy is noncriminal, it is first necessary to define what it means to be *criminal*. One obvious way to approach the problem would be to ask whether particular kinds of mental elements, harms, or wrongs characterize the acts we call criminal. Unfortunately, this approach has proved problematic.[3] For every putative criminal offense that requires a mental element of intent or knowledge, a significant harm that is of interest to the public at large, or a wrongful violation of a victim's rights, there is another that involves minimal harms, trivial wrongs, and no *mens rea.*

A better approach is one originally suggested by Glanville Williams.[4] The idea is to offer a formal definition of crime that considers the legal *consequences* of the act as determinative. Under this approach, crimes are acts that (1) subject defendants to the possibility of various characteristic forms of punishment (such as imprisonment, criminal fines, and probation), (2) are initiated exclusively, or almost exclusively, by government prosecutors by means of grand jury indictment or criminal information, and (3) trigger certain basic constitutional rights (such as the rights to effective assistance of counsel, confrontation of witnesses, and a jury of one's peers).[5]

Assuming that this characterization is sufficient, the main question to be addressed in this chapter can be reframed. Under this formal approach, the question is why, in general, should certain kinds of thievery be subject to these characteristic forms of punishment and procedure? Are there certain kinds of stealing that are more (or less) likely to justify criminal penalties and procedures than others?

Civil Law Remedies for Stealing

Near the end of *Lush Life,* Richard Price's gritty crime novel set on Manhattan's Lower East Side, the book's antihero, Eric Cash, confesses to his boss, restaurant owner Harry Steele, that he's been skimming money from the tip pool. Steele is perplexed as to how Cash expects him to respond. "What, your conscience is bothering you?" Steele asks. "And so you want me to do what. Fire you, sue you, press charges, what. . . ."[6] For a layman, Steele is surprisingly well informed. All three kinds of remedy—informal private sanctions such as firing, a civil suit for tortious conversion or fraud, and criminal charges of theft—would potentially be applicable in such circumstances. This section considers the overlap that exists between the criminal law of theft; the civil law of conversion, misrepresentation, trespass to chattel, and misappropriation; and various nonlegal approaches.

Tortious Conversion

The tort of conversion is typically defined as "an intentional exercise of dominion and control over a chattel which so seriously interferes with the right of another to control it that the actor may justly be required to pay the other the full value of the chattel."[7] Only very serious interference with the right of control over, or possession of, property constitutes conversion.

The most significant differences between the crime of theft and the tort of conversion (beyond the procedural and remedial differences that exist between all crimes and torts) concern the required mental element and the defenses available. Conversion is an intentional tort in the sense that the defendant must intend to take or otherwise appropriate property in a manner that is inconsistent with the owner's rights.[8] But, unlike the thief, the converter need not have an intent to interfere with another's rights in property.[9] Thus, while every case of theft also constitutes conversion, not every case of conversion constitutes theft. For example, one who takes property belonging to another in the mistaken belief that it has been abandoned, or who purchases stolen goods in the good faith belief that they are not stolen, is a converter but not a thief.

The remedy for conversion is usually in the form of damages equal to the fair market value of the chattel at the time of conversion. The converter can, as an alternative, offer to return possession of the chattel to the complainant, but the complainant has no obligation to accept.[10]

Many of the issues that have arisen in the context of theft have also surfaced in that of conversion. Most significantly, for present purposes, is the question of what constitutes property subject to taking—the subject of Chapter 4. As with the law of theft, the law of conversion has seen a gradual widening in the definition of what constitutes property. Originally, only tangible, personal property was subject to conversion. Thus, neither interests in real property, choses in action, nor nonproprietary rights (such as rights in bodily tissue and corpses) could be subject to conversion at early common law.[11] But by the nineteenth century, it was possible to convert promissory notes, checks, and bills of lading—tangible documents that represented intangible rights in property—and, later, property that was wholly intangible, such as shareholders' interests in a corporation.[12]

Today, the law of conversion, like the law of theft, continues to grapple with difficult questions about the extent to which it should be applied to the improper exercise of control over intangible property such as Internet domain names, photographic images, and business goodwill.[13] Some states allow conversion to apply to "every species of personal property" both tangible and intangible,[14] while others recognize no remedy for conversion of intangible property at all.[15] Most states seem to fall somewhere in between, requiring that intangible property rights be merged into a document that effectively represents these rights. However, there remain questions about the extent to which the document into which intangible property rights are merged must itself be tangible, as opposed to electronic or digital in nature.

Trespass to Chattel

Another tort that bears significant relation to the crime of theft is trespass to chattel, which is defined as the "intentional interference with the possession of personal property [that] proximately cause[s] injury."[16] Trespass to chattel developed earlier than conversion (or *trover*, as it was originally known) as an outgrowth of trespass to real property. In its earliest form, trespass to chattel encompassed a broad range of kinds of interference with an owner's property rights, including unauthorized use, damage or destruction, and removal. With the subsequent development of conversion, however, the scope of trespass to chattel was narrowed to apply primarily to the unauthorized use or removal of property, as opposed to its wrongful possession.

The difference between trespass to chattel and conversion is mostly a difference of degree rather than of kind. Conversion constitutes a more significant interference with the owner's right than trespass to chattel.[17] The distinction is roughly analogous to that between larceny and joyriding, respectively. Like theft, conversion involves a near complete interference with the owner's property rights; like joyriding, trespass to chattel involves only a partial or temporary deprivation of such rights. It is thus understandable why the defendant in a suit for conversion is liable for the whole value of the property, while a defendant in a suit for trespass to chattel is liable only for actual damage done to the chattel.

Like the law of theft and conversion, the law of trespass to chattel has had to deal with the emergence of new forms of property. Indeed, it is precisely the development of new forms of intellectual and intangible property that has breathed new life into the tort. Defendants sometimes infringe plaintiffs' rights in intellectual property in ways that do not constitute the complete or near complete deprivation of property rights that conversion would seem to require. For example, plaintiffs who own computer systems have sought to exclude unwanted uses of such systems, such as unsolicited commercial e-mail.[18] Given the difficulties of proving complete or near complete deprivation of property rights in such cases, it is no surprise that trespass to chattel has reemerged as a viable claim.

Civil Fraud, Misrepresentation, and Fraudulent Inducement

Although the tort of misrepresentation (also known as civil fraud, deceit, or fraudulent inducement) potentially applies to an almost limitless range of human activity, its most common application occurs in the realm of business and commerce and, as such, generally involves an infringement of property rights. In this context, the gist of misrepresentation consists in a plaintiff's reliance on material misrepresentations of fact that lead to transfers of property and the making of contracts and other bargains.[19] Examples of tortious misrepresentation include a homeowner's inducing a sale by falsely representing that the basement does not flood and an employer's recruiting employees by falsely representing that it had no plans to move or close.[20]

There is little, if any, difference between the substantive elements of civil fraud and those of criminal fraud. Indeed, most scholars say that, other than the usual differences in procedure and penalties, the two acts are indistinguishable.[21] Many of the same issues that arise in the case of criminal fraud also surface in the case of civil fraud. Among these are whether (1) the plaintiff actually relied on the defendant's representation, (2) such reliance was justifiable, (3) the defendant's representations were material, (4) such representations were merely puffing or dealer's talk, (5) such representations can be in the form of a statement of law or opinion or promise rather than a statement of fact, and (6) a misleading nondisclosure will suffice as a misrepresentation.

Misappropriation

Another body of law that creates civil remedies for at least certain forms of what is arguably theft is the misappropriation doctrine, a species of unfair competition law recognized by the Supreme Court in *International News Service v. Associated Press*.[22] The misappropriation doctrine establishes tort protection for various kinds of intangible quasi–property not protected by intellectual property law, such as ideas, information, formulas, designs, and artistic creations. The doctrine is premised on the notion that a commercial rival should not be allowed to profit unfairly from the costly investment and labor of one who produces information. As precedent, *International News* is not without its problems.[23] Nevertheless, in some recent cases, the claim of misappropriation has been successful, and it remains important in cases involving intangible property, a subject that will be explored further in Chapter 4.[24]

Civil Statutory Remedies

Beyond all of these common law forms of relief available to victims of stealing exists a broad range of statutory civil remedies. The most obvious are so-called civil theft statutes, which allow for recovery of punitive damages by the victim of theft as it is defined in criminal law. Sometimes these statutes are limited to theft of particular kinds of things, such as livestock, cable television services, or money paid to a contractor.[25] Other times they are more general in their application.[26] There are also numerous federal statutes that allow for civil forfeiture proceedings to recover stolen property as well as for damages in cases of alleged theft of intellectual property.[27] Finally, as discussed later in the chapter, some specialized statutes provide civil or quasi-civil remedies for shoplifting and for failure to return lost or misdelivered property.

Nonlegal Approaches to Stealing

Despite the focus here on civil law alternatives to criminal prosecution for theft, the importance of nonlegal alternatives should not be underestimated. Probably the most effective way to prevent theft of one's property is to employ locks, fences, lighting, alarm systems, watch dogs, security guards, closed-circuit television surveillance, passwords, computer security devices, and the like.[28] Even marking goods with the label "Property of X" can do a good deal to deter thefts (by indicating that goods are traceable). We also rely on various informal means of social control, such as expressing disapproval of, and even ostracizing, those who steal. (Think of the public reaction to celebrity shoplifter cases such as those involving actress Winona Ryder, Olympic gymnast Olga Korbut, tennis star Jennifer Capriati, movie critic Rex Reed, and former Miss America Bess Myerson.) Finally, there are various, more formal, but nevertheless private, forms of social control that are relevant here. For example, offenders who are caught stealing from an employer or other institution with which they are affiliated are often subject to termination, expulsion, or other internal disciplinary procedures.

CRIMINALIZING THEFT

Given the civil and nonlaw alternatives, if and when is it appropriate to treat theft as a crime? What conduct should be subject to criminal sanctions is one of the most complex questions in all of criminal law theory. Given the scope of my project, it would not be practicable to try to derive a set of criminalization principles from scratch. Instead, I shall seek to build on the work of others.

Framework for Analysis

Joel Feinberg devotes almost all of his magisterial four-volume *The Moral Limits of the Criminal Law* to addressing just one aspect of the problem, namely, the extent to which various forms of conduct satisfy the harm or offense principles. But, as Feinberg acknowledges, even if the harm principle is satisfied, a legislature must consider many other issues before properly deciding whether some conduct should be treated as criminal. Among these further questions, which Feinberg explicitly sets aside, is the extent to which the benefits of criminalizing some particular conduct would outweigh its costs.[29] In a sense, the present book picks up where Feinberg left off.

The most ambitious attempt to develop a comprehensive theory of criminalization comes from Douglas Husak.[30] Husak's approach relies on "seven general principles or constraints designed to limit the authority of the state to enact penal offenses."[31] He divides them into two categories, which he calls internal and external constraints. Internal constraints, he says, are best understood as being addressed to the persons who are being punished.[32] These consist of the "non-trivial harm or evil" constraint, the "wrongfulness" constraint, the "desert" constraint, and the "burden of proof" constraint. External constraints address not only the persons who are punished but also the citizens who are asked to create and maintain a system of punitive sanctions. These consist of asking if the state has a "substantial interest in whatever objective the statute is designed to achieve," if the law "directly advance[s] that interest," and if the statute is "no more extensive than necessary to achieve its purpose."[33]

Elsewhere, I have offered a critique of Husak's complex and subtle theory.[34] For the moment, I simply note several points on which I depart from his approach. First, although I dealt with the concepts of harmfulness and wrongfulness separately in the previous chapter, I conflate them here for purposes of considering the censuring function of criminal law. Second, I bypass Husak's concern with the procedural rights of a defendant to have the state prove its case beyond a reasonable doubt, not because I view such rights as unimportant but because I do not view them as directly relevant to the question of which forms of theft should be criminalized. Third, while Husak says that his principal concern is with the authority of the legislature to "enact" penal offenses, I am concerned as well with the factors that a prosecutor should consider in deciding whether to seek criminal penalties in an individual case. Fourth, while Husak tends at times to view criminal and civil sanctions as if they were mutually exclusive remedies, I am more explicit in acknowledging the overlap between the two.

In approaching the task of determining whether a particular crime type or token should be criminalized, it will be helpful to think of the procedural context in which such questions are likely to arise. The process of criminalization ordinarily begins with the legislature, which must decide whether a given crime type, however defined, should be subject to criminal penalties. Having determined that it should, the legislature must then decide how much punishment to authorize. In the United States, legislatures will ordinarily prescribe a range from minimum to maximum. The decision-making process then shifts to the prosecutor, who must decide whether and how to bring criminal charges in a given case. Finally, assuming that the defendant is convicted, a court will have to decide the punishment to be imposed.

So what factors should be taken into account in deciding whether theft in its various forms should be treated as a crime? Influenced by the method developed by Feinberg and Husak and by Jonathan Schonsheck,[35] I propose seven basic questions: (1) Is the form of theft deserving of the kind of censure that criminal sanctions are intended to impose? (2) Is there a significant advantage to be gained by having the prosecution of such conduct initiated by the state rather than, or in addition to, an action initiated by a private party? (3) Does the state have a substantial interest in preventing the harm caused by theft? (4) What would an optimal system of theft-deterring criminal sanctions include? (5) How could it be determined if criminal sanctions provided an effective means of preventing the harms of theft? (6) Do the benefits of criminalizing theft outweigh its costs, including not only the costs of prosecution and incarceration but also the costs of chilling otherwise socially beneficial conduct? (7) Should criminalization of theft should be viewed as a last resort, and, if so, when?

Is Theft the Kind of Conduct the Criminal Law Should Want to Censure?

One of the most important functions of the criminal law, as Feinberg famously explained in an earlier work, is to convey to both the offender and to the broader community the wrongfulness of criminal ways. As Feinberg put it:

> [P]unishment is a conventional device for the expression of attitudes of resentment and indignation, and of judgments of disapproval and

reprobation, on the part either of the punishing authority himself or of those "in whose name" the punishment is inflicted. Punishment, in short, has a *symbolic significance* largely missing from other kinds of penalties.[36]

On a mostly parallel track, Antony Duff has emphasized the "communicative" function of criminal sanctions—the ability of such sanctions to communicate to offenders the censure or condemnation that they deserve for their crimes.[37]

Civil sanctions, such as damages for breach of contract or tort, simply do not have the expressive or communicative quality of criminal sanctions like imprisonment and even criminal fines. Thus, one of the reasons to impose criminal penalties on theft, rather than or in addition to civil sanctions, is to express resentment, indignation, disapproval, or reprobation for such conduct. Moreover, such expressivity in criminal law also has an instrumental function: criminal law is believed to have the power to shape, change, and reinforce social norms by making statements that create and sustain such norms, rather than controlling behavior directly.[38]

So, are such censure and disapprobation justified in the case of theft? In general, the answer is yes, though the situation is considerably more complex than in the case of crimes like murder, rape, and assault. People ordinarily do feel a sense of violation when their property is involuntarily taken from them. Those who steal challenge the authority of property rules; they express contempt for the property owner and for society more generally; they trample over others' rights in pursuit of their own selfish interests.

An argument for why and how theft should be subject to criminal punishment is offered, interestingly, by Kant. In the *Metaphysics of Morals,* he explains the kind and amount of punishment the state has a right (and an obligation) to inflict. What Kant expresses is a form of *lex talionis*: "Whatever undeserved evil you inflict upon another," he says, "you inflict upon yourself."[39] He then goes on to elaborate this more general point by referring specifically to theft:

> Whoever steals makes the property of everyone else insecure and therefore deprives himself (by the principle of retribution) of security in any possible property. He has nothing and can also acquire nothing; but still wants to live, and this is now possible only if others provide for him. But since the state will not provide for him free of charge, he

must let it have his powers for any kind of work it pleases (in convict or prison labor) and is reduced to the status of a slave for a certain time, or permanently if the state sees fit.[40]

What Kant seems to be saying is that one who commits theft is engaging in a kind of contradiction: his stealing undermines the very system of property from which he seeks to benefit. The only way the contradiction can be resolved is by imposing its consequences on the offender—in this case, by forcing the convicted thief to give his labor to the state.[41]

To say that theft in most or even all of its forms is deserving of criminal law's censure, however, hardly means that it is deserving of the same amount of censure in all cases. Implicit in the retributivist conception of crime is the notion that the severity of a criminal sentence should be a function of the seriousness of the crime.[42] And, as I argue throughout this book, the wrongfulness of theft varies greatly, depending on a number of variables.

Among the most important factors in judging the blameworthiness of a given act of theft is the value of the property stolen. This is consistent with the idea that theft is first and foremost an assault on a victim's property rights. Thus, other things being equal, the more valuable the property stolen, the greater the wrong to the victim, and the more extensive the offender's desert. And, indeed, criminological studies show that the greater the value of the property stolen, the more lay subjects believe it should be punished.[43] For example, in the *National Survey of Crime Severity* led by Marvin Wolfgang, the scenario in which a person breaks into a bank at night and steals $100,000 was ranked as far more serious than that in which a person breaks into a department store and steals merchandise worth $1,000.[44]

In this respect, the current MPC scheme of grading—which makes theft of property worth less than $50 a petty misdemeanor, theft of goods valued at $50 to $500 a misdemeanor, and theft of property worth more than $500 a third degree felony—is woefully deficient.[45] It seems obvious that, at least at the high end, the MPC grading curve is far too flat. On the other hand, the highly graded approach used by the federal Sentencing Guidelines, in which thefts of very large amounts of money can lead to extremely long prison sentences, equal to or exceeding the sentence for serious offenses like rape and aggravated assault, may strike some readers as overly harsh. Whether stealing a very large sum of money *should* be regarded as comparable in seriousness to crimes like rape and assault is a difficult question that I do not seek to resolve here.

A second factor in determining how much censure is due is the means by which the theft is committed, dealt with at length in Chapter 2. Judgment of a given act of theft's blameworthiness does, and ought to, vary significantly depending on the wrongful means by which the theft was committed—whether through violence, stealth, invasion of privacy, coercion, deception, breach of trust, or exploitation of an emergency situation.

Another factor in determining the blameworthiness of a given act of theft is the type of property involved. Once again, the empirical study that Kugler and I conducted indicates that even where the value of property was held constant, subjects consistently ranked theft of goods as more serious than theft of services and theft of intangible property.

A final factor relevant to determining the appropriate amount of censure is the extent to which a given act of theft is regarded as morally ambiguous. As seen in Chapter 2, whether a particular act of property appropriation is regarded as stealing depends to a significant degree on the definition of such contested civil law concepts as property, ownership, possession, abandonment, and title. In general, the more *malum prohibitum*-like a given act of theft is, the weaker the case for criminalization. The problem of moral ambiguity in theft law is particularly evident in the case of offenses such as failing to return lost or misdelivered property, writing a bad check, breaching a contract based on a false promise, and certain cases of extortion (all examined later in this chapter); as well as the misappropriation of intellectual property and other intangibles (covered in the next chapter).

Why Should the State Seek Redress against Those Who Steal?

In Roman law, the great majority of thefts were treated as delicts, or civil wrongs, rather than crimes.[46] In the normal case, the choice between a civil and criminal action typically lay with the victim, who could choose either to go to the civil courts and obtain compensation or bring the thief before the *praefectus vigilum* (city prefect or warden). Yet there were some theft offenses that fell exclusively within the public criminal domain. These included *abigeatus* (rustling), *latrocinium* and *rapina* (banditry and robbery), *effractura* (burglary), and *plagium* (kidnapping). Such offenses were, according to Olivia Robinson, "identified as posing a greater threat to society because of their audacity, or the frequency or scale of their operations; the enhanced threat was to be met with an aggravated penalty [beyond mere compensation]." Under this approach, it was appropriate to use state-initiated criminal proceedings "when something outrageous needed to be marked for public disapproval."[47]

Today, criminal proceedings are distinguished from civil actions by the fact that the former are brought by a public prosecutor on behalf of the "The State," "The People," or the "The Crown" and are ultimately subject to punishment brought in the name of such entities. Yet the fact that a prosecution is brought on behalf of the state is neither a necessary nor sufficient condition of its being criminal. It is not necessary because in many Anglo-American jurisdictions, there once was, and may still be, the possibility of criminal proceedings initiated not by a state prosecutor but rather by a private plaintiff.[48] Nor is the public nature of prosecution a sufficient condition, since there are many cases in which governments bring civil suits seeking tort or contract or equitable remedies, rather than criminal prosecutions. Nevertheless, the idea that a prosecution is brought by a public prosecutor on behalf of the state does seem central to what makes an action criminal. So why, in general, are prosecutions brought by the state on behalf of the people, and why is state prosecution an appropriate response to theft in particular?

One explanation is that some crimes involve circumstances in which plaintiffs are unavailable to bring suit on their own. Theoretically this is true in the case of murder, since the primary victim is, by definition, deceased (though there may well be surviving family members or friends who could bring a wrongful death action). It is also true for crimes that have no specifically identifiable victim (such as bribery and treason) or which have a large number of diffuse victims (such as certain environmental crimes). But in the present context, this explanation seems inapplicable for the obvious reason that theft ordinarily does involve an identifiable victim—namely, the owner of the property stolen.

A related argument in favor of state-initiated criminal proceedings is that, even when there is an individual victim, such victim, though aggrieved, often has an insufficient economic incentive to bring suit.

This is particularly so when the defendant is judgment proof. Were the government not to act, the wrong might go unaddressed. Once again, however, there are problems with this rationale. It fails to explain why people who commit acts like murder and rape and who have the means to pay a large fine should nonetheless be subject to prosecution by the government. In addition, it fails to explain why impecunious tortfeasors who commit merely negligent acts are generally *not* subject to state criminal prosecution.

On the other hand, to the extent that the economic incentive argument holds up anywhere in the criminal law, it does so fairly well in the case of theft. According to Department of Justice statistics, the average value of property stolen per theft incident in the United States during 2009 was less than a thousand dollars.[49] Particularly in jurisdictions where each party pays its own attorney fees, the high costs of litigation will therefore make most would-be privately initiated theft suits economically nonviable. This is on top of the fact that many would-be theft defendants are indigent, and therefore judgment proof, to begin with.[50]

Another explanation for why criminal proceedings should be brought by the state rather than private plaintiffs is suggested by Lawrence Becker, who has argued that society's response is, or has the potential to be, much more "volatile" when serious harm is caused intentionally (as in the case of traditional *malum in se* crimes) than when accidentally (as in the case of most torts).[51] The idea seems to be that the first kind of act may cause a "chain reaction breakdown," while the latter would create primarily sympathy and "public support" for the victim's family. By taking the "administration of justice out of the hands of injured parties," Becker says, we "prevent blood feuds and vicious self perpetuating cycles of revenge they spawn."[52] We thus punish to "satisfy the desire for retaliation felt by victims of crime and to satisfy the public outrage generated by those crimes."[53] Becker's provocative argument may well help make sense of why we treat intentional acts like murder as a crime and negligent acts such as wrongful death as a tort, but it does little to explain why we treat theft as a crime and conversion and misrepresentation as torts.

Yet another possibility, advanced by Susan Dimock, is that criminal law is meant to respond to those acts which "if performed by any sizable minority with any frequency, would undermine basic trust between members of a community."[54] Unfortunately, this approach is also unhelpful in the present context. While there is certainly something to the notion that crimes involve an undermining of trust, Dimock never explains how such acts should be distinguished from widespread instances of breach of contract and trespass, which are not ordinarily treated as criminal. Moreover, it seems likely that we should want to treat as criminal serious crimes like murder and rape even though (thankfully) they are not performed by a sizable minority with any frequency.

A better approach to understanding the need for state-initiated proceedings is to ask whether there is some sense in which criminal acts constitute harms to the public at large or ought to concern the public at large. In the case of crimes like bribery, treason, and perhaps some environmental offenses, it seems obvious that harm is done, or risked, to large numbers of citizens or to public institutions. But this is less immediately obvious in the case of theft. When D steals property from V, it would appear that the principal person harmed is V. So why should a public prosecutor step in and prosecute on behalf of the people or the state, even in cases where the individual victim has no interest in seeing such a case brought?

One of the most insightful explanations of why criminal prosecutions are brought on behalf of the state comes from Sandra Marshall and Antony Duff. According to their view, the wrongs and harms involved in crimes are public not so much in the sense that they are wrongs and harms *against* the public, but rather wrongs and harms in which the public is properly interested.[55] "[T]o believe that a certain kind of conduct should be criminal," they say, is to believe "that it is conduct which should be declared wrong by the community: that it is a matter on which the community should take a shared and public view, and claim normative authority over its members."[56] Thus, it is the *quality* or *character* of the wrong involved in crimes that is different, not merely or even necessarily the extent of the harm or wrong or the degree of their seriousness. Such wrongs are, as Marshall and Duff have put it, "non-negotiable" wrongs.[57] The rape victim and her attacker are involved in more than merely a "conflict" that can be "negotiated" and "resolved." Even if the victim does not cooperate with the government in agreeing to give evidence, the state may still proceed with its case. Moreover, the kind of conduct at issue in criminal law is the kind of conduct that people should (and should be able to) categorically refrain from, even in cases in which the victim has in some sense contributed to the crime by making it easier for the offender to commit such a wrong or by tempting him to do so.[58] The public "shares" in the wrong that the individual victim has suffered. "[I]t is not 'our' wrong *instead of* hers," they say, "it is 'our' wrong *because* it is a wrong done to her, as one of us—as a fellow member of our community whose identity and whose good is found within that community."[59]

This approach to understanding what it is that makes crime a matter of public concern seems to me essentially correct, at least as far as it goes. What it fails to acknowledge, however, is the fact that so many kinds of conduct are subject to both criminal *and* civil penalties. At times, Marshall and Duff seem to imply that, with respect to any given offense, there will be some "presumptive or default position"—*either* civil *or* criminal.[60] But this either/or approach seems to me problematic.

To be sure, a few civil law wrongs are exclusively the province of private law. For example, there is no criminal law corollary to breach of contract, at least in cases in which the defendant intended to honor the contract at the time he entered into it and only subsequently decided to breach. Conversely, some criminal wrongs will be exclusively public. For example, there is no clear civil law corollary to bribery, perjury, or treason.

More commonly, however, conduct that is subject to criminal penalties will also be subject to civil remedies, and vice versa. Public and private proceedings are not mutually exclusive but instead run on parallel tracks subject to different procedures and burdens of proof, and sometimes requiring proof of slightly different elements. This is true not only of newer statutory provisions involving matters such as insider trading, price fixing, and the environment, but also of more traditional, common law–based, core offenses like murder and criminal assault. Each such offense can be, and often is, also addressed through corresponding civil tort proceedings.

As an alternative to Marshall and Duff's approach, then, I propose a two-step inquiry. The first step of the inquiry would apply at the legislative stage; it would deal with crime types. Here we would ask whether the crime type *typically* or *normally* involved (1) the kind of conduct that is properly declared wrong by the community as a whole, (2) a nonnegotiable wrong of the sort that one should expect to be categorically safe from, and (3) something more than a mere conflict that can be negotiated and resolved. If the answer to each of those questions is yes, we would proceed to step two of the inquiry. This step would apply at the prosecutorial stage and would focus on crime tokens. The same three questions would apply as before, but this time in the context of the particular case in which criminal sanctions are contemplated.

So is the conduct that underlies the offense of theft likely to satisfy such demands? It would be a mistake to try to answer that question across the board for all kinds of theft at once. Some kinds of theft—such as shoplifting and intentional bad check writing—look more like disputes between private parties that can be negotiated and resolved in civil court or out of court entirely than like disputes in which the community as a whole ought to take an interest. From this perspective, we need to be even more selective when applying criminal penalties to theft than to various other core crimes.

Does the State Have a Substantial Interest in Preventing Theft-Caused Harm?

So far, I have been considering the question of criminalization primarily from a retributivist point of view. Under this approach, criminal penalties are imposed to subject defendants to public censure. However, the fact that conduct is blameworthy, while a necessary condition to justify state sanctions, is not sufficient. Under the hybrid approach to criminalization being followed here, there are also other important consequentialist justifications for criminalization that need to be considered—including, crucially, prevention. Does the state have a substantial interest in preventing the kind of harm that theft statutes are designed to prevent, and does the criminal law provide an effective means of preventing such harms from occurring? Note that the subject here is different from that dealt with in the discussion of harm in Chapter 2. There the concern was with the way in which the harm-causing effects of stealing inform the determination of desert. Here, the focus is on the extent to which the state has an interest in preventing such harms.

So what harms does stealing cause? As I have argued above, theft can be harmful both to individual victims and to society more generally. In cases where the offender steals state property, the state has the strongest interest in preventing the resulting harm.[61] More commonly, the thief steals from private individuals and entities. In many cases, the loss of property through theft reduces the victim's standard of living. And, even if the property owner does not personally bear the burden of the loss, an insurance company may.

The harms caused to society by theft and other property crimes are truly staggering. The FBI estimates that there were approximately 9.3 million property crimes committed in the United States during 2009, a rate of about 3,000 offenses per 100,000 inhabitants, resulting in an estimated $15.2 billion in losses.[62] Of the property crimes committed, "larceny-theft" accounted for an estimated 67.9 percent (a rate of approximately 2,061 per 100,000 inhabitants[63]), burglary for 23.6 percent, and motor vehicle theft for 8.5 percent.[64] The total value of property stolen during 2009 was approximately $13.2 billion, of which only about $3.15 billion was recovered.[65] The average value of property taken during larceny-thefts was $864 per offense.[66]

Also significant are theft's indirect costs. Theft can lower property values, reduce people's sense of life satisfaction, cause psychological distress and apprehension, and hasten the decline of whole neighborhoods.[67] In post-invasion Iraq, for example, the occurrence of theft was said to be so pervasive that many citizens reported feelings of shame, desperation, and powerlessness.[68] And in China, fraudulent practices in business, education, and scientific research are believed to be retarding the nation's climb to the next rung on the economic ladder.[69]

This is hardly to say that every act of stealing will necessarily be to society's overall detriment. Despite what many economists would say, there will undoubtedly be cases in which a poor person's stealing property from a rich person will result in an "economically efficient" redistribution of wealth.[70] For example, a poor person without other means of transportation may well be able to make better use of a wealthy person's rarely-driven backup vehicle (imagine Antonio of the *Bicycle Thief* stealing from Robin Williams). The transfer of such property, even when involuntary, would seem to reflect a net social benefit. And this is true even in situations that would not be recognized by the defense of necessity or choice of evils.

As such, the kinds of harm caused by theft and other property crimes should be distinguished from those caused by offenses like murder and rape. The circumstances in which the commission of a rape would be socially beneficial must be exceedingly rare, if they exist at all; and cases where murder would be socially beneficial, though perhaps slightly more common, are still extremely limited.[71] It is much easier to imagine scenarios in which a theft would lead to at least a *prima facie* net social benefit. If nothing else, this suggests yet another reason to be more cautious about using criminal sanctions to respond to theft than to other core offenses.

What Would an Optimal System of Theft-Deterring Criminal Sanctions Look Like?

Putting aside for now the problem of socially beneficial thefts, assume that theft ordinarily *is* a bad thing and that society normally will have an interest in preventing it. The next question is whether and how the threat of criminal sanctions can provide an effective means of prevention. Here it will be helpful to compare the extent to which criminal sanctions are effective in preventing stealing with their ability to prevent other kinds of criminal and antisocial conduct.

Law and economics scholars have conceptualized what they view as the principal rationale for criminal sanctions in terms of what Guido Calabresi and Douglas Melamed famously referred to as "kickers."[72] Simply requiring a defendant to compensate the victim for a loss after it has occurred is inadequate to serve as a deterrent. We need, in Richard Posner's words, "to impose additional costs on unlawful conduct where the conventional damages remedy alone would be insufficient to limit that conduct to the efficient level."[73] In the context of criminal law, we call such kickers *punishment*.

Stephen Garvey offers a concise summary of the argument:

> For the economist, theft is a crime because it consists of my taking something of yours, say your car, without your consent, when I could have—and should have—bargained to get it from you within the free market. Getting-by-taking, as compared to getting-by-bargaining, is inefficient. If I really wanted your car, I should have bargained with you to get it. Moreover, even if I am required to compensate you *ex post*, I have still not acted efficiently because, again, I could have bargained with you *ex ante*. I thus commit a crime when I bypass an existing market—here the market in used cars—and secure possession of an

entitlement outside that market. Economic analysis, therefore, treats punishment as a form of supracompensatory damages, or "kicker," that I must pay on top of compensation. Its purpose is to give me an incentive to get what I want through a market transaction, at least when the relevant market exists.[74]

In other words, we impose criminal sanctions on potential thieves (those who have not internalized the norm against stealing) to raise their potential costs to some level above the value of the goods stolen.

Most normatively inclined criminal law scholars have been critical of this traditional law and economics approach. For example, as Claire Finkelstein has emphasized, the economic approach fails to offer an adequate explanation for why mental states such as intent and knowledge play such a crucial role in the criminal law.[75] Moreover, the law and economics approach conspicuously ignores the retributive and expressive aims of criminal sanctions. And, dependent as it is on the assumption that people make rational cost-benefit calculations in deciding what conduct to engage in, it does little to explain the criminalization of irrational offenses like heat of passion manslaughter (though it should be noted that a newer body of behavioral economics scholarship seeks to fill this void).[76]

If there is one kind of criminal conduct for which the classical economic approach seems potentially promising, however, it is theft. Empirical studies suggest that the majority of property crimes are committed by a relatively small number of repeat career criminal offenders, who are motivated primarily by the desire for monetary gain.[77]

Suppose that a potential thief is considering stealing an item that would cost a hundred dollars if acquired through lawful means.[78] Further assume that the probability that the thief will be identified, prosecuted or sued, and have a judgment entered against him is 25 percent. This means that the expected cost of acquiring the item unlawfully is only twenty five dollars ($100 × .25). If the only penalty imposed for theft was that the thief had to return the property stolen, the potential offender would be seriously underdeterred. Therefore, the argument goes, to dissuade the potential thief from engaging in this course of action, the law must impose a penalty such that the expected cost of the illegal activity would exceed the expected cost of the legal activity. One way to do this would be to impose a fine in an amount greater than $400 ($100 × 4). Another way would be to impose a sanction that involves taking away something more valuable than money, such as the potential thief's liberty.

Even if such an approach made sense in the abstract, however, there are a number of complications that would need to be dealt with before an optimal and just scheme of sanctions could be worked out.

First, it should be observed that the deterrent approach would focus on what the thief *intends* to steal rather than on what he actually does steal. Second, we would need to know how well-informed potential offenders actually are about both applicable penalties and the probability that they'll be caught and convicted. Third, to determine penalties, the difficulty of detecting and proving various forms of theft should presumably be taken into account. For example, if embezzlement was significantly harder to detect or prove than extortion, then, other things being equal, embezzlement would warrant a higher penalty. Fourth, we would need to consider how finely calibrated the system of sanctions should be, recognizing that at some point the benefits of precision would be outweighed by the costs of complexity (as is also true in the case of offense labeling, discussed in Chapter 1). Fifth, whatever sanctions were determined to be optimal from the perspective of deterrence would still need to comply with the demands of desert as a side constraint (as discussed in Chapter 2). For example, suppose that embezzlement was twice as hard to deter and three times as hard to detect as extortion. Would this mean that subjecting the embezzler to five times the punishment imposed on the extortionist would be justified? The answer is almost certainly no since it is wholly implausible that, other things being equal, an embezzler would be deserving of five times more punishment than an extortionist.[79]

In short, formulating criminal sanctions that are both optimally efficient and retributively just poses significant challenges for the criminal law codifier. I have not sought to resolve these issues here. I have been content merely to identify some of the greatest difficulties.

Do Criminal Sanctions Provide an Effective Means of Deterring Theft?

Determining whether criminal sanctions for theft are worth the cost would also involve knowing how effective such sanctions actually were in advancing the state's interest in preventing stealing. To make this determination, we would need to know the extent to which such laws were effective in changing people's behavior. Proving that any given criminal sanction actually has a deterrent effect has been notoriously difficult.[80] And proving that theft sanctions in particular have a significant deterrent effect would seem to be especially challenging. Because theft in its most basic forms has always, in every known society, been penalized, there is no baseline from which to measure how much stealing would occur in the absence of such laws.

Nevertheless, at least two kinds of data might be developed. First, we could do a longitudinal study of the effect various *changes* in the law have had on the incidence of theft among the same population over time. For example, as noted in Chapter 1, theft by false pretenses was not recognized as a crime in England until 1757. If we observed a *decrease* in the extent to which such acts were committed by the same population *after* criminalization, we should be able to infer that such laws provided an effective form of prevention (assuming, of course, that other plausible factors could not explain the decrease). Similarly, if we observed an *increase* in the commission of certain kinds of thievery after decriminalization, then once again we could infer that such laws had been effective. Second, we could do a cross-jurisdictional study to see if, other things being equal, the amount of punishment imposed on theft affects the rate of its incidence. If the law and economics hypothesis proved to be true, presumably, *ceteris paribus,* rates of theft would be lower in jurisdictions where penalties were higher.[81]

Unfortunately, the availability of such data—both longitudinal and cross-jurisdictional—is limited. There is evidence indicating that the incidence of poaching decreased in England following the passage of the Poaching Prevention Act 1862 and Ground Game Act 1880[82] and that the incidence of pickpocketing in England *increased* after the penalty was *reduced* in 1808 from death to transportation for life.[83] Moreover, as will be covered in the next chapter, the incidence of certain intellectual property "theft" crimes does seem to have decreased following the enactment of legislation such as the Copyright Felony Act and No Electronic Theft Act. The problem is it is difficult to say how much such changes are attributable to changes in threatened sanctions, how much to changing public norms, and how much to changes in technology (whether it was barbed wire in the late nineteenth century or various computer encryption technologies in the late twentieth and early twenty-first).

Moreover, just because some particular form of theft was previously subject to lesser, or no, *criminal* sanctions does not necessarily mean that it was not subject to other forms of deterrence, such as civil sanctions of some sort. Thus, what we should want to measure is not the difference between rates of thievery when criminalized and when not sanctioned at all, but instead the marginal difference between rates of thievery when fully criminalized (at some particular level of punishment) and when merely subject to some lesser form of deterrence. Such data would no doubt be difficult to compile.

Are the Benefits of Criminalization Worth the Costs?

Assume, at least for purposes of discussion, that theft does involve wrongful harms, that such wrongful harms are the proper concern of the state, and that criminal sanctions are effective not only at censuring blameworthy conduct but also at preventing it. Further assume that criminalization provides others benefits as well, such as emotional relief for victims and the incapacitation of potential repeat offenders. The next question is whether such benefits would be worth the costs of criminalization.

All forms of criminalization entail costs, in terms of investigation, prosecution, adjudication, and punishment.[84] Sometimes these costs are direct, such as paying salaries to police, prosecutors, public defenders, judges, prison guards, and probation officers. Other times they are indirect, such as when family members suffer because a parent or spouse is in prison or when an offender has difficulty finding a job after release.[85] Offenders who are in prison rather than out earning a living are generally unable to pay off debts they have incurred. It is hard to say, however, whether costs associated with the investigation, prosecution, adjudication, and punishment of theft are any greater than in the case of other crimes. In general, the costs of criminal sanctions fall more heavily on the poor than they do on the middle class and wealthy. Thus, if it could be shown that offenders who commit theft were more likely to be poor than offenders who commit other crimes, we might conclude that the costs of prosecuting and punishing theft were also higher.

As in the case of the analysis of wrongs, harms, and preventive effects, the analysis of costs is likely to differ for different kinds of theft. For example, many retailers seem to believe that the direct costs of prosecuting shoplifters, in terms of processing the necessary paperwork and having employees available for police interviews and trial testimony, are in fact greater than the benefits of doing so. As a result, they would prefer to use civil or informal remedies. Something similar appears to be true with respect to many cases of employee theft, where the favored remedy, often, is firing (recall the passage from Price's *Lush Life*).

The kind of theft subject to criminal sanctions will also determine the probability that socially beneficial conduct will be chilled. There seems to be a greater likelihood that legitimate business conduct will be hindered by the criminalization of certain cases of hard bargaining extortion, bad check writing, failing to return lost property, and receiving stolen property than by the criminalization of robbery, larceny, and theft by housebreaking. Economic growth would be stymied if people feared that they would face criminal sanctions every time they bought property the provenance of which was uncertain; took possession of goods that appeared to be lost; wrote a check believing incorrectly there was enough money in their account to cover it; or made a threat that they would engage in some unwanted but legal conduct unless paid. Such chilling effects can also be observed in the case of so-called theft of intellectual property.

Are Criminal Sanctions Justified as a Last Resort?

Yet another possible element in determining whether and to what extent theft in its various forms should be criminalized can be found in the traditional common law principle of *ultima ratio,* criminal law as last resort. Does the principle of last resort actually add anything to the analysis so far, and, if it does, what application should it have in this context?

The principle of *ultima ratio,* in its most familiar formulation, says that because criminal punishment is the most severe, stigmatizing, and intrusive means of enforcement that can be applied to antisocial behavior, it should be used sparingly and only when no alternative, noncriminal sanction will adequately serve the ends that criminal punishment would be intended to achieve.[86] The principle is, as Andrew Ashworth has put it, one of "minimum criminalization."[87]

Private or administrative law procedures are to be preferred if they would achieve the same results as criminal law sanctions.

The principle of last resort rests on a number of broad premises about the proper role of government in a liberal society, which are mostly beyond the scope of this study. Suffice it to say that our form of government is founded on the principle that personal autonomy is to be valued and that the government is entitled to restrict such autonomy only when there is a good reason to do so. Thus, it follows that, if we are to respect the interest that citizens have in preserving their autonomy and privacy, we should use means of control that are no more restrictive of autonomy and privacy than necessary.

There is also a purely instrumental reason for respecting the principle of last resort: the uniquely powerful expressive and communicative functions of criminal sanctions rely to some extent on their rarity. If a sanction is over-applied, and if conduct is overcriminalized, the sanction begins to lose its meaning; its expressive value is diluted; and being labeled a *criminal* has less meaning than it otherwise would have.

As in the case of other limits on criminalization, the principle of last resort can be applied in the legislative, prosecutorial, and judicial contexts. In authorizing criminal penalties for certain types of criminal conduct, a legislature would need to ask whether the conduct being criminalized is such that alternative, noncriminal sanctions would ordinarily be sufficient to serve the ends that criminal punishment would be intended to achieve. In authorizing criminal penalties in the prosecutorial or judicial context, the prosecutor or judge would need to ask whether alternative sanctions would be sufficient in a particular case.

So how does the principle of last resort play out in the context of theft? Recall that the same thievery is subject to both civil and criminal penalties in many instances. Under *ultima ratio*, such overlaps are hard to justify. Assuming that the legislature's goal in authorizing criminal sanctions is to achieve both retributive and preventive ends (as it must be in a hybrid consequentialist/nonconsequentialist system), it is hard to see how civil sanctions alone could achieve both.[88] In our current system, criminal penalties are the only truly realistic means to achieve censure. If, on the other hand, the legislature's goal is to achieve only prevention (as where the legislature is considering the possibility of applying criminal sanctions to certain regulatory or *malum prohibitum* crimes), then criminal sanctions would fail to satisfy the separate demand of retributivism. In such circumstances, application of the principle of last resort would be, as Douglas Husak has put it, "trivial and unimportant. . . . Its application would achieve nothing that was not already accomplished by insisting that crime and punishment are and ought to be expressive."[89]

BORDERLINE CASES OF THEFT

Having set forth a conceptual framework for determining whether a given act of theft should be criminalized, the task now is to apply that framework to a collection of what I contend are particularly problematic, borderline cases of theft. These are (1) *de minimis* thefts, (2) theft by failing to return lost or misdelivered property, (3) receiving stolen property, (4) theft by false promise, (5) writing bad checks, and (6) extortion that involves a threat to do an unwanted but otherwise lawful act. Under the MPC (and, to a lesser degree, under the English Theft Act), most of these forms of conduct are subject to the same level of punishment, and proof of one is sufficient to constitute proof of any other. The analysis in this section shows why the MPC's treatment is misguided.

De Minimis Thefts

How should the law treat thefts involving property that is of *de minimis* or trivial value? Should they be subject to lesser penalties than thefts of more valuable property or perhaps even exempt from prosecution entirely? And should such differential treatment be a matter of prosecutorial or judicial discretion, or should it be built into the offense definition itself? In this section, I survey the law in this area, consider the underlying policy and theoretical issues, and look at two particular areas in which the question of *de minimis* thefts often arises: shoplifting and thefts by employees.

The *De Minimis* Defense Generally

Before considering what it means for a theft to be *de minimis,* it will be helpful to consider what it means for a crime generally to be *de minimis.* The idea that a crime is *de minimis* can be traced to the traditional common law maxim of *de minimis non curat lex*: the law does not concern itself with trifling matters.[90] To say that a criminal act is *de minimis* is to say, at least in part, that it entails little in the way of blameworthiness. This can mean that the harms it causes are *de minimis*. Alternatively, it may refer to the *de minimis* nature of the wrong. Note, however, that the issue here is different from the issue in the Robin Hood and anti-vivisectionist "choice of evils" cases. To say that a crime is *de minimis* is not to say that the harm caused is outweighed by the harm prevented, but rather that the harm or wrong itself is so trivial that the criminal law ought not to be concerned with it in the first place.

We can talk about *de minimis* harms and wrongs in connection with both crime types and crime tokens. In the former case, *de minimis* acts as a constraint on criminalization: a particular kind of conduct is deemed the sort that would not ordinarily justify criminal sanctions. This decision will almost invariably be made by the legislature. This is also the issue that has tended to occupy those few criminal law theorists who have addressed the question of *de minimis* harms. Feinberg, for example, offers two examples of the kind of conduct that should not be criminalized because it is too trivial. One is "repeated rude and disrespectful remarks to parents, spouses, teachers, and others who have a right to better treatment;" the other is "mischievous party hosts . . . putting too much gin in their unsuspecting (and nondriving) guests' drinks."[91] According to Feinberg, "bare minimal invasions of interest just above the threshold of harm are not the appropriate objects of legal coercion."[92] Similarly, Ashworth notes that, "[a] great deal of modern criminal law consists of relatively minor offences designed as a more or less remote threat to those who may jeopardize the smooth running of road traffic, licensing procedures, urban planning, commercial and financial regulations, and so on." And he asks, "since the criminal law is a condemnatory mechanism which may lead to the infliction of punishment, do not offences of this nature contradict any principle that a certain degree of wrongfulness should be required before any conduct or omission is made criminal?"[93] These points seem to me undeniable from the perspective of the liberal theory of criminal law. It is surely a corollary of the harm principle that crime types that tend to cause only trivial harm should be exempt from criminal sanctions.

A separate issue, however, is whether a given crime *token* is *de minimis*. Should a particular instance of the sort of conduct that *has* been criminalized be prosecuted criminally? Most often, prosecutors will deal with this issue in the behind-the-scenes exercise of their discretion to prosecute. Less often, judges consider this issue in deciding whether to dismiss charges that have already been brought.

In the latter context, the issue arises as an affirmative defense. Historically, the *de minimis* maxim was applied only to civil law matters, and some courts continue to be reluctant to recognize the doctrine in criminal cases.[94] For example, in a civil rights case involving the alleged theft by police of three soda cans, Judge Posner wrote:

> The law does not excuse crimes . . . merely because the harm inflicted is small. You are not privileged to kill a person because he has only one minute to live, or to steal a penny from a Rockefeller. The size of the loss is relevant sometimes to jurisdiction, often to punishment, and always to damages, but rarely if ever to the existence of a legal wrong. It would be a strange doctrine that theft is permissible so long as the amount taken is small—that police who conduct searches can with impunity steal, say, $10 of the owner's property, but not more.[95]

The MPC departs from this traditional approach in offering a surprising mandatory rule concerning dismissal of what it calls "*De minimis* Infractions." Section 2.12 states as follows:

> The court shall dismiss a prosecution if, having regard to the nature of the conduct charged to constitute an offense and the nature of the attendant circumstances, it finds that the defendant's conduct:
>
> (1) was within a customary license or tolerance, neither expressly negatived by the person whose interest was infringed nor inconsistent with the purpose of the law defining the offense; or
>
> (2) did not actually cause or threaten the harm or evil sought to be prevented by the law defining the offense or did so only to an extent too trivial to warrant the condemnation of conviction; or
>
> (3) present such other extenuations that it cannot reasonably be regarded as envisaged by the legislature in forbidding the offense.

Section 2.12 reflects a thoroughgoing muddle. Of its three subsections, only one expressly involves the subject of *minimis* infractions. Let us look at each in turn.

Subsection (1) applies to cases in which the defendant's conduct "was within a customary license or tolerance." The example given is of a defendant trespassing on posted land where the landowner has expressed no objection to observed trespassing in the past. As properly understood, the defense described here is one of consent, not *de minimis* harm.[96] Obviously, one can consent even to a substantial harm (though the fact that a harm is *de minimis* may make it more reasonable for the offender to assume that the victim has consented).

Subsection (3) applies to "such other extenuations that it cannot reasonably be regarded as envisaged by the legislature in forbidding the offense." It is hard to know exactly what to make of this provision. It sounds like a general excuse of unavoidability for exceptional and unanticipated circumstances. According to Stanislaw Pomorski, it is probably best understood as "a delegation of discretionary authority to dismiss prosecutions on 'equitable' grounds . . . [which could] serve as a vehicle for developing new, judicially created defenses."[97]

Section (2) is the only section that properly involves *de minimis* infractions, and then only in part. The first part of Section (2) says that the act did not "actually cause or threaten the harm or evil sought to be prevented." According to the Commentary, this language is a "generalization" of the provision in Section 5.05(2), which creates a defense of "utter impossibility" in cases involving inchoate offenses like attempt, solicitation, and conspiracy.[98]

Only the second part of Section (2)—that the act caused or threatened the harm or evil sought to be prevented by the law defining the offense "only to an extent too trivial to warrant the condemnation of conviction"—actually constitutes a *de minimis* offense. The example given by the Commentary is of "unconsented-to contacts" which "might constitute a technical assault in some jurisdictions even though the harm that was threatened and that in fact occurred was too trivial for the law to take into account."[99] No reference is made to the use of the *de minimis* defense specifically in the context of theft.

Section 2.12 has had a relatively modest impact on American law. To date, the defense has been adopted in only five jurisdictions—Guam, Hawaii, Maine, New Jersey and Pennsylvania—and several of these have watered down its effect by making the exception permissive rather than mandatory.[100] It is unclear why Section 2.12 has had as little impact as it has. Perhaps it's because it *is* such a muddle. Or perhaps it's because legislatures are wary of the potential problems that recognition of such a defense would create in practice.

The *De Minimis* Defense in the Context of Theft

So far, I have looked at the extent to which the criminal law in general does, or ought to, recognize a *de minimis* defense. How applicable is the *de minimis* defense in the particular context of theft? More precisely, should a certain subcategory of thefts—those involving the stealing of very low value property—be routinely exempt from criminal prosecution, whether through statutory exemptions, a policy of prosecutorial discretion, or as an affirmative defense? The nature of the question posed is different from that dealt with by Feinberg and Ashworth. Beginning from the premise that the behavior in question normally is properly subject to criminal sanctions, the question is whether criminalization is still justified even in those special cases where the quantum of harm is very small.

Different legal systems have dealt with the question of *de minimis* thefts in different ways. Jewish law has tended to reject any distinction based on the value of the property, viewing even thefts of property worth less than a *perutah* (an ancient copper coin of negligible value) as productive of bad character.[101] At least one Canadian court followed a similar rule, holding in a case involving the theft of a drill bit valued at less than one dollar that the *de minimis* defense simply had no application in the criminal law.[102] An alternative approach is to disallow *de minimis* considerations at the guilt stage but permit them to come in at sentencing. This is more or less the approach followed by English common law, which had no exemption for thefts of small amounts of property, but did draw a line between grand and petit larceny by imposing capital punishment for the former and only whipping or imprisonment for the latter.[103] A third approach occurs in Islamic law, where the stealing of property that is of *de minimis* value or of value only to non-Muslims (such as pork and alcoholic drinks) is treated not as theft *(Hadd)* but rather as the lesser offense of *Tazeer.*[104]

And what about those few jurisdictions, like the MPC, that do recognize the possibility of *de minimis* as a complete defense? Is the defense more likely to apply in the case of theft than other crimes? At first glance, one would think so. It is much easier to imagine a theft that involves *de minimis* harm than a murder that does. Even the mercy killing of a person who is in pain and close to death is not a case of per se *de minimis* harm; rather, it is more properly thought of as involving a choice of evils.

Nevertheless, I am aware of only two reported U.S decisions concerning theft in which a court recognized the validity of the *de minimis* defense.[105] Both cases come from New Jersey, one of the five jurisdictions that have adopted the generalized MPC *de minimis* provision. In *State v. Smith*, the court held that shoplifting three pieces of bubble gum was a *de minimis* infraction in light of the particular circumstances surrounding the offense.[106] The decision in *State v. Nevens* is similar.[107] The defendant was convicted of stealing two bananas, an orange, an apple, and a pear from a restaurant buffet. In reversing the conviction as properly exempt from prosecution, the court noted that there were no signs posted indicating that food should not be taken out of the restaurant and that the defendant could have eaten as much fruit as he wanted if he had stayed inside.[108]

Such acceptance of the defense is clearly the exception rather than the rule. For example, several theft cases in Pennsylvania have construed Section 2.12 so narrowly that it is hard to imagine any case in which it would apply. In *Commonwealth v. Campbell*, the court refused to dismiss on *de minimis* grounds a conviction for shoplifting $1.59 worth of goods.[109] In *Commonwealth v. Moses*, the court declined to dismiss a prosecution of a defendant who robbed a ten-year-old boy of 35 cents in candy money, stating that the state would protect a child and his meager possession with the same vigilance as it protected an adult with great wealth.[110]

So which rule is right? Should there be a viable *de minimis* defense in the case of theft or not? In answering this question, we need to return to first principles: What makes an offender deserving of criminal punishment in the first place, and how, if at all, would a *de minimis* defense relieve him of such culpability?

Moral blameworthiness, according to the analysis offered in Chapter 2, is a function of harm and wrongfulness (as well as intent). One kind of harm that theft causes is harm to the individual victim whose property is stolen. By definition, this kind of harm is minimal in cases of *de minimis* thefts unless there is an aggregation of many discrete thefts (e.g., suppose that everyone shopping at the Whole Foods surreptitiously took a couple of olives from the olive bar; before long, there would be none left[111]). A second kind of harm is that caused to the community at large, which suffers a loss in the security of the system of property rights. The quantum of this latter harm seems less dependent on the value of the property stolen; in terms of systemic harms, the fact that there was a theft at all seems more important than the amount stolen.

What is even harder to evaluate is such acts' wrongfulness. On the one hand, the extent to which the victim's rights are violated does seem to be, at least in part, a function of the stolen property's value: the lower the value of the property, the less significant the violation of the victim's rights. The disrespect such an offender expresses for the moral worth of the injured party in such a case seems fairly minimal. Moreover, some *de minimis* thefts may be so close to the range of what is considered socially acceptable that criminalization should be considered inappropriate.

On the other hand, theft of even low value property involves a violation of the norm against stealing and of the victim's rights. Like non-*de minimis* thefts, *de minimis* thefts are unlawful, without consent, and dishonest. A person who is the victim of even a very minor theft might well feel strong reactive emotions such as anger and resentment.[112] Similarly, a person who commits even a minor theft may feel significant pangs of guilt, shame, and remorse. (For a particularly extreme example, think of Saint Augustine's account of his adolescent theft of the pears.[113]) According to this view, theft remains the sort of matter in which the community should (as Marshall and Duff put it) "take a shared and public view, and claim normative authority over its members."[114]

Assume, if only for purposes of discussion, that the harm and wrongfulness in a theft involving property of very low value is so minimal that criminal penalties are unjustified. What effect should this judgment have in practice? This brings me back to the distinction between types and tokens. If we really believed that all thefts of property worth less than, say, ten dollars were not worth criminalizing, then it seems that we should write that judgment into the statute. But doing so would obviously create a moral hazard. Thieves could go around stealing items worth $9.99 or less knowing that they would be immune from prosecution. Such a rule would, in effect, give them a "license to steal."

Another approach would be to look at the cases on an individual basis, as tokens. The traditional way to do this is in terms of a criminal law defense, whether a justification defense or an excuse defense. Douglas Husak has considered *de minimis* defenses in terms of both paradigms and has concluded that neither fits very comfortably.[115] Justification defenses require that the harm sought to be avoided by the defendant's conduct be greater than that sought to be prevented by the law defining the offense charged. In the case of *de minimis* thefts, as Husak correctly observes, "[c]learly, no greater good is achieved when the defendants commit *de minimis* offences."[116] As for excuse defenses, they are supposed to "cancel or eliminate altogether the blame deserved by a defendant who commits a criminal act."[117] But once again, Husak properly concludes that "[d]e minimis offenders are not totally blameless." The best we can do, he says, is to assert that the *de minimis* offender's conduct is "not wrongful enough" to merit criminal prosecution.[118]

Even assuming that *de minimis* offenders *deserve* to be punished, however, we would still need to ask whether their prosecution meets the additional requirements of criminalization—in particular, whether the benefits of prosecuting and punishing someone who stole, say, three pieces of bubblegum from a candy store would outweigh its costs.

The benefits are fairly straightforward. A robust practice of prosecuting those who commit such thefts would entail a significant deterrent effect—a particular attraction in the case of repeat offenders.[119] It would also serve the expressive or communicative function of the criminal law—to send a message about the evils of stealing.[120]

The costs, however, are more complex and, I believe, ultimately outweigh the benefits. First are the direct costs of prosecution, which are unlikely to be appreciably lower in the case of bubblegum larceny than in the case of auto theft. Indeed, given the various evidentiary issues that might arise in such cases, the costs of prosecuting *de minimis* thefts may sometimes be higher than the costs of prosecuting non-*de minimis* thefts. For example, a defendant who takes home a small amount of goods from his workplace may have a plausible argument that he reasonably believed that such taking was consented to by his employer and that it fell within what the MPC calls "customary tolerance." Second are the opportunity costs arising from the fact that prosecutors and judges, with limited time and resources, will have to forgo other, possibly more important, cases.[121] Third is the fact that aggressive enforcement policies in such cases might have a chilling effect on innocent people who would avoid certain legal, and even socially beneficial, behaviors so as to foreclose the possibility of misunderstandings or untrue allegations in borderline cases. Fourth are indirect costs to victims, such as time and effort spent testifying. Finally, there are costs to the defendants, who arguably will suffer harm, as Feinberg puts it, "out of all proportion both to their guilt *and* to the harm they would otherwise cause, even when the priority of innocent interests is taken into account."[122]

Shoplifting and Employee Theft

The question of how best to deal with *de minimis* thefts is not limited to quaint cases of bubblegum and breakfast buffet larceny. It is in fact an issue that arises in the context of two widespread and socially significant forms of criminality: shoplifting and employee theft.

On its face, there is no obvious reason to treat shoplifting (or retail theft, as it is often labeled) as a distinct offense, separate from other forms of larceny. The fact that the victim is a business rather than an individual should hardly matter in light of equal protection norms. Yet more than half the states have specific statutory prohibitions on such behavior.[123] The offense is typically narrower than ordinary larceny in that it must be committed within "an establishment in which merchandise is displayed for sale."[124] But there is also a sense in which it is broader. Theft normally requires that the defendant actually steal, take, obtain, or remove some property. Shoplifting, by contrast, typically includes several inchoate alternatives. A defendant need not actually remove any property from the premises to commit shoplifting. So long as the shoplifter has the intent to deprive the owner of the property, it is enough to "conceal" it or "transfer it from one container to another" or "alter, remove, or substitute one label or price tag for another."[125] Some shoplifting statutes also specify that the goods taken be of relatively low monetary value, at least for a first offense.[126] Curiously, such statutes do not typically require that the offender be, or pretend to be, a customer of the store from which he is stealing, though this seems to be an element that most people would associate with the offense.

What is most significant about such legislation, however, is not so much that shoplifting is treated as a distinct offense, but that it is so often *not* treated as a criminal offense. At least twenty-nine states explicitly provide, as an alternative to criminal sanctions for shoplifting, statutory civil liability, typically including actual damages, a specific statutory fine, and in some cases punitive or treble damages.[127] A few states also impose liability on the parent or legal guardian having custody over a minor who commits shoplifting.[128] In addition, many states provide specific procedures for the detention of suspected shoplifters by law enforcement or merchants[129] or immunity for shopkeepers who are sued for false imprisonment.[130] The effect in many jurisdictions is that shoplifting has been largely decriminalized.[131]

The question is why. Why have legislatures created a separate, specialized scheme of enforcement for conduct that could clearly be dealt with under generalized larceny statutes? Why is the legislative approach to shoplifting seemingly so at odds with the MPC-inspired, one-size-fits-all approach to theft seen elsewhere? And, is that approach the right one?

At least five factors help explain why the law of shoplifting has developed in this manner. First is the apparently forgiving attitude the public seems to hold towards such conduct. To say that *D* shoplifted is generally less stigmatizing than to say that *D* stole or committed theft or larceny. One reason for this is that the value of the property is ordinarily low, and the value of stolen property is taken to be a morally relevant factor in assessing a given theft's blameworthiness. Another reason is that the victims of shoplifting are often large, impersonal retail stores with deep pockets, rather than individuals (though it is worth asking whether judgments are likely to differ when the victim is a small "mom and pop" store). Yet another explanation is related to the fact that a shockingly high number of people have themselves engaged in such conduct. Studies suggest that as many as *60 percent* of American consumers have shoplifted at some time in their lives.[132] Although some shoplifters are professional thieves or drug users who steal to feed their habit, the vast majority appear to be otherwise law-abiding amateurs with no known history of criminal activity who steal sporadically for their own consumption rather than for resale.[133] Shoplifting is particularly common among adolescents, who account for approximately 40 percent of all incidents. What studies exist suggest that shoplifting by adolescents is behavior, often brought on by peer pressure and hormonal changes, that will likely be grown out of. (Think again of the 16-year-old Saint Augustine, stealing pears with his youthful companions.)

Second is the peculiar psychology of shoplifting. Some, although a relatively small number, shoplifters are diagnosed as suffering from kleptomania, an impulse disorder listed in the Diagnostic and Statistical Manual of Mental Disorders (DSM-IV).[134] Many others use shoplifting as a relief mechanism for anxiety, frustration, boredom, or depression.[135] People who shoplift steal items they often don't need, sometimes don't use, and typically have the money to pay for.[136] For many, shoplifting is an addictive behavior that even arrest cannot stop.

Third is the fact that shopkeepers have long been subject to tort liability for false imprisonment, assault, and battery for erroneously interfering with suspected shoplifters.[137] Shopkeepers are therefore reluctant to get involved, meaning that many shoplifters get away without ever being apprehended.

Fourth, there are some cases involving items of small value where genuine confusion exists about whether the owner consents to a given taking. Consider shampoo and other toiletries left for guests in hotel bathrooms. Is a guest entitled to take them home at the end of his stay, or may they be used only while in the hotel? What about food from a hotel buffet? Must all the food be eaten while in the dining room, or can the guest lawfully take a bagel or piece of fruit with her when she leaves? The answer to all of these questions is far from clear.

Fifth, and perhaps most importantly, is the economics of shoplifting. In the United States, more than an estimated 200 million shoplifting incidents occur annually, accounting for as much as $13 billion in losses to business per year.[138] The costs of prosecuting and punishing every such incident would overwhelm both the government and the private sector. As Wal-Mart's chief of asset protection put it in announcing that the company had backed away from its previous zero-tolerance policy and would no longer press charges against those who steal less than $25 in merchandise, "If I have somebody being paid $12 an hour processing a $5 theft, I have just lost money. I have also lost the time to catch somebody stealing $100 or an organized group stealing $3,000."[139]

As a result of such economic realities, businesses have sought less costly ways to deal with the problem. Many invest significant resources in surveillance cameras, security tags, uniformed and undercover guards, exit inspections, locked cases for merchandise, and the like. But beyond that they have lobbied for what they believe will be the most effective legislative solutions.[140] Among other things, business groups have sought statutory authority to detain suspected shoplifters without incurring civil liability for doing so—the so-called "shopkeeper's privilege."[141] And they have generally preferred civil remedies that would provide restitution to the victim rather than retributive justice brought in the name of the state. In the New York area, for example, suspected shoplifters at grocery stores owned by Chinese immigrants, following the practice in China, are subjected to what are essentially privately inflicted shame sanctions: they are photographed holding up the items they are accused of attempting to steal and threatened that the photographs will be publicly displayed unless they pay the store owners a fine.[142] In effect, many modern businesses have been successful in turning theft—otherwise viewed as an offense against the state—into a private dispute between retailer and offender.[143]

A similar phenomenon has occurred in the context of employee thefts. Studies indicate that approximately 60 percent of American office workers admit to having taken office supplies, such as pens, paper, and post-its, from work to use at home for matters unrelated to their jobs.[144] Many employees also make personal use of intangible or semi-tangible goods and services, such as workplace telephone, mail, and computer time.[145] Relatively few of these thefts are ever prosecuted. Of course, the vast majority are never detected. But even in those cases in which they are detected, the result is often either no discipline at all, minor discipline, or, in the most serious cases, employee dismissal. Employers and the police seem to regard such thefts not as "conduct which should be declared wrong by the community" (as Marshall and Duff would have it), but rather as essentially private disputes between employer and employee. Thus, to a large degree, employee thefts of low-value property, like shoplifting, have been functionally decriminalized.

What is there about thefts from employers that make them susceptible to such treatment? As in the case of shoplifting, economic realities seem to be controlling. The direct costs of detecting, apprehending, and prosecuting every employee who heads home with a clutch of magic markers or paper clips hidden in his or her briefcase would be prohibitive. This is not to mention the high transaction costs involved in having employees pay for every personal fax, telephone call, and sticky note, or the indirect costs associated with employees spying and reporting on each other.

Moreover, as in the case of hotel guests taking shampoo with them when they leave, many employees say they believe that their employers would not object to their taking home low-value items for their personal use.[146] And this may well be the case. I suspect that employers anticipate that employees will appropriate some small amounts of company property for their own use and in some sense thereby consent to it.[147] In that sense, many employee appropriations of small value items should not be regarded as theft to begin with.

Who Should Decide Whether the *De Minimis* Exception Applies?

Based on the foregoing, it seems reasonable to conclude that some cases of theft involving small amounts of property should be, and functionally are, exempt from criminal prosecution. The question remains whether such exemption should be implemented by the legislature (in drafting the theft statute), by the prosecutor (in using her discretion whether to prosecute), or by the judge (in applying the defense and dismissing the case).

In some criminal law contexts, it is practicable to draft a statute that includes a *de minimis* exception. In the case of assault, for example, the MPC defines the offense to preclude even what it calls technical liability by limiting the relevant harm to bodily injury (defined as "physical pain, illness or any impairment of physical condition") or serious bodily injury (defined as "bodily injury which creates a substantial risk of death or which causes serious, permanent disfigurement, or protracted loss or impairment of the function of any bodily member or organ").[148] One could imagine a similar approach to theft, which could be defined as the unlawful taking only of property worth more than, say, ten dollars, or perhaps (more vaguely) of property of some "significant" value. All other thefts could be treated as non-criminal infractions.

I am skeptical, however, that such an approach would work. By creating a license to steal low value items, it would undermine the norm against theft generally and potentially raise the aggregate level of employee theft to intolerable levels. In the end, the better approach would be to allow prosecutors and judges to make the decision that a particular case of theft should be regarded as *de minimis* retrospectively, on a case-by-case basis.

Theft by Failing to Return Lost or Misdelivered Property

At common law, beginning late in the fifteenth century, one who found lost goods and failed to return them to the owner upon demand was liable in tort for trover.[149] It was not until several centuries later, apparently as late as the nineteenth century, that one who took into his possession lost, mislaid, or misdelivered property and failed to make a reasonable effort to find the owner, could be held guilty of larceny.[150] A failure to make an effort to find the owner was considered unreasonable if the finder knew the owner's identity or could reasonably discover it (for example, from earmarkings on the property or from the circumstances of its finding). Merely picking up or possessing the lost property did not constitute a crime; the finder had to fail to make an effort to find the owner. If the finder took possession of property intending to look for its owner and restore the thing to him, he did not assume the rights of the owner and did not commit larceny. This was true even if he picked up the property intending to return it to the owner and subsequently decided not to do so.

Theft by finding lost or misdelivered property is among the bundle of common law offenses that the MPC incorporated into its undifferentiated offense of theft, and it is thereby subject to the same punishment as theft by unlawful taking, theft by deception, theft by extortion, theft of services, and receiving stolen property. Section 223.5 of the MPC provides as follows:

> A person who comes into control of property of another that he knows
> to have been lost, mislaid, or delivered under a mistake as to the nature
> or amount of the property or the identity of the recipient is guilty of
> theft if, with purpose to deprive the owner thereof, he fails to take rea-
> sonable steps to restore the property to a person entitled to have it.[151]

The MPC formulation is thus both broader and narrower than the common law offense. It is narrower in the sense that a defendant can avoid liability if he has the intent to steal at the time he takes possession but subsequently changes his mind and takes reasonable steps to find the owner. It is broader in the sense that the defendant cannot avoid liability by postponing his intent to deprive until some time after taking possession of the property.

The Theft Act 1968 makes no explicit reference to theft by finding, though as *Smith's Law of Theft* notes, with one important exception, the Act is "obviously intended" to preserve the substance of the common law rule.[152] The exception is found in Section 3(1), which states that "[a]ny assumption by a person of the rights of an owner amounts to an appropriation, and this includes, where he has come by the property (innocently or not) without stealing it, any later assumption of a right to it by keeping or dealing with it as owner."[153] What this means is that, under the Theft Act, as under the MPC (and Canadian law[154]), and contrary to the common law, a finder who forms the intent to deprive the owner of property only after taking possession will nonetheless be guilty of theft. Also, like the MPC, the Theft Act implicitly views theft by finding as morally equivalent to, and interchangeable with, theft by other means.

Theft by failing to return lost or misdelivered property is a complex and interesting offense, though one that the scholarly literature has almost completely ignored. The criminalization of theft by failing to return poses a number of significant problems. First, to the extent that it imposes a duty to act, rather than a duty not to act, it goes against the grain of a criminal law that tends to disfavor crimes of omission. Second, the offense embraces a surprisingly wide range of conduct, some of which would be viewed as unequivocally wrongful and some of which would not. In particular, theft by taking control of property that is lost or mislaid and theft by taking control of property that has been misdelivered are quite different acts, and they ought not be treated as functionally equivalent. Third, the criminal law of theft by finding depends on the complex civil law of lost property in a way that poses problems for the principle of legality and suggests that civil liability is typically a better alternative. Accordingly, rather than treating theft by omission as subject to the same punishment as theft by commission, we should consider subjecting it to lesser penalties, decriminalizing it entirely, or providing finders of lost property with positive incentives—such as cash rewards—to return it.

Theft by Omission

Theft by failing to return can be said to involve the criminalization of an omission in two senses. The first arises out of the requirement that the offender, having taken possession of some property, subsequently fails to take reasonable steps to restore the property to a person entitled to have it. The second sense occurs in those cases in which the defendant's coming into possession of the property is itself passive, as where the property was misdelivered to his house.

In considering the criminalization of omissions, I begin with an approach developed by Tony Honoré, who divides conduct into doings and not-doings.[155] When a doing is contrary to a norm, it is a commission; when a *non*-doing is contrary to a norm, it is an omission. Norms, in turn, are divided into ordinary norms and norms that impose distinct duties. The distinct-duties theory holds that we have, beyond the background duties we owe to all, special duties to other people and entities, which vary from person to person according to individual circumstances and past dealings between them. A classic example is the duty that parents owe to their children. Under this approach, harms caused by omission are, other things being equal, comparable in their wrongfulness to harms caused by an affirmative act when the person who omits to perform some act is under a distinct duty to do so. When only background duties are operative, however, omissions are normally less bad than positive acts.

One question, then, is whether the offense of theft by finding involves a distinct duty and, if so, what form it takes. According to Honoré, there are five types of situation that yield distinct duties: (1) The agent, by a positive act, causes a harm or increases a risk to others, and thereby incurs an affirmative duty to mitigate such harm or risk. For example, a motorist who runs over a pedestrian has a duty to summon help even if his initial act was not at fault (e.g., where he has blamelessly struck a pedestrian who has run into the street). (2) The agent occupies a position or office or fills a role which may require him to act positively. An example would be that of a parent who is obliged to act affirmatively in caring for a child, even when he did not create the initial danger. (3) Society imposes a duty to act positively because of a need or dependency which the agent is well placed to fulfill, as where an agent takes custody of another and thereby deprives him of normal opportunities of being rescued. (4) Receipt of a gift or other benefit sometimes imposes an obligation on the recipient to act. (5) People have specific duties to act affirmatively when they have voluntarily agreed to do so, as in the case of promises. Of course, not all of these situations create duties in law, let alone criminal law; in some cases, the duty is merely a moral one.

So, what kind of duty, if any, is at play in the case of theft by finding? For a start, we can rule out, as obviously inapplicable, the second, fourth, and fifth grounds noted above. This leaves as potential candidates the first and third grounds cited. Considering the first ground, can we say that the finder of lost property has, by a positive act, caused a harm or created a risk to others, and thereby incurred an affirmative duty to mitigate such harm? Assuming, as will normally be the case, that the finder has had no role in the owner's loss of the property, it seems to me wrong to say that the finder of lost property has caused a harm or created a risk. This is therefore not like the case of the motorist who runs over a pedestrian and is then legally obligated to summon help.

A more plausible basis for finding a duty is the third ground— namely, that the finder, by taking possession of the lost property, thereby deprives the owner of a normal opportunity to find it. Consider the case of Geoffrey Rowlett, an English magistrate who found a £3,200 Rolex watch on the floor of a supermarket, made no effort to find the real owner, and gave it to his wife as a sixtieth birthday present.[156] He was subsequently convicted of theft. Rowlett's case seems to reflect the core case of theft by finding.

Upon finding the lost watch, Rowlett had three basic choices: He could have taken possession of the property and then tried to find its owner, such as by alerting the store manager of his find or putting up a notice on the store's bulletin board. Such conduct would have been proper, even praiseworthy. Alternatively, he could have done nothing; he could have simply walked on by, leaving the watch lying on the floor. Most people in our society today would probably say that, if Rowlett had done this, he would have done nothing wrong, and that his conduct would therefore have been morally neutral (though it is worth noting that Jewish law seems to disagree on this point, also viewing as morally culpable those who leave lost property lying where they found it.[157]) Finally, Rowlett could have done what he actually did, which was to take the property for his own use and make no effort to find the owner. Most people, I assume, would regard such conduct as in some respect wrong. By taking possession of the watch, rather than leaving it lying on the floor, he deprived the owner of the opportunity to return to the store and find the watch in the location where it was lost. The owner of the watch became (in Honoré's term) "dependent" on Rowlett by virtue of Rowlett's having taking possession of it.

Even if we were to agree, however, that it is morally wrong to take possession of lost property and then fail to make any effort to find the owner, it hardly follows that such an omission should constitute a crime, let alone that it should be treated as equivalent to theft. Let me suggest a number of reasons why this is so.

The first is that the harm caused by the offender's failure to look for the owner of found property seems less serious than that caused by an affirmative act of stealing. If Rowlett had affirmatively stolen O's watch, say, by picking his pocket, he would certainly have caused O a significant harm. But where O has already lost the watch, the *additional* harm caused by Rowlett's preventing him from having an opportunity to recover it is relatively small. The difference, in short, is between worsening a situation and merely failing to improve it.

Second, even if Rowlett's preventing O from recovering his lost watch were as harmful as his stealing it in the first place, it is doubtful that the harm would be sufficient to merit criminal sanctions. In almost all of those cases in which the law imposes on one who creates a dependency on another a duty to act, the risk involved is one of serious physical harm. This is true even in the case of so-called Bad Samaritan statutes, which normally say that the victim must be "in peril" before the defendant is required to act.[158] In the case of omissive theft, in contrast, the harm is the loss of property.[159] The criminal law simply does not regard such property-related harms as equal in seriousness to harms to one's physical well-being.

Third, it seems a more significant violation of O's rights that D wrongly takes property that is in O's possession than that D fails to return property that is not in O's possession to begin with.[160] Certainly, making an effort to find the owner of the watch would be the decent thing for D to do. But to what extent would D's failing to make such an effort constitute a wrong to the owner? Consider how you would feel if you lost your watch and had it returned to you the next day by its finder. You would, I think, feel grateful. You might even think that the finder had acted supererogatorily.[161] You might think it appropriate to give the finder a reward for his virtuous act. For example, a Newark cabdriver named Mohammed Khalil recently returned to its caretaker a $4 million Stradivarius violin left in the backseat of his cab.[162] For his honesty, Khalil was given a cash reward, a special private recital by the grateful violinist, Philippe Quint, and Newark's highest honor, the Medallion, presented by Mayor Cory Booker. Indeed, many jurisdictions now *require* that the true owner give the finder a reward for his trouble.[163] Assuming that all of this is true, it seems odd to say that it is morally wrongful to fail to do that which, had one done it, would merit a reward.[164]

Fourth, people are presumably less certain about the moral and legal obligations to return found property than they are about the moral and legal prohibitions on the out-and-out taking of property from another's possession. The norms associated with returning found property where the owner can easily be located are simply not as strong or as deeply rooted as those associated with the prohibition on taking others' property outright. The schoolyard slogan of "finders keepers, losers weepers," though neither an accurate reflection of the law nor a particularly admirable sentiment, nevertheless seems to have had some lasting effect on many people's moral sensibilities. (Similar is the nonsensical saying that "possession is nine-tenths of the law.")

Fifth, and closely related, is the fact that the criminal law in this area is unusually dependent on somewhat esoteric concepts in the civil law of property. This suggests that theft by failing to return lost property is even more *malum prohibitum*-like in character than other forms of theft.

Finally, it is worth noting that the norms concerning the return of lost property seem, to a degree perhaps unusual in the law of theft, culturally specific. For example, a recent study suggests that residents of Tokyo are significantly more likely to return lost property than residents of New York.[165] Undoubtedly this gap reflects the fact that Japan, in contrast to the United States, has a widely recognized, accessible, and efficient system for reporting lost objects, one that rewards good behavior and punishes bad—a coherent system of "carrots and sticks," as Saul Levmore puts it in his discussion of finders' law.[166] To what extent these norms have been internalized, in the sense that residents of Tokyo could be said to be more honest than New Yorkers, seems somewhat harder to say.

Lost Property versus Misdelivered Property

In the previous section, I argued that the reasons for criminalization are weaker in the case of the non-return of lost or misdelivered property than in the case of affirmative takings of property. The question here is whether there is a morally relevant difference between failing to look for the owner when one takes possession of property that has been *lost* and failing to look for the owner when one takes possession of property that has been *misdelivered*. Weak as the arguments are for criminalizing the first sort of omission, the arguments for criminalizing the second sort of omission are even more so. If I am right, we can observe yet another respect in which the MPC improperly conflates morally distinct forms of theft.

The MPC provides that theft is committed when a person "comes into control of property of another that he knows to have been . . . delivered under a mistake as to the . . . identity of the recipient" and then "with purpose to deprive the owner thereof . . . fails to take reasonable steps to restore the property to a person entitled to have it."[167] The Theft Act says that in committing theft by failing to return lost or misdelivered property, one must "assume" the rights of the owner, by "keeping" it or "dealing with it as owner."[168]

In the case of lost property, it will normally be clear when the offender comes into control of the property of another. In the case of misdelivered property, however, the existence of such control is less likely to be clear. Imagine, for example, that a box containing a Rolex watch, addressed to someone other than Magistrate Rowlett, is mistakenly delivered to his house by the letter carrier. And imagine that Rowlett disposes of the box or takes it into his house and puts in a closet without ever using it. Should we say that Rowlett has come into control of the property?

Even assuming that Rowlett has come into control of the watch, the idea that he should be subject to criminal sanctions for failing to take steps to return it to its owner seems troubling. Rowlett's conduct in the case of the misdelivered Rolex is even more passive and therefore arguably even less wrongful than in the case of the lost Rolex. In the actual case, it was Rowlett's own act of taking the lost watch into his possession that created the risk that its owner would be unable to recover it. In the hypothetical case of the misdelivered Rolex, by contrast, the risk that the owner of the watch will be unable to recover her lost property was created by a third party—namely, the letter carrier who misdelivered the mail.

One can easily imagine a case in which O, the former occupant of some premises, has moved away, and that day after day mail addressed to him is received by the new occupant, R. If R fails to send some of the mail on, and instead discards it or keeps it piled up on a table by the door, there is a reasonable argument that R is guilty of theft. Yet to impose sanctions for failing to return misdelivered property in such

circumstances would seem to compound the problem of omission liability discussed in the previous section.

To treat as criminal those who come into control of misdelivered
property and fail to look for the owner becomes even more problematic in the context of intangible property. Imagine that (1) Rowlett's
bank mistakenly credits to his account a sum that should have been
credited to another depositor's account, (2) Rowlett is aware of the
mistake but never tells the bank about it, and (3) the money remains
in his account, accruing interest. Has Rowlett committed "Theft of
Property . . . Delivered by Mistake"? Must he use or transfer the funds
to assert control over them?[169] Or can he come into control by simply
knowing that the funds have been incorrectly credited to his account
and allowing them to remain there? Assuming that he comes into control of the funds as soon as he becomes aware that they are in his
account, it would appear that Rowlett has violated MPC Section 233.5.
The problem is that Rowlett's conduct in this case seems even more
passive than in the previous case, since he has not even done so much
as take physical control of the property.

Legality, Omissive Theft, and the Civil Law of Found Property

Another problem with the offense of theft by failing to return lost or
misdelivered property is that it criminalizes conduct the wrongfulness
vel non of which is dependent on sometimes arcane issues in the civil
law of found property. Indeed, questions concerning the ownership of
lost property are among the most difficult and contested in all of personal property law.[170] Such complexity raises serious concerns about
the legality of criminalizing this sort of conduct. Difficult questions
must be resolved about when property can properly be said to be abandoned; who owns salvage, treasure trove, property found at sea, and
property found underground; and the possible distinction between
lost and mislaid property.

Regarding the law of abandonment, consider the case of Fabio Piras,
a Sardinian tourist vacationing in London shortly after the death of
Princess Diana. Tens of thousands of flowers, teddy bears, letters, and
other tributes to her memory had been left outside various royal pal-
aces. Piras took one of the teddy bears from outside the gates of St.
James's Palace and, not surprisingly, made no effort to find the owner.

He was convicted of theft and initially given a sentence of one week in prison. He later had his sentenced reduced to a £100 fine but was punched in the face by a member of the public when he left the court, having won his appeal.[171]

The obvious question is whether the property taken by Piras should properly be regarded as abandoned. Theft is committed only if the defendant takes the property *of another*. Abandoned property is deemed not to be property belonging to another. So did the teddy bear belong to another, and, if so, to whom? It seems unlikely that property left *outside* the gates of St. James's Palace should be said to belong to the royal family (who own the palace) or to the British government. Nor is it likely that it still belonged to the person who left it there; such leaving was surely not intended to be temporary. On the other hand, the property does not seem to have been entirely abandoned. It was presumably intended to remain where it was, at least for a time, as a tribute to the late princess, and perhaps later to be given to charity (though it's unclear whether this latter possibility would even have been contemplated by the person who left it there). In taking the teddy bear for his own use, Fabio surely violated some expectation of the person who left it there. What seems doubtful, however, is that this is the kind of property violation that theft law is meant to prohibit.[172]

The difficulty of determining whether property is truly abandoned and, if it is, who should get subsequent title to it, is reflected in a number of important dichotomies in the civil law of personal property, such as those between property found at sea and property found underground; property found on land owned by third parties and property found on public lands; property buried intentionally by owners since deceased and property lost unintentionally; property lost, property mislaid, and property unclaimed; property found by a trespasser and property found by one lawfully on property; and between treasure trove and salvage.

Consider the case of the container ship, *MSC Napoli*, loaded with brand new BMW motorcycles and other goods and stranded in the English Channel off the coast of Devon in January 2007.[173] After containers from the wreck began washing up on the shore, around 200 people ventured onto the beach to scavenge the flotsam. At first, the police tolerated the acts as "salvage," but later they branded them as "despicable," closed the beach, and threatened prosecution.[174] As far as can be determined, there seems to have been genuine confusion among both the scavengers and the police about whether such conduct was permissible.

The law concerning such finding is complex and varies significantly from jurisdiction. The term *treasure trove* refers to valuable property, such as gold, silver, gemstones, or money, hidden underground, in cellars, or in attics, where the property is old enough to presume that the true owner is dead and the heirs undiscoverable. Unlike the Rolex watch lost by its owner and found by Magistrate Rowlett, treasure trove is property that has been hidden by its owner with a view to its subsequent discovery. (Thus, shipwrecks like the *Napoli* and *Titanic* should not be regarded as containing treasure.) In Britain, the traditional rule was that treasure trove should be regarded as property of the crown. (This is so even if the property was hidden on private land.) One who takes such property for his own is therefore committing theft. In most American states, by contrast, the finder is allowed to keep the property[175] (though in Louisiana, following the "civilian" tradition, the rule has been that the property is divided between the finder and the owner of the land on which it is found[176]).

The rights of finders vary depending on where property is found, how it was lost or abandoned, and how long ago it was lost or abandoned. For example, if abandoned personal property is found embedded in the soil, it will ordinarily be awarded to the landowner rather than the finder.[177] Abandoned chattels found in public places will normally be awarded to the finder, in contrast to chattels found on private property (such as a store or a restaurant), which will go to the property owner.[178]

Another traditional distinction is that between lost, mislaid, and unclaimed property. Property is considered lost if its owner parted with it involuntarily: A cell phone that drops unnoticed onto the street through a hole in its owner's pocket is considered lost; the owner will probably not know where to look for it. Property is considered mislaid if the owner parts with it intentionally, but forgets where he puts it: a phone put down on a table in a restaurant and then forgotten would be regarded as mislaid; its owner may well remember where she placed it and retrace her steps to retrieve it. Unclaimed property is (typically, intangible) property, such as securities or cash, that is held by a bank or other institution and is unclaimed by its owner for some lengthy period of time. The law traditionally held that the owner of lost property lost possession, while the owner of mislaid property maintained construc-tive possession.[179] In criminal law terms, this meant that one who took possession of mislaid property was more likely to be held guilty of theft than one who took possession of lost property. Modern theft statutes, following the MPC approach, abrogate the distinction between lost and mislaid property on the grounds that the distinction is too elusive in practice; after all, how exactly is a finder supposed to know whether property is lost or mislaid?

By this point in the discussion, it will, I hope, be clear that the legal status of lost and misdelivered property often depends on finely drawn and contested distinctions in the civil law of property. To premise criminal liability on such distinctions is to introduce serious questions of notice and legality.

From a larger social policy perspective, one of the main goals of the law in this area is to reunite owners with their lost property, and, where it is not possible to find the owner, the law aims to encourage the prop-erty's use by someone else so that its value is not lost to the community entirely.[180] Often, but not always, the finder of the chattel will have a better claim to it than anyone other than the original owner.

One way to achieve such a societal goal would be to reward people— to give them a carrot—for their honesty in returning found property. This is not to say that there should be no role in this area for sticks as well, including, certainly, tort actions for conversion and, perhaps, civil fines. What role the criminal law should play in furthering such a policy is another question. What seems clear, at a minimum, is that certain kinds of theft by omission should be viewed as less unambigu-ously wrongful, and therefore subject to less severe punishment, than most kinds of affirmative theft—a point that is consistent with the empirical study of public perceptions of theft wrongfulness.

Receiving Stolen Property

Should the possession (or receiving or handling[181]) of stolen property be treated as a crime separate from that of theft; and if so, how should it be punished?[182] Anglo-American law has responded to this question in a variety of ways. Until 1692, possessing stolen property was no crime at all. In that year, Parliament enacted legislation that subjected one who knowingly possessed stolen property to liability as an accessory after the fact, a less serious form of liability than being a principal in the first or second degree.[183] In 1827, new legislation made receiving stolen property a free-standing crime, but one that was still subject to lesser penalties than larceny and other theft offenses.[184] Twentieth-century law took a different tack: under the MPC, receiving stolen property was treated as interchangeable with various forms of theft and subject to the same penalties.[185] The Canadian Criminal Code also subjected theft and receiving to the same punishment scheme, though it treated them as distinct, non-interchangeable offenses.[186] The English Theft Act took yet another approach. It both continued to treat handling stolen goods as a separate offense and subjected it to the possibility of even harsher maximum penalties than theft itself.[187]

Which of these various approaches makes the most sense today? The question is worth asking not only because receiving is a commonly committed and widely prosecuted offense that the theoretical litera-ture has virtually ignored, but also because it bears interesting com-parison to various possession offenses that *have* been the focus of recent literature and because an understanding of receiving is essen-tial to an understanding of theft law more generally.

Based on their history and rhetoric, it appears that receiving statutes are intended to punish and deter two distinct, yet complementary, aspects of the offender's conduct, which I shall call *backward–looking* and *forward–looking*. From a backward–looking perspective, the receiver can be said to perpetuate the wrongful deprivation of the victim owner's property rights, effected in the first instance by the thief, and perhaps to conceal the thief's offense from discovery. From a forward–looking perspective, the act of receiving can, at least in some cases, be said to encourage the commission of future thefts by helping to create a ready market for stolen goods. In this latter sense, receiving would be viewed as similar to various other possession offenses.

The problem is that the offense in its current statutory formulation reflects only the backward-looking perspective. Receiving statutes require nothing more than that the offender possess or receive stolen property (knowing that it is stolen); they say nothing about the future effects of his act. And because perpetuating an owner's loss of prop-erty is a lesser wrong than causing him to lose his property to begin with (or so I shall argue), it appears that the receiver deserves less blame and punishment than the thief. To the extent that receiving, as currently formulated, is subject to the same punishment as theft, it is therefore overcriminalized.

This is not to say that receiving statutes could not be formulated differently. Such statutes could incorporate the forward-looking perspective by, say, requiring that the offender's conduct not only perpetuate the owner's loss of property but also that it make future thefts more likely. Or statutes could criminalize two degrees of receiving: a lesser offense that was solely backward–looking and a greater offense that was both backward– and forward–looking. For statutes of this latter sort, enhanced punishment might well be justified.

A Brief History of Receiving

In the 1602 case of *R. v. Dawson*, the defendant was sued for slander after he allegedly said to the plaintiff, "Thou art an arrant knave, for thou hast bought stolen swine, and a stolen cow, knowing them to be stolen."[188] The court dismissed the case, holding that the plaintiff had failed to state a claim. Merely making a statement that would harm the plaintiff's reputation was not sufficient to constitute slander. To be actionable, the statement had to attribute to the plaintiff the commission of a felony or serious crime involving moral turpitude.[189] In this case, the court said, the defendant had failed to make such a statement in that "the receipt or sale of goods stolen is not a felony, nor makes any accessory, unless it is joined with a receipt or abetment of the felon himself."[190]

Although occurring in a somewhat peculiar procedural context, the decision in *Dawson* accurately reflects the state of English law during most of the seventeenth century and earlier. While it was a crime to harbor a *thief* or other felon as early as the Middle Ages,[191] there was no criminal offense of possessing stolen *property* until 1692, when Parliament enacted a law that made one who knowingly received stolen property an accessory after the fact, a less serious form of liability than being a principal in the first or second degree.[192]

The Industrial Revolution of the late eighteenth and early nineteenth centuries prompted yet more changes in the crime of receiving, culminating in the Larceny Act of 1827, which removed receiving "from its position as an appendage of theft and elevated [it] to the dignity of a separate substantive crime."[193] Passage of such legislation can be attributed to several factors. Proving that a defendant was in possession of stolen property could be considerably easier than proving that the defendant had actually stolen it. As Bruce Smith has explained, for those of modest means, "wealth . . . frequently resided in humble goods such as wood, metal, rope, and vegetables, which were virtually indistinguishable from similar items held by others."[194] Such nondescript goods were simply "too commonplace for property owners to identify credibly at trial as their own."[195] Whereas prosecution for larceny required the prosecutor to prove from whom the goods had been stolen, prosecution for receiving did not. To be convicted of receiving, a defendant merely had to be in possession of goods suspected of having been stolen and unable to offer a "satisfactory account."[196] Valuable goods, for the first time in history subject to mass production, also became harder to identify and therefore easier to sell.[197] In addition, many of the technicalities that burdened the law of theft (concerning the means of stealing and type of property stolen) did not apply to prosecutions for receiving.

Another factor that helps explain the emergence of receiving as a separate offense was the fact that during the eighteenth and nineteenth centuries, the sale and purchase of stolen property was becoming big business, the most spectacular evidence of which was the dramatic rise and fall of Jonathan Wild.[198] At a time when there was no professional police force, Wild ran an ingenious crime syndicate in which his agents would steal property, keep the goods, and wait for the crime to be announced in the press. Wild would then claim that his "thief taking agents" (who constituted a kind of private police force) had recovered the stolen merchandise. The property would then be returned to its rightful owners for a reward (ostensibly to cover the expenses of running his agents).

Until well into the twentieth century, receiving remained a distinct offense, subject to a lesser penalty than larceny, embezzlement, false pretenses, and other leading theft offenses. All of this began to change by mid-century, however. Under the MPC, receiving stolen property was treated as an alternative means of committing theft and therefore subject to the same penalty as the other theft and theft-like offenses. The supposed justifications for such consolidation were the same that underlay the movement toward consolidation of theft offenses more generally. One particular concern was that a defendant charged with theft could argue that he had actually committed receiving, and vice versa.[199] As elsewhere, the MPC avoided this "bait and switch" problem by the familiar means of Section 223.1, which says that "[a]n accusation of theft may be supported by evidence that it was committed in any manner that would be theft under this Article, notwithstanding the specification of a different manner in the indictment or information."[200]

Judging the Blameworthiness of Receiving

How should we judge the moral blameworthiness of receiving? Recall the results of the empirical study. Subjects were asked to rank twelve hypothetical scenarios involving different means of misappropriating a $350 bicycle: by armed robbery, simple robbery, extortion, blackmail, burglary, larceny, embezzlement, looting, passing a bad check, false pretenses, failing to return misdelivered property, and receiving stolen property. The receiving stolen property scenario read as follows:

> Tom was walking along a street. The previous day, Owen's bike had been stolen. A person Tom did not know rode Owen's bike up to him and said, "I stole this bike and I'll sell it to you for just $20." Tom bought the bike and rode it away, intending to keep it for himself.

Virtually all of the participants in the study ranked this scenario as significantly less blameworthy, and deserving of significantly less punishment, than all but one of the eleven other theft and theft-related scenarios that were part of the study (the exception was failing to return misdelivered property, which was rated as more or less equivalent to receiving stolen property).

The question is why. Why is it that, despite the MPC's treatment of receiving as interchangeable with and subject to the same punishment as embezzlement, larceny, false pretenses, and the like, members of the public viewed this scenario as worthy of substantially less punishment? Informal, post-study discussions with subjects revealed an intuitive, but not very well developed, judgment that receiving stolen property was somehow less wrongful than theft proper. Some more fully articulated, critical analysis seems called for.

Formulating the Offense. To understand the underlying moral content of receiving, we need first to understand the various ways in which the offense has been formulated. Under Section 223.6 of the MPC, a person is guilty of receiving stolen property "if he purposely receives, retains, or disposes of movable property of another knowing that it is has been stolen, or believing that it has probably been stolen."[201] *Receiving,* in turn, is defined as "acquiring possession, control or title, or lending on the security of the property."[202] Section 22 of the Theft Act says that a person handles stolen goods "if (otherwise than in the course of stealing) knowing or believing them to be stolen goods he dishonestly receives the goods, or dishonestly undertakes or assists in their retention, removal, disposal or realization by or for the benefit of another."[203] Under Section 354 of the Canadian Criminal Code, one commits "possession of property obtained by crime" if one "has in his possession any property or thing or any proceeds of any property or thing knowing that all or part of the property or thing or of the proceeds was obtained by or derived directly or indirectly from . . . the commission in Canada of an offence punishable by indictment."[204]

There is thus a significant variation in the way the offense is formulated in the various Anglophone jurisdictions. The Canadian formulation is both broader and narrower than the MPC and the Theft Act formulations. It is broader in terms of *actus reus*—the defendant need do nothing more than "possess" property (worth more than $5,000) that has been stolen to be guilty of the offense,[205] whereas under the MPC, the defendant must "acquir[e] possession, control or title" of the stolen property, and under the Theft Act the defendant must "receive" the goods or undertake or assist in their "retention, removal, or disposal." The Canadian formulation is narrower, however, with respect to *mens rea*; the defendant must "know" that the property has been stolen, whereas under the MPC and the Theft Act the defendant must "know" *or* "believe" that it has been stolen.[206]

In terms of *mens rea*, which approach makes more sense, the Canadian or the Anglo-American? Should a defendant have to *know* that the property has been stolen, or is it enough to *believe* that it is stolen to commit receiving? Presumably, the Anglo-American rule is more likely to encourage potential buyers to investigate the provenance of suspicious-looking goods, thereby reducing the market for stolen goods and ultimately the incentive to steal. It is also more likely to prevent the transfer of stolen goods to third parties, thereby potentially making the recovery of such goods easier. On the other hand, the Anglo-American rule probably inhibits some lawful transactions that the Canadian rule does not (such as sales that might otherwise occur at flea markets, antique stores, and garage sales). In that sense, the Canadian rule could arguably be said to promote economic efficiency.

What if one neither knows nor believes that goods are stolen, but is merely negligent with respect to their ownership status? Why not require those who are considering buying goods to ascertain their provenance before doing so, at least in circumstances that are suspicious? The conflict, as Victor Tadros has described it in the context of rape law, is basically between subjectivists, who argue that one should be criminally responsible only if one is actually aware of the risk that the *actus reus* might result from her conduct, and objectivists, who hold that criminal responsibility should properly be attributed on the ground that the defendant ought to have been aware that the *actus reus* would, or might, come about as a result of her action.[207] Whatever the right rule, it is striking how different the *mens rea* required in receiving is from that of rape, which, according to Tadros, says, in essence, that "I am not permitted to have intercourse with a person unless I have taken sufficient steps to ensure that the person I am having intercourse with is consenting."[208]

As for the *actus reus* of the offense, by stating that anyone who "possesses" stolen property commits the offense, the Canadian Criminal Code presents the possibility that everyone who commits theft (at least of property worth more than $5,000) will also automatically be guilty of possession, since one cannot steal property without coming into actual or constructive possession of it. The American provision seems to work the same way. The English provision, by contrast, avoids this problem of "double dipping" by expressly providing that a "person handles stolen goods if *(otherwise than in the course of the stealing)* . . . he dishonestly receives the goods," meaning that under English law one cannot be guilty of both theft and receiving simultaneously.[209]

The MPC formulation, in fact, is doubly redundant. A separate theft provision, Section 223.2, entitled "Theft by Unlawful Taking or Disposition," says that "a person is guilty of theft if he unlawfully takes, or *exercises unlawful control over,* movable property of another with purpose to deprive him thereof."[210] Under this definition, not only does every act of thieving constitute receiving, but also every act of receiving also constitutes thieving. Indeed, this is exactly the point made by the Commentary to Section 223.6, which states, "[a]nalytically, the receiver does precisely what is forbidden by Section 223.2(1)— namely, he exercises unlawful control over property by another with a purpose to deprive."[211]

As a matter of statutory construction, this approach is problematic. If the act of receiving really were intended to be covered by the broad language of Section 223.2, there would be no need for the separate provision of Section 223.6; it would be superfluous. In fact, the framers of the Code titled Section 223.2 "theft by unlawful *taking or disposition*," and they presumably intended it to apply to cases in which a defendant actually takes or disposes of another's property. I suspect that the real reason Section 232.2 used such broad language was to avoid the problems that arose out of the common law requirements of caption and asportation, including particularly the difficulties of distinguishing between attempted and completed theft.[212]

To avoid such redundancy and superfluity, I propose that we follow the English approach and treat thieving and receiving as separate offenses. Under this approach, the crime of theft would require something more than merely possessing stolen property, while the crime of receiving would consist in possessing stolen property that one has obtained by some means other than stealing it oneself. The paradigm case would thus be one in which the defendant bought or received property from another, knowing (or believing) that it had been stolen. Why should this be a crime? What harms does such conduct cause? What forms of wrongfulness does it entail?

Two Rationales for the Law of Receiving. To understand why we criminalize receiving, we need to consider how it both perpetuates prior harms and, in some cases, arguably encourages future harms. Like the thief, the receiver of stolen property wrongfully deprives the owner of his rights in such property and therefore deserves blame. I am skeptical, however, that the deprivation perpetuated by the receiver should be thought of as equivalent to the deprivation initiated by the thief. It is, after all, the thief who has caused the radical, involuntary change in the owner's relationship to his property—from possession to non-possession. Stealing is a specific kind of act, with a specific moral status. Stealing involves a transfer of property, as I argued in Chapter 2, not just an ongoing deprivation.[213]

Unlike the thief, the receiver does not cause any *change* in the status of the owner's rights. To be sure, he benefits from the change that the thief has effected by perpetuating the deprivation of the owner's rights. He may in some cases make it harder for the owner to recover her property (in this, the offense of receiving is like that of failing to return lost or misdelivered property). No doubt the receiver has done a wrongful and dishonest thing. But he does not wrong the owner in the same way and, I would say, to the same extent, as the thief. His role, as I will explain below, is essentially a subsidiary one.

The fact that the receiver perpetuates the owner's loss of property, however, is not the only reason receiving is criminalized. In addition to the past harms that he perpetuates, the receiver is also said to encourage future harms. The dynamic works as follows: many thieves steal property not to keep or make use of the property themselves but rather to sell it to a third party, known as a *fence,* for a quick profit. The fence thus creates the market that makes theft profitable. Understood this way, receiving becomes the *raison d'être* of stealing.

Maimonides made this point more than 800 years ago: "It is prohibited to buy from a thief any property he has stolen, such buying being a great sin, since it encourages criminals and causes the thief to steal other property. For if a thief finds no buyer, he will not steal."[214] More recently, criminologists Duncan Chappell and Marilyn Walsh have argued that:

> Once we have seen the fence as author of both the incentive and the opportunity for theft, we can appreciate more fully the compelling nature of his exchange relationship with the thief. We can also begin to see the thief as little more than an instrument of the fence—a highly visible but relatively minor cog in a giant distribution circuit.[215]

It has thus often been said that without receivers there would be no thieves,[216] and while this statement is obviously not literally true, it is certainly the case that, without an efficient and profitable market in which stolen goods could be bought and sold, we would have a lot less thievery.[217]

It is important to note, however, that, viewed from this perspective, receiving causes not harm itself but merely the *risk* of harm. In this sense, receiving is reminiscent of other proxy crimes such as possession of illegal drugs, unlicensed firearms, tools for counterfeiting, tools for burglary, and things that can be used to commit terrorist acts.[218] Each offense is said to be justified by the risk it poses of some future harmful act, whether it be drug use, firearm use, counterfeiting, burglary, or terrorism, respectively.

Offenses of this sort have come under attack from a number of recent commentators.[219] First, they are said to be overly inchoate or anticipatory in character; rather than punishing actual harms, they punish the mere threat of harm, without even the "substantial step" or "dangerous proximity" requirement that is characteristic of attempt liability. Second, possession statutes have been said to do the work that was once done by now-disfavored vagrancy laws. They are easy to detect and easy to prove, and give police a pretext to stop, search, and incapacitate. Third, at least some possession statutes are overbroad in that they criminalize innocent conduct (a good example is possession of burglary tools).

I am sympathetic to these concerns, which seem particularly apt when the thing illegally possessed is stolen property. Indeed, one could argue that such criticisms are *a fortiori* true in this context. Although the probability that one who possesses tools designed for the commission of burglary, counterfeiting, or terrorism will herself attempt to commit these offense seems fairly high, the probability that one who possesses stolen property will cause another to commit theft seems relatively low. The causal chain is more attenuated precisely because a second party—namely, the thief—is involved.

Receiving as a Form of Complicity. In addition to considering the harms that it causes or risks, it will be helpful to think about receiving as a form of complicity. To say that an accomplice is complicit in the act of a principal is to say that the accomplice's liability is derivative of the principal's act—that, in Sanford Kadish's words, it is "incurred by virtue of a violation of a law by the primary party to which the secondary party contributed."[220] The accomplice, or secondary party, shares in the liability of the principal, or primary party, because he has contributed to the actions of the principal that gave rise to her liability.

So what would it mean to say that a receiver, R, was complicit in the act of a thief, T? Here, we can imagine at least three scenarios: Consider, first, a case in which R promises T that, if T steals a bike from its owner, R will purchase it from her; and imagine further that T does steal the bike and that R does in fact buy the stolen bike from T. Here we would say that R had specifically encouraged T in the commission of *this* theft, that he has influenced her decision to commit the crime, and that he therefore shares, to some degree, in the blameworthiness of T's act.[221] In such a case, we should charge R as an accomplice to T's theft.[222] But note that R would be an accomplice in T's theft regardless of whether he ultimately bought, or even possessed, the stolen bike. At most, the fact that he bought the bike would provide evidence of R's contribution to the scheme.

Now consider a case of a different sort: Assume that R buys a bike from T that T stole, but imagine that prior to T's stealing the bike, R had no knowledge of T's plan to steal it, and T had no knowledge of R's interest in buying it. Assume, further, that this was the first bike that T had ever stolen and the first stolen bike that R had ever purchased; both were "theft virgins." In fact, when T stole the bike, she planned to keep it for herself, but she subsequently changed her mind and sold it to the first person she could find who wanted to buy it, who happened to be R. R had never before contemplated buying stolen property. Moreover, neither R nor T has any intention of ever stealing or receiving again; going forward, both plan to be "theft celibate."

A good example is provided by a case recently in the news.[223] Brian Hogan was in a bar in Redwood, California, when he found a cell phone lost by an Apple computer software engineer named Gray Powell. Hogan took the cell phone home and quickly realized that what he had in his hands was something quite valuable: a prototype of Apple's 4G iPhone, not scheduled for commercial release for another six months. Hogan allegedly made no reasonable effort to return the lost property to Apple and as such committed theft under California law. Instead, he allegedly got in touch with Sage Robert Wallower, a graduate student at Berkeley, who allegedly helped Hogan contact technology Web sites that would be interested in buying the phone. Jason Chen, the editor of a technology blog called Gizmodo.com, paid $5,000 for the phone and subsequently posted various photos of and articles about the device on Gizmodo's Web site.[224] As far as can be determined, this was the first (and presumably last) time that Hogan, Wallower, or Chen would be involved in such conduct.

In such one-off, after-the-fact, noncausative cases, can we say that receivers like Wallower and Chen have been complicit in the thief's act? Following an approach suggested by Christopher Kutz in a somewhat different context,[225] I would say that Wallower and Chen could be viewed as complicit insofar as they "ratified" or "endorsed" the acts of Hogan.[226] One who purchases property he knows to have been stolen benefits from the thief's prior wrongdoing. By wrongfully possessing property belonging to another, the receiver says in effect that he does not respect the owner's property rights, and he elevates his own interests above the owner's.[227]

Even if *R* can properly be viewed as *morally* complicit in *T*'s act, however, I am skeptical that we would be justified in holding *R criminally* liable as an accomplice to *T*. *R* has not in any familiar sense aided or abetted *T* in the commission of any crime. The criminal law is concerned with punishing those who cause or risk harm, and that is something *R* has not done. To extend criminal liability to those who, after the fact, ratify or endorse the criminal acts of others strikes me as a significant and potentially dangerous expansion in the scope of accomplice liability.[228]

Finally, consider a third type of scenario exemplified in the extreme by the case of the notorious Toronto bike thief, Igor Kent, a kind of modern-day Jonathan Wild.[229] Kent was arrested in 2008 after a police sting operation uncovered 2,865 stolen bicycles that had been stashed in garages and warehouses throughout the city. Kent had bought the bikes from the thieves who had stolen them, often bartering for them with illegal drugs, and then resold them in his bike shop, in many cases to the very people from whom they had been stolen.

Assume, at least for purposes of discussion, that the Toronto bike thieves normally had no knowledge of Kent's interest in buying any specific bike prior to the thefts, and that Kent in turn normally had no specific knowledge of the thieves' plans to steal it. That would make this case distinguishable from the first scenario, in which *R* specifically promised *T* that, if *T* stole a bike from its owner, *R* would purchase it. But it would also be distinguishable from the second scenario in that *R* and *T* are most definitely not theft virgins: they are both veterans of the stolen property trade, they have dealt with each other on various occasions in the past, and they plan to do so again in the future. When *T* steals the bike from its owner, she is aware that there is a high probability that *R* (or others like him) will want to buy it. *R*, likewise, is always on the lookout for stolen bikes and other goods to buy. He has made it known to various thieves, including T, that he is a potential buyer of their stolen goods. And on this occasion he does in fact buy T's bike.

Is criminal liability for R justified? It's a close call, but I believe that such a case can be made. Note that R does more than merely endorse T's past wrongdoing; he encourages T in a continued course of wrongdoing. It should not be necessary for R to encourage a specific act of stealing to say that he has aided and abetted. Thief and receiver exist in an ongoing and reciprocal, if informal, economic relationship. In such circumstances, it makes sense to say that the receiver provides encouragement to the thief.

Punishing Possession of Stolen Property

Having surveyed the moral content of receiving, we are now in a position to assess its appropriate level of punishment, particularly in comparison to the offense of theft. As noted, the modern trend is to subject receiving to the same (or, in the case of the English Theft Act, even greater[230]) punishment than theft, though the empirical study indicated that most subjects believed that receiving should be punished less.

I argued earlier that, as the offense is currently formulated, the only legitimate retributive basis for punishing receiving is the backward-looking one—namely, the idea that the receiver perpetuates the wrongful deprivation of the owner's property. By contrast, the forward-looking rationale—the idea that the receiver encourages future acts of theft—should not be viewed as a legitimate basis for punishment since the crime, as presently formulated, requires nothing more than the knowing possession of stolen property and is satisfied regardless of whether the thief or receiver have ever stolen or received or are ever likely to do so again.

Indeed, I assume that this is exactly how the subjects in the empirical study read the receiving scenario, specifying that Tom knowingly purchased, from a person he did not know, a bike stolen from Owen. Given that the focus of all of the other scenarios in the study was Tom's deprivation of Owen's property, it seems likely that the subjects focused on this backward-looking aspect of the crime rather than on the possibility that Tom's act would encourage future acts of stealing.

If I am right about the priority of the backward-looking perspective, then what are the implications for punishment? The relationship between thieving and receiving can be understood as closely analogous to the relationship between the production of certain kinds of contraband and their possession. Our criminal law often (though not always) treats those who produce, sell, or supply illegal goods more harshly than those who buy or possess them. For example, in New York, a person who possesses materials depicting an obscene sexual performance by a child is guilty of a class E felony (punishable by up to four years in prison), whereas a person who produces, directs, promotes, sells, or disseminates such material is guilty of a more serious class D felony (punishable by up to seven years imprisonment).[231]

Like those who possess stolen property, those who possess child pornography arguably create a market for such material and thereby encourage its future production and dissemination. But as in the case of stolen property possession, such forward-looking effects do not figure in the formulation of child pornography possession statutes themselves. That is, an offender would be guilty of possessing child pornography even if no such material was ever again produced. Instead, the most appropriate rationale for child pornography possession statutes is the backward-looking one—namely, that such conduct perpetuates the exploitation of children initiated by the pornography maker. In the case of both stolen property and child pornography, possession of the banned substance is therefore subordinate to its creation. Under such a model, possession of stolen property should be subject to less punishment than theft.

There is also another possible approach. Assuming that we intend to take seriously the forward-looking aspect of receiving, we could enact statutes that criminalized two grades of the offense. Grade A would constitute simple receiving: it would require nothing more than that the offender possess property (otherwise than in the course of stealing) knowing or believing that it has been stolen, and it would be subject to a lesser penalty than theft proper. Grade B would be aggravated receiving: it would require that the defendant not only possess stolen property, but also that he do so in circumstances in which his conduct was likely to encourage the commission of additional thefts. And when would such circumstances properly be presumed? A receiver who engaged in a pattern or practice of receiving (say, a minimum of two or three such acts within a specified time period) might be presumed to have helped establish a market for stolen goods.[232] In such circumstances, a penalty equal to or even higher than that given to theft would be appropriate.[233]

Theft by False Promise, Writing Bad Checks, and Extortion

There are two additional methods of stealing property to consider: by deception and by coercion. Because I have written about both concepts fairly extensively in earlier work,[234] I will do so only briefly here, focusing on three particular offenses: theft by false promise, writing a bad check, and extortion. All three of the offenses follow the same basic pattern. Conduct at the core reflects the kind of harmfulness and wrongfulness to which criminal sanctions are properly addressed. Yet, outside the core, such conduct overlaps with, and blurs into, lawful and even socially beneficial conduct. The result is both significant problems of proof and significant dangers of chilling effects. For this reason, with respect to such offenses, criminal sanctions should be used only sparingly, and civil alternatives should be seriously considered.

Obtaining Property by False Promise

To understand the current state of the law of theft by deception, it is helpful to recall some of the history of the offense recounted in Chapter 1. At early English common law, one who obtained title to another's property by deception (as opposed to force or stealth) was generally held not to have committed a criminal offense. Rather, the doctrine of *caveat emptor* prevailed. As Perkins and Boyce put it, "A person who deprived another of his property by force or stealth was regarded by all as a very evil person, but he who got the better of another in a bargain by means of falsehood was more likely to be regarded by his neighbors as clever than as criminal."[235]

There were two important exceptions to this early rule. The first was the offense of common law cheat, which consisted of fraud perpetrated by means of a false token, such as false weights and measures. Unlike other forms of theft by deception, the use of false weights and measures was said to be something against which common care and prudence could not guard. Observing this distinction in *R v. Wheatly*, the court held that it was not a crime to fraudulently sell and deliver to a customer a container with sixteen gallons of beer while falsely representing that it contained eighteen gallons.[236] The court reasoned that the case involved what was really only a civil wrong, "an inconvenience and injury to a private person," not a deceptive practice used in the "general course of . . . dealing," which would affect "all or many of . . . customers."[237] The second exception to the rule of *caveat emptor* was the offense of forgery. Starting with the statute of 1562, Parliament made it a crime to forge publicly recorded, officially sealed documents with the intent to affect title to land, as well as to knowingly use such documents as evidence in court.[238]

Over time, however, the definition of what constituted theft by deception broadened. In 1757, Parliament enacted a statute that made it a crime for any person "knowingly or designedly" by false pretenses to obtain title to "money, goods, wares or merchandizes" from another person "with the intent to cheat or defraud."[239] Although significantly broader in scope than earlier theft by deception offenses like forgery and common law cheat, the original offense of false pretenses was still more limited than the modern version. In the leading 1821 case of *R. v. Goodhall*, the 1757 Act was read narrowly to exclude insincere promising, thus restricting its application to misrepresentations of past or existing fact.[240] Although the jury had found that *D* had obtained meat by making a promise to pay that he never intended to keep, the appellate court reversed the conviction, finding that the misrepresentation was "merely a promise of future conduct, and common prudence and caution would have prevented any injury arising from it."[241] A similar rule was subsequently adopted by American courts.[242]

By the middle of the twentieth century, this so-called existing fact dogma was beginning to erode. A majority of courts and scholars believed that a distinction between false representations and false promises was no longer warranted.[243] As a result, the MPC explicitly included within the scope of Theft by Deception not only deception as to false statements regarding "law" or "value" of some property, but also "false impressions" and "states of mind."[244] By 2005, forty-five states and the District of Columbia had criminalized theft by false promise, whether through express legislation or judicial interpretation.[245] The

English Fraud Act 2006 reflects a similar approach. Included within the definition of what constitutes fraud by false representation are not just representations as to "fact or law," but also representations as to the defendant's "state of mind"—that is, false promises.[246] Thus, in almost every state and in England, one who obtains goods by promising to pay money he intends not to pay commits fraud or theft. For example, in the scenario contained in the empirical study described in Chapter 1, Tom committed theft by riding Owen's bike away after falsely promising to return the next day with the money owed.

Although there are undoubtedly good reasons for criminalizing at least some appropriations of property effected through false promise, there are also reasons for caution. The first is that, as a matter of proof, it is often difficult to tell what D's intent was at the time he entered into the contract. To criminalize in this area is thus to raise the possibility of criminalizing contracts honestly entered into but subsequently breached. The second problem is that criminalization might deter parties to contracts that are no longer economically efficient from engaging in "efficient breach."[247] As the court in *Chaplin v. United States* (one of the leading American cases to follow the rule in *Goodhall*) put it, "[b]usiness affairs would be materially encumbered by the ever present threat that a debtor might be subjected to criminal penalties if the prosecutor and jury were of the view that at the time of borrowing he was mentally a cheat."[248]

So how should the dilemma be resolved? One approach would be to return to the regime of *Goodhall* and decriminalize all frauds based on false promise. But such an approach would go too far. At least in the core cases, people who steal by means of false promises are no less deserving of blame and punishment than people who steal by means of false statements. What we need is a way to distinguish between those cases of alleged false promise that should be criminalized and those that should not.

A helpful approach is suggested by Ian Ayres and Gregory Klass. They offer us the case of Max Bialystock, Mel Brooks's maniacal Broadway producer/con artist in *The Producers*, who knowingly sells more than one thousand percent of the interest in the intended-to-flop *Springtime for Hitler*.[249] The fact that he makes a promise that is mathematically impossible to honor makes it beyond doubt that Max affirmatively intends not to perform on his promise. In such a case, there is no difficulty in saying that what Max did was stealing. He takes money from his gullible investors with the promise to return it, with interest, in the event that the show makes a profit. The fact that he will be unable to fulfill his promise, whether or not the show makes a profit, makes it clear that he has no intent to return the property due and that he is thereby violating his victims' property rights. This is theft every bit as much as theft based on misrepresentations of fact. In such cases, criminal sanctions are appropriate.[250]

A similar result should occur where the contract breacher has engaged in a pattern of promises that are subsequently not honored. Here, Ayres and Klass offer the case of Ray Brent Marsh, the owner of a Georgia crematorium who, on more than three hundred occasions, accepted money promising to conduct a cremation and then failed to do so.[251] Again, there is no reason to distinguish false promise cases of this sort from those in which a defendant makes a misrepresentation about the quantity, quality, or price of goods.

More generally, Ayres and Klass distinguish between cases in which a promisor affirmatively *intends not* to perform and cases in which she does *not intend* to perform.[252] Given the circumstances, Bialystock and Marsh almost certainly had an affirmative intention not to perform. But often people make promises that reflect not an intention not to perform but rather (1) an intention to perform only under certain (undisclosed) conditions, (2) an intention to perform *or* pay damages if they do not, or (3) a lack of understanding of what was being promised. Promises of this sort are not fraudulent and should not be treated as a crime. For example, a bank promises to return its depositors' funds upon demand. Because banks' loan practices are structured in a certain way, however, it is impossible for them to satisfy every depositors' demands at once.[253] If a bank promises to return money and then fails to do so because of a run by depositors, it has not committed fraud simply because its promise was qualified by an undisclosed condition. Similarly, if an airline sells a seat which turns out to be unavailable because of overbooking, that is not fraud either. At the time it entered into the agreement, the airline lacked the affirmative intent not to perform.

In light of these considerations, Ayres and Klass recommend not complete decriminalization of the offense of theft by false promise, but rather a narrowing of how the offense is defined, and caution in how it is prosecuted.[254] They argue that prosecutors should have to offer proof that the defendant affirmatively intended not to perform, rather than merely proof of no intent to perform (since no intent is compatible with, for example, a conditional or an irrelevant intention).

A good example of how such an approach might be reflected in law can be seen in the New York Larceny by False Promises statute, which provides as follows:

> In any prosecution for larceny based on false promise, the defendant's intention or belief that a promise would not be performed may not be established by or inferred from the fact alone that such promise was not performed. Such a finding may be based only upon evidence establishing that the *facts and circumstances of the case are wholly consistent with guilty intent or belief and wholly inconsistent with innocent intent or belief,* and excluding to a moral certainty every hypothesis except that of the defendant's intention or belief that the promise would not be performed.[255]

Such an approach, in my view, is much preferable to that of Section 223.3 of the MPC, which includes no such limitations. Evidence establishing guilty intent or belief would presumably exist where it could be shown that a promisor knew that it would be impossible to perform, that he had repeatedly broken promises of the same sort, or that a pattern of deceptions and other actions demonstrated a preconceived scheme to defraud.

Passing Bad Checks

Closely related to, perhaps even a specialized subset of, theft by false statement or false promise is the offense of passing bad checks, which in most American jurisdictions, following the MPC, is treated under a specialized provision separate from theft.[256] (Passing a bad check is to be distinguished from using a forged check, which is invariably treated as a form of false pretenses.[257]) As in the case of theft by false promise statutes, bad check laws seem sound at their core; but at the periphery, there remains a potential for overcriminalization and abuse.

Why do we need a separate statute covering bad checks? The mere fact that a check writer writes a check for which there are insufficient funds is insufficient to establish that the writer had the intent to defraud. The check writer might not have known that there were insufficient funds in her account, or she might have intended to deposit additional funds in her account prior to the check's being presented to the bank. To get around this difficult problem of proof, specialized bad check statutes incorporate a permissive presumption of fraud. The presumption says, in the language of the MPC, that it will be *prima facie* evidence that the defendant intended to defraud "if payment was refused by the drawee for lack of funds, upon presentation within thirty days after issue, and the issuer failed to make good within ten days after receiving notice of that refusal."[258]

There are at least two basic problems with this permissive presumption. The first is that the presumption on its own terms sweeps too broadly. Under such a provision, merely bouncing a check and failing to make good within ten days would constitute a crime. And the crime is a potentially serious one. In *Bordenkircher v. Hayes*, for example, the Supreme Court upheld a life sentence for a habitual offender who had violated Kentucky's bad check law by uttering a bad check in the amount of $88.30.[259] The presumption is particularly hard to defend in cases where the shortfall is minimal. As Ayres and Klass explain, banks typically refuse to honor a check for a given amount unless there is enough in the drawer's account to cover the entire amount.[260] Thus, a check for $1,000 is likely not to be honored even if the check writer has $999 in his account. And if he fails to pay in the additional dollar within ten days, he will be found guilty of the crime of writing a bad check.

Second are the practical abuses to which such statutes are put. It is not uncommon for recipients of checks written on insufficient funds to threaten criminal proceedings to gain leverage in what is essentially a commercial transaction. The problem is particularly serious in the context of the payday loan industry.[261] Payday loans are small, short-term, extremely high interest loans that are intended to cover a borrower's expenses until his or her next payday. To obtain a loan from a payday lender, the borrower typically writes a postdated check for the combined value of the loan and the finance charge. Unless the loan is repaid or refinanced within a specific period of time (usually two weeks), the lender deposits the check.[262]

If, however, by the time the loan comes due, the borrower does not have the money in his account, the lender is entitled under the bad check laws in many jurisdictions to threaten criminal prosecution. By permitting borrowers to be criminally prosecuted for writing bad checks, the law essentially allows them to be prosecuted for defaulting on their debts. As one commentator has put it:

"Payday loan prosecutions concern the breach of a contract to repay a loan, not the deceptive practice of convincing a creditor that a bad check was good." Unlike innocent merchants who unknowingly receive bad checks for their wares, payday lenders are fully aware that borrowers do not have sufficient funds in their accounts to cover the check; otherwise, the borrower would not be seeking a payday loan. Payday lenders insist on receiving a postdated check from a borrower with full knowledge that the borrower does not currently have sufficient funds in her account.[263]

Business interests have lobbied for specialized laws in this area that will serve their special concerns. In this respect, bad check laws are reminiscent of specialized shoplifting laws. But unlike shoplifting laws, which have had the effect of alleviating the harsh impact of criminal prosecution, bad check laws have had just the opposite effect. Rather than offering alternatives to criminal prosecution, they have tended to give payday lenders the means to leverage the threat of criminal prosecution to their advantage.

Extortion

Under MPC Section 223.4, a person is guilty of the redundantly named[264] offense of Theft by Extortion if he:

purposely obtains property of another by threatening to

1. inflict bodily injury on anyone or commit any other criminal offense; or
2. accuse anyone of a criminal offense; or
3. expose any secret tending to subject any person to hatred, contempt or ridicule, or to impair his credit or business repute; or
4. take or withhold action as an official, or cause an official to take or withhold action; or
5. bring about or continue a strike, boycott, or other collective unofficial action, if the property is not demanded or received for the benefit of the group in whose interest the actor purports to act; or

    6. testify or provide information or withhold testimony or infor-
       mation with respect to another's legal claim or defense; or
    7. inflict any other harm which would not benefit the actor.[265]

Like the other theft offenses, extortion is regarded by the MPC as
interchangeable with other forms of theft. Thus, evidence of extortion
is sufficient to support a charge of theft by deception, embezzlement,
or larceny; and evidence of theft by deception, embezzlement, or larceny is sufficient to support a charge of extortion.[266]

Two basic modes of committing extortion can be identified as
defined in the MPC. In mode 1, the extortionist, E, threatens his
victim, V, that, unless V gives him some property, E will commit an
unambiguously *unlawful* act that, if committed, would cause harm to
V. This is essentially the kind of extortion described by subsection (1)
of the MPC provision. For example, E threatens that, unless V gives
him a thousand dollars, E will break V's knees or burn down his house.
In mode 2, by contrast, E threatens his victim, V, that unless V gives
him some property, E will commit a *lawful* act that would nevertheless
be harmful to, and unwanted by, V. This is essentially the kind of extortion described by subsections (2)–(7) of the MPC provision, which
include an astonishingly broad collection of conduct. Extortion of this
latter sort is multifaceted. The offender can commit it by threatening
that unless he is paid, he will accuse another of a crime, take or fail to
take some official action, say something embarrassing (but true) about
another, call a labor strike, engage in a boycott, offer or withhold testimony, or *inflict any other harm which would not benefit the actor.*

Extortion in mode 1 is clearly the sort of conduct that should be
treated as criminal. From a moral perspective, it is never acceptable to
obtain money from another by threatening criminal harm. Indeed, as
the study from Chapter 1 indicates, most people view theft of this sort
as even more blameworthy than basic larceny, and therefore deserving
of even greater punishment, as in fact it is treated in the Theft Act
(which subjects it to twice the maximum penalty as ordinary theft),[267]
though not in the MPC (which subjects it to exactly the same penalty
scheme as theft by unlawful taking).[268]

Mode 2 extortion presents a much different situation, however. In
many circumstances in business, political, and professional life, people
threaten to do lawful, even if aggressive and unwanted, acts unless

paid. For example, lawyers threaten to report crimes and bring law-suits unless settlement is reached. Labor leaders threaten to strike unless management meets certain demands (some of which may benefit the leaders personally). Investors threaten to take over companies unless their stock is bought out at a premium price. Politicians threaten to inflict political damage or withhold political support unless consideration is given. Employers threaten to fire, or fail to hire, employees unless money is paid.[269] And so on.

To treat all of this hard bargaining as criminal, even though the threatened act itself is not criminal, is to create a web of confusion. Conduct that is socially acceptable within the specialized realms of business, finance, labor, politics, and law will potentially become subject to criminal sanctions. Socially valuable conduct will be chilled. The criminal law will be overextended.

My preferred solution, as I have argued elsewhere,[270] is to draw a bright line between threats to do what is lawful and threats to do what is unlawful. The latter would be treated as extortion. The former would be treated as criminal only where specialized legislation made them so. (The most obvious such legislation would be that concerning informational blackmail.) This does not mean that threats to do lawful but unwanted acts unless paid would uniformly be condoned. Such conduct could be handled by means of civil litigation or administrative proceedings.

*　　*　　*

The case for criminalizing theft is far more complex than that for offenses like murder and rape. Even at its core, theft law reflects a significant overlap with civil remedies such as tortious conversion. On the periphery, the moral status of theft law is even more ambiguous. To treat all kinds of theft as equivalent, as the MPC does, is to deprive theft law of much of its meaning. In determining whether and to what extent criminal penalties should be authorized and applied, each kind of theft needs to be assessed separately.

FOUR

Property in Theft Law

Virtually all of the cases of theft I have considered so far, both real and imagined, have involved the stealing of a tangible good—whether it was bicycles, a painting by Leonardo da Vinci, the *Arbeit macht frei* sign at Auschwitz, three pieces of bubble gum, a prototype iPhone, a fresh baguette, or a teddy bear left as a memorial to Princess Diana. All of these items have been the sort of thing that can be physically touched, carried away, and bought or sold.

But what about cases in which the item said to be stolen isn't a physical thing at all, but rather a firm's secret plans for the marketing of a new product or the services of one of its employees? What if what was "stolen" wasn't an actual bicycle, but was instead the patented design for a new derailleur or a secret new technique for manufacturing handlebars? And what if an offender took a ride in a bicycle taxi after falsely promising to pay for the service? How, if at all, should the law of theft apply to the misappropriation of such things?

The empirical study described in Chapter 1 suggested that people's attitudes concerning the blameworthiness of misappropriating services and intangible things differ from their attitudes concerning the misappropriation of tangibles. Subjects were asked to compare the blameworthiness of four cases, each involving the theft of a test preparation tool prepared by ABC Test Prep and valued at fifty dollars. In each case, the property existed in a distinct form: as a tangible good (a book); as an intangible good (a computer file downloaded from a Web site); as a limited-supply service (attendance at a lecture in a full hall);

and as an unlimited-supply service (attendance at a lecture in a half-empty hall). The results of the study indicated that people tended to think of taking the physical book as more blameworthy than downloading the electronic book or attending the lecture (regardless of whether the hall was empty or full).

Part of my goal in this chapter is to develop a conceptual framework that will explain why the study's subjects might have made the intuitive judgments they did. More generally, I am interested in developing an account of what kinds of things should count as property for purposes of theft law. I make no attempt to be comprehensive; instead, I focus on those forms of property that raise what I regard as the most interesting and timely issues.[1]

The discussion is important from both a theoretical and a practical standpoint. Theft law originally developed at a time when property was mostly tangible. Today, our economy is increasingly based on the production and sale of information and other intangibles. The overall value that intellectual capital—including copyrights, trademarks, patents, and related information assets—represents for American business is enormous, about a third of its total economic value, or approximately $5 trillion.[2] The intellectual property industry, the fastest growing sector in the U.S. economy, now accounts for more exports than any other sector.[3] Along with such growth has come growth in related crime: the misappropriation of intellectual property is now estimated to cost American businesses several hundred billion dollars every year, with total losses estimated at more than $1 trillion.[4]

What role the criminal law, and specifically the law of theft, should play in protecting such property, however, is unclear. We seem to be in a period of transition. The Department of Justice, Congress, and the movie and music industries have consistently asserted that infringement is morally equivalent to—indeed, is a form of—theft. Yet the general public and most intellectual property scholars remain skeptical: Abbie Hoffman notwithstanding,[5] it has frequently been observed that citizens who would never think of walking into a store and shoplifting a book, CD, or DVD seem to have little hesitation in illegally downloading text, music, and video from the Internet.[6] The question is why.

CONCEPTUAL FRAMEWORK

In establishing a framework for analyzing the types of property that theft law should protect, this chapter will focus on (1) the relationship between theft law and "other" law; (2) the importance of the label *theft*; and (3) the key concepts of commodifiability, rivalrousness, excludability, and zero-sumness.

Balancing the Concerns of Theft Law with Those of Other Law

As suggested in Chapter 2, the concept of theft is informed by two competing normative approaches. One approach reflects a prelegal, universal, and naturalistic conception that stealing is in some sense morally wrong. The other involves a highly legalized, culturally specific, and positivist conception that turns on often technical conceptions of property, ownership, abandonment, and the like. In determining what should count as property for purposes of theft law, we need to balance the concerns of theft law itself with those of other law, if any, that governs the property at issue.

The bundle of rights that characterizes a given property interest can be thought of as more or less "thick" or "thin," as Pamela Samuelson has put it.[7] Any bundle of rights that rises to the level of "ownership" is likely to involve, at a minimum, the rights of possession, use, and enjoyment; the right of transfer; and the right to exclude others.[8] But beyond that, there can be significant differences concerning, for example, the precise scope and duration of such rights and the question of who has standing to assert them—factors that will be determined with reference to the underlying policy concerns of the body of law in question.

Modern theft law provides a broadly sweeping, general purpose safety net, which is intended to protect both the rights of the individual property owner/victim and society's interest in a regime of property security more generally. As such, the bundle of rights protected by theft law is quite thick. For example, theft law has traditionally included no *de minimis* exception; any theft, no matter how trivial, is potentially subject to prosecution. Moreover, theft law does not, except in the extreme case of necessity, require a weighing of costs and benefits; even a transfer of property from a wealthy owner victim who has little use for it to an impoverished thief who could barely survive without it will be regarded as criminal. At the same time, the *consequences* of deciding that a misappropriated item constitutes property for purposes of theft law—namely, criminal conviction and imprisonment—can be much more severe than the consequences of determining that an item is property for purposes of, say, patent law or the Fifth Amendment's Takings Clause. The bundle of rights that characterizes property in other areas can, by contrast, be much thinner. For example, copyright law has what is essentially a built-in *de minimis* exception. Under the doctrine of fair use, copying relatively brief excerpts of copyrighted texts for noncommercial purposes is not considered infringement. Intellectual property rights are also normally limited in time. More generally, intellectual property law is designed to balance the economic interests of creators in reaping the rewards of their efforts against those of society in having access to a free flow of new ideas.

Clearly, what counts as property in one area of the law is not necessarily what counts as property in another.[9] Treating something as property in the context of the Due Process or Taking Clause,[10] for example, will reflect different concerns and have different consequences than calling something property in the context of the mail fraud statute.[11] Determining whether things like body parts, contraband, and trade secrets should count as property for purposes of theft law thus requires a complex analysis. We will need to consider both the goals (and consequences) of theft law itself and the underlying concerns that color the "propertization" of such things on their own terms.

Why the Label *Theft* Matters

Much of the analysis that follows focuses on the extent to which it is proper to apply the label *theft* or *stealing* to describe certain violations of an owner's property rights. In some cases, I will contrast the concept of theft to concepts of trespass, infringement, and unauthorized use or joyriding. (I shall use the general term *misappropriation* to refer to all of these various types of property violations across the board.) At some point, such distinctions may seem formalistic. Tony Smith, for example, has suggested that the debate over whether information is or is not property (and therefore subject to theft) is a "sterile" one, and that the real question should be "whether or not the criminal law [generally] is a proper vehicle for the protection of" such things.[12]

Certainly, the question of criminalization is important. But, as described in Chapter 2, whether we call something *theft* rather than *trespass, unauthorized use,* or *joyriding* does in fact matter. Each term connotes a specific kind of property violation. Trespass, unauthorized use, and joyriding all refer to an unauthorized, though temporary, use of another's property. These offenses violate a property owner's right to *exclude.* Theft, by contrast, connotes something more permanent and more substantial. To say that some property has been stolen is to say that its owner has not only been denied the right to exclude others from use, but that he has also been denied the right to possess and make full use of the property himself.

The importance of such labeling is well illustrated by the practice of the Department of Justice, Congress, courts, and the movie and music industries, each of which has sought to invoke the image of stealing or theft (or piracy) when they refer to copyright infringement, trademark infringement, and misappropriation of trade secrets.[13] Congress and the state legislatures have also passed laws applying to "identity theft" and "stolen valor." To label something as "theft" or "stealing" is a significant rhetorical move and it deserves scrutiny. From a practical standpoint, calling something "theft" matters in terms of how an offense is formulated, classified, and codified; how such lawbreaking is viewed by the general public; the level at which punishment will be assigned; and how prosecutorial policy will be carried out. It also matters from a theoretical standpoint: Since the goal of this book is to develop a coherent and comprehensive account of theft law, we need to know which cases are at the core, which are the outliers, and which are outside the category entirely.

Conceptual Tools

To determine what should count as property for purposes of theft law, it will be helpful to consider the basic economic concepts of commodifiability, rivalrousness, excludability, and zero-sumness.

Commodifiability

The concept of commodifiability is most familiar in the context of debates over whether to permit the sale of things such as sex (as in prostitution), reproductive capacity (as in surrogacy), and bodily organs (as in kidneys for transplant). Law and economics and libertarian scholars tend to argue that, the broader we commodify, the better for society, because markets offer an efficient means of distributing scarce resources.[14] Liberal theorists, by contrast, argue that, while markets do have their uses, too much commodification undermines other important social values, such as personal dignity and social justice.[15] Scholars also raise the question of commodifiability in literature on intellectual property law, seeking to explain what kinds of information, if any, should be subject to legal protection.[16]

Rather than speaking of commodifiability in the prescriptive sense (i.e., whether a particular good or service *should* be allowed to be bought or sold), I use it here primarily in the descriptive sense (i.e., whether something *can* be bought or sold). For purposes of this discussion, I distinguish among three different kinds of noncommodifiability: (1) things that are illegal to possess, buy, or sell (such as contraband drugs and weapons); (2) things that are illegal to buy or sell but not to possess (such as human organs); and (3) things that are not illegal to buy, sell, or possess, but which seem to be intrinsically incapable of being bought or sold (such as love and admiration).

A thing's ability to be bought or sold, whether legally or illegally, is a necessary condition for its being subject to theft. Things that are incapable of being bought or sold should therefore fall outside the reach of theft law. This is consistent with the approach taken in the Model Penal Code Commentary, which defines property as something "that is a part of one person's wealth and that another person can appropriate."[17] It is also consistent with the idea that the purpose of theft law is to protect our system of property rights. In addition, some things, though capable of being bought and sold, should nevertheless fall outside the scope of theft law on account of independent policy concerns (I have in mind here things like slaves and human corpses).

Rivalrousness and Excludability

Rivalrous goods are goods the use or consumption of which by one consumer prevents simultaneous consumption by other consumers.[18]

Some goods are rivalrous because they are "used up" and can no longer be used by others. For example, after I drink my glass of Pinot Noir, there will be none left for you. Other goods are rivalrous because of crowding effects: if I'm using my razor to shave, you can't use it at the same time. There are also rivalrous *services*: If Dr. Freud is treating Rat Man, he cannot also be simultaneously treating Wolf Man (unless they are in group therapy). In contrast, *nonrivalrous goods* may be used or consumed by one consumer without preventing simultaneous consumption by others. Most examples of nonrivalrous goods and services are intangible. Broadcast radio is an example: when a consumer turns on a radio set, this does not prevent the radio in another consumer's house from working. Similarly, if the singer Norah Jones were to perform live in Central Park, one person's enjoyment of the concert would not preclude others' (at least up to the point at which there was overcrowding).

A good or service is *excludable* when it is possible to prevent access by people who have not paid for it.[19] It is *nonexcludable* when it is not possible to do so (or, more precisely, when the cost of keeping nonpayers from enjoying the benefits of the good or service is prohibitive). An example of an excludable good is my rickety old Trek bicycle, which I store in a shed behind my house. If Jones played Carnegie Hall, her performance would also be excludable. An architecturally appealing structure, such as the Chrysler Building, by contrast, creates an aesthetic, nonexcludable good, which can be enjoyed by anyone who happens to look at it.[20]

Goods that are both rivalrous and excludable are called *private goods*.[21] Examples include essentially any tangible consumer good (jelly beans, grandfather clocks, umbrellas, etc.). If I own an umbrella, my use of it tends to diminish your ability to use it; our use is therefore rivalrous. It is also excludable because I can put the umbrella in my briefcase and thereby prevent you from using it. Virtually all of the things I have so far talked about as being subject to theft are private goods.

Goods that are neither rivalrous nor excludable are called *public goods*.[22] An example frequently given is national defense, which is nonrivalrous because the fact that citizen *X* is protected does not diminish the protection that citizen *Y* receives and is nonexcludable because it is not possible to exclude protection for *X* if he lives in the same locale as *Y*.

There are also two intermediate categories. Goods that are rivalrous without being subject to exclusion are referred to as *common goods.*[23] Examples are natural resources, such as fish that are found outside national waters. Goods that are excludable without being rivalrous (at least until congestion occurs) are known as *toll goods* or *club goods.*[24] Examples include baseball games played in stadiums and movies seen in movie theatres. Also typically included in the category of toll goods are things protected by intellectual property laws—copyright, patent, trademark, and trade secrets. Without such laws, the words, ideas, images, and sounds that underlie such property would be pure public goods; there would be nothing to prevent them from being copied endlessly, thereby resulting in a "tragedy of the commons." By enforcing copyrights and patents through the threat of sanctions—by introducing excludability (though not rivalrousness)—intellectual property law thus *transforms* information from a public good to a toll good.[25] Theft law itself also has the potential for making what would otherwise be public goods, such as intangible information, into excludable, and thereby protectable, toll goods.

Theft as a Zero-Sum Transaction

Which of these various categories a given good or service falls into will, along with its commodifiability or noncommodifiability, determine whether, and in what manner, it is subject to theft. Theft, crucially, involves a transfer of property from owner to offender. As described in Chapter 2, this transfer can be thought of in terms of a common sense (if not strict economic) notion of "zero-sumness":[26] what the thief gains, the victim must lose.

Private goods are obviously subject to zero-sum transactions and therefore (assuming they are also commodifiable) are potentially subject to theft. If a thief steals my bicycle, for example, I no longer have it. Indeed, theft law was originally designed with exactly these kinds of goods in mind.

The harder question concerns the theft of public goods. Because public goods are nonrivalrous, it would seem that they are not subject to zero-sum transactions. What would it mean, for example, to steal national defense? So long as I live in the geographic location that is protected, my protection will not be diminished by your use. People receive the benefits of public goods regardless of whether they pay for them. (The only possible context in which a person might be said to have stolen a public good like national defense is if he failed to pay taxes and yet continued to reap the benefits of residence. Some commentators have indeed spoken of tax evasion as a form of theft, though in an earlier work I explained why I think this characterization is inaccurate.)[27]

In other circumstances, however, public goods do seem potentially subject to zero-sum transactions. For example, if I have information that is valuable in virtue of its being confidential, and you take that information from me and make it public, I still have the information, though it is now clearly worth less (or possibly nothing) to me. Does this taking count as a zero-sum transaction? Should it count as theft?

STEALING NONCOMMODIFIABLES

Despite the broad language with which property is defined under modern consolidated theft law, clearly not every thing of value can be stolen. I propose that we begin narrowing the field by considering (1) things that are illegal to buy, sell, or possess; (2) things that are illegal to buy and sell, but not to possess; and (3) things that are seemingly incapable of being bought or sold.

Things Illegal to Buy, Sell, or Possess: Contraband and Stolen Goods

Imagine that a *D* misappropriates drugs from their illegal possessor. Should *D* be prosecuted for theft? The problem, it seems, is that the possessor lacks any lawful proprietary interest in the property stolen. Were she to bring a civil suit for tortious conversion, trespass to chattel, or misappropriation, she would likely fail.[28] Given this, can an argument be made that the possessor's unlawful claim to property should also not be protected by the law of theft? Should we be satisfied with prosecuting the drug thief for drug possession as well? Might prosecuting the drug thief for theft have the perverse effect of reinforcing the arguably antisocial idea that people should have proprietary rights in illegal goods? Or are the concerns of theft law so broad that it is meant to apply even when the person from whom the property is stolen has no lawful interest in it?

If ever there was a case in which the "contraband is not property subject to theft" argument should have seemed plausible, it was the 1923 New York Court of Appeals decision in *People v. Otis*.[29] The defendant was charged with stealing a quantity of whiskey, which, under the provisions of the National Prohibition Act, was then illegal to possess.[30] The act expressly stated that "no property rights shall exist" in liquor illegally possessed. "How then," the court asked, "may there be larceny of such liquor? If we give the broadest possible construction to these words, there is no answer; for it must be conceded that to enforce [Prohibition], Congress may declare that to steal liquor shall no longer be a crime. It might think it wise to license theft so as to discourage intoxication."[31]

Despite such language, however, the court ultimately rejected this approach, concluding that the statute in question was "merely a police regulation, adapted to aid the enforcement of the prohibition law and to be applied with that end in view."[32] It was not intended to make liquor exempt from theft. Thus, even in the face of language to the effect that no property rights shall exist, the court held that contraband was still property for purposes of theft.

Virtually all Anglo-American authorities agree that stealing contraband does constitute theft, notwithstanding the status of such property in civil law. For example, the MPC specifically says that the term *property of another* is intended to include within its meaning even property that could not be recovered by the theft victim by civil means because it was used in an unlawful transaction or was subject to forfeiture as contraband.[33] Case law is also clear that one who steals property which itself has been stolen by another may be prosecuted for theft or robbery notwithstanding the illegality of the victim's possession.[34]

This seems to me basically the right approach. As I argued in Chapter 2, theft, as a criminal offense, is intended not merely, or even primarily, to protect the interests of individual property owners; that is the purpose of the private law of conversion, misappropriation, and trespass to chattel. Rather, the law of theft is largely intended to protect the interests that society as a whole has in the system of private property. If people were free to steal each other's illegal drugs and weapons with impunity, that would undermine society's sense of property security and create a potential for violence, notwithstanding the fact that such things are illegal to own.[35]

And what about stealing property that is already stolen? In Wagner's opera *Das Rheingold,* the Nibelung Alberich steals the *Rheingold* from the Rhine maidens and makes a ring of power. Wotan, the king of the gods, wants the ring for himself. Loge, the god of fire, advises Wotan: "What a thief stole, you steal from the thief."[36] Loge seems to be saying that there is no wrong in Wotan's stealing from Alberich since Alberich himself has stolen. Is he right? Should stealing stolen property count as theft or shouldn't it? More precisely, should stealing stolen property count as (1) theft, (2) possessing stolen property, (3) both theft and possessing stolen property, or (4) no crime at all?

In Chapter 3, I argued that possessing stolen property should be regarded as a lesser form of criminality than theft proper; although the receiver perpetuates the deprivation of property caused by the thief, he does not cause it himself. The rights that Wotan would be violating would be the Rhine maidens', not Alberich's, since Alberich has no legitimate property interest in the *Rheingold.* This would suggest that Wotan should be charged with possessing. On the other hand, Wotan is not *merely* possessing. He takes the ring from Alberich through a combination of deceit and force. There is a broader societal interest, as in the case of stolen contraband drugs and weapons, in preventing people from stealing each other's things, even when such things have already been stolen. For these reasons, the more appropriate charge would be theft. (Charging both receiving *and* theft, however, would be overkill in the same way that it would be overkill to charge any thief, who by definition is also possessing stolen property, with both offenses.)

Things Illegal to Buy and Sell, but Not to Possess

While illegal drugs and weapons and stolen property are illegal to buy, sell, *or* possess, other kinds of things, though they are (or arguably should be) illegal to buy or sell, are not illegal to possess. In this section, I consider the theft of human beings, body parts, sex, and animals.

Human Beings

In slave-owning societies like ancient Rome and the pre-Emancipation American South, human beings were treated as property, and those who stole them could be prosecuted for theft.[37] This was true whether the slave stealer's motives were virtuous (say, he wanted to help the slave attain freedom), or base (he wanted the slave to work on his plantation rather than for his "lawful owner"). Children were also viewed as a kind of property, and the crime of child-stealing, known in Roman law as *plagium,* constituted a form of theft as well.[38]

Although international human rights law and all decent people today condemn slavery as among the most fundamental violations of human dignity, the practice, sadly, still exists. Human trafficking—involving both sexual exploitation and forced labor—remains an immense, and growing, problem.[39] Given how valuable a "commodity" human beings are in the international slave trade, it is no surprise that there are cases in which captives are "stolen" by one trafficker from another.[40] Should such cases be treated as theft?

Following the analogy of contraband drugs and weapons, one might think that the answer should be yes and that the trafficker/thief should be prosecuted for both trafficking and stealing. I am skeptical, however, about such reasoning. I argued above that if people were free to steal each other's illegal drugs and weapons, that would have the effect of undermining society's sense of property security. I doubt that the same can be said of people stealing other people's slaves. Indeed, one could not prosecute the stealing of human beings without implicitly endorsing their commodification. To bring such prosecutions would thus lend credibility to the morally noxious practice of slavery itself.

Dead Bodies, Tissue, and Body Parts

Consideration of how the law should treat the stealing of living persons leads naturally to the question of how to treat the stealing of corpses and dead body parts, as well as bodily tissue obtained from living persons. As one commentator has put it, the view that it is anathema to treat human beings as chattel has "indelibly influenced the development of the law concerning [corpses and] separated bodily materials."[41] The focus here is on three characteristic cases:

- In the early 2000s, a dentist named Michael Mastromarino allegedly masterminded a scheme in which hundreds of corpses, obtained from funeral homes around the New York area, were cut up and their bones, skin, and tendons sold for use in transplants and other medical procedures. The body parts were taken without the consent of the decedents' families and often against their express wishes. Among the decedents whose body parts were taken was Alistair Cooke, the long-time host of the PBS series *Masterpiece Theatre.*[42]

- In the early 1990s, doctors at the University of California Irvine Center for Reproductive Health fertility clinic allegedly took eggs from as many as sixty unsuspecting women during examinations, fertilized the eggs with sperm from unspecified donors, and planted the resulting zygotes and embryos in other women, who in some cases bore children.[43]

- In 1976, a man named John Moore started treatment for leukemia at the UCLA Medical Center. His doctors quickly became aware that some of his blood products were potentially of great commercial value. They took numerous samples of various bodily fluids, in some cases without any independent medical rationale. Without Moore's knowledge or consent, one of his doctors produced a cell line from Moore's tissue, patented it, and sold rights to the cell line to a biotechnology firm.[44]

For each case, can what the defendants did reasonably be treated as theft?

Let us begin with Mastromarino. As with contraband drugs, body parts are valuable commodities that can fetch high prices on the black market. In virtually every jurisdiction, they are illegal to buy or sell.[45] Unlike contraband drugs, however, body parts are obviously not illegal to possess. Yet to say that a body is capable of being possessed is not necessarily to say that a body can be stolen. At common law, corpses were not considered property for purposes of the law of larceny.[46] Was the common law approach the right one, or would it have made sense to treat Mastromarino's misappropriation of corpses and body parts as a form of theft?

In the actual case, Mastromarino pled guilty to numerous counts of "body stealing," racketeering, and reckless endangerment and was sentenced to eighteen to fifty-four years in prison. Despite its title, however, New York's "Body Stealing" statute is not really about theft. The statute makes it a crime to "remove[] the dead body of a human being, or any tissue, organ, or part thereof from a grave, vault, or other place, where the same has been buried, or from a place where the same has been deposited while awaiting burial, without authority of law."[47] This strikes me as the right approach. The main concern of such laws, like all grave-robbing and corpse-desecration laws, should be to protect the sanctity of human bodies after death.[48] Whatever proprietary rights the decedent's family might have in the remains of their loved one are limited.[49] Once again, the idea that persons, even after they have died, should not be propertized should prevail.

When body parts are used as the raw material to create some new "product," however, a different result arguably should follow. Under the Australian case of *Doodeward v. Spence,* "when a person has by the lawful exercise of work or skill so dealt with a human body or part of a human body in his lawful possession that it has acquired some attributes differentiating it from a mere corpse awaiting burial, he acquires a right to retain possession of it."[50] *Doodeward* constitutes an important exception to the traditional rule that body parts cannot constitute property. Thus, in the English case of *R. v. Kelly,* forty human body parts, all of which had been preserved as anatomical specimens, were taken from the Royal College of Surgeons without permission for use by an artist. Consistent with the doctrine in *Doodeward,* the court held that such parts *did* constitute the College of Surgeons' property within the meaning of Section 4(1) of the Theft Act.[51]

How should such considerations bear on the resolution of the Irvine fertility case? Despite the fact that the women who had their ova appropriated without their permission were (in contrast to the decedents in the Mastromarino case) very much still alive, it would, I believe, still be wrong to say that the rights they had violated were proprietary. The wrongs that such women must have felt upon learning that their eggs had been taken without their permission, fertilized with a stranger's sperm, and implanted in another's woman's uterus, were not at all like the wrongs that one feels as a result of a theft. These women suffered a severe blow to their procreative autonomy and sense of privacy—more like rape, I would think, than stealing.

In fact, this is more or less the logic that the actual Irvine case followed. Orange County prosecutors (apparently following the reasoning in the *Moore* case, discussed below) concluded that they could not charge the doctors with theft because human eggs did not constitute property for purposes of California's theft statute.[52] Instead, the two doctors at the center of the scandal were indicted for insurance fraud (they fled the country, however, and were never tried); more than a hundred civil suits for fraud and negligence were brought by former patients of the clinic; and California law was ultimately amended to include a separate offense of unauthorized use of sperm, ova, or embryos[53]—in essence, a "tissue desecration" statute."[54] This nonproperty approach seems to me essentially the right approach.

Finally, there is *Moore v. Regents of the University of California*. Moore sued for civil conversion, and the California Supreme Court denied his claim, holding that his tissue did not constitute property for purposes of conversion law (though it also indicated that his right to informed consent *had* been violated). The decision seems largely driven by the public policy concern that extending property rights to include organs would have a chilling effect on medical research. There is no indication that prosecutors ever considered bringing a theft charge.

Moore raises a host of complex, evolving, and controversial issues that go well beyond the scope of our concerns here and which have spawned a large body of academic commentary.[55] For the moment, I simply want to observe that, from the perspective of theft law, the case should be regarded as even easier than the Irvine fertility cases. In contrast to those cases, the plaintiff here essentially abandoned whatever claim he might have had to property in his bodily tissue and fluids at the time the samples were given. He never had a proprietary interest in his excised spleen, and it did not become valuable until a significant amount of skill and expertise was applied to transform it into a marketable cell line. Accordingly, the exception articulated in *Doodeward* and *Kelly* should not apply. For this reason, I think it is clear that *Moore* did not involve a theft.

Sex

In addition to goods that are illegal to buy or sell but not to possess, there are also services that are illegal to buy or sell but not to partake of. I am thinking here primarily of sexual services, which, under prostitution laws that exist in most jurisdictions, may not legally be bought or sold. The question is whether sex can nevertheless be the subject of theft.

The issue arose in the Canadian case of *R. v. Petrozzi*.[56] The defendant was charged with rape. The complainant was a prostitute who had agreed to have sex with the defendant for one hundred dollars. The defendant conceded that he had lied when he told the complainant that he intended to pay for sex and that he had therefore committed fraud; but he contended that the act was nevertheless consensual and therefore did not constitute rape. Is the argument valid?

One possible solution turns on the traditional distinction in the law of rape between fraud in the factum and fraud in the inducement.[57] If sexual intercourse was obtained as a result of deception that caused the victim to misunderstand the very nature of the conduct in which she is engaging ("fraud in the factum"), then we say that her consent is vitiated. For example, it is rape if the victim is unaware that she has consented to the act of sexual intercourse itself, as where she was tricked by her doctor (or someone posing as a doctor) into believing that what was taking place was a vaginal examination or surgical operation when in fact it was sexual intercourse.[58] However, if the victim understands the basic nature of the transaction but is mistaken about certain material facts ("fraud in the inducement"), then her consent will not normally be vitiated. For example, it is not rape if the victim consented to sex, knowing that it was sex, but was misled into believing that her partner was a certain celebrity or that he intended to marry her.[59]

Theft law reflects no such distinctions. A defendant who obtains property from a victim by misleading her regarding the specific material terms of the agreement is just as guilty of fraud as one who misleads her regarding the basic nature of the agreement. The fact that fraud was used in the inducement rather than in the factum is no defense in the criminal law of theft, although it may in some cases affect the validity of contracts entered into.[60]

On the facts of *Petrozzi*, it seems reasonable to say that what the defendant committed was fraud in the inducement rather than fraud in the factum (assuming that the defendant's version of events is taken as true). The complainant seems to have had no misconception about the nature of the conduct in which she was engaging. What she was mistaken about was whether she would be paid for her services. Under such a reading, I would argue that the offense the defendant committed was theft by deception (false pretenses) rather than rape.

Against this analysis, one might argue that (1) to treat as theft a human trafficker's abduction of another human trafficker's slave would have the perverse effect of reinforcing the propertization of human beings; and (2) analogously, to treat as theft a case like *Petrozzi* would reinforce the arguably antisocial, demeaning, and immoral notion that sex is a commodity that can be bought and sold. Perhaps. But I am inclined to think that there are significant differences between the two cases. First, even assuming that voluntary prostitution is wrong, it is obviously not nearly as wrong as slavery. Second, it makes a difference that in cases like *Petrozzi*, it is the prostitute herself who has participated in the supposedly wrongful commodification of sex.[61] Third, to fail to prosecute the john for theft would be to allow him to escape punishment for what is clearly a dishonest act (the same is not true of the drug thief). For these reasons, I believe the better analogy is to theft of contraband drugs rather than to theft of human beings.[62]

Animals

Finally, there is the question of stealing animals. The English common law distinguished between *ferae naturae* (wild animals) and *mansuetae naturae* (domesticated animals).[63] *Ferae naturae* belonged to no one and hence could not be stolen. The only kinds of animal that could be stolen were *mansuetae naturae,* and, then, only some of these. Many early cases, reflecting the fact that larceny was a capital offense at common law, held that dogs, cats, and monkeys were not subject to theft; these cases reasoned that only animals that could be used for food and whose theft would therefore potentially cause its owner to go hungry could justify such a harsh penalty; as Coke put it, it was not fit that a "person should die for a dog."[64]

Modern law makes no such distinction among domesticated animals, any of which can constitute property for purposes of theft law. Wild animals held in captivity (as in a zoo) will also count as property. Thus, the MPC defines property to include both captured and domestic animals, and the Theft Act is understood to apply to both domesticated animals and wild animals that have been reduced to possession, so long as such reduction was made by someone other than the defendant (and provided that such person has retained possession).[65] The modern approach seems clearly right to me. That cows could be stolen while dogs could not was surely among the most arbitrary and ad hoc rule in the common law of theft; there is simply no justification for it in a world in which theft is no longer a capital offense.

However, another issue should be mentioned, one that presumably would not have occurred to the framers of the MPC or the Theft Act, but which is related to the issues I have just been considering regarding the stealing of persons, body parts, embryos, and sexual services. Various animal rights theorists have argued that animals should not be considered property to begin with.[66] While I am skeptical of this approach, its implication for theft law is worth considering. If we really were to have a regime in which animals (like people) could not be property, then it would seem to follow that animals (like people) also could not be the subject of theft. And how would we deal with cases in which animals were abducted from their human "protectors"?[67] Presumably, we would need to employ some alternative statutory scheme, one which was not premised on the idea that animals could be owned.

Things Incapable of Being Bought or Sold

Having considered the theft of things that are illegal to possess, buy, or sell, and things that are not illegal to possess, but are, or arguably should be, illegal to buy or sell, we now come to the third form of noncommodifiability—namely, things that are not illegal to buy, sell, or possess, but are in some sense *incapable* of being bought or sold. The focus here is on plagiarism and the federal Stolen Valor Act. These subjects also require a return to the concept of rivalrousness.

Plagiarism

Plagiarists have often been referred to as *thieves* or *criminals,* and plagiarism as a *crime, stealing, robbery, piracy,* or *larceny.*[68] Even some dictionaries define plagiarism as "literary theft," a definition that is consistent with the term's etymological origin, the Latin word *plagium* (which, at Roman law, referred to the stealing of a slave or child). Yet, despite such talk, the fact is that no plagiarist has ever been prosecuted for theft. The questions that need to be asked are: (1) What, if anything, does the plagiarist steal? (2) Should whatever the plagiarist steals count as property for purposes of theft law? and (3) Is the notion of plagiarism as theft anything more than just a recurring metaphorical use of the term?

In determining what, if anything, the plagiarist steals, let us consider the dynamic of the act: An author offers her work to the world by publishing it in a book or magazine or on the Internet. Anyone may read it or take ideas from it. Under widely accepted academic, literary, and journalistic norms and practices, however, the author's presentation of her ideas constitutes an offer to the effect that one may use them only on the condition that attribution is made to their originator. Under this model, A "pays" for the privilege of copying B's words or ideas by giving B credit for having been their author. Plagiarism, of course, occurs when A uses words or ideas originated by B but fails to pay B proper credit. Plagiarism, in other words, involves what Leo Katz has called the "misappropriation of glory."[69]

But is glory or, more prosaically, credit for words or ideas the sort of thing that should be considered property for purposes of theft law? There are really two questions here: (1) Is credit for words or ideas commodifiable? and (2) Is credit for words or ideas sufficiently rivalrous to meet the zero-sum requirement of stealing described earlier? In other words, does consumption of credit by the plagiarist deprive the rightful author of the good?

First, is credit for words or ideas the sort of thing that is capable of being bought or sold? Is it, in the language of the MPC Commentary, something "that is a part of one person's wealth and that another person can appropriate"? Although there are surely exceptions (one thinks, for example, of writers of instruction manuals, ghostwriters, copywriters, pseudonymous writers, and, I assume, contributors to *Wikipedia*), most writers do have an interest in public credit for their work. Indeed, for many literary and academic writers, garnering recognition is at least as, if not more, important than receiving financial compensation. Receiving credit for one's ideas offers psychic rewards that, for novelists, poets, playwrights, and scholars, are quite significant.

But to say that something is valuable is not necessarily to say that it is commodifiable. We often say that X has stolen "love" or "affection," a "kiss" or a "look," the "election" or the "show." I doubt we literally mean that X has committed a form of theft that could be prosecuted. Instead, I assume that these are figurative uses of the term, like saying that a real estate developer "raped the land" or that a lawyer's fees constituted "highway robbery." When we say that X has "stolen the election" from Y, what we mean is that X has taken something to which he is not entitled. We believe that X has wronged Y by taking something which Y has (or previously had) a claim to, but not in a way that involves the kind of proprietary harm that is characteristic of theft proper. In that sense, the usage is metaphorical.

So, when we say that a plagiarist has stolen credit from the true author, are we using the term in a metaphorical sense, or are we really saying that credit for authorship is a commodity? The question is a hard one. Certainly, recognition of one's work and the development of a reputation as a creative scholar or artist in a given field often do result, even if indirectly, in significant tangible rewards, such as tenure and promotion, pay increases, grants and fellowships, publishing contracts, job offers, lectures and exhibitions, invitations to conferences, client referrals, appointment to political or judicial office, and other forms of career advancement and compensation.[70] Indeed, the number and prestige of citations received are regarded by some academics as a means of "keeping score." In the absence of universally accepted criteria for determining academic and scholarly achievement, faculties and individual professors are often ranked by the frequency with which their work is cited. Such rankings, in turn, may be relevant to important judgments about status and reputation.

But none of this is to say that credit itself, much as we value it, can be bought or sold, borrowed, or even given away. Credit for words or ideas is something that one must earn. It cannot be bought or sold, and it is therefore noncommodifiable. Indeed, that is precisely what makes such credit so valuable within certain communities, and plagiarism so reprehensible. I would therefore conclude that the credit that the plagiarist steals cannot be property for purposes of theft law.[71] Plagiarism as theft should be understood as a metaphor, and its commission should be addressed by nonlegal means.[72]

The second question is whether, even if (contrary to what I have just argued) credit for words or ideas were commodifiable, such credit would be sufficiently rivalrous to meet the zero-sum requirement that I have argued is a necessary requirement of stealing. The answer here, I believe, is yes. The plagiarist who misrepresents himself as author of a work created by someone else deprives the true author of something—namely, credit—that the author is entitled to. The act of plagiarism therefore meets the requirement of zero-sumness.

Stolen Valor Act

Analogous in some important respects to plagiarism is the offense created by the federal Stolen Valor Act of 2005, which makes it a crime to "falsely [represent oneself], verbally or in writing, to have been awarded any decoration or medal authorized by Congress for the Armed Forces of the United States."[73] The penalty is a fine or six months in prison, enhanced to one year if the decoration involved is the Congressional Medal of Honor, a distinguished-service cross, a Navy cross, an Air Force cross, a silver star, or a Purple Heart.[74] The question I want to ask is whether use of the term *stolen* in the title of the statute and in its legislative history is anything more than a metaphor. Does it really make sense to say that a person who misrepresents himself as, say, a Medal of Honor winner, however ignoble that act, should be regarded as a thief? (I put to the side concerns about whether the statute is unconstitutional.[75]) Once again, we need to ask whether whatever it is the bogus Medal of Honor claimant is stealing is both commodifiable and rivalrous.

The Medal of Honor is the highest military distinction awarded by the U.S. government, "in the name of Congress," often personally by the president, to one who distinguishes him or herself "conspicuously by gallantry and intrepidity at the risk of his or her life above and beyond the call of duty while engaged in an action against an enemy of the United States."[76] Fewer than 4,000 Medals of Honor have been awarded (many of them posthumously) since the award was created during the Civil War.

When one falsely represents himself as a recipient of this honor, what, if anything, is he stealing? Who, if anyone, is harmed or wronged? Medal of Honor recipients are entitled to a number of material benefits from the government, including a special pension, supplemental uniform allowance, transportation, commissary privileges, a distinctive license plate, and invitations to presidential inaugurations.[77] One can also imagine a putative Medal of Honor recipient being the recipient of gifts spontaneously given by fellow citizens—say, free meals, drinks, tickets to ball games, and the like. Thus, to the extent that the putative Medal of Honor recipient is an impostor, and obtains such material things as a result of deceiving others into believing that he is the real thing, it seems appropriate to say that he has indeed committed false pretenses. But, as far as I can tell, this is not the sort of harm with which the Stolen Valor is principally concerned. And such false pretenses would in any event be covered by any number of federal false claims and fraud statutes.[78]

As in the case of plagiarism, the real focus of the Stolen Valor Act is the act of dishonestly claiming *credit* for something one has not earned—in this case, glory on the battlefield.[79] The offender induces others to think well of him by means of deception. As such, the violation of the act does not involve a harm to a proprietary interest. Like credit for literary or academic achievement, military honor is not the sort of thing that can be transferred, legally or illegally. One either earns it or one does not. Claiming credit for military honors one has not earned may or may not be the sort of act that the government should want to criminalize (I tend to think not), but it should not in any event be conceptualized as theft because the thing that is "stolen," being noncommodifiable, is not properly regarded as property.

As to whether credit for military honor is rivalrous, the result is different from the case of plagiarism. Whereas the plagiarist claims credit for a particular idea or string of words created by a particular author, the bogus Medal of Honor impostor is not ordinarily seeking credit for any *particular* act of heroism; he is not normally claiming, for example, to have performed the feats of Audie Murphy at the Battle of Holtzwihr. The plagiarist fails to give proper attribution to a particular deserving author, whereas the bogus Medal of Honor claimant misrepresents himself as one of the 4,000 or so people who have won the medal. In that sense, the bogus Medal of Honor claimant is hoping to benefit unfairly from a shared public good.

We can think of the sum total of honor conveyed by the granting of all Medals of Honor as constituting a pie. The fewer pieces of pie that are distributed, the bigger each slice will be. So, if there were, say, one hundred genuine winners and one fraudulent claimant, the value of the slices held by the genuine winners would be diminished by 1 percent. (Given this, it may seem fitting that in a 1996 case, an elderly Florida man who was convicted of wearing a fraudulent medal was required as part of his sentence to write a letter of apology to each of the then-living 171 recipients of the medal.[80]) Bogus claimants may cause some fractional harm to genuine recipients, but it is not the kind of substantial, zero-sum harm that is caused by the plagiarist.

STEALING SEMI-TANGIBLES

In this section, I consider the susceptibility to theft of several kinds of property that I shall refer to as *semi-tangibles*. These are grouped into three categories: (1) electricity, cable television transmissions, and Wi-Fi; (2) private services; and (3) public services.

Electricity, Cable, and Wi-Fi

In a vintage episode of *The Simpsons*, Homer gets a cable TV hookup and spends all of his time watching television.[81] His daughter, Lisa, becomes suspicious that the hookup is illegal (which in fact it is), and following a Sunday school lesson on the nature of hell, she is terrified that that is where Homer is headed as a result of his having violated the eighth commandment's prohibition on stealing. Lisa becomes aware of common thievery all around her. For example, she convinces Marge to pay for two grapes she's sampled in the grocery store. Eventually, Homer's conscience bothers him, and he agrees to terminate the illegal cable hookup. Reluctantly, Homer climbs to the top of the power pole in front of his house. He looks over the wires, not knowing which one to cut. The first wire he snips causes the power to go out on one side of the street; the second wire snipped causes the other side of the street to lose power. When Homer snips a third wire, the screen suddenly cuts to TV static and the credits begin to roll.

Was Lisa right? Does accessing cable television through an unauthorized hookup constitute stealing? What about illegally appropriating electricity or Wi-Fi Internet service? The law of theft has always viewed the illegal appropriation of such things with awkwardness. The problem is as old as the myth of Prometheus, who stole fire from Zeus and gave it to mortals.[82] (After Prometheus took it, did Zeus really no longer have the fire?) Despite their obvious commodifiability, such things are seemingly less tangible than things like jewelry and automobiles (though more tangible than things like copyrighted texts and Internet domain names). Moreover, they seem to exist on the borderline of goods and services.

At least as to electricity, the Theft Act and MPC take opposite approaches. The framers of the Theft Act viewed electricity, "owing to its nature," as falling outside the definition of stealing in Section 1(1).[83] Instead, they included a separate provision entitled "Abstracting of Electricity," which imposes a less serious penalty on anyone who "uses without due authority, or dishonestly causes to be wasted or diverted, any electricity."[84] The framers of the MPC, on the other hand, saw no problem in including "electric or other power" within the general definition of property in Section 223.0(6).[85] Yet most states and the federal government have nevertheless enacted a complex range of specialized provisions, both criminal and civil, regarding misappropriation not only of electricity, but also natural gas, cable transmissions, telephone connections, satellite, and other communications technologies.[86]

Was the MPC right to treat electricity and other semi-tangibles simply as goods subject to theft, like furniture or jewelry? Or should such things be treated under a separate, non-theft-based statutory framework? Part of the challenge here is simply understanding the physical realities that inform such acts of misappropriation.[87]

Electric current consists of a flow of electrically charged particles (most commonly, electrons), the intensity of which is measured in amperes.[88] Electrical power is normally generated by electromechanical generators driven by steam produced from fossil fuel combustion or by heat released in nuclear reactors. Since electrical energy cannot easily be stored in quantities large enough to meet demands on a national scale, it is produced locally by electrical utility companies that make only as much as is required. Electricity is transferred in bulk from generating power plants to substations located near population centers. It is then distributed to individual customers over wires running between the substation and the consumers' meter sockets. Consumers are typically billed by the electric company for the number of kilowatt hours used per month.

Electricity can be "stolen" in at least two ways. Some consumers tamper with the meters in their houses so as to be billed at a rate lower than their actual usage.[89] This is essentially false pretenses. Others "tap into" the wire between the substation and their homes, thereby bypassing the meter entirely. This is a kind of larceny. In both cases, the offenders are receiving electricity they have not paid for. Does this meet my paradigm of theft?

Electricity is obviously commodifiable. The harder question is whether it is also rivalrous. If I am right about the idea that theft must involve a zero-sum game, then we need to know not only what the thief gets but also what the victim, or victims, lose. There are three possibilities here.

One possibility is that the electric company is losing the revenue it *would have* earned had the user paid for the electricity used. The problem is that we can't know whether and how much electricity the user would have used had he been required to pay for it; people often tend to be less careful about electricity consumption if they know they don't have to pay the bill (witness my three children). Under this approach, the best we could do is estimate how much electricity the offender would have used in a manner analogous to the way we estimate how much in lost profits the holder of a copyright, trademark, or patent has suffered as the result of infringement.[90]

A second possibility is to say that the legal regime has essentially determined that producers of electricity have a right to be paid for their product and that those who take such goods without paying for them have committed theft. This likely accords with our intuitions, but it begs the question. Specifically, it fails to explain why unauthorized use of electricity should count as theft to begin with.

A final possibility is that what the electric company is losing is the misappropriated electricity itself. Unlike credit for intellectual creations and valor in battle, electricity has a physical reality. Only one consumer or group of consumers can use each electron flow at a given time. In that sense, electricity is a rivalrous, if dynamic and somewhat ephemeral, good. Electricity flow is often described in terms of a hydraulic metaphor, under which what is generated is pressure. When electricity is diverted from a transmission wire, the pressure in the line is reduced downstream. If enough electricity is diverted, this will result in a degradation in service to other customers. At some point, the electric company will have to build more capacity in its generators to meet increased demand. In consequence, rates to consumers are likely to increase. For these reasons, misappropriation of electricity, at least in large quantities, meets the requirement of zero-sumness.

Theft of cable television transmissions, à la Homer Simpson, presents a not quite analogous case. The Federal Communications Commission assigns every television station a specific section of bandwidth of approximately 6 megahertz.[91] The stations transmit their signals to satellites that orbit the earth. These signals are picked up and sorted by cable companies through antennas and satellite dishes, or in some cases through fiber optic networks. The cable companies pay royalties to the stations based on various methodologies that take account of their subscriber base. Once the cable companies receive the signals, they send them to cable subscribers as an electrical current through a coaxial or fiber optic cable network. When the cable signals enter a subscriber's home through the cable network, a cable box translates the signal into an image the subscriber can see on a television screen. Subscribers normally pay the cable provider a monthly subscription fee based on the selection of channels they receive.

Offenders typically "steal" cable television by making an illegal physical connection to the cable system (such as by splicing into a neighbor's cable service) or by attaching equipment (referred to as a "black box") that allows for unauthorized receipt of programming. The signal is scrambled at the main control center before transmission in encrypted form. The black box allows for unauthorized descrambling, typically allowing the offender to receive premium programming he hasn't paid for.

There are several possible ways in which the unauthorized receipt of cable television arguably deprives the cable company of a thing of value. First, the cable thief (unlike the electricity thief) normally makes unauthorized use of copyrighted material. (Whether this actually constitutes theft is discussed below.) Second, there are cases in which the cable television thief, like the electricity thief, would have paid the cable company for the service but for his misappropriation; the cable company thus potentially loses income. Third, there might be cases in which the unauthorized cable user is depriving the cable company of some physical thing, as the electricity thief does. As a general matter, however, the hydraulic metaphor is less apt in the case of cable television than it is in the case of electricity. While illegal cable hookups may cause some bona fide users to experience some degradation in service (such as lower image resolution), unauthorized usage does not normally cause the same sort of drag on resources for cable companies as it does for electric companies. The theft paradigm is therefore harder to sustain.

Finally, there is the misappropriation of Wi-Fi, a short-range networking technology that enables computers to connect wirelessly to the Internet.[92] Internet service providers (ISPs) provide access to the Internet for a fee, typically calculated on a flat monthly basis. ISPs connect to their customers using data transmission technologies such as dial-up, DSL, cable modem, wireless, or dedicated high-speed interconnects. Networks operating wirelessly must be able to receive and send data through a system of routers and adapters.

Some network operators, intentionally or unintentionally, leave their networks unprotected, allowing roaming users to access the Internet through their networks without obtaining prior consent. A roaming Wi-Fi user thus obtains a valuable service without paying for it. In a few cases, such conduct has been treated as a crime. For example, in 2006, a man in Washington State was arrested and charged with theft of services for regularly parking his car outside a coffee shop and accessing the shop's wireless network without buying any products.[93] There have been similar cases in Alaska, London, and Singapore.[94] Normally, such cases are prosecuted under specialized telecommunications or computer misuse statutes. Do they satisfy the paradigm of theft more generally?[95]

In my view, the case for treating Wi-Fi piggybacking as theft is harder to make than the case for treating an appropriation of electricity or cable as such. For one thing, there are essentially no circumstances in which tapping into an electric or cable line without paying would be regarded as permissible. There are, by contrast, many cases in which using another's Wi-Fi connection is acceptable. Many Internet network operators have no objection at all to others piggybacking on their service. Indeed, coffee shops and hotels now routinely offer their customers complimentary Wi-Fi connections. The point is not that failing to take an easy precaution against having one's property taken ipso facto constitutes consent: leaving my car sitting overnight in a high-crime neighborhood with the doors unlocked, the windows down, and the key in the ignition may be foolish, but it clearly does not constitute consent to having it taken. The point is rather that the norms of Internet usage are still evolving, and people may be genuinely confused about when piggybacking is acceptable and when it is not.[96]

The loss caused by Wi-Fi piggybacking to ISPs also tends, on average, to be less significant than the loss caused by electricity theft to the electric company. Radio waves sent out by a wireless network are in some sense abandoned if not used. If I'm not currently using my wireless connection and my neighbor piggybacks on it without my permission, no loss is suffered; my neighbor is truly a free rider. On the other hand, if the amount of piggybacking reaches a high level, there will be noticeable degradation in service, just as there is in the case of electric and cable piggybacking.[97] When wireless technologies run at or near capacity, they tend to run slower than when they are under capacity, just as traffic in the Lincoln Tunnel tends to run slower when there are more cars driving through it. Thus, one solution would be to treat as theft only piggybacking that results in an actual degradation of service.

Services

Theft law has traditionally distinguished between theft of goods and theft of services. Indeed, at common law, misappropriation of services was no crime at all.[98] For example, in *Chappel v. United States,* a pre-MPC, federal case, an Air Force sergeant was charged with theft for having ordered a subordinate during duty hours to paint an apartment that he owned.[99] Citing Blackstone's *Commentaries* as authority, the Ninth Circuit held that services do not constitute property for purposes of the federal theft statute.

American and English law both now criminalize theft of services, but their approaches to doing so differ. The MPC defines services to "include[] labor, professional service, transportation, telephone or other public service, accommodation in hotels, restaurants or elsewhere, admission to exhibitions, use of vehicles or other movable property."[100] It states that a person commits theft of services if he "purposely obtains services which he knows are available only for compensation, by deception or threat, or by false token or other means to avoid payment for service."[101]

The MPC treats theft of services as interchangeable with, and subject to the same punishment as, theft by various means (deception, coercion, failure to make required disposition of funds, and so forth).[102] As such, it makes a category mistake. Theft of services obviously does not involve a difference in the *means* by which a theft is committed. What makes theft of services distinctive is the type of property being stolen. Theft of services is thus properly contrasted to theft of goods or theft of intangibles. Theft of services can be committed by a variety of means—for example, by deception or by coercion.

The Theft Act 1968 contained no specific provision regarding theft of services. Today, the offense of obtaining services dishonestly is contained in Section 11 of the Fraud Act 2006, which replaced the former offense of obtaining services by deception under Section 1 of the Theft Act 1978.[103] Section 11 subjects a convicted defendant to a maximum penalty of five years (less than the seven years to which a theft of goods would subject him).[104] The Fraud Act contains no definition of the term *services,* although the Theft Act 1978 stated that it "is an obtaining of services where the other is induced to confer a benefit by doing some act, or causing or permitting some act to be done, on the understanding that the benefit has been or will be paid for."[105]

Both approaches—the MPC's and the Fraud Act's—present interesting issues. Services are said to be distinguishable from goods in four respects: intangibility (services involve performances and actions rather than physical objects), heterogeneity (no two services will be precisely alike), simultaneous production and consumption, and perishability.[106] Nevertheless, the line between services and goods is often unclear. Most theorists place products somewhere on a continuum between pure commodity goods on one end and pure services on the other.[107] Bespoke clothing, for example, seems in equal parts a good and a service (at least if one is the person for whom the clothes are being made). So, if *D* tricked or coerced *T* into making him a custom-made suit, should that constitute theft of goods or theft of services? Under the MPC, it would make no difference, because the Code treats both the same. But it would matter under the Theft Act, because the Act treats theft of services as a less serious crime.[108]

Unfortunately, things are even more complicated than that. In fact, there are two kinds of services, or at least two ends of a continuum along which services run. I shall refer to these two kinds of service as *private services* and *public services*. An example of a private service is a haircut provided by a barber, which is both rivalrous and excludable.[109] It is rivalrous because *D*'s consumption of the haircut prevents simultaneous use by other consumers; it is excludable because other consumers can be prevented from use. Imagine that *D* falsely promises to pay for a haircut from *H, H* performs the haircut, and *D* fails to pay. Here, *D*'s act is closely analogous to cases in which *D* deceives *H* into turning over a tangible good. Having given *D* whatever time and effort it took to cut his hair, *H* has effectively been foreclosed from using that time to earn a living. From a moral perspective, there is virtually no distinction between *D*'s tricking *H* into giving him a fifteen-dollar haircut and *D*'s tricking *H* into handing over a fifteen-dollar bottle of wine. In each case, we should say that *D* has committed theft. To the extent that the MPC would treat the two cases as equivalent, it gets things right; to the extent that English law would treat theft of a haircut as a less serious offense, it gets things wrong.

This assessment is reversed, however, when we look at the theft of *public* services. Imagine that *D* sneaks into a theater in which *P* is performing and watches *P*'s performance without paying for it. *P*'s performance is excludable, but not rivalrous. It is excludable because nonpaying consumers can ordinarily be excluded from use, but it is not rivalrous because the use of *P*'s performance by *D* does not preclude simultaneous use by other viewers, at least as long as there is no overcrowding. This situation is essentially the same as that contained in the empirical study, described in Chapter 1, involving a person who attended a lecture without paying admission. Our subjects ranked this as less blameworthy than taking the physical book. Were they right to do so? That is one of the questions I will consider in the next section.

For the moment, however, two other issues merit brief mention. First, note that in both of the theft of services hypotheticals offered, it was stipulated that *D*'s intent to deprive his victim of the money owed to him existed *at the same time* he sneaked into the theater or asked for a haircut. One can, however, imagine a different sort of case in which *D* decides not to pay *V* what he owes him until *after* he's already received his haircut. Following the argument in Chapter 2, concerning promissory fraud, it is clear that while the first case would properly be treated as theft, the second case would be merely a breach of contract.

Finally, imagine a case in which the situation is reversed and the one who fails to perform is not the employer but the employee. For example, suppose the employee spends most of the day, every day, updating his Facebook page rather than doing the work assigned to him. In some sense, the employee is dishonestly getting something (his salary) for nothing, and for this reason some commentators have argued that this should be viewed as a kind of theft.[110] But this approach seems wrong unless it can be shown that, at the time he undertook to do the job, the employee deceived his employer into paying him for a job he had no intention of performing. Absent that, such cases should also be handled as breach of contract.

Public Services

In the previous section, I offered a distinction between private services and public services, arguing that theft of private services should be treated in a manner that is closely analogous to theft of private goods. But to what extent might theft include the misappropriation of public services as well?

Recall again the results of the empirical study from Chapter 1. Subjects were asked which they regarded as more blameworthy: Sally's illegally taking a fifty-dollar physical book or illegally attending a fifty-dollar lecture. Sixty-seven percent said that taking the physical book was more blameworthy, 10 percent said that listening to the lecture without paying was more blameworthy, and 22 percent said there was no difference. In addition, 55 percent said it was worse for Sally to sneak into the hall if it was full, 7 percent said it was worse to sneak into a partially empty hall, and 38 percent said there was no difference. On a scale from 1 to 9, the average blameworthiness score was 7.65 for taking the physical book, 6.01 for sneaking into the full hall, and 5.17 for sneaking into the partially empty hall.

How can these data be explained? Why did a majority of subjects view Sally's taking the physical book as more blameworthy than misappropriating the lecture? And why did a majority think it was worse to sneak into a full hall than a partially empty one?

The first thing to note is that, unlike a haircut or massage, a lecture can ordinarily be consumed by multiple people at the same time. Sally's attendance does not preclude ABC from offering the lecture to others. A lecture is therefore not a rivalrous service in the way that a haircut or massage would be (though lectures are typically excludable). This would explain why the subjects rated taking the physical book as more wrongful than sneaking into the lecture.

This is not to say that Sally's sneaking into the lecture deprived ABC of nothing. Sally is a classic free rider; if everyone failed to pay for admission as she did, ABC would not have enough revenues to con-tinuing operating. In both cases (full hall and partially empty hall), it could be argued that Sally deprived ABC of the profits it would have received had she paid the price of admission. The problem is that the argument rests, once again, on a hard-to-prove, counterfactual assump-tion: namely, that *but for* her sneaking into the lecture, Sally *would have* paid the price of admission.

And what about the difference between sneaking into the full hall and sneaking into the partially empty hall? Why did the subjects rank the first scenario as more blameworthy? Recall that Sally "listened to the entire lecture without paying for it. The auditorium that day was full. *As a result, ABC could not sell Sally's seat to someone else who wanted to attend the lecture.*" The italicized language suggests that, in this case, someone *was* willing to pay for admission to the lecture. Sally was thus not the free rider she was in the case of the partially empty hall. But for Sally's sneaking in, ABC *would have* received the price of admission from that other person.

The loss to ABC is thus less speculative in the case of the full hall than in the case of the partially empty hall. Given the importance that the subjects apparently attached to the speculative nature of the loss, perhaps the law, in the interest of fair labeling, should reflect such a distinction. One possibility would be to require the government to prove as part of its case-in-chief that, but for the illegal admission, either the defendant or another would-be customer would have paid for a seat. This is not as far-fetched as it may seem. As noted above, copyright, trademark, and patent law all measure damages in terms of lost profits.[111] Requiring the government to prove what profits were lost as part of its case-in-chief would essentially shift the inquiry from the damages phase of the proceedings to the liability stage.

STEALING INTANGIBLES

At early common law, as discussed in Chapter 1, only property of a certain type could be subject to larceny: movable chattels such as cash, jewelry, furniture, vehicles, and other merchandise. Excluded from the protection of theft law were things at two ends of the property continuum: real property and intangible property.[112] The requirement of asportation meant that neither land nor any form of intangible property could be subject to theft.[113]

By the nineteenth century, however, the definition of what constituted property for purposes of theft law had begun to expand. Old statutes were interpreted more broadly, and new, specialized statutes were enacted to deal with the misappropriation of certain kinds of intangible and semi-tangible property. As things like licenses, franchises, business good will, and interests in stock began to occupy an increasingly important place in the economy, it is not surprising that society sought protection—wisely or not—in the criminal law.[114]

By the time theft law was consolidated in the twentieth century, the definition of property subject to theft had become strikingly broad. As described in Chapter 1, an early draft of the MPC included within the list of things that would be treated as property subject to theft "patents, copyrights, and trademarks."[115] The final draft omitted references to these specific forms of intellectual property and instead simply referred to "tangible and intangible personal property."[116] The Theft Act similarly defined property as "money and all other property, real or personal, including things in action and other intangible property."[117] And the Canadian Criminal Code said simply that one commits theft if he steals "anything, whether animate or inanimate."[118] The question to consider is not so much how these specific provisions should be interpreted, but rather the extent to which theft should be understood *from a conceptual standpoint* to encompass misappropriation of intangibles.

Information and Ideas Not Protected by Intellectual Property Law

Later in this chapter, I will consider the misappropriation of things intellectual property law *does* protect, but for now I want to consider several forms of economically valuable information to which copyright, patent, trademark, and trade secrets law does *not* apply.[119] Information itself is a hugely complicated concept, the science and theory of which have given rise to a new academic field of study.[120] I use the term here, loosely, to refer to things like compilations of names and addresses, data about stocks and bonds, patient medical histories, employee records, and diplomatic communiques. Precisely because such things do not enjoy the independent protection of intellectual property law, prosecutors have sought to rely on the general safety net provided by the law of theft to address their misappropriation.[121]

Such attempts have not always been successful. As a general matter, English and Canadian courts have tended to exclude information from the scope of property subject to theft. American courts have normally been more open to the possibility, but they have not been consistent in doing so.

Typical are three U.S. cases that send mixed signals. In the Supreme Court case of *Carpenter v. United States,* the defendant, Winans, was a reporter for the *Wall Street Journal,* one of two writers of the daily "Heard on the Street" column, which offered recommendations concerning the advisability of investing in selected stocks.[122] *Journal* policy treated such information as confidential and prohibited its use, prior to publication, by anyone other than the *Journal* itself. Winans conspired with others to trade securities on the basis of prepublication information. In affirming his conviction for, *inter alia,* fraudulently misappropriating property from the newspaper, the Court said that the intangible nature of the information misappropriated "does not make it any less 'property' " than other forms of property traditionally protected by the mail and wire fraud statutes.[123] It did not matter that the *Journal* still "had" the information even after Winans had used it.

Analogous is the Wyoming case of *Dreiman v. State.* The defendant in that case had previously been in a romantic relationship with the victim, which she broke off. After the victim changed to an unlisted telephone number, the defendant broke into her house and copied the phone number, her social security number, and her insurance policy numbers.[124] He also took tangible property. In upholding Dreiman's conviction for burglary, the Wyoming Supreme Court held that, regardless of whether he had actually taken any tangible property, he would still have been guilty of the offense, since the confidential information he took *did* constitute property for purposes of burglary law.[125]

In contrast is the Colorado case of *People v. Home Insurance Co.,* in which the defendants, investigators working on behalf of an insurance company, obtained confidential medical information concerning two patients at a Denver hospital. The physical records themselves never left the hospital file room; rather, the information in the records was conveyed over the telephone. Despite the broad definition of property in its statute, the Colorado Supreme Court applied a rule of "strict construction," and held that confidential medical information did not constitute a "thing of value" for purposes of theft.[126]

The law in England and Canada is more uniform, if only because neither country has the profusion of separate jurisdictions the United States has. In the English case of *Oxford v. Moss,* a university student dishonestly gained access to a copy of an examination in advance of its administration.[127] After reading its contents, he returned the paper to where he had found it, at no time having had an intention to steal the tangible paper itself. The question was whether such confidential information was intangible property for purposes of the Theft Act. The appellate court said no, but provided little in the way of analysis. Judge Smith said simply that it was "clear" that civil cases involving the misappropriation of confidential information were inapposite.[128] Judge Wein said that the defendant had "no intention permanently to deprive the owner of" property.[129]

Finally, in the Canadian case of *R. v. Stewart,* the defendant, as part of an effort to organize a hotel union, attempted to obtain confidential employee information, including names, addresses, and telephone numbers.[130] Had the scheme been carried out, no physical object would have been taken, just information. On appeal to the Canadian Supreme Court, the defendant's conviction for encouraging theft was reversed on the grounds that confidential information of this sort did not constitute a "thing" for purposes of the theft statute. In reaching this conclusion, the court identified the same two factors I have identified as crucial to determining whether something should be regarded as property for purposes of theft law. It said that, to be the subject of theft, a thing (1) "must be of a nature such that it can be the subject of a proprietary right" and (2) "must be capable of being taken or converted in a manner that results in the deprivation of the victim."[131]

With respect to the first factor, although it conceded that confidential information had been subject to protection in various civil cases, the *Stewart* court reasoned that such protections had "arise[n] more from an obligation of good faith or a fiduciary relationship than from a proprietary interest."[132] With respect to the second factor, the court said that, as a general matter, only tangible objects can be subject to the kind of deprivation that theft law requires "because if one appropriates confidential information without taking a physical object, for example by memorizing or copying the information or by intercepting a private conversation, the alleged owner is not deprived of the use or possession thereof."[133] In the end, however, the court seems to have decided the case primarily on the basis of judicial restraint, stating that "the realm of information must be approached in a comprehensive way, taking into account the competing interests in the free flow of information. . . . The choices to be made rest upon political judgments that . . . are matters of legislative action and not of judicial decision."[134]

So, should the information at issue in these cases have been considered property subject to theft or not? In each case, I think the information taken was indeed commodifiable, since information of these sorts is sold, legally and illegally, all the time.[135] The harder question is whether the taking of such information was rivalrous in the way that theft law requires. To answer that question, we need to look at each case individually.

At first glance, information seems to be a classic, nonrivalrous public good: even if you copy down, without my permission, my telephone number, social security number, insurance policy numbers, medical information, exam questions, or employee information, I have not, it would appear, lost anything. On first look, then, the zero-sum paradigm seems unfulfilled.[136] But a fuller, more meaningful inquiry would consider whether the value of the information taken in each case was so substantially reduced as to cast doubt on its continued usefulness. The principle is similar to that found in Section 77 of the draft Scottish Criminal Code (proposed in 2003 but never enacted), which says that a person (1) commits theft if he steals, (2) steals if he deprives another of property, and (3) deprives another of property if, *inter alia*, he "*depriv[es] that person of its value.*"[137]

Was this test met in these five cases? In *Dreiman*, the defendant copied an unlisted phone number, social security number, and insurance policy numbers. The social security number and insurance policy numbers were not confidential, and there is no reason to believe they lost their value when the defendant copied them down. But a different analysis should apply with respect to the victim's unlisted phone number. The whole point of having such a number was to avoid contact with her former boyfriend. By copying the number and thereby eliminating its confidentiality as to him, the defendant deprived the victim of the number's essential value. In that sense, the unlisted phone number was stolen while the social security and insurance policy numbers were not. A similar analysis should probably apply in the case of *Moss.* In my view, where even a single student obtains the questions in advance, the integrity of the exam is compromised and its basic value negated. In such a case, it makes sense to say that a theft has occurred. A harder question is presented by the other three cases. Without more information than is given in the opinions, it is difficult to say whether or not the prepublication information at issue in *Carpenter* (traded on by only a small handful of investors), the medical information at issue in *Home Insurance,* and the employee information at issue in *Stewart* retained their basic value even after being copied and used.[138]

And what about the recent case of WikiLeaks founder Julian Assange, who obtained copies of hundreds of thousands of confidential U.S. State Department documents from a leaker, believed to be Army intelligence analyst Bradley Manning? In late 2010, Assange began giving the files to leading news organizations around the world to publish in their respective publications. Assange subsequently published the information on his own site. Putting aside questions about whether Assange and others violated the Espionage Act, it is worth asking whether any theft-related crimes might have been committed. To answer this question, we first need to ask whether information of this sort constitutes property that can be stolen. I assume that such information is commodifiable (if only on the black market). The harder question, again, is whether it is rivalrous. It appears that the State Department was not actually deprived of any physical documents; everything that was disseminated consisted of computer copies of documents of which the State Department retained the "original." Once again, then, we need to ask whether the revelation of such confidential information deprived the State Department of its basic value. I would say yes; if there is any kind of information the value of which is tied to its confidentiality, it is probably information related to international diplomacy and national security.

If I am right about this, then we would need to ask what theft and theft-related crimes were committed and who committed them. First, I would say that Manning, the Army analyst who allegedly leaked the documents, breached his duty of confidentiality to the Army and converted the information to his own use; he therefore committed a kind of embezzlement. Assuming that Assange encouraged, aided, or abetted Manning in his act, then Assange could be regarded as an accomplice to theft or possibly a coconspirator. As for the news organizations, I assume that they were not involved until after the theft had already occurred. Nevertheless, they certainly knew that the information had been stolen, and instead of "returning" it to the State Department, they published it in their publications. The media companies could then, theoretically at least, be prosecuted for receiving stolen property. Of course, whether any of these sorts of prosecution would be good policy—especially in light of the public's supposed "right to know"—is an entirely different question.

At this point, it is worth noting a certain conceptual convergence that has occurred. To commit theft, one must take or assume control over another's property with the intent to deprive him of it permanently. The focus of this chapter is on the kinds of property subject to theft. But, as I have just shown with respect to information, simply because something counts as property for purposes of theft in one context does not necessarily mean it will count as property for purposes of theft in another. Whether something should count as property subject to theft will often turn not only on whether it *can* in some conceivable case be taken from its owner permanently, but also whether its owner actually *has* in some particular case been deprived of his property.

Identity Theft

Probably no theft-related crime has received more media and government attention in recent years than identity theft. It has been called the "fastest growing crime in America" and the "crime of the new millennium."[139] According to a study conducted by Javelin Strategy & Research, the number of consumer victims of identity fraud in the United States increased 12 percent to 11.1 million adults in 2009, while the total annual fraud amount increased by 12.5 percent to $54 billion.[140]

The term *identity theft* first became common starting in the late 1990s as the Internet was coming into widespread use.[141] States began passing laws specifically aimed at combating the problem,[142] and Congress in 1998 enacted the Identity Theft Assumption and Deterrence Act.[143] The subject of identity theft has also generated a significant amount of attention from social scientists, legal academics, and government agencies, who have sought to measure the prevalence of the crime, the means by which it is committed, its impact on victims, and the means by which it might be controlled.[144] But identity theft has attracted relatively little attention from criminal law theorists.[145] In this section, I aim to develop a conceptual analysis of this important crime.

Under both federal and state law, the term *identity theft* typically refers to the unauthorized use of another's identity or personal information for the purpose of (1) obtaining property or economic benefit of some sort or (2) committing some other, nonproperty offense, such as drug trafficking or terrorism.[146] I shall not be focused on cases in which the offender seeks to obtain property or commit some other crime by means of using a *false* identity, as opposed to using the identity of a *real* person. Nor shall I be directly concerned with cases in which the identity used belongs to a decedent.[147]

Understood in the first sense of using another's identity or personal information to obtain property, identity theft typically involves two distinct *actus reus* elements and two distinct kinds of victim. With respect to *actus reus,* the identity thief must, first, obtain or possess another's personal information (such as credit card numbers, date of birth, social security number, mother's maiden name, password, or personal identification number). Often, this obtaining will be done by illicit means, such as housebreaking, deception, threats, force, computer hacking, phishing, telemarketing frauds, or intercepting mail. Indeed, there is evidence that obtaining personal information for use in identity theft is now one of the main motives for much burglary, robbery, theft from cars, and pickpocketing.[148] But identity information can also be obtained by legal means, such as where a waiter, clerk, sales representative, hospital employee, or landlord comes into possession of such information in the course of performing his job (we can think of this as a kind of "identity embezzlement"[149]), or where the identity thief rummages through a trashcan or dumpster looking for personal information.[150]

The second *actus reus* element consists of using the information to obtain property or credit or to avoid arrest or otherwise hide one's identity from law enforcement. This second step is carried out by taking over an existing account, opening a new account, using a credit or debit card, filing for a tax refund, obtaining a rental car, giving false information to a police officer, and the like. Typically, the identity thief will use the assumed identity repeatedly until the identity's usefulness is exhausted. Often, the victim of identity theft will not even know that he has been victimized until long after the fact.[151] Some identity thieves also sell identity information to others and "breed" additional identity-related documents such as driver's licenses, passports, and visas.

Identity theft also typically involves two kinds of victim. The first is the individual whose identity is stolen, usually referred to as a *consumer* victim. Such a person can suffer inconvenience, embarrassment, reputational injury, time wasted, bad credit, and monetary loss. The second kind of victim is the financial institution duped by the use of the stolen identity—the credit card company, bank, retailer, rental car agency, or other seller of goods or services. These institutions are typically the ones who absorb most of the financial loss.

With respect to the institutional or business victims, identity theft is basically indistinguishable from false pretenses. The identity thief uses a particular form of deception—the assumption of a false identity—to trick the institutional victim into handing over property. Although the scope of modern identity thefts may be larger than traditional frauds,[152] and may be carried out using new computer technologies, the basic moral content of the act—in terms of harms and wrongs—is no different from other frauds. And to the extent that false pretenses is properly understood as a form of theft, it is therefore also appropriate to think of this aspect of identity theft as a form of stealing.

What is especially interesting, and seemingly novel, about identity theft, however, are the harms and wrongs caused to the individual or consumer victim, the person whose identity is used without his permission. Such harms can be painful and traumatizing. In T. C. Boyle's novel *Talk Talk,* for example, a "high-living lowlife"[153] named Peck Wilson obtains a driver's license and credit card using the identity of a young deaf woman named Dana Halter. Such use causes Dana great inconvenience and embarrassment: she's arrested and jailed for an offense Peck committed, she loses her job, and finds herself being dunned by bill collectors for past-due accounts she never opened. A victim's assistance counselor tells Dana she's not alone in having had her identity misappropriated:

> [S]he trot[s] out one horror story after another: the woman who had her rental application swiped from the desk in her landlord's office

and wound up with some thirty thousand dollars in charges for elaborate meals and services in a hotel in a city she'd never been to, as well as the lease on a new Cadillac, the purchase price and registry of two standard poodles and $4,500 for liposuction; the twelve-year old whose mother's boyfriend assumed his identity till the kid turned sixteen and was arrested when he applied for a driver's license for crimes the boyfriend had committed; the retiree whose mail mysteriously stopped coming and who eventually discovered that thieves had not only filed a change of address but requested his credit reports from the three credit reporting agencies so that they could drain his retirement accounts, cash his social security checks and even appropriate the 200,000 frequent flier miles he'd accumulated. And it got worse: deprived of income, the old man in question—a disabled Korean War veteran—wound up being evicted from his apartment for non-payment of rent and was reduced to living on the street and foraging from Dumpsters.[154]

As traumatic and invasive as this aspect of the crime undoubtedly is, however, does it make sense, conceptually, to call it theft? Exactly what kind of property, if any, is the identity thief misappropriating when he passes himself off as someone else? Can such misappropriation really be understood as stealing?

The identity thief could be stealing two kinds of thing. The first thing he seems to take is personal *information* about his consumer victim, such as her driver's license number, credit card numbers, passwords, and the like. Such information is obviously commodifiable; there is a tremendous market for its sale. The problem, however, is determining whether such information should be regarded as rivalrous. Once again, we need to know the precise nature of the defendant's interference with his victim's property.

In cases where the identity thief uses O's identity information just once or twice, O will probably not lose the ability to use such information herself. O still has her property. The classic zero-sum paradigm of tangible property theft is thus not satisfied. D has committed, at most, trespass or unauthorized use.

But one can also imagine cases in which the use of O's identity information is so extensive that O would lose the ability to use the information herself. A difference in degree thus becomes a difference in kind.

The principle is roughly analogous to one discussed in Chapter 2. There I presented cases in which the unauthorized borrowing of property was treated as theft when such borrowing resulted in a major portion of the property's economic value being lost (think again of a formerly fresh baguette borrowed, without the owner's permission, for the week). Here, the suggestion is not that the identity thief merely intended to borrow the victim's identity. Rather, it's that unauthorized use of another's identity information should be treated as theft in those cases where such use causes the victim to effectively lose the use of her property. At some point, the value of such information becomes so depleted that it makes sense to say that it has been stolen. Crucially, in such cases, the identity theft victim is deprived not only of her ability to exclude others from use of her property but also of the ability to use the property herself. This is essentially what happened in Boyle's fictional case. Peck's use of Dana's identity information was so damaging that it had the effect of substantially reducing the value of the information to Dana herself, at least in the commercial setting. With Peck using her identity, Dana could no longer get a loan, use her credit card, or avoid custodial arrest.

The idea that a relatively limited taking of information does not constitute a theft while a more substantial one does finds a useful analogy in American constitutional law. Under the Takings Clause of the Fifth Amendment, governmental regulations that impact property rights do not normally constitute a constitutional taking requiring the payment of just compensation, but when those regulations go "too far," in Justice Holmes' words, just compensation is required.[155] Exactly how far is too far, of course, can be quite difficult to say, both in the Takings context and in the theft context. Conceptually, however, the basic principle that a difference in degree can constitute a difference in kind seems sound.

The second candidate for property taken by the identity thief is, as the name of the offense would suggest, the victim's personal identity itself. Whether such a thing should count as property presents a tough issue. On the one hand, it is true that, in many states, the right of publicity affords individuals a property-like interest in the use of their name, likeness, photograph, portrait, voice, and other personal characteristics in connection with the marketing of products and services.[156] Individuals who have their names or images used commercially must be compensated, and if they are not, they can sue for damages. On the other hand, there is a difference between allowing one's name, likeness, or other personal characteristics to be used in return for payment and actually selling one's identity. I would argue that personal identities are nontransferable and therefore noncommodifiable. My identity is mine and yours is yours, and we could not transfer them to each other even if we wanted to.

To the extent that we are concerned about the injury to the victim's identity (as opposed to the injury to his personal information), a better model than theft would be the common law crime of false personation. False personation has traditionally involved passing oneself off as a police officer or other public official. For example, the federal false personation statute applies to anyone who "falsely assumes or pretends to be an officer or employee acting under the authority of the United States" and "in such pretended character demands or obtains any money, paper, document, or thing of value."[157] But the crime has also sometimes been more broadly defined to include any passing off as another person to obtain some benefit or avoid some penalty, including cases where a person stopped by the police gives a false name to avoid arrest.[158] Whichever way it is defined, false personation involves a distinct, noneconomic harm that results from the offender's passing himself off as someone else.

Intellectual Property

Whether intellectual property of various sorts should constitute property for purposes of theft law presents among the most complex and pressing set of issues dealt with in this book. I begin by considering (1) how government and the entertainment industry have used the rhetoric of theft law to characterize the infringement of intellectual property; (2) the extent to which social norms are consistent or inconsistent with such rhetoric; and (3) some of the broader conceptual and policy issues that are implicated. I then evaluate a range of specific forms of intellectual property in which the infringement-as-theft claim has been made: copyright, patent, trademark, and trade secrets. I shall argue that the fact that one form of intellectual property infringement does or does not meet the criteria for theft does not necessarily mean that other forms of intellectual property infringement will yield the same result.

Intellectual Property and the Rhetoric of Theft

The idea that infringement of intellectual property should be conceived of as a form of "theft" or "piracy" shows up in a range of contexts on the American scene. The terms are used most commonly in connection with copyright infringement, which is probably the intellectual property offense most likely to be committed by members of the general public, and therefore the offense about which those who use the terms most want to see the public "reeducated." (Infringement of patents and misappropriation of trade secrets both tend to be the province of commercial firms in competition with the owner of intellectual property; infringement of trademarks is committed both by those who produce and those who consume counterfeit goods.)

My main focus here will be on use of the term *theft* rather than *piracy*. Piracy is arguably a subcategory of theft. Its core meaning is violent theft or kidnapping at sea, but it has also been used, at least since the early eighteenth century, to refer to the unlawful reproduction of copyrighted works or plagiarism.[159] As such, the term is doubly problematic. Not only does it imply that misappropriation of intangibles is like misappropriation of tangibles, but it also implies that violent theft is like nonviolent theft. For present purposes, it is unnecessary to deal much with intellectual property piracy except to note its rhetorical force. Instead, I shall focus mainly on intellectual property theft.

As early as 1999, in announcing the U.S. Justice Department's initiative to make intellectual property crimes a "major law enforcement priority," then-Deputy Attorney General (now Attorney General) Eric Holder emphasized that unauthorized downloading of intellectual property is "theft, pure and simple," and that "those who steal our intellectual property will be prosecuted.[160] Similarly, Deputy Assistant Attorney General John Malcolm, whose department oversees copyright infringement cases, said to expect more of these kinds of prosecutions because "there does have to be some kind of public message that stealing is stealing is stealing."[161]

The Departments of Justice and Commerce have also sought to use educational and public relations campaigns to convince the public, especially young people, that Internet "piracy is theft" and that "pirates are thieves."[162] One of the first such efforts grew out of a Department of Commerce white paper recommending that:

Certain core concepts should be introduced at the elementary school level—at least during initial instructions on computers or the Internet, but perhaps even before such instruction. For example, the concepts of property and ownership are easily explained to children because they can relate to the underlying notions of property—what is "mine" versus what is "not mine," just as they do for a jacket, a ball, or a pencil. At the same time that children learn basic civics, such as asking permission to use somebody else's pencil, they should also learn that works on a computer system may also be property that belongs to someone else.[163]

The white paper was followed by the launching of the Justice Department's brightly colored, cartoon-filled "Cyberethics for Kids" Web site laying out "Rules in Cyberspace" in an easy-to-follow list of dos and don'ts, which includes:

DON'T steal copyrighted computer programs ("software") by copying it from the Internet. This is the same as stealing it from a store. People work hard to develop new programs and deserve to be paid for them. If software designers don't get paid for their work, they can't continue creating new software, such as new educational games or tools that help with schoolwork.[164]

The Obama administration has in no way backed down from such rhetoric,[165] and the idea that intellectual property infringement is theft continues to be reflected in the practice of the Department of Justice's Bureau of Justice Statistics, the most important collector of data on criminal justice matters in the United States, which classifies statistics on all enforcement of federal intellectual property laws under the general rubric of *Intellectual Property Theft*.[166]

The movie and music industries, meanwhile, have waged their own campaigns to convince the public that infringement is a kind of theft.[167] For example, in 2004, the Motion Picture Association of America (MPAA) produced a brief video that appeared before program content on many DVDs. The voiceover and text of the ad said:

> You wouldn't steal a car.
> You wouldn't steal a handbag.
> You wouldn't steal a mobile phone.
> You wouldn't steal a DVD.
> Downloading pirated films is stealing.

> Stealing is against the law.
> Piracy: it's a crime.[168]

In addition, in a raft of civil lawsuits brought against major distributors of peer-to-peer file sharing software such as Napster, Grokster, and Scour.com, as well as thousands of individual alleged file sharers, the entertainment industry again repeatedly invoked the language of theft.[169] As the longtime MPAA President Jack Valenti, echoing Justice Department officials, put it in announcing the filing of a lawsuit against Scour.com, "This is about stealing, plain and simple. Creative works are valuable property and taking them without permission is stealing, whether you download movies illegally or shoplift them from a store. Technology may make stealing easy. But it doesn't make it right."[170]

The same equation of illegal use of intellectual property with theft shows up in the legislative context (presumably owing, at least in part, to heavy lobbying by the entertainment industry). For example, when Congress chose to criminalize copyright infringement not involving an economic motive or commercial benefit, it did so in a statute entitled the "No Electronic Theft Act."[171] When it enacted the Economic Espionage Act of 1996, it made it a crime to "steal" confidential information, and explicitly labeled the offense "theft of trade secrets."[172] And when it passed the Prioritizing Resources and Organization for Intellectual Property Act of 2008 ("PRO-IP Act"), which increases civil and criminal penalties for trademark and copyright infringement, members of both houses repeatedly emphasized the view that such activities constitute a form of theft.[173]

Social Norms

To what extent do ordinary citizens (at least in the United States) agree with the view espoused by their government and the entertainment industry that infringement of intellectual property is akin to theft?[174] Most citizens have relatively little opportunity to infringe patents or steal trade secrets, or to be the victims of such conduct, and probably do not have strong views on its wrongfulness. Ordinary citizens are more likely to have the opportunity to infringe copyrights (and perhaps trademarks, when considering whether to purchase counterfeit goods), and there are in fact a significant amount of data regarding people's practices and attitudes with respect to such conduct.

According to studies conducted by the Pew Internet & American Life Project in the middle of the last decade, somewhere between 14 and 29 percent of respondents reported that they had downloaded music files from the Internet.[175] Another 15 percent said they had downloaded video files. About a third of these users said they were using peer-to-peer networks, on which downloads are usually illegal. Fifty-eight percent of music downloaders said they "did not care about the copyright" on the files they downloaded, as opposed to the 27 to 37 percent who said they did care.[176] Certainly, the incidence of unauthorized downloading of material from the Internet remains far higher than the incidence of theft of tangible goods.[177] For example, it has been estimated that between 50 and 90 percent of all computer software used is unauthorized.[178] The music industry contends that more than 2.6 billion infringing music files are downloaded every month.[179] Copyright infringement alone is estimated to cost about $58 billion and 373,000 jobs a year.[180] One can hardly imagine the kind of dystopian society we would be living in if the incidence of tangible property theft were even a fraction of that rate.

At the same time, it appears that significantly fewer people were making illegal downloads when the last Pew study was conducted in 2004 than when the earlier studies were conducted in 2002 and 2003—exactly the period in which the music and motion picture industries were most aggressive in pursuing lawsuits and in employing their public relations campaigns. Thus, in 2004, about a third of the former music downloaders—close to six million Internet users—said they had "turned away from downloading."[181] If nothing else, we can say that social norms in this area are in flux.

Exactly why many people seem to have abandoned such practices, at least for a time, is unclear, however. Four possibilities come to mind: One is that former downloaders now refrain from such conduct because they have been convinced that illegal downloading really is equivalent to theft, or at least is morally wrong to some extent. A second is that, whether or not they believe that illegal downloading is morally wrong, the former downloaders are afraid of possible lawsuits and criminal prosecutions if they download and get caught. A third possibility is that, with the closure of Web sites such as Napster, illegal downloading has become more difficult. A final possibility is that, with the advent of popular electronic services like iTunes, legal downloading has become more convenient.[182]

The empirical study described in Chapter 1 offers some useful insights here. Recall that subjects were asked which they regarded as more blameworthy: illegally taking a fifty-dollar physical book or illegally downloading a fifty-dollar computer file. Fifty-six percent said that taking the physical book was more blameworthy, 3 percent said that downloading the computer file was more blameworthy, and 41 percent said there was no difference. On a scale of 1 to 9, the average blameworthiness score was 7.65 for taking the physical book as compared to 6.30 for taking the computer file.

These data suggest that the general population may well be split on the question of infringement/theft equivalence. While a majority of people believe that, other things being equal, illegal downloading is *not* as blameworthy as stealing a tangible object, a significant minority of people (44 percent) believe that it is. A significant percentage of people also seem to believe that, even if illegal downloading is not *as wrong as* physical stealing, it is still wrong to some significant degree.

Background Issues in Intellectual Property Law

As suggested at the beginning of this chapter, one of the challenges in deciding what kinds of property should be subject to theft is balancing the demands of theft law with the demands of other law that governs the property sought to be protected. The challenge is particularly acute in the context of intellectual property law—a highly complex subject, with an ever growing body of legislation and an immense academic literature that reflects a wide range of fiercely fought policy and conceptual debates. For present purposes, it will have to suffice to identify only the most prominent landmarks.

One question is whether and to what extent intellectual property should even be regarded as "property" in the first place.[183] From a conceptual standpoint, the question is an important one because, if one assumes that intellectual property *is* analogous to tangible property, a range of implications about how to protect such property follows. Among these is the notion that the wrongful taking of intellectual property potentially constitutes theft. If one believed that intellectual property was *not* property, however, it is hard to see how theft law could ever apply. As a means of control, one would presumably have to look to other approaches, such as regulatory or tort law.

A second and even more important question is, regardless of whether intellectual property is or is not property, how should it be regulated? There are two competing policy demands here. On the one hand is the problem of free riders. Anyone with access to a photocopier or a computer, broadband Internet connection, and peer-to-peer sharing software can easily engage in low-cost, large-scale copying.[184] If competition from subsequent copies reduces the price to the marginal cost of production, then the initial publisher will have little or no incentive to distribute the work in the first place.[185] To ensure sufficient incentive, intellectual property law gives creators limited rights in their creative outputs so that they may profit from their innovation and be motivated to produce even more new ideas.[186] Copyright, in other words, substitutes legal excludability for physical excludability.[187] The public, in turn, benefits from the opportunity to obtain ideas and inventions it would not otherwise have access to.

On the other hand, we should be cautious about providing *too much* protection to intellectual property. The purpose of copyright (and, by extension, other forms of intellectual property law) is, in the words of the Constitution, to "promote the progress of science and the useful arts."[188] While restrictive intellectual property laws protect ideas from free riding, they also potentially impose barriers to others who want to use those ideas to make new inventions of their own, or to create new works of art, or write new works of scholarship. For this reason, intellectual property rights tend to be more limited in time and scope than rights in tangible property, and such rights are granted only when certain basic threshold requirements for protection are met. As Eduardo Moisés Peñalver and Sonia Katyal have put it, "[i]ntellectual property rights, though robust, are nonetheless frequently relativized by countervailing interests like freedom of expression, freedom of imagination, the right to innovate, and other public-welfare considerations."[189] The question of how exactly to balance creators' incentives to create with the public's right to access new ideas is, in essence, *the* question that divides so-called intellectual property (IP) minimalists from IP maximalists. Maximalists maintain that intellectual property should be heavily protected so that people will continue to have economic incentives to produce more intellectual property. Minimalists maintain that intellectual property should be only loosely controlled to allow the free flow of information.

Yet another question concerns the extent to which criminal law, whether in the guise of theft or not, plays an appropriate role in regulating intellectual property. The criminal law offers the most severe sanctions that can be imposed in a civil society and presents the risk that not only socially harmful conduct but also socially beneficial conduct will be deterred. Minimalists almost invariably reject the use of criminal sanctions, except perhaps for the most egregious violations.[190] But even those maximalists who favor an expansive approach to intellectual property rights would presumably concede that civil sanctions are ordinarily to be preferred over criminal ones.

Although I cannot hope to resolve these issues here, they are worth keeping in mind as the discussion proceeds.

Distinguishing among Types of Intellectual Property

Intellectual property law is hardly a monolith. While all forms of intellectual property share some important characteristics, there are also significant differences.[191] Even if we were to determine that one form of intellectual property infringement was or was not theft-like, we could not thereby conclude that other forms of intellectual property infringement were or were not necessarily theft-like as well.[192] We need to look at each of the major forms of intellectual property—copyright, patent, trademark, and trade secrets—on an individual basis.

Before beginning, I offer four brief clarifications. First, for purposes of discussion, I shall be focusing on the basic elements of these various forms of intellectual property as they exist, and as they differ from each other, under American law, while recognizing that they may not be formulated the same way in other jurisdictions. Second, I shall be focusing for the most part on worst-case scenarios—cases in which the infringer intended to infringe and in which the infringement was unambiguous. Third, the various forms of intellectual property that I will be dealing with should not be thought of as mutually exclusive. For example, when people say, loosely, that Facebook founder Mark Zuckerberg was sued for allegedly "stealing the idea" for his social network site from several Harvard classmates who allegedly had it first,[193] they are (or should be) using that as a shorthand for describing a lawsuit that alleges both copyright infringement and misappropriation of trade secrets (as well as breach of contract, breach of fiduciary duty, unjust enrichment, unfair business practices, and intentional interference with prospective business advantage).[194] Fourth, and perhaps most importantly, my goal at this point is not to determine whether it would be good policy, from the perspective of intellectual property law, to allow prosecution for misappropriation of copyright, trademark, patent, and trade secrets (though I touch on this issue in the final section of the chapter), but simply whether it makes sense within the conceptual framework I have been developing to think of misappropriation of intellectual property as a form of theft.

Copyright. Copyright law is meant to protect "original works of authorship" that are fixed in a tangible form of expression.[195] These include literary works, musical compositions, plays, motion pictures, sound recordings, architectural works, photographs, visual art, computer software, even, apparently, yoga postures and tattoos.[196] Copyright protection extends only to the expression of an idea, not the idea itself.[197] Copyright law gives the author a number of exclusive rights in the protected work, including the right to make copies and to distribute it to the public, have it performed, and displayed. It also provides the right to control derivative works, such as translations and screenplays that are based on the protected work. Such exclusive rights are limited by several important doctrines, the most important of which is the fair use doctrine, which allows limited unauthorized use of copyrighted works in contexts such as educational activities, news reporting, literary and social criticism, and parodies.[198] Rights in copyright are also limited in terms of duration—the life of the author plus seventy years.[199]

Copyright infringement occurs when someone other than the copyright owner violates any of the itemized rights without the owner's permission.[200] Thus, it is infringement to copy, adapt, distribute, perform, or display a protected work unless the act is expressly exempted (as in the case of fair use or first sale). Infringement actions can lead to injunctive relief, damages, and criminal sanctions. Criminal sanctions are reserved for cases in which the infringement (1) was committed for purposes of commercial advantage or private financial gain or (2) involved copyrighted works having a total retail value of more than $1,000.[201]

Is copyright infringement properly understood as a form of theft? (I put to the side the practical question whether, given the preemptive effect of federal copyright law, a state criminal prosecution for theft could actually be brought.[202]) Authorities significantly disagree on this question. On the one hand are statements from prosecutors, legislators, the entertainment industry, and at least some commentators to the effect that copyright infringement by downloading should be thought of as "stealing," "piracy," or "theft pure and simple."[203] On the other hand, various authorities have expressed skepticism about such an approach. Most significant is the Supreme Court's 1985 decision in *Dowling v. United States*, in which the defendant was charged with violating the National Stolen Property Act, which makes it a crime to transport over state lines stolen "goods, wares, [or] merchandise."[204] The defendant had allegedly conspired to transport unauthorized recordings he had made of copyrighted songs performed by Elvis Presley. In reversing the conviction, the Supreme Court rejected the government's argument that copyright infringement was an attack on the value of a copyright owner's property tantamount to or actually theft. The Court reasoned that:

> The copyright owner . . . holds no ordinary chattel. A copyright, like other intellectual property, comprises a series of carefully defined and carefully delimited interests to which the law affords correspondingly exact protections. . . . Thus, the property rights of a copyright holder have a character distinct from the possessory interest of the owner of simple "goods, wares, [or] merchandise," for the copyright holder's dominion is subjected to precisely defined limits.
>
> While one may colloquially link infringement with some general notion of wrongful appropriation, infringement plainly implicates a more complex set of property interests than does run-of-the-mill theft, conversion, or fraud. As a result, it fits but awkwardly with the language Congress chose—"stolen, converted or taken by fraud"—to describe the sorts of goods whose interstate shipment [the statute] makes criminal.[205]

The majority opinion in *Dowling* thus makes clear that, at least within the context of the National Stolen Property Act, the Court does not regard copyright infringement as a species of theft. And there is English law to the same effect.[206]

Thinking of copyright infringement as theft is indeed problematic, but for reasons different than those emphasized by the Court in *Dowling*.

The real problem is not that copyright is "carefully defined and carefully delimited" by doctrines such as fair use. There are many cases in which rights in real or personal property are limited in duration and by various restrictions on use, and yet theft law would still apply. Imagine, for example, that F establishes a trust that gives his son, S, the right to live in Blackacre Manor during S's lifetime and to have use of all of the fixtures therein. Assume that under the trust, ownership of the house and fixtures will pass to F's granddaughter upon S's death. Assume further that the trust also prohibits S from removing, disposing of, assigning, alienating, or encumbering any of the fixtures in the house. Now imagine that D breaks into Blackacre Manor one night and steals a valuable painting hanging on the wall. Despite the fact that S's interest in the painting was limited in duration and scope of use, we would have no problem at all saying that the painting was clearly property that could be stolen and that D had therefore committed theft. By analogy, the fact that rights in copyright are limited in duration and scope of use should not by itself preclude the applicability of theft law.[207]

The real question is whether the kind of property protected by copyright law, though clearly commodifiable, is rivalrous and therefore subject to the kind of zero-sum transaction that theft law requires.[208]

To answer that question, consider the following hypothetical and its three variations. O has written a copyrighted monograph with a limited market potential (just for fun, we can say it's an obscure book on the moral theory of theft law). The work is available for downloading from the publisher's Web site for forty dollars. The publisher anticipates that it will sell about a thousand copies of the work and that almost all of these will be purchased by libraries and by a relatively small group of readers in O's field, most of whom belong to the same small number of professional associations.

> *Variation 1*: D^1 wants to read the monograph but does not want to pay the price charged, so she makes an illegal download for her own personal use.
> *Variation 2*: D^2 thinks that forty dollars is too much for anyone to pay, so she downloads the book from the publisher's Web site, makes a thousand digital copies, and sells them (or gives them away—it makes no difference) to libraries and individuals whom she has reason to believe would otherwise buy the book.[209]

Variation 3: The paywall on the Web site where O's book is being sold is easily circumvented, and a thousand of the otherwise most likely buyers—librarians and readers D^3 through $D^{1,002}$—each acting independently of each other, make illegal downloads of the work for their own use.

Which, if any, of these cases involves stealing?

The first thing to observe is that, in all three cases, O and O's publisher still "have" the work even after the illegal downloads have occurred: in none of the cases has D taken the only copy that O has. The material protected by copyright is thus a nonrivalrous public good and the classic zero-sum paradigm of tangible property theft would seem not to be satisfied.[210]

Nevertheless, in each case, O has lost, or potentially lost, something of value. In the first variation, D^1 potentially deprives O of the income he might have received had D^1 paid for the download. The situation is analogous to the case of Sally, who sneaked into the hall to hear ABC's lecture in the empirical study. O has suffered a limited setback to his interests in property: D^1 has used O's property without his permission, but he has not deprived him of it. We can say at most that D^1's conduct involves an act of trespass, unauthorized use, or unjust enrichment.[211]

In the second variation, by contrast, D^2 potentially deprives O not only of the income he would have received had D^2 paid for the work, but also of the income he would have received had the thousand other potential buyers paid for it. D^2 has cut into O's potential revenues much more significantly than D^1. Indeed, the economic value of O's property has been virtually negated. The situation here is analogous to the case of extreme identity theft in Boyle's novel. Once again, a difference in degree becomes a difference in kind. As in the case where D borrowed O's fresh baguette for a week, D^2's conduct here satisfies, or comes close to satisfying, the zero-sum paradigm that exists in cases of tangible goods. In such cases, we should be able to say that a theft has occurred.

As for the third variation, note that the total loss to O is the same as in the second variation. The difference is that no single agent is responsible for such loss. Instead, the responsibility is spread among a thousand independently acting agents, each of whose individual culpability is indistinguishable from D^1's. The harm is significant in the aggregate, but no single offender or group of offenders is sufficiently culpable to justify criminalization.[212]

Patent. Patent law provides rights to inventors of new, useful, and nonobvious inventions, including chemical, electrical, and mechanical products and processes, as well as other pragmatic innovations in fields ranging from biotechnology to business methods.[213] An invention is judged useful if it is minimally operable towards some practical purpose; and it is judged nonobvious if it is beyond the ordinary abilities of a skilled artisan knowledgeable in the appropriate field.[214] To receive a patent, an inventor must file a patent application with the United States Patent and Trademark Office (PTO). The PTO examines applications to ensure that the invention meets the requirements of patent law. As in the case of copyrights, the term of patents is limited. Under current law, for patents filed on or after June 8, 1995, the term of the patent is twenty years from the earliest claimed filing date.[215] Granted patents confer the right to exclude others from making, using, or selling the patented invention. They may also be assigned or licensed to others.

Patent infringement occurs where the infringer "without authority makes, uses, offers to sell, or sells any patented invention."[216] Patentees may file a civil suit to enjoin infringers and obtain monetary damages. Under current U.S. law, patent infringement is not a crime, though it is treated as such in a number of other countries, including Japan, Brazil, and Thailand; and proposals to make patent infringement a crime have been raised from time to time in the context of international law.[217]

Patent infringement has on occasion been spoken of as a form of theft, though such usage is less common than in the context of copyright or trade secrets.[218] Is there an argument that patent infringement should properly be understood as such? Under U.S. law, the infringer's intent is mostly irrelevant. An individual who was previously unaware of the existence of the patent in question, or even of the whole patent system, may nevertheless be found to be an infringer.[219] Furthermore, a large percentage of patents do not hold up upon scrutiny. One study of around three hundred litigated patents found that 46 percent of them were invalidated.[220] Thus, a potential infringer often cannot be certain whether she is violating a legitimate patent.[221]

For purposes of analysis, however, I will focus on cases of clear, direct, and willful patent infringement.[222] The facts of *Avia Group International, Inc. v. L.A. Gear California, Inc.* provide a good example.[223] L.A. Gear sold a shoe known as Model No. 584 ("Boy's Thrasher") that was designed and manufactured by the Taiwanese firm Sheng Chun. Avia, believing that the L.A. Gear shoe infringed its patent for an ornamental design used on an athletic shoe outer sole, sent L.A. Gear a letter demanding that it desist from selling the Boy's Thrasher model. L.A. Gear then sent a letter to Sheng Chun stating, "[u]rgently need pattern corrections on Style 584 as to avoid infringement on AVIA Model 750. Sending these fax ideas for possible solutions." Sheng Chun responded by stating that pattern modifications were "impossible." L.A. Gear proceeded to place an order for manufacture of the shoe with the infringing patent anyway. A court subsequently determined that Avia's patent had been infringed. It permanently enjoined L.A. Gear from further infringement and awarded Avia substantial damages and attorney's fees.

Is an intentional patent infringement case such as this (admittedly, not the typical case of patent infringement) properly understood as theft? The analysis is similar to that of copyright infringement. L.A. Gear's use of Avia's patent was nonrivalrous in the sense that it did not impact Avia's ability to use the invention in any way. But this is not to say that Avia did not suffer a loss. Because L.A. Gear did not pay a license fee for use of the patent, Avia lost income it might otherwise have earned. That, by itself, would not be enough to constitute theft on my account, however, since it only speaks to Avia's ability to exclude, not its ability to use. At most, it would constitute unauthorized use.

Based on the facts as presented in the opinion, it is impossible to say whether L.A. Gear's unauthorized use of the patent was so extensive that it deprived the patent owner of the basic value of the patent. Such cases certainly do exist, however. An example is arguably provided by the case of Bob Kearns, the inventor of the intermittent windshield wiper, for which he obtained his first patent in 1964. Kearns tried to interest the American Big Three automakers in his invention, but none took him up on his offer.[224] Within a couple of years, however, each company began to install intermittent windshield wipers on their cars, allegedly in violation of Kearns's patents. As a result of their infringement, the value of the patent was essentially lost.[225] By the time the lawsuits were decided (and Kearns was awarded substantial damages) the patents had expired. In such a case, we might say that the defendants' trespass was so significant that it deprived the owner of the economic value of his property and thereby crossed the threshold to become theft.

Trademark. Trademark law protects words and symbols used by a merchant to identify its goods or services and to distinguish them from those of others.[226] The symbol can be a word, a phrase, a design, an image, a sound, a color, or even a fragrance. Trademarks protect goods like *Knopf Borzoi* books, and service marks protect services like *Westlaw* computer research. To qualify as a mark, a symbol must "identify and distinguish" the good or service. A symbol becomes a mark upon bona fide use in commerce in connection with relevant goods or services. Trademarks have an initial validity of ten years upon issuance by the PTO, but owners can renew them indefinitely every ten years if the marks continue being used.[227] Trademarks can also be obtained under state common law.

To infringe a trademark, an infringer must use the mark in commerce in connection with the sale of goods or services in such a way that it is likely to cause confusion, mistake, or deception.[228] Like copyright law, trademark law has a number of doctrines that carve out certain areas of expression from control of the trademark owner, such as parodies and comparative advertising.[229] Trademark law tends to rely more heavily on private enforcement than on criminal prosecutions. Criminal penalties have applied in the realm of trademark in the United States only since the adoption in 1984 of the Trademark Counterfeiting Act, which makes it a crime to engage in the intentional trafficking of counterfeit goods or services.[230] Only the most egregious, "absolute core case of trademark infringement"—where a defendant uses the identical mark owned by a plaintiff on the same type of goods and sells those goods in direct competition in the same geographic area—leads to criminal prosecution.[231] Such cases are referred to as trademark *counterfeiting, infringement,* or *passing off.* The term *theft* is sometimes used as well, though such rhetoric is less pervasive in the realm of trademarks than in the case of copyright and trade secrets.[232]

As an example of a core case of trademark infringement, consider the facts of *Burger King v. Mason.*[233] The defendants had entered into a franchise agreement with Burger King, which gave them the right to operate a number of Burger King restaurants and use the Burger King name and various associated trademarks and forms of trade dress. The relationship then soured, and Burger King terminated the agreements, as it was entitled to do. When the defendants nevertheless continued using the Burger King trademarks, Burger King sued for infringement. The court agreed that the defendants had violated Burger King's trademarks and awarded it post-termination profits earned by the former franchisees. The suit was a civil suit, but the facts nevertheless provide an appropriate vehicle to ask whether a defendant's intentional trademark infringement can properly be understood as a kind of theft.

Trademark infringement potentially affects two kinds of victim. The first are those consumers who believe that they are buying a genuine Whopper hamburger, iPhone, or Louis Vuitton hand bag when they are really buying a counterfeit knock off. In the *Burger King* case, it is doubtful that consumers suffered much harm. Since the defendants had previously been longtime Burger King franchisees, it seems unlikely that there was much difference between the genuine licensed Whoppers they were selling prior to termination and the counterfeit Whoppers they were selling post-termination. In cases where the defendant is selling, say, counterfeit pharmaceuticals or medical devices, however, and they prove to be ineffective or unsafe, the harm can be significant. In either case, though, selling counterfeit goods under a false trademark is a kind of fraud. The seller deceives the buyer into believing that he is buying something different from what he is actually buying. What is stolen is the consumer's money, just as it would be in any case of consumer fraud.

Trademark infringement also potentially causes harm to the owner of the mark. In some cases, the holder of the mark will lose a sale when his potential customer buys the counterfeit good rather than the real thing. (This is not always true, of course; many people who buy counterfeit Louis Vuitton purses on the street corner undoubtedly know that they are fakes and have no intention of buying the more expensive, genuine article.) In such cases, we might say that what has been stolen from the trademark holder is the money he might otherwise have earned had the customer bought the real thing rather than the fake. The situation is analogous to the case in which the copyright owner loses a sale as a result of an illegal download or photocopy. The problem, once again, is that it's hard to know if, but for the infringement, the would-be infringer would have paid for the trademarked good.

In other cases, the owner of the mark is harmed by being deprived of the license fee he might otherwise have received had the seller of the counterfeit goods properly licensed the trademark. Once again we must speculate about counterfactuals. I would guess that many people who sell counterfeit Louis Vuitton purses on the street corner lack the money or inclination to pay whatever the Louis Vuitton company charges for the privilege of selling goods with its trademark. Except in those cases in which there is evidence that the infringer *would have* paid the license fee, it's hard to conclude that this is what is being stolen.

Finally, it is often said that trademark infringement has the effect of devaluing the trademark owner's brand. For example, if a consumer believes she is buying a (presumably) high-quality Louis Vuitton handbag, but actually receives a cheap Taiwanese knock off, she is likely to think less of the brand in the long run. Trademarks are thus at least semi-rivalrous in the sense that if anyone other than the trademark owner uses the mark, it will normally interfere with the benefits the owner derives from the mark.[234]

This last kind of harm is analogous to the harm caused to individuals by identity theft. Just as the identity thief makes use of the good reputation *V* has developed by paying his bills on time and staying out of trouble, the trademark infringer makes use of the good reputation built up around another's mark. In normal cases, such use will not rise to the level of theft; it will once again be closer to unauthorized use or trespass. But there are extreme cases in which the use of an owner's mark is so pervasive, the level of confusion so high, and the value of the mark so depleted, that one could say that a theft has occurred. For example, through a process referred to as "genericide," formerly trademarked names such as *Thermos, Aspirin, Yo-Yo, Escalator,* and *Cellophane* all have passed into the public domain as a result of their generic use.[235] As a result, these marks have lost virtually all value to their owners. Were this to happen as a result of intentional infringement, we might conclude that a theft had occurred.

Trade Secrets. Thomas' English Muffins are known for their distinctive "nooks and crannies," the tracery of air pockets that covers their inside surface. The technique for making Thomas' muffins is so secret that it has been split up into several pieces, including the basic recipe, the moisture level of the muffin mixture, the equipment used, and the manner in which the muffins are baked.[236] While many of Thomas' employees know one or more pieces of the technique, only seven employees in the whole company are said (at any given time) to know every step. One of these was Ralph Botticella, formerly a vice president in charge of bakery operations for the company that owns Thomas'. In January 2010, Botticella left Thomas' and accepted a job with rival baker Hostess Brands, which apparently has long wanted to know Thomas' secrets. In the actual case, Thomas' gained an injunction barring Botticella's move, and Hostess withdrew its offer of employment. But, if Botticella had gone to work for Hostess, and if he had shared Thomas' secret technique for making English muffins (which he had agreed not to share), would that have constituted stealing? More generally, should misappropriation of trade secrets be regarded as a form of theft?

To qualify as a trade secret, information must (1) have been the subject of reasonable efforts to maintain its secrecy; and (2) derive commercial value from not being generally known or readily ascertainable by others.[237] The case law reveals an enormous variety of information subject to the trade secrets laws, including lists of customers, marketing data, bid price information, technical designs, manufacturing know-how, computer programs, and chemical formulae.[238]

Misappropriation of a trade secret can occur in two basic ways. Sometimes, trade secrets are obtained by breach of a confidential relationship, as where an employee leaves her old employer and starts work on her own or for a competitor.[239] This is exactly what Thomas' feared would happen in the Botticella case. Trade secrets can also be misappropriated by those who have no special relationship to the trade secret holder, by illegal means, such as wiretapping, bribery, fraud, or theft of personal property.[240]

Traditionally, misappropriation of trade secrets was treated as a matter of state civil law under the Restatement (Third) of Unfair Competition, the Uniform Trade Secrets Act, and the Restatement of Torts.[241] Since 1996, misappropriation of trade secrets has also been treated as a federal crime under the Economic Espionage Act, which

provides for imprisonment of up to ten years and fines as high as
$5 million.[242]

There is a lively debate about exactly how misappropriation of trade
secrets should be conceptualized. Under the traditional common law
view, trade secrets law was conceived of as a means to enforce certain
standards of commercial conduct.[243] The law of trade secrets sought to
balance the need to protect business assets from interference with the
need to promote competition between businesses.[244] Under this view,
infringement of trade secrets constituted a type of unfair competition.[245]
A second view is that misappropriation of trade secrets consists of what
is essentially a breach of contract.[246] Yet another theory holds that trade
secret infringement constitutes a kind of unjust enrichment.[247]

According to what is probably the dominant view, however, trade
secrets are properly understood as a form of property. In *Ruckelshaus
v. Monsanto,* this meant that research data submitted to a federal
agency documenting the safety of the submitter's product would be
considered property within the meaning of the Fifth Amendment's
Takings Clause, and that due compensation would therefore be
required.[248] But the view that trade secrets are a form of property is
also quite relevant in the context of theft law. Indeed, in no area of
intellectual property law are the language and conceptual apparatus
of *property* and *theft* more present than in the case of trade secrets law.
Most notable is the Economic Espionage Act, which uses the term
owner to refer to one who seeks to enforce a right in a trade secret, *steal*
to refer to what the infringer does to the secret, and *theft* to refer to its
misappropriation.[249]

Like copyright law, the law of trade secrets offers less expansive
property rights than is typically found with respect to tangible property. One who holds a trade secret does not have a guaranteed right to
the exclusive use of the secret. The right to sue is triggered only when
the secret is wrongfully used or taken. If someone else independently
discovers the secret information—whether through purposeful scrutiny, luck, or accident—the original owner loses exclusive rights in it.
Thus, as Gerry Moohr has put it, trade secrets are property only in a
"conditional sense."[250] (On the other hand, unlike copyright and
patent, trade secrets law is not limited in duration; trade secrets remain
enforceable as long as they remain subject to reasonable efforts to

maintain their secrecy and derive commercial value from not being generally known or readily ascertainable by others.)

As I argued above, however, the mere fact that a property right is limited in duration or scope is not sufficient to rule out its eligibility for propertization under the law of theft. We need to consider the extent to which the owner loses and the thief gains. Consider again the case of Thomas' English Muffins. If Botticella were to share with Hostess Thomas' secret technique for achieving nooks and crannies, Thomas' would still have the information. In that sense, trade secrets are nonrivalrous. But there is also an important sense in which Thomas' would be losing something that victims of copyright, patent, and trademark infringement do not lose—namely, the confidentiality of the information. Once possessed by Hostess, one of Thomas' main rivals in the baking business, the knowledge of how to make nooks and crannies becomes significantly less valuable to Thomas'. The case is thus analogous to the "theft of confidential information" cases—*Dreiman, Moss,* Wikileaks, and possibly *Carpenter, Stewart,* and *Home Insurance*—discussed earlier. In that sense, of all the kinds of intellectual property infringement discussed, infringement of trade secrets is the one most appropriately characterized as a form of theft.

Again, this is not to say that trade secret misappropriation necessarily should be treated as a crime. There may well be compelling public policy reasons for refraining from doing so, including concerns (expressed by the court in *Stewart*) about employee mobility and incentives to produce new products and ideas. It is merely to say that the paradigm of theft seems to fit misappropriation of trade secrets more closely than it does the misappropriation of copyright, patent, or trademark.

Virtual Property

My discussion of the types of property that can properly be subject to theft concludes with a consideration of so-called *virtual goods.* To understand what is meant by this term, it is necessary to recognize two different ways that computer code functions.[251] Most computer code is nonrivalrous; one person's use does not prevent others' use. Computer code of this type is analogous to various forms of intellectual property and is most appropriately protected by the law of copyright and patent, discussed previously.[252] But there is also another type of computer code that, as Joshua Fairfield puts it, is "designed to act more like land or chattel than ideas."[253] Examples include the code associated with domain names, URLs, Web sites, e-mail accounts, and certain aspects of online "virtual world" computer games. These codes are rivalrous because, if one person "owns" the property they create, others normally cannot. For this reason, various commentators have considered the possibility that the virtual goods associated with such code should be protected not by the law of intellectual property, but rather by law that is closer to that which applies to traditional forms of tangible property.[254] To what extent should property of this type be governed by the law of theft?

The issue of domain name theft is famously presented by the case of *Kremen v. Cohen*.[255] Kremen had registered the domain name *sex.com* with the domain registrar Network Solutions. Cohen, recognizing the tremendous commercial potential of the name, came up with a plan to steal it from Kremen. He sent Network Solutions a forged letter he claimed to have received from Kremen stating that Kremen had abandoned his interest in *sex.com* and authorizing its transfer to Cohen. Network Solutions accepted the letter at face value and transferred ownership of the domain name to Cohen, who subsequently turned it into a highly profitable pornography site.

In an effort to recover the domain name and lost earnings, Kremen brought various claims against Cohen and Network Solutions, including civil conversion. In holding that a domain name did constitute property subject to conversion, and therefore allowing the claim to proceed, the Ninth Circuit, in an opinion by Judge Kozinski, reasoned that "[registering] a domain name is like staking a claim to a plot of land at the title office. It informs others that the domain name is the registrant's and no one else's."[256]

Cohen never was, as far as can be determined, prosecuted for theft or fraud.[257] With creditors at his heels (he'd been ordered to pay Kremen $65 million in damages), Cohen apparently fled to Mexico.[258] But would such a prosecution have been proper? I believe the answer is yes. Theft of domain names involves a zero-sum result in a way that theft of intellectual property ordinarily does not. Trademarks can be used by several firms simultaneously;[259] domain names cannot. Cohen's gain was very much Kremen's loss. The paradigm of theft is thus satisfied.

A final form of supposed property that raises intriguing questions for the law of theft is virtual property generated within complex online computer games known as massively multiplayer online role playing games (MMORPG). These games (the most popular one of which is *World of Warcraft*) involve computer-simulated fantasy environments in which thousands of players around the world interact with each other. MMORPG players typically pay a subscription fee to a game company for access. Players adopt alter egos known as avatars, develop relationships, achieve goals, build reputations, and accumulate virtual assets, such as "swords, armor, potions, food, jewelry, or other accessories . . . that enhance the character's ability to fight, cast spells, or move within a virtual world."[260]

Although MMORPGs are only games, the assets accumulated by their players often have significant value, both personal and economic.[261] Accumulating assets takes time and effort, which some players do not want to invest. There has thus grown up an outside, secondary "gray market" (not sanctioned, at least officially, by the gaming companies) in which virtual property is bought and sold, with real money exchanging hands on Web sites like eBay. Industry analysts estimate that trade in virtual goods of this sort ranges from $200 million to $2 billion a year.[262]

Inevitably, where goods are bought or sold, they are also stolen (and fenced). Such thefts occur both inside the game and out. Inside the game, a player may commit larceny by taking items that another player has "put down" on the ground, embezzlement by taking goods that have been entrusted to her, false pretenses by taking goods by means of a trick, or even robbery by using an "unbeatable bot—a type of computer program executed to perform automated tasks—to beat up other players' characters to acquire their goods."[263] Outside the game, hackers go phishing to obtain a video gamer's login data, use the data to log in to the game's account, and then "grab all virtual items of value in the account."[264] One estimate puts the amount of thefts in MMORPG virtual goods stolen every year at one million dollars and rising.[265]

For people who play these games seriously, these misappropriations can be quite traumatic. But so can cheating in any game or sport. Is that any reason to treat such acts as theft and prosecute them as such? Although American law has so far rejected such treatment,[266] arrests and prosecutions for MMORPG theft have occurred in China, Taiwan, South Korea, the Netherlands, and England.[267] But are virtual goods generated by MMORPGs the sort of property that is properly subject to theft as that concept has been developed in this book?

Ownership of MMORPG property, despite its intangibility, conveys a right to possess, use, transfer, and exclude. Such property is clearly commodifiable, both within the game and in the real world. Moreover, like domain names, virtual property in MMORPGs seems rivalrous in a way that various forms of intellectual property generally are not. If player *A* steals player *B*'s virtual battleaxe, player *B* typically no longer possesses it.[268] Theft of MMORPG property thus does reflect theft law's zero-sum paradigm: *D*'s gain is *O*'s loss.[269] The rights associated with such property are also, in some respects, broader than those associated with patents and copyright. For example, they are not limited by a statutory term of protection, the copyright fair use exception and first use doctrine, or the complexities of patent invalidation procedures. On the other hand, there is something admittedly impermanent about MMORPG virtual property. If a gaming company decided to "pull the plug" on its game, or even if a gamer failed to pay his monthly fee, the property might simply disappear into thin air.

CRIMINALIZATION REDUX

This chapter has focused on the question of whether the misappropriation of ostensibly nonrivalrous and noncommodifiable forms of property should be regarded as stealing for purposes of theft law. I have argued that answering this rather narrow conceptual question is crucial in determining how to formulate offenses, determine punishments, and educate the public. The mere fact that an act satisfies the paradigm of theft, however, does not necessarily mean that it should be prosecuted as such. As shown in Chapter 3, a range of prudential and practical considerations must be taken into account.

The first consideration is whether the conduct at issue is viewed by the public as unambiguously morally wrongful. There are really two sub-issues here. One is whether a given kind of property, *in general,* is the kind of property that people feel comfortable saying can be stolen. With respect to tangible things like contraband drugs, dogs, and cadavers, semi-tangibles like electricity, and private services like haircuts, this is quite plausible. As the empirical study data indicate, however, there is less consensus about the wrongfulness of misappropriating intangibles like information and public services. Norms in this area are "sticky."[270] There is a large gap between what the law regards as wrongful and what is regarded as wrongful by a significant segment of society. Moreover, as Peñalver and Katyal have explained, because of doctrines such as fair use and patentability, "intellectual property rights [are] far more complex for the average layperson to navigate than the more familiar world of tangible property."[271] Therefore, just as I previously urged caution in using the criminal law to prosecute morally ambiguous offenses such as failing to return found or misdelivered property and writing a bad check, so too would I urge caution with respect to prosecuting theft of intellectual property, information, and other intangibles.

The other sub-issue concerns not the kind of property per se, but rather the *particulars* of a given act of theft. I argued earlier that, for certain kinds of property, such as information and patented inventions, not all misappropriations will constitute theft; only those misappropriations that deprive the owner of substantial use of his property should qualify. Admittedly, my analysis involved some fairly fine distinctions. From a theoretical standpoint, I believe these distinctions are defensible and significant. I am less confident that they would be readily administrable in practice. Both offenders and juries might have difficulty in knowing whether a given instance of information misappropriation would qualify as theft. Once again, I would recommend special caution before criminalizing.

The second major issue concerns the function that theft law plays in practice. I envision at least three distinct models here. Under one model, theft would function as a freestanding crime. I am thinking here of cases involving theft of stolen noncopyrighted information (as in *Dreiman* and *Moss*), body parts, and human tissue. In such cases, there would ordinarily be no criminal offense other than theft with which an offender could be charged. Under this model, if such cases were determined to fall outside the scope of theft, the offender would go unpunished. It is in such cases that the "safety net" claim of theft law would be at its strongest.

Under the second model, theft would provide a conceptual template that would exist within an independent statutory framework. Imagine, for example, that Congress decided it wanted to enact a law intended to halt the misappropriation of copyrighted or trademarked material. In formulating its approach, it might decide to rely on the paradigm of theft, or it might not. It might decide, within the logic of "other" law, to rely solely on civil actions (as it has done in the realm of patent) or to use a different criminal law paradigm, such as trespass, unauthorized use, or regulatory violation. It might also decide that state theft remedies should be preempted by federal law. The important point is that, even in the absence of theft law, there would be plenty of alternative remedies. Treatment as theft under this model thus seems less urgent.

There is also a third model. A legislature might decide that, with respect to some conduct, even though the paradigm of theft might in some technical sense be satisfied, it would nevertheless be better not to regulate at all. I am thinking here especially of plagiarism and MMORPG theft. Conduct of both sorts matters intensely to those within the narrow community where it occurs, but relatively little to society at large. The decision to criminalize must ultimately reflect the judgment that (in Marshall and Duff's words) the conduct at issue "is a matter on which the community should take a shared and public view, and claim normative authority over its members."[272] In my view, plagiarism and virtual game theft do not meet that standard. Despite the harm such conduct causes to those affected, these offenses should be dealt with primarily by nonlegal means within the local communities in which they occur.

Conclusion

In this book, I have sought to develop an account of the theoretical foundations of theft law. My method has to been to focus on those problems that seemed to me most in need of analysis: I have not sought to cover theft law doctrine comprehensively; nor have I endeavored to develop a full-scale proposal for reform. Nevertheless, I have been unsparing in my criticism of others' attempts at theft law reform, and a reader might well wonder whether I could do any better. I believe I can, and toward that end I now offer a "how-to" guide for writing a better theft statute, featuring a checklist of eight principles I hope future theft reformers will want to take into account. Inasmuch as the checklist is derived from the analysis that precedes it, I hope it will also serve as an appropriate summing up.

Before I offer my list of principles, however, I need to explain why I have decided not to offer a "model theft statute" instead. Theft law, as we have seen, has been a much under-theorized field. This book constitutes something like a "first cut"—an attempt to identity issues, clear away conceptual underbrush, and challenge orthodoxies. My goal has been to persuade other scholars, law reformers, and, ultimately, policymakers to subject the law of theft to a thorough reconsideration. To offer a model statute at this point would be distracting; it would draw attention away from the broad underlying principles that I have sought to explore and toward the exact details of drafting. It would also be premature, in the sense that any attempt to draft an offense provision in isolation, without first deciding general structural issues concerning culpability, grading, classification, and the like, would be premature.[1]

Some of the recommendations I offer are quite broad in their scope and are therefore unlikely to elicit much objection, while others are quite specific (and therefore more likely to be controversial). None of the recommendations should be evaluated without reference to the analysis and argument that precedes them in the rest of the book. Even if future theft law reformers disagree with my substantive recommendations, I would hope that the list could at least provide a useful focus for debate.

1. Avoid overcriminalization. A theft statute should make clear which theft-related conduct will be subject to criminal prosecution, which to civil action, which to both, and which to neither. Even more than in many other areas of criminal law, overuse of criminal sanctions in the realm of theft can chill socially neutral or even socially beneficial conduct. When drafting statutes, deciding whether to prosecute, and imposing punishment, legislatures, prosecutors, and courts, respectively, should consider the extent to which the conduct in question is deserving of censure, whether it makes sense for the state (rather than, or in addition to, individuals) to pursue proceedings, whether the criminal law would be effective in preventing the alleged harms, and whether the benefits of criminalization would outweigh its costs. (These issues are dealt with in Chapter 3.)

2. Balance concerns of fair labeling with administrability. Theft provisions should respect and signal "widely felt distinctions between kinds of offences and degrees of wrongdoing" and should be "divided and labeled so as to represent fairly the nature and magnitude of the law-breaking."[2] At the same time, they should avoid overspecificity, be understandable by the general public and juries, and be readily administrable by prosecutors and the judiciary. For example, enacting a statutory scheme that distinguished between theft by deceit and theft by force would seem sensible, as would distinguishing between theft of tangibles and theft of intangibles. But enacting, as one set of commentators has recommended, a specialized identity theft statute that would distinguish among "identity larceny," "identity larceny by trick," "identity embezzlement," "identity theft by aggravated means," and "identity burglary" would constitute over-particularism.[3] (See Chapters 1 and 2.)

3. Define the *actus reus* element.   A theft statute should avoid the "taking and carrying away" language of the common law and instead include an element of "exercising control over" or "depriving another of" property. The statute should reflect the idea that theft involves a zero-sum game—that, loosely speaking, what the thief gains, the victim loses. At the same time, the statute should leave open the possibility that theft can occur even when the victim still "has" the property in question (as in the case of intangible and semi-tangible goods and some services), so long as he has been deprived of the basic value of the property. (See Chapters 2 and 4.)

4. Define the *mens rea* element.   A theft statute should require an intent or purpose to deprive the owner of his property either (1) permanently or (2) temporarily, where such temporary deprivation is for such an extended period of time that its borrowing would constitute an appropriation of a major part of the property's value. Acts involving temporary deprivation that do not meet the requirement of depriving the owner of a major part of the property's value should be dealt with under separate provisions making it a crime to engage in unauthorized use, joyriding, and the like.

- Among the elements of the statute should be *lack of consent* and *dishonesty.*
- Good faith mistakes, whether reasonable or unreasonable, that negate a defendant's intent to deprive another of property should provide a defense, but the legislature should at the same time consider creating a lesser offense of reckless or negligent appropriation of property. (See Chapter 2.)

5. Define *property* for purposes of theft law.   A theft statute needs to define *property* clearly, avoiding overly broad formulations such as *anything of value.* One possibility would be to list specific types of property that could be subject to theft, but this seems almost certain to create unintended gaps. An alternative would be to rely solely on the meaning of property as defined in civil law, but this would arguably elevate the concerns of civil law over theft law. The recommended approach would be to define property according to two basic requirements: that the good or service is commodifiable (meaning that it is capable of being bought and sold), and rivalrous (meaning that consumption of it by one consumer will prevent simultaneous consumption by others). In the case of intangible and semi-tangible goods and public services, the requirement of rivalrousness would be presumed to have been satisfied only where the prosecution has proven that the victim has been deprived of the property's basic value. (See Chapter 4.)

6. Grade theft offenses according to three independent variables: the value of property stolen, the means by which the theft was carried out, and the type of property stolen. In accordance with the goals of deterrence, a theft statute should impose penalties that are high enough to deter would-be thieves from stealing without at the same time over-deterring socially beneficial or neutral behavior. In accordance with the goals of retributivism, it should impose penalties that are proportional both horizontally (in the sense that comparably blameworthy offenders receive comparable punishments) and vertically (in the sense that more blameworthy offenders receive severer punishments than less blameworthy ones, and vice versa).

(a) Value of property stolen. A theft statute should be graded with sufficient detail to reflect significant differences in the value of the property stolen. As discussed in Chapter 1, I recommend a system of grading similar to that used in Section 2B1.1 of the Federal Sentencing Guidelines. The precise dollar amount cut offs will vary greatly depending on the wealth of a given society, and should be regularly adjusted to reflect inflation.

- Consistent with constitutional, evidentiary, and prudential concerns, courts should consider the possibility of admitting evidence regarding the specific adverse impact of the theft upon the individual victim. Such a factor could potentially serve as an aggravating factor at sentencing.
- Prosecutors should be urged to use their discretion not to bring, and courts not to convict, thefts that are considered de minimis and which can be adequately dealt with through civil proceedings or informal means.

(See Chapters 1 and 2.)

(b) Means by which theft is carried out. A theft statute should be graded with sufficient detail to reflect significant differences in the means by which the theft is carried out. I recommend four "bands" of seriousness:

1. The highest seriousness band would be reserved for
   - aggravated or armed robbery (thefts that involve the use of weapons or the infliction, or threat, of immediate serious bodily injury); and
   - aggravated looting.
2. The next most serious band would include
   - simple robbery (theft committed through the infliction or threat of non-serious bodily injury);
   - theft by means of a coercive threat to engage in unlawful conduct; and
   - theft by housebreaking (burglary).
3. The baseline band of seriousness would consist of
   - simple theft (i.e., theft committed without any of the enumerated aggravating or mitigating circumstances);
   - theft by breach of trust (embezzlement);
   - theft by deception other than that involving a false promise;
   - theft by false promise where the promise is impossible to honor or where the offender has engaged in a pattern of promises that have not been honored; and
   - theft by means of an otherwise lawful threat to expose embarrassing information unless the victim pays (i.e., informational blackmail). No other threats to engage in lawful behavior unless paid would be criminalized.
   - possession of stolen property where such possession is part of a pattern or practice of theft.
   - theft by passing a bad check where there is a pattern or practice of passing bad checks.
4. The lowest band of seriousness would contain
   - failing to return lost or misdelivered property where there is some clear duty to do so;
   - theft by false promise or deception where the evidence does not support a finding that the promise is impossible to honor or

that the offender has engaged in a pattern of promises that have not been honored;

- possession of stolen property where the evidence is insufficient to support a finding that such possession was part of a larger pattern or practice of theft; and
- theft by passing a bad check where the evidence is insufficient to support a finding that the defendant was engaged in a pattern or practice of passing bad checks.

(See Chapters 2 and 3.)

(c) Kind of property stolen. A theft statute should be graded with sufficient detail to reflect significant differences in the kind of property stolen. I recommend at least two bands of seriousness:

1. The baseline should include tangible goods (e.g., a bicycle) and private services (e.g., a haircut).
2. The less serious band should include public services (e.g., unauthorized attendance at a theater or stadium), intangible property (such as information and trade secrets), and semi-tangible property (such as electricity) where the misappropriation of such property has the effect of substantially depriving the owner of its value. If such misappropriation does not have such an effect, it should not be regarded as theft, though it may subject the perpetrator to other forms of criminal or civil liability, such as conversion, trespass, misappropriation, or unauthorized use.

(See Chapter 4.)

7. Specify how to allege and prove theft. A theft statute should specify that evidence that the defendant has committed one form of theft will *not* be sufficient to support a conviction for a different form of theft. Where an offender has allegedly used more than one means to commit a given theft, the prosecution may make use of alternative pleading, but the convicted defendant may be punished for only one form of the offense. (See Chapter 1.)

8. Reprosecution. A theft statute should provide that, if the defendant is successful in obtaining an acquittal or reversal on the grounds that he committed a form of theft different from that charged, there should ordinarily be no procedural bar to his subsequent prosecution for an alternative form of theft provided that double jeopardy rules are complied with. The defendant who has used such a defense successfully in a prior prosecution shall be estopped from arguing in the later prosecution that he actually committed the earlier offense charged. (See Chapter 1.)

*   *   *

Fifty years have passed since the promulgation of the Model Penal Code, and almost forty-five years since the enactment of the Theft Act. The world is a very different place than it was then, and our way of conceptualizing the criminal law has changed dramatically in the interim. Yet subsequent reform of theft law has been negligible, and scholarly critique has been slight. It is my hope that the analysis presented in this book will provide the impetus for needed reform.

NOTES

INDEX

Notes

INTRODUCTION

1. Regarding the number of victims and dollar loss, see Federal
   Bureau Investigation, U.S. Dept. of Justice, *Crime in the United States:
   Uniform Crime Reports,* at 6 (2010), http://www2.fbi.gov/ucr/cius2009
   /offenses/property_crime/larceny-theft.html. (During 2009, there
   were approximately 6.3 million "larceny-thefts" committed in the
   United States, accounting for some $5.5 billion in losses, excluding
   robberies, frauds, and so-called thefts of intellectual property).
   Regarding the number of offenders, studies suggest that as many as
   60 percent of American consumers have shoplifted at some point in
   their lives. Dena Cox et al., "When Consumer Behavior Goes Bad: An
   Investigation of Adolescent Shoplifting," 17 *J. Consumer Research* 149
   (1990). By way of comparison, between 30 and 60 percent of adult
   Americans (depending on age) say that at some point in their lives
   they have used illegal drugs. Office of National Drug Control Policy,
   "Drug Use Trends (October 2009)," http://www.oas.samhsa.gov
   /NSDUH/2k9NSDUH/2k9ResultsP.pdf, at pp. 95–96.

I. THEFT LAW ADRIFT

1. Quoting, respectively: Rollin M. Perkins and Ronald N. Boyce,
   Criminal Law (Mineola, NY: Foundation Press, 3d ed. 1982) 389;
   Herbert Wechsler, "The Challenge of the Model Penal Code," 65
   Harvard L. Rev. 1097, 1112–1113 (1952); James Fitzjames Stephen,

History of the Criminal Law of England (Buffalo: William S. Hein, reprint ed. 1883), vol. 3, at 143; Dale E. Bennett, "The Louisiana Criminal Code: A Comparison with Prior Louisiana Law," 5 *Louisiana L. Rev.* 6, 37 (1942); *Commonwealth v. Ryan*, 30 N. E. 364, 365 (Mass. 1892) (Holmes, J.).

2. One exception is the Australian scholar Alex Steel, whose work is discussed below.

3. See, e.g., Robert S. Jackson, "Some Comparative Legal History: Robbery and Brigandage," 1 *Georgia International & Comparative L. J.* 45, 87 (1970). The other common law offenses were Murder, Rape, Manslaughter, Sodomy, Arson, Mayhem, and Burglary.

4. William Blackstone, *Commentaries on the Law of England* (Chicago: University of Chicago Press, reprint ed. 1979), vol. 4, at *230; Perkins and Boyce, *Criminal Law*, at 343.

5. Perkins and Boyce, *Criminal Law*, at 343.

6. George Fletcher, "The Metamorphosis of Larceny," 89 *Harvard L. Rev.* 469, 474 (1976).

7. Id. at 498.

8. David Ormerod and David Huw Williams, *Smith's Law of Theft* (Oxford: Oxford University Press, 9th ed. 2007), at 1.

9. Wayne LaFave, *Criminal Law* (St. Paul: Thomson West, 4th ed. 2003), at 919–20.

10. Undoubtedly, the victim of such acts, discovering that he had been duped or betrayed into parting with his property, would be angry at the wrongdoer. Yet, as Wayne LaFave puts it, "the malefactor in these two cases is generally less available for retaliatory measures than when the owner discovers him in the process of taking the property out of his possession." Id. at 920.

11. *Anon. v. The Sheriff of London (The Carrier's Case)*, Year Book 3 Edw. IV pl. 5 (Ex. Ch. 1473), reprinted in 64 *Selden Society* 30 (1945) (creating legal fiction of "breaking bulk" where carrier had been given lawful possession of goods which he subsequently converted to his own use).

12. There are generally said to be two kinds of extortion: extortion under color of official right and extortion by means of coercion. The former offense, which was made a crime as early as 1275, is essentially indistinguishable from the crime of receiving or soliciting a bribe. Extortion of this type is not properly viewed as a form of theft and is therefore not directly relevant here. See generally James Lindgren, "The Elusive Distinction between Bribery and Extortion: From the Common Law to the Hobbs Act," 35 *UCLA L. Rev.* 815, 838 et seq. (1988).

13. 9 Geo. I, ch. 22, § 1 (1722) (repealed). See generally E. P. Thompson, *Whigs and Hunters: The Origin of the Black Act* (New York: Pantheon, 1975). Earlier, in 1567, Scotland had made it a crime to obtain property by certain written threats of physical harm to the person or property. 1567 Scot. Parl. Acts, ch. 27.

14. *R. v. Pear,* 1 Leach 212, 168 Eng. Rep. 208 (1779). The defendant hired a horse from a stable, intending from the outset to steal it. Once again, there seemed to be no trespass in the taking, since the owner of the horse had consented to Pear's possession of it. This time, the court held that a new species of larceny, which it called "larceny by trick," had been committed, a majority of the judges reasoning that the owner of the horse retained possession until the time of its conversion by the defendant.

15. 30 Geo. II, c. 24, § 1 (1757); *R. v. Young* [1789] 100 E. R. 475; Jerome Hall, *Theft, Law and Society* (Indianapolis: Bobbs-Merrill, 1935; rev. ed. 1952), at 45–52.

16. LaFave, *Criminal Law,* at 957.

17. Joshua Dressler, *Understanding Criminal Law* (Newark: LexisNexis, 5th ed. 2009) at 611–612. Another way to think about the distinction is in terms of using deception to buy property (false pretenses) and using deception to borrow or rent it (larceny by trick). LaFave, *Criminal Law,* at 928.

18. Even as late as the early nineteenth century, some judges questioned whether lost property could be the subject of larceny. E.g., *State v. Roper,* 14 N.C. 473 (1832).

19. See, e.g., F. David Reisman, Jr., "Possession and the Law of Finders," 52 *Harvard L. Rev.* 1105, 1130 (1939); Fowler V. Harper, Fleming James, Jr., and Oscar S. Gray, *Harper, James and Gray on Torts,* vol. 1, at 113–115 (3d ed. Wolters Kluwer, 2006); William L. Prosser, "The Nature of Conversion," 42 *Cornell L. Rev.* 168, 169 (1957).

20. *Wynne's Case,* 2 East P. C. 664 (K. B. 1786) (hackney-coachman convicted of larceny for keeping article left in cab).

21. Embezzlement Act 1799, 39 and 40 Geo. III, c. 89; *R. v. Bazeley,* 2 East P.c. 571 (Cr. Cas. Res. 1799) (acquitting defendant bank clerk who pocketed money given him by customer for deposit in the customer's account on the grounds that the bank never had "possession" of the money since defendant had put it in his pocket without first putting it in the cash drawer). This statute was part of a broader movement during the eighteenth century in which the expansion of theft law ceased to be a matter primarily for the courts and became instead

largely the concern of Parliament. Model Penal Code § 223.1, Comment at 128.

22. LaFave, *Criminal Law,* at 947; see also Hall, *Theft, Law and Society,* at 35–40.

23. 7 & 8 Geo. IV, c. 29, § 54 (1827); 3 Will. & M. c. 9, § 4 (1691).

24. LaFave, *Criminal Law,* at 985.

25. See Gerald H. Gordon, *The Criminal Law of Scotland* (Edinburgh: W. Green & Son, 2d ed. 1978) 515 (citing Scottish cases).

26. 12 Anne c.7 (1713).

27. 6 & 7 Vict., ch. 96, @ 3 (1843) (repealed).

28. Comment, "Criminal Law—A Study of Statutory Blackmail and Extortion in the Several States," 44 *Michigan L. Rev.* 461 (1945).

29. Perkins and Boyce, *Criminal Law,* at 335.

30. Stephen, *History of the Criminal Law of England,* vol. 3, at 128; Joel Prentiss Bishop, *New Commentaries on the Criminal Law* c.X (Chicago: T. H. Flood, 8th ed. 1892).

31. Stephen, *History of the Criminal Law of England,* vol. 3, at 153. American statutes treated it either as a misdemeanor or as a felony. Perkins and Boyce, *Criminal Law,* at 351 n.1.

32. Larceny Act 1916 (repealed).

33. Gordon, *The Criminal Law of Scotland,* at 515 (citing Baron Hume, *Commentaries on the Law of Scotland Respecting Crimes*).

34. 4 Geo. 4, c. 54. See generally Stephen, *History of the Criminal Law of England,* vol.3, at 149–150.

35. Reisman, "Possession and the Law of Finders," at 1132–1133.

36. Hall, *Theft, Law and Society,* at 56.

37. For a helpful overview, see Alex Steel, "Problematic and Unnecessary? Issues with the Use of the Theft Offence to Protect Intangible Property," *30 Sydney L. Rev.* 575 (2008). *See also* Sir William Holdsworth, *A History of English Law* (London: Methuen, 1938), vol. XI, at 530–31.

38. Geraldine Szott Moohr, "Federal Criminal Fraud and the Development of Intangible Property Rights in Information," 2000 *University of Illinois L. Rev.* 683, 687; A. T. H. Smith, *Property Offences* (London: Sweet and Maxwell, 1994), at 45.

39. Blackstone, *Commentaries on the Law of England,* at *232.

40. Dressler, *Understanding Criminal Law,* at 601.

41. LaFave, *Criminal Law,* at 934; Hall, *Theft, Law and Society,* at 84.

42. Perkins and Boyce, *Criminal Law,* at 293.

43. See generally Sir John Baker, *The Oxford History of the Laws of England* (Oxford: Oxford University Press, 2003), vol. VI, at 564–566.

44. Hall, *Theft, Law and Society,* at 82.
45. Perkins and Boyce, *Criminal Law,* at 294. As Perkins and Boyce explain, "there is no reason to suppose that English judges did not share the traditional Englishman's fondness for dogs"; the rule must be explained on other grounds—namely, concern with the harshness of the death penalty as a remedy for thefts of animals that typically had relatively little monetary value. Id.
46. Stephen, *History of the Criminal Law of England,* vol. 3, at 126.
47. LaFave, *Criminal Law,* at 295.
48. Hall, *Theft, Law and Society,* at 89.
49. Id. at 90.
50. 2 Geo. 2, ch. 25 (1729), overruling *Calye's Case,* 8 Co. Rep. 32a, 77 Eng. Rep. 520 (K.B. 1584).
51. Hall, *Theft, Law and Society,* at 89.
52. Id.
53. Thompson, *Whigs and Hunters.*
54. See, e.g., *State v. Miles,* 2 Nott and McCord 1 (S.C. 1819), cited in Hall, *Theft, Law and Society,* at 91 n.40; Texas, Act of Jan. 26, 1839, Laws of the Republic of Texas (2 Laws of Texas, 1833–1846).
55. Edward Livingston, *Complete Works of Edward Livingston on Criminal Jurisprudence* (Montclair, NJ: Patterson Smith, 1968 ed., orig. publ. 1873), vol. 2, at 163–177. Livingston offered a slightly stripped down version of the common law of theft, eliminating the term "larceny" and reference to concepts such as possession, custody, caption, and asportation, and defining "property" broadly to include anything "that can be taken," but maintaining separate provisions for theft from the person, theft by housebreaking, fraudulent breach of trust, false pretenses, robbery, receiving, and extortion, and continuing to exclude "incorporeal" property from the scope of things that could be stolen.
56. *First Report of Her Majesty's Commissioners on Criminal Law* (1834) (on common law of theft), reprinted in Parliamentary Papers, XXVI, 117 (I.U.P. 1971); *Fourth Report* (1839) (on crimes against persons and property), reprinted in Parliamentary Papers, XIX, 235; *Seventh Report* (1843) (digest of the criminal law), reprinted in Parliamentary Papers, XIX, 1183. See generally Lindsay Farmer, "Reconstructing the English Codification Debate: The Criminal Law Commissioners, 1833–1845," 18 *Law and History Review* 397 (2000). The English Law Commissioners of this period took a surprisingly "modern" view of theft, suggesting, for example, that the distinction between larceny and embezzlement is not "available on any grounds of natural justice,

civil policy, or legal analogy [and is] useless as a legal distinction for penal purposes." *Fourth Report* (1839), xlix.

57. *A Penal Code Prepared by the Indian Law Commissioners* (Union, NJ: Lawbook Exchange, 2002) (orig. publ. 1838), 48–53. Macaulay's approach was similar to Livingston's in that it eliminated reference to larceny, custody, asportation, and the like, while maintaining separate provisions for criminal breach of trust, extortion, blackmail, false pretenses, receiving stolen property, and fraud. On the creation of the Indian Penal Code generally, see Wing-Cheong Chan, Barry Wright, and Stanley Yeo (eds.), *Codification, Macaulay and the Indian Penal Code: The Legacies and Modern Challenges of Criminal Law Reform* (Farnham, Surrey: Ashgate, 2011).

58. *Report of the Royal Commission Appointed to Consider the Law Relating to Indictable Offenses* (1879), reprinted in Parliamentary Papers, VI. The Canadian Criminal Code of 1892, which was based on the 1879 report, is discussed later in this chapter.

59. Stephen, *History of the Criminal Law of England,* vol 3, at 122.

60. Id.at 143, 146.

61. Id. at 153.

62. Id. at 162.

63. James Fitzjames Stephen, *General View of the Criminal Law of England* (1863 ed.) at 129–132.

64. Id.

65. Id. at 129–130. For further discussion of Stephen's views on the reform of theft law, see Alex Steel, "The Meanings of Dishonesty in Theft," 38 *Common Law World Review* 103 (2009).

66. *Commonwealth v. Ryan,* 30 N.E. 364, 364–365 (Mass. 1892) (Holmes, J.).

67. See, e.g., Note, "Larceny by Trick: False Pretenses," 2 *California L. Rev.* 334 (1914); Note, "Larceny, Embezzlement and Obtaining Property by False Pretenses," 20 *Columbia L. Rev.* 318 (1920); Note, "Larceny—Embezzlement—Obtaining Property by False Pretenses— Effect of Minnesota Statute," 22 *Minnesota L. Rev.* 211 (1938); George Wilfred Stumberg, Note, "Criminal Appropriation of Movables—A Need for Legislative Reform," 19 *Texas L. Rev.* 117 (1941); Austin W. Scott, Jr., Comment, "Larceny, Embezzlement and False Pretenses in Colorado—A Need for Consolidation," 23 *Rocky Mountain L. Rev.* 446 (1950); J. E. Hall Williams, "Reform of the Law of Larceny: An Urgent Task," 21 *Modern L. Rev.* 43 (1958); Arthur L. Goodhart, "The Obsolescent Law of Larceny," 16 *Washington & Lee L. Rev.* 42 (1959).

68. Perkins and Boyce, *Criminal Law,* at 389; Wechsler, "The Challenge of the Model Penal Code," at 1112–1113.

69. Dale Bennett, "The Louisiana Criminal Code: A Comparison with Prior Louisiana Law," 5 *Louisiana L. Rev.* 6, 37 (1942).

70. Kansas 1968 Judicial Council Comments, K.S.A. 21–3701 (quoted in *State v. Washburn*, 979 P.2d 1272 (Kan. App. 1998)).

71. Perkins and Boyce, *Criminal Law*, at 389.

72. Note, "Larceny by Trick: False Pretenses," 2 *California L. Rev.* 334 (1914).

73. J. Edwards, "Possession and Larceny," 3 *Current Legal Problems* 127, 128 (1950).

74. *Moynes v. Cooper* [1956] 2 W.L.R. 562.

75. Dressler, *Understanding Criminal Law*, at 615.

76. Lindsay Farmer also argues for a "second metamorphosis" in theft law, though one that is still ongoing. Lindsay Farmer, "The Metamorphosis of Theft: Property and Criminalisation" (circulating draft).

77. Criminal Code (1892) § 305. For the history of the 1892 Code, see Desmond Brown, *The Genesis Of the Canadian Criminal Code Of 1892* (Toronto: University of Toronto Press, 1989); Winifred H. Holland, *The Law of Theft and Related Offences* (Scarborough, Ontario: Carswell, 1998) 35–38.

78. Canadian Criminal Code § 305 (now codified as § 322).

79. Id. at § 302 (blackmail), § 346 (extortion); § 354 (receiving stolen property); § 361 (false pretenses); § 380 (obtaining property by means of deceit).

80. Id. at § § 303, 304.

81. Winifred Holland, *The Law of Theft and Related Offences* (1998), 38. What was originally Section 305 is now Section 322. For a helpful summary of Canadian theft law, see Richard Barnhorst and Sherrie Barnhorst, *Criminal Law and the Canadian Criminal Code* (Toronto: McGraw-Hill/Ryerson, 5th ed. 2009) 303–332.

82. Law Reform Commission of Canada, *Theft and Fraud Offences* (Ottawa: Law Reform Commission of Canada, Working Paper 19, 1977); Law Reform Commission of Canada, *Theft and Fraud Offences* (Ottawa: Law Reform Commission of Canada, Report 12, 1979).

83. Mass. Stat. 1899, c. 316, § 1, Mass. Rev. Laws (1902) c. 208, § 26 (discussed in Note, "Larceny, Embezzlement and Obtaining Property by False Pretenses," 20 *Colum. L. Rev.* 318, 323 (1920)).

84. N.Y. Penal Law § 1290, N.Y. Consol. Laws c. 40 (Laws of 1909 c.88) § 1290 (discussed in Note, "Larceny, Embezzlement and Obtaining Property by False Pretenses," at 323).

85. Ariz. Code Ann. 43–5501 (1939); Cal. Penal Code Calif. § 484 (1927); La. Crim. Code Art. 67 (Act 43 of 1942); Minn. Stat. § 622.01 (1945); Mont. Rev. Code § 94–2701 (1947); Wash. Rev. Stat. § 2601 (1932).

86. *People v. Meyers*, 275 P. 219, 221 (Cal. 1929).

87. For a brief history, see Stuart P. Green, *The Louisiana Criminal Code: Ten Proposals for Reform* (New Orleans: Louisiana Bar Foundation, 2002); see also Dale E. Bennett, "The Louisiana Criminal Code: A Comparison with Prior Louisiana Criminal Law," 5 *Louisiana L. Rev.* 7 (1942).

88. Lee Hargrave, "Theft in the Louisiana Criminal Code of 1942," 52 *Louisiana L. Rev.* 1109 (1992).

89. La. Rev. Stat. 14:67.

90. La. Rev. Stat. Art. 14:67(A); La. Rev. Stat. Art. 14:2(2).

91. La. Rev. Stat. Art. 14:60 (burglary); La. Rev. Stat. Art. 14:65 (robbery); La. Rev. Stat. Art, 14:66 (extortion); La. Rev. Stat. Art. 14:68 (unauthorized use of movable); La. Rev. Stat. Art, 14:69 (illegal possession of stolen things); La. Rev. Stat. Art. 14:71 (issuing worthless checks). For further discussion of the Louisiana approach to theft, see below.

92. Quoted in Markus D. Dubber, *Criminal Law: Model Penal Code* (New York: Foundation Press, 2002), 8.

93. In 1937, Wechsler and his Columbia colleague Jerome Michael wrote a two-part article recognizing the previous lack of serious reform in the area of the criminal law and calling for a "rationalization" of the subject. Jerome Michael and Herbert Wechsler, "A Rationale of the Law of Homicide (Parts I and II)," 37 *Columbia L. Rev.* 701, 1261 (1937).

94. Charles McClain and Dan M. Kahan, "Criminal Law Reform: Historical Development in the United States—Twentieth-century Developments," in Joshua Dressler (ed.), *Encyclopedia of Crime and Justice* (New York: Macmillan, 2d ed. 2001), 412.

95. Wechsler died in 2000 at the age of 90, Schwartz in 2003 at the age of 89. In 1980, the ALI had published a final "Official Draft" of the Code with Revised Comments taking account of developments since the Code was promulgated in 1962. The reportorial staff for the revised commentary on Part II of the Code consisted of Professors R. Kent Greenawalt, Peter W. Low, and John Calvin Jeffries, Jr.

96. Wechsler, "Challenge of the Model Penal Code," at 1112–1113. Later, once the Code was finished, Wechsler would write, "[t]he undisciplined proliferation of offenses, with concomitant complexity of content and frequent inequality in grading, is nowhere better illustrated than in theft." Herbert Wechsler, "Codification of Criminal Law in the United States: The Model Penal Code," 68 *Columbia L. Rev.* 1425 (1968).

97. Discussion Draft No. 1—Property Offenses, Ch.2 (Nov. 17, 1952), in Model Penal Code Record, American Law Institute Archives, Biddle Law Library, University of Pennsylvania (1942–1985) [hereinafter MPC Archive].
98. Id., comments at 1.
99. Id.
100. Id. at 1.
101. Id.
102. Id.
103. Discussion Draft No. 3—Property Offenses, Ch.2 (Nov. 20, 1953), in MPC Archive. Discussion Draft No. 2 covered sentencing and treatment, rather than property offenses.
104. Id. at 1.
105. Id.
106. Model Penal Code § 222(2) (robbery); MPC § 224.5 (writing bad check); MPC § 221.1 (burglary).
107. The theft provisions were not the only part of the Model Penal Code's Special Part that reflected a form of consolidation. Something similar occurred in the case of murder, which merged into a single offense "purposely" causing death, "knowingly" causing death, and causing death by "extreme or depraved indifference." Model Penal Code § 210.2 (a) and (b). And, indeed, the tendency of the Code to blur important distinctions in this area as well has been criticized. See, e.g., David Crump, "Murder, Pennsylvania Style: Comparing Traditional American Homicide Law to the Statutes of Model Penal Code Jurisdictions," 109 *West Virginia L. Rev.* 257, 351 (2007). Yet the manner in which the MPC consolidates the law of theft—combining eight formerly distinct offenses into one—seems far more thoroughgoing, and therefore more problematic, than the form of "consolidation" that the MPC applies in the case of murder.
108. Model Penal Code § 223.1(2). Once again, robbery and writing a bad check were exceptions. Writing a bad check was treated as a misdemeanor. Robbery was treated as a felony of the second degree if it involved the infliction or threat of serious bodily injury and as a felony of the first degree if the actor attempted to kill someone or purposely inflicted or attempted to inflict serious bodily injury. MPC § 222(2).
109. Council Draft No. 4 (March 4, 1953), at b.
110. Model Penal Code § 223.0(6).
111. Model Penal Code § 223.7 (Theft of Services); MPC § 223.1(1) (consolidation provision).

112. Proceedings (1954) in University of Pennsylvania archive, box 4–18.

113. Proceedings (1954)—from box 4–18.

114. Discussion Draft No. 1, at 9–10.

115. Model Penal Code § 1.02(1)(a).

116. Model Penal Code § 1.02(2)(c). Recently, however, proposed revisions to the MPC sentencing provisions have explicitly identified as one of their goals "to render sentences in all cases within a range of severity proportionate to the gravity of offenses, the harms done to crime victims, and the blameworthiness of offenders." Model Penal Code: Sentencing—Tentative Draft No. 1 (2007), § 1.02(2)(a)(i).

117. Model Penal Code § 102, Commentary at 132–134.

118. This is in contrast to their decision generally to focus on treatmentism rather than punishment and to include the death penalty as a possible punishment, both issues about which there was considerable controversy. See Anders Walker, "American Oresteia: Herbert Wechsler, the Model Penal Code, and the Uses of Revenge," 2009 *Wisconsin L. Rev.* 1017.

119. A.L.I. Proceedings 44–200 (1954) (unpublished), in MPC Archive [box 4–18], at 149 (statement of Emory Niles).

120. Id. at 150 (statement of Floyd Thompson).

121. Id. at 150 (statement of Louis Schwartz).

122. Id. at 150 (statement of Louis Schwartz).

123. McClain and Kahan, "Criminal Law Reform: Historical Development in the United States," at 424. On the relative lack of influence of the Special Part, see Gerald E. Lynch, "Towards a Model Penal Code, Second (Federal?): The Challenge of the Special Part," 2 *Buffalo Criminal L. Rev.* 297, 297 (1998).

124. These states are: Arkansas, Colorado, Delaware, Idaho, Illinois, Kansas, Maine, Montana, Nebraska, New Hampshire, New Jersey, New York, North Dakota, Oregon, Pennsylvania, South Dakota, Texas, and Utah.

125. These states are: Alabama, Alaska, Arizona, California, Connecticut, District of Columbia, Florida, Hawaii, Indiana, Iowa, Louisiana, Maryland, Massachusetts, Minnesota, Missouri, Nevada, Ohio, Tennessee, Washington, Wisconsin, and Wyoming.

126. States with consolidation of all theft crimes except extortion: Alaska, Arizona, Florida, Hawaii, Iowa, Maryland, Massachusetts, Minnesota, Nevada, Tennessee, and Wyoming.

127. States with consolidation of all theft crimes except extortion and receiving stolen goods: California, District of Columbia, Louisiana, Washington, and Wisconsin.

128. State with consolidation of all crimes except extortion and theft of lost property: Alabama.

129. State with consolidation of all theft crimes except receiving stolen Property: Missouri.

130. States with consolidation of all theft crimes except a general unauthorized use statute: Connecticut, Ohio, and Indiana.

131. These states are: Georgia, Kentucky, Michigan, Mississippi, New Mexico, North Carolina, Oklahoma, Rhode Island, South Carolina, Vermont, Virginia, and West Virginia.

132. Model Penal Code § 223.1(1). This rule is "subject only to the power of the Court to ensure fair trial by granting a continuance or other appropriate relief where the conduct of the defense would be prejudiced by lack of fair notice or by surprise."

133. 445 A.2d 798 (Pa. Super. Ct. 1982).

134. Id. at 800. For similar reasoning in a different Pennsylvania case, see *Commonwealth v. Robichow,* 487 A.2d 1000 (Pa. Super. Ct. 1985) (finding no difference between proof required for charge of theft by deception and proof required for charge of failure to make required disposition of funds received).

135. 694 N.W.2d 651 (Neb. 2005).

136. Id. at 655.

137. 466 A.2d 78 (N.J. 1983).

138. Id. at 81–82.

139. *State v. Hill,* 332 A.2d 182 (N.H. 1975).

140. Id. at 184.

141. Maryland Sentencing Guidelines Offense Table, Appendix A at 43; Minnesota Sentencing Guidelines at 57; Pennsylvania Sentencing Guidelines at 25–30; Utah Sentencing Guidelines at 13; Washington Adult Sentencing Manual 2008, Table 2; Wisconsin Sentencing Commission, Wisconsin Sentencing Guidelines at 1. The value of property stolen is also the most important factor in the federal sentencing guidelines. U.S. Sentencing Guidelines Manual § 2B1.1(b)(1) (containing detailed enhancement schedule based on value of property stolen);

142. Minnesota Sentencing Guidelines at 73–74.

143. Wisconsin Sentencing Guidelines: Worksheet, Theft—More than $10,000.

144. Wisconsin Sentencing Guidelines at 4.

145. See USSG Manual § 3B1.3 ; Guidelines on Theft, Part E3 (England); Maryland Sentencing Guidelines Manual at p. 43; Minnesota Guidelines; Wisconsin Guidelines.

146. U.S. Department of Justice, Bureau of Justice Statistics, Felony Defendants in Large Urban Counties—2004, Table 26, http://www .ojp.usdoj.gov/bjs/pub/html/fdluc/2004/tables/fdluc04st26.htm. For a study examining the differences between sentences for armed and unarmed robbery, larceny, and burglary, see Henry R. Glick and George W. Pruett, Jr., "Crime, Public Opinion and Trial Courts: Analysis of Sentencing Policy," 2 *Justice Quarterly* 319 (1985).

147. For a discussion of the variables that most affected the length of sentence in theft cases, see Roger Douglas, "Sentencing in the Suburbs I: Theft and Violence," 13 *Australian & New Zealand J. Criminology* 241 (1980); Matthew Zingraff and Randall Thomson, "Differential Sentencing of Women and Men in the U.S.A.," 12 *Int'l J. Sociology of Law* 401 (1984); Robert Tillman and Henry N. Pontell, "Is Justice 'Collar-Blind'? Punishing Medicaid Provider Fraud," 30 *Criminology* 547 (1992).

148. Washington State, Sentencing Guidelines Commission, Statistical Summary of Adult Felony Sentencing (Fiscal Year 2008).

149. Maryland State Commission on Criminal Sentencing Policy, Maryland Sentencing Guidelines Compliance and *Average Sentence for the Most Common Person, Drug and Property* (Fiscal Year 2007) (unpaginated).

150. Florida Department of Corrections, Bureau of Research and Data Analysis, *Florida's Criminal Punishment Code: A Comparative Assessment* (Sept. 2007).

151. Ronald L. Gainer, "Federal Criminal Code Reform: Past and Future," 2 *Buffalo Criminal L. Rev.* 45 62 (1998).

152. California Penal Code § 487.

153. Discussed in Robinson and Cahill, "Can a Model Penal Code Second Save the States from Themselves?," 1 *Ohio State Journal of Criminal Law* 169, 170 (2003). See also Ellen S. Podgor, "Do We Need a 'Beanie Baby' Fraud Statute?," 49 *American University L. Rev.* 1031 (2000).

154. 18 U.S.C. § 408.

155. La. Rev. Stat. Arts. 14:67.1 (theft of livestock); 14:67.2 (theft of animals); RS 14:67.5 (theft of crawfish); penalty; RS 14:67.6 (theft of utility service); RS 14:67.7 (theft of petroleum products); RS 14:67.8 (theft of oilfield geological survey, seismograph, and production maps); RS 14:67.9 (theft of oil and gas equipment); RS 14:67.10 (theft of goods); RS 14:67.12 (theft of timber); RS 14:67.13 (theft of an alligator); RS 14:67.15(theft of a firearm); RS 14:67.17 (theft of motor vehicle fuel); RS 14:67.19 (theft of anhydrous ammonia).

156. 18 U.S.C. § 1347 (health care fraud), 18 U.S.C. § 1344 (bank fraud), 18 U.S.C. § 157 (bankruptcy fraud), 18 U.S.C. § 1520 (accounting fraud).

157. 18 U.S.C. § 641 (theft of federal money or property), § 664 (theft from employee pension funds); § 668 (theft of artwork from museums); 18 U.S.C. § 1163 (theft from Indian tribal organizations).

158. 18 U.S.C. § 1341 (mail fraud), 18 U.S.C. 1341 (wire fraud), 18 U.S.C. § 1030 (computer fraud).

159. For an excellent discussion of this phenomenon, see William J. Stuntz, "The Pathological Politics of Criminal Law," 100 *Michigan L. Rev.* 505, 558 (2001).

160. O. F. Robinson, *The Criminal Law of Ancient Rome* (Baltimore: Johns Hopkins, 1995) 21–35.

161. Bernard S. Jackson, *Theft in Early Jewish Law* (Oxford: Oxford University Press, 1972) 58–67, 76–82.

162. Hisham Ramadan, "Larceny Offenses in Islamic Law," 2006 *Michigan State L. Rev.* 1609, 1617. Cf. Kevin M. Trainor, "When Is a Theft Not a Theft? Relic Theft and the Cult of the Buddha's Relics in Sri Lanka," 39 *Numen* 1 (1992).

163. J. M. Beattie, *Crime and the Courts in England, 1660–1800* (Princeton, NJ: Princeton University Press, 1986) 145.

164. Judy Dempsey, "Sign Over Auschwitz Gate is Stolen," *N.Y. Times* (December 18, 2009), http://www.nytimes.com/2009/12/19/world /europe/19poland.html?scp=1&sq=arbeit%20macht%20frei%20 theft%20auschwitz&st=cse; Jennifer Medina, "California: Woman Arrested in Relic's Disappearance," *N.Y. Times* (June 17, 2011), http://www.nytimes.com/2011/06/18/us/18brfs-California.html? _r=1&emc=tnt&tntemail1=y; "National Briefing: Three Guilty in Theft of Moon Rocks," *N.Y. Times* (December 25, 2002), http://www .nytimes.com/2002/12/25/us/national-briefing-washington-3-guilty -in-theft-of-moon-rocks.html.

165. See generally Douglas Husak, *Overcriminalization: The Limits of the Criminal Law* (Oxford: Oxford University Press, 2008), 36–37; Stuntz, "Pathological Politics."

166. Larceny Act 1861 (c.96); Larceny Act 1916 (c.50).

167. Criminal Law Revision Committee, *Eighth Report: Theft and Related Offences,* Cmnd. 2977 (1967), at 5.

168. My thanks to Lindsay Farmer for his insight on this point.

169. Griew, *The Theft Acts 1968 and 1978,* at 2. Parliament would subsequently enact two additional pieces of legislation meant to deal with

problematic aspects of the deception offenses: the Theft Act 1978 and the Fraud Act 2006.

170. *Eighth Report: Theft and Related Offences,* at 6.

171. Id. at 9.

172. Ormerod and Williams, *Smith's Law of Theft,* at 3.

173. Theft Act 1968 s. 1.

174. Theft Act 1968 s. 9 (burglary); id. at s. 8 (robbery); Fraud Act 2006, ss. 1–4 (fraud and false pretenses) (replacing earlier set of provisions concerning fraud in the Theft Act 1968, ss. 15–17); Theft Act 1968, s. 21 (blackmail and extortion); id. at s 22 (handling stolen goods); id. at s.17 (false accounting); Theft Act 1978 s. 3 ("making off" without paying). Perhaps for this reason, John Gardner has written:

> Whether one is a victim of theft, deception, criminal damage or making off, one is harmed by being deprived of one's belongings. Yet this codification did not seek to eradicate the different themes of different offences. . . . [I]n the realm of property offences, the harm does not capture all that is interesting, or rationally significant, about the wrong.
>
> [T]he differences marked in the Theft Act between theft, obtaining by deception, false accounting, making off with payment, [and] handling stolen goods . . . single out for specific prohibition . . . different modes of wrongdoing . . . [a]nd they single them out in ways which resonate in the moral imagination of the ordinary people to whom the law must provide its clear guidance.

John Gardner, "Rationality and the Rule of Law in Offences Against the Person," in *Offences and Defenses* (Oxford: Oxford University Press 2007) 42, 47. For reasons indicated in the text, I think Gardner overstates the case for the Theft Act's preservation of theft law's moral content.

175. J. C. Smith, *The Law of Theft* (London: Butterworths, 8th ed. 1997), § 2–117, at 70–71. The exception can be found in Section 3(1), which states that "[a]ny assumption by a person of the rights of an owner amounts to an appropriation, and this includes, where he has come by the property (innocently or not) without stealing it, any later assumption of a right to it by keeping or dealing with it as owner."

176. Ormerod and Williams, *Smith's Law of Theft,* at 152–153.

177. *Eighth Report: Theft and Related Offences,* at 20.

178. Theft Act 1968, s. 3(1).

179. *Eighth Report: Theft and Related Offences,* at 7–8. The current penalty is seven years. Theft Act 1968 s. 7.

180. Fraud Act 2006 s11 (replacing section 1 of Theft Act 1978).
181. Theft Act 1968 s 4.
182. *Eighth Report: Theft and Related Offences,* at ¶¶ 110–112, at 7–9.
183. I am indebted to Alex Steel for his help in explaining Australian theft law to me. For a helpful overview, see Alex Steel, "The Meanings of Dishonesty in Theft," 38 *Common Law World Review* 103, 119 et seq. (2009).
184. See David Brown et al., *Criminal Laws: Materials and Commentary on Criminal Law and Process of New South Wales* (Leichardt, NSW: The Federation Press, 4th ed. 2006), 973 et seq.
185. 77 Criminal Code Act 1899 (Qld) s. 391(1); Criminal Code Compilation Act 1913 (WA) s. 371(1).
186. 1995 report on Theft, Fraud, Bribery, and Related Offences ("Chapter 3") by the Model Criminal Code Officers Committee of the Standing Committee of Attorneys-General.
187. Criminal Code Act 1995, s.131.1.
188. The other authors were Eric Clive, Pamela Ferguson, and Christopher Gane. *A Draft Criminal Code for Scotland with Commentary* (Edinburgh: Scottish Law Commission, 2003), http://www.scotlawcom.gov.uk /publications/consultation-papers-and-other-documents/.
189. Id. at § § 77(1) and (2). "Appropriating" was defined broadly to include "taking, keeping, or disposing of the property, or dealing with it as if it were one's own." § 77(3)(a).
190. Id. at § 77(3)(b). Chapter 4 will cover this provision more extensively.
191. Id. at § 112(h).
192. Commentary to § 77, at 146.
193. Draft Code § § 75, 76, 85, 86, 87, 88, 89, and 90
194. Described in Eric Clive, "Codification of the Criminal Law," in James Chalmers, Lindsay Farmer, and Fiona Leverick (eds.), *Essays in Criminal Law in Honour of Sir Gerald Gordon* (Edinburgh: Edinburgh University Press, 2010).
195. Dressler, *Understanding Criminal Law,* at 615.
196. See George P. Fletcher, "Dogmas of the Model Penal Code," 2 *Buffalo Crim. L. Rev.* 1, 11 (1998) (making similar point). One rare exception is a passing reference in the MPC Commentary to the French Penal Code's offense of *escroquerie* (swindling). Discussion Draft No. 1, Commentary at 8.
197. German Criminal Code (1998) (translation by Federal Ministry of Justice), http://www.iuscomp.org/gla/statutes/StGB.htm; see also Michael Bohlander, *Principles of German Criminal Law* (Oxford: Hart Publishing, 2009).

198. Compare StGB Section 263 with Section 265a (*Erschleichen von Leistungen*).
199. Código Penal (Argentina), http://www.justiniano.com/codigos _juridicos/codigo_penal.htm, Articles 162, 172, 173 section 7, 168–171, 173–175.
200. Marcelo Ferrante, "The Criminal Law of Argentina," in Kevin Jon Heller and Markus Dubber (eds.), *The Handbook of Comparative Criminal Law* (Stanford, CA: Stanford University Press, 2010) 12, 40.
201. Id.
202. Id.
203. Articles 277(1)(c) et seq. Thanks to José Milton Peralta for bringing this provision to my attention.
204. *Austria:* Austrian Penal Act (South Hackensak, NJ: Fred B. Rothman, 1966) (Norbert D. West and Samuel I. Shuman, trans.), § 171 (larceny), § 181 (embezzlement), § 197 (fraud). *Finland:* Penal Code of Finland (Littleton, Co: Fred B. Rothman, 1987) (Matti Joutsen, trans.), ch. 28 (larceny), ch. 29 (embezzlement), ch. 31 (extortion), ch. 32 (possessing stolen property). *France:* Code Penal (France), http://www.adminet.com/code/index-CPENALLL.html, § 311–1 (*vol*/larceny), § 312–1 (*l'extorsion*/extortion), § 312–10 (*chantage*/ blackmail), § 313–1 (*l'escroquerie*/ fraudulent obtaining), § 314–1 (*l'abus de confiance*/theft by breach of trust), § 321–1 (*recel*/receiving stolen property); see generally Catherine Elliott, *French Criminal Law* (Portland, OR: Willan Publishing, 2001) 179–200 (including appendix with translation of selected provisions of the Code). *Japan:* Japan Penal Code art. 235 (larceny), art. 236 (robbery), art. 246 (fraud), art. 247 (breach of trust), art. 249 (extortion), art. 252 (embezzlement), art. 256 (accepting stolen property); see generally John O. Haley, "The Criminal Law of Japan" in Heller and Dubber, *Handbook of Comparative Criminal Law,* at 393, 409. *Netherlands:* Netherlands Penal Code (Littleton, CO: Fred B. Rothman, 1997) (Louise Rayar and Stafford Wadsworth, trans.), § 310 (larceny), § 317 (extortion /blackmail), § 321 (embezzlement), § 326 (theft by deception). *Nigeria:* Nigerian Criminal Code (1990), http://www.nigeria-law .org/Criminal%20Code%20Act-Tables.htm, § 383 (stealing), § 401 (robbery), § 408 (extortion), § 419 (false pretenses), § 427 (receiving stolen property). *Spain:* Código Penal (Spain), http://noticias. juridicas.com/base_datos/Penal/lo10-1995.html, Ar. 234 (*hurtos*/ larceny—defined as the nonconsensual taking of the property of another with intent to profit from the taking, punishable by up to eighteen months imprisonment), Art. 238 (*robos*/robbery—taking

property by using force against person or against property), Art. 248 (*estafas*/false pretenses—obtaining property from another by way of fraud with the intent to profit from the conduct, punishable by up to three months in prison). There are also two distinct types of embezzlement offenses: one type criminalizes the embezzlement of movable goods while the other criminalizes the embezzlement of money. Carlos Gómez-Jara Díez and Luis E. Chiesa, "Spanish Criminal Law," in Heller and Dubber, *Handbook of Comparative Criminal Law,* at 488, 520.; *Sweden:* Swedish Penal Code http://wings.buffalo.edu/law/bclc /sweden.pdf, ch. 8, § 1 (theft), ch. 8, § 13 (receiving stolen property), ch. 9 § 1 (fraud/theft by deception), ch.8, § 4 (extortion theft by coercion), ch.10, § 1 (embezzlement).

205. See, respectively, Robinson, *The Criminal Law of Ancient Rome,* at 23–40; Moses Jung, *The Jewish Law of Theft* (Philadelphia: Dropsie College, 1929) 28–32.

206. John Wesley Bartram, Note, "Pleading for Theft Consolidation in Virginia: Larceny, Embezzlement, False Pretenses and § 19.2–294," 56 *Washington & Lee L. Rev.* 249 (1999); John G. Douglass, "Rethinking Theft Crimes in Virginia," 38 *University of Richmond L. Rev.* 13 (2003).

207. Hall's views of criminal law reform are discussed in Jerome Hall, "The Proposal to Prepare a Model Penal Code," 4 *J. Legal Studies* 91 (1951), reprinted as an appendix to *Theft, Law and Society,* p. 349.

208. See, e.g., Herbert Wechsler, "Book Review," 49 *Columbia L. Rev.* 425, 428 (1949) (reviewing first edition of Hall's *General Principles of Criminal Law* and accusing him of the "sheerest kind of dogmatism").

209. George P. Fletcher, *Rethinking Criminal Law* (Boston: Little Brown, 1978; reprinted by Oxford University Press in 2000).

210. Fletcher's account of that history was the subject of a sharp colloquy with Lloyd Weinreb. See George P. Fletcher, "The Metamorphosis of Larceny," 89 *Harvard L. Rev.* 469 (1976); Lloyd L. Weinreb, "Manifest Criminality, Criminal Intent, and 'The Metamorphosis of Larceny,' " 90 *Yale L.J.* 294 (1980); George P. Fletcher, "Manifest Criminality, Criminal Intent, and the Metamorphosis of Lloyd Weinreb," 90 *Yale L.J.* 319 (1980).

211. Fletcher, *Rethinking Criminal Law,* at 30.

212. Authorship of J.C. Smith's treatise passed to David Ormerod and David Huw Williams after Smith's death in 2003. Ormerod and Williams, *Smith's Law of Theft.* The other works referred to in the text are Winifred H. Holland, *The Law of Theft and Related Offences* (Scarborough, Ontario: Carswell, 1998); C. R. Williams and M. S.

Weinberg, *Property Offences* (Sydney: The Law Book Co., 2d ed. 1986); A. T. H. Smith, *Property Offences* (London: Sweet & Maxwell, 1994); Edward Griew, *The Theft Acts 1968 and 1978* (London: Sweet & Maxwell, 7th ed. 1995); Edward Phillips, Paul Dobson, and Charlotte Walsh, *Law Relating to Theft* (Abingdon: Routledge-Cavendish, 2001).

213. For law review literature in a similar vein, see Glanville Williams, "Theft, Consent and Illegality" (Parts 1 and 2) *Criminal L. Rev.* 127, 205 (1977); Stephen Shute, "Appropriation and the Law of Theft," *Criminal L. Rev.* 445 (2002); Alan L. Bogg and John Stanton-Ife, "Protecting the Vulnerable: Legality, Harm and Theft," 23 *Legal Studies* 402 (2003); D. W. Elliott, "Dishonesty in Theft: A Dispensable Concept," *Criminal L. Rev.* 395 (1982).

214. Steel offers what is in essence a sophisticated defense of the common law of theft, focusing on several related points. First, he believes that it was a mistake for modern theft law to abandon the common law's commitment to larceny as an offense against possession. Possession, he says, offers a "strong and principled boundary to the offence," and abandoning it has led to the loss of an essential moral component in theft. Second, he rejects the view that theft law should be primarily about protecting property rights per se. He says that the goal of preventing violence that might arise when an offender takes property from the possession of another should remain key, and that the harms and wrongs that result from such dispossession are very different from the harms and wrongs that result from deception offenses. Third, he takes issue with the view that theft law is meant to protect the regime of property rights generally as much as, or more than, it is meant to protect the rights of individual property holders. Finally, Steel rejects the idea that theft law should be extended to apply to the misappropriation of intangible property. See Alex Steel, "Taking Possession: The Defining Element in Theft?," 32 *Melbourne University L. Rev.* 1030 (2008); Alex Steel, "The Harms and Wrongs of Stealing: The Harm Principle and Dishonesty in Theft," 31 *University of New South Wales L.J.* 712 (2008); Alex Steel, "Problematic and Unnecessary? Issues with the Use of the Theft Offence to Protect Intangible Property," 30 *Sydney Law Review* 575 (2008). It is worth noting that Steel lives and works in New South Wales, one of the few Anglo-American jurisdictions that has never abandoned the common law of theft.

215. E.g., Kathleen F. Brickey, "The Jurisprudence of Larceny: A Historical Inquiry and Interest Analysis," 33 *Vanderbilt L. Rev.* 1101 (1980);

Michael Tigar, "The Right of Property and the Law of Theft," 62 *Texas L. Rev.* 1443 (1984).

216. Model Penal Code § 223.1(2).

217. Model Penal Code § 6.06(3).

218. See Paul H. Robinson, "Reforming the Federal Criminal Code: A Top Ten List," 1 *Buffalo Crim. L. Rev.* 225, 247 (1997).

219. Congressional Research Service, Federal Sentencing Guidelines: Background, Legal Analysis, and Policy Options (2007), CRS-14, at note 71, http://www.fas.org/sgp/crs/misc/RL32766.pdf.

220. Model Penal Code § 223.0(6).

221. Thanks to Alex Steel for pressing me on this point.

222. Loosely adapted from Dressler, *Understanding Criminal Law,* at 560.

223. I suppose there is a slight difference in the fact that one case involves a breach of D's *employer's* trust, while the other involves a breach of D's *customer's* trust, but that seems like a vanishingly fine distinction to me.

224. For the record, I would treat both cases as embezzlement on the theory that larceny represents the baseline form of theft and embezzlement an aggravated form of wrongfulness owing to the breach of trust. To treat this case merely as larceny would therefore arguably be to undercriminalize it.

225. E.g., *United States v. Delano,* 55 F.3d 720, 727 (2d Cir. 1995) (reversing RICO conviction where evidence showed that defendant had used unlawfully obtained services, rather than "property" as defined by statute defining predicate act of extortion); see also "Criminal Law—Property Subject to Larceny in North Carolina," 19 *North Carolina L. Rev.* 221 (1941).

226. Model Penal Code § 223.1, Commentary at p. 134.

227. See *Baker v. Commonwealth,* 388 S.E2d 837 (Va. Ct. App. 1990) (reversing conviction for false pretenses where defendant absconded with car taken for test drive at automobile dealership after leaving as security a truck previously obtained by fraud elsewhere; the court held that the proper charge was larceny by trick); *Sparr v. People,* 219 P.2d 317 (Colo. 1950) (reversing conviction for false pretenses where D, a foreman in the employ of X, a warehouseman who stored beans and other farm products, went to V and offered to sell him 100 sacks of beans, which D falsely said he owned but which actually belonged to X. V accepted the offer and paid D $700. At no time were the beans delivered to V; the court held that since there was no conversion of X's property, the proper charge was embezzlement).

228. Sherry A. Moore, Note, "Nevada's Comprehensive Theft Statute: Consolidation or Confusion," 8 *Nevada L.J.* 672, 687 (2008). Despite statutory consolidation of Nevada theft law, prosecutors in many cases apparently continue to use common law terminology in charging documents.

229. 92 F.2d 753 (9th Cir. 1937).

230. Id.

231. 284 U.S. 299, 304 (1932); see also *Dixon v. United States,* 509 U.S. 688 (1993) (reaffirming *Blockburger* approach to determining whether offenses are the "same").

232. Thanks to George Thomas for his help in sorting this out.

233. [1956] 1 Q.B. 439.

234. Id.

235. See, e.g., Tom Tyler, *Why People Obey the Law* (New Haven: Yale University Press, 1990).

236. Paul H. Robinson and John M. Darley, "Intuitions of Justice: Implications for Criminal Law and Justice Policy," 81 *Southern California L. Rev.* 1, 21 (2007). See also Paul H. Robinson and John M. Darley, *Justice, Liability, and Blame: Community Views and the Criminal Law* (Denver: Westview Press, 1995); Paul H. Robinson and John M. Darley, "Testing Competing Theories of Justification," 76 *North Carolina L. Rev.* 1095 (1998); John M. Darley et al., "Community Standards for Defining Attempt: Inconsistencies with the Model Penal Code," 39 *American Behavioral Scientist* 405 (1996).

237. See Janice Nadler, "Flouting the Law," 83 *Texas L. Rev.* 1399 (2005); Elizabeth Mullen and Janice Nadler, "Moral Spillovers: The Effect of Moral Mandate Violations on Deviant Behavior," 44 *J. Experimental Social Psychology* 1239 (2008); William Stuntz, "Self-Defeating Crimes," 86 *Virginia L. Rev.* 1871 (2000).

238. Andrew Ashworth, *Principles of Criminal Law* (Oxford: Oxford University Press, 4th ed. 2003) 89–90.

239. Id. at 90.

240. On the virtues and vices of more particularized crime definitions generally, see Jeremy Horder, "Rethinking Non-Fatal Offences Against the Person," 14 *Oxford J.L.S.* 335 (1994); Kenneth W. Simons, "Understanding the Topography of Moral and Criminal Law Norms," in R. A. Duff and Stuart P. Green, (eds.), *Philosophical Foundations of Criminal Law* (Oxford: Oxford University Press, 2011) 228, 230–234; R. A. Duff and Stuart P. Green, "Introduction," in Duff and Green, *Defining Crimes: Essays on the Special Part of the Criminal Law* (Oxford: Oxford University Press, 2005) 1, 10–16.

241. For a discussion of fair labeling in the context of theft, see C. M. V. Clarkson, "Theft and Fair Labelling," 56 *Modern L. Rev.* 554 (1993); Stephen Shute and Jeremy Horder, "Thieving and Deceiving: What is the Difference?" 56 *Modern L. Rev.* 548 (1993); P. R. Glazebrook, "Thief or Swindler: Who Cares?" 50 *Cambridge L.J.* 389 (1991).

242. James Chalmers and Fiona Leverick, "Fair Labelling in Criminal Law," 71 *Modern L. Rev.* 217, 239 (2008). For an example of what I regard as overspecificity in proposed theft legislation, see Shane Pennington, Guha Krishnamurthi, Jon Reidy, and Michael J. Stephan, "A Precise Model for Identity Theft Statutes," 46 *Crim. L. Bulletin* 5 (2010) (proposing elaborate statutory scheme for criminalizing identity theft, consisting of "identity larceny," "identity larceny by trick," "identity embezzlement," "identity theft by aggravated means," and "identity burglary").

243. Michael O'Connell and Anthony Whelan, "Taking Wrongs Seriously: Public Perceptions of Crime Seriousness," 36 *Brit. J. Criminology* 299 (1996).

244. See, e.g., Marvin Wolfgang et al., *National Survey of Crime Severity* (Washington, D.C.: U.S. Department of Justice—Bureau of Justice Statistics) (1985) (comparing the seriousness of acts such as "A person armed with a gun, robs a bank of $100,000 during business hours. No one is physically hurt," "A person, armed with a lead pipe, robs a victim of $1,000. The victim is injured and requires treatment by a doctor but not hospitalization," "A person illegally gets monthly welfare checks of $200," and "A person steals property worth $50 from outside a building"); Paul H. Robinson and Robert Kurzban, "Concordance and Conflict in Intuitions of Justice," 91 *Minnesota L. Rev.* 1829 (2007) (comparing the seriousness of shoplifting a fifteen-dollar t-shirt from a family-owned music store with a cabdriver's tricking a young passenger out of $20 change); M. Levi and S. Jones, "Public and Police Perception of Crime Seriousness in England and Wales," 25 *British J. Criminology* 234 (1985).

245. See generally Joshua Knobe and Shaun Nichols (eds.), *Experimental Philosophy* (New York: Oxford University Press, 2008); Kwame Anthony Appiah, *Experiments in Ethics* (Cambridge, MA: Harvard University Press, 2008); see also Experimental Philosophy blog, http://experimentalphilosophy.typepad.com/experimental _philosophy/.

246. 22 *Philosophical Psychology* 711 (2009).

247. Id. at 722.

248. Cf. Adam J. Kolber, "How to Improve Empirical Desert," 75 *Brooklyn L. Rev.* 433, 436 (2009) (even if a large majority of people believed that "it is immoral to permit people of the same sex to marry each other, we might resist the idea that such intuitions alone, even if they represent a consensus view, provide *any* moral support for prohibiting same-sex marriage").

249. Cf. Mary Sigler, "The Methodology of Desert," 42 *Arizona State L.J.* 1173 (2011); Christopher Slobogin, "Is Justice Just Us? Using Social Science to Inform Substantive Criminal Law," 87 *J. Criminal Law & Criminology* 315 (1996); Kenneth W. Simons, "The Relevance of Community Values to Just Deserts: Criminal Law, Punishment Rationales, and Democracy," 28 *Hofstra L. Rev.* 635 (2000) (all criticizing empirical desert approach on this ground).

250. Cf. Kolber, "How to Improve Empirical Desert," at 441–443 (criticizing work of Paul Robinson on this ground).

251. Cf. Zachary R. Calo, "Empirical Desert and the Moral Economy of Punishment," 42 *Arizona State L.J.* 1123, 1136–1137 (2011) (discussing the relationship between empirical desert and universal moral judgments).

252. I gratefully acknowledge the contributions of Matthew Kugler to this section of the chapter. The full results of our study appear in Stuart P. Green and Matthew B. Kugler, "Community Perception of Theft Seriousness: A Challenge to Model Penal Code and English Theft Act Consolidation," 7 *Journal of Empirical Legal Studies* 511 (2010).

253. Of the 172 students who participated in the study, six left some of the study incomplete and their data were excluded. Of the remaining 166 participants, 80 were male, 85 were female, and one did not report his or her sex. The sample was predominantly white (109), though there were also African American (19), Hispanic (13), and South or East Asian (18) students. Seven participants did not report ethnicity or were multiracial. On the use of law student subjects in such studies, see Joshua Dressler et al., "Effect of Legal Education upon Perceptions of Crime Seriousness: A Response to *Rummel v. Estelle*," 28 *Wayne L. Rev.* 1247 (1982).

254. All data were converted into weeks for the purpose of analysis. For sentences of less than three months, duration was rounded to the half week. Sentences of less than half a week were rounded up to half a week if they were greater than one day (which was rounded down to zero weeks).

255. Before the transformation, the sentence scores of nine of the twelve scenarios were extremely skewed (skew >3) and nine had extreme

kurtosis (>10). After the transformation, none of the twelve had extreme skew or kurtosis. It is thus appropriate to assume that the transformed scores have sufficiently normal distributions for parametric analysis. See Rex B. Kline, *Principles and Practice of Structural Equation Modeling* (New York: Guilford Press, 2nd ed. 1998).

256. Data were analyzed using ANOVAs with crime type as a within subjects factor. Crime type affected ratings of blameworthiness F $(6.77, 1112.8) = 160.03$, $p < .001$ $[[eta]]^2 = .49$; the assigned sentence F $(3.05, 500.25) = 267.50$, $p < .001$ $[[eta]]^2 = .62$; and ranking order F $(6.43, 1050.17) = 325.71$, $p < .001$ $[[eta]]^2 = .66$. Greenhouse-Geisser corrections were performed for all analyses due to violations of sphericity. Crimes with nonoverlapping 95 percent confidence intervals for a given measure were deemed to have differed significantly on that measure. Analyzing the rank order data with a nonparametric Wilcoxon test yields identical results.

257. The various ways in which robbery is categorized and punished are discussed in Chapter 2.

258. Model Penal Code § 223.0(6).

259. MPC § 223.7.

260. Theft Act 1968, s. 4.

261. Fraud Act 2006, s. 11.

262. Fraud Act 2006, s. 11(3)(b).

2. THE GIST OF THEFT

1. Neil MacCormick, "Reconstruction after Deconstruction: A Response to CLS," 10 *Oxford J. Legal Studies* 539, 556 (1999).

2. Joel Feinberg, "Punishment," in Joel Feinberg and Hyman Gross (eds.), *Philosophy of Law* (Belmont, CA: Wadsworth, 2d ed. 1980) 515.

3. In so doing, I follow Duff and others. Antony Duff, *Punishment, Communication, and Community* (Oxford: Oxford University Press, 2001), at 11–14.

4. The approach in this paragraph is borrowed from Stuart P. Green, *Lying, Cheating, and Stealing: A Moral Theory of White Collar Crime* (Oxford: Oxford University Press, 2006), at 23.

5. Id. at 30–47.

6. Feinberg, *Harms to Others*, at 31–36.

7. The distinction among these three concepts will sometimes be less than sharp. For example, in the case in which Tom took Owen's bike by mistake, we might say not only that Tom's act was not intentional but also that it was not wrongful.

8. John Stuart Mill, *On Liberty* (London: Longman, 1869); Joel Feinberg, *The Moral Limits of the Criminal Law* (New York, Oxford University Press, 4 vols, 1984, 1985, 1986, 1988).

9. For a useful discussion, see Joseph William Singer, *Introduction to Property* (Boston: Aspen, 2d ed. 2005), at 2.

10. Id.

11. A. M. Honoré, "Ownership," in Anthony G. Guest (ed.), *Oxford Essays in Jurisprudence* (Oxford: Clarendon Press, 1961) 107.

12. A. P. Simester and Andrew von Hirsch, "Rethinking the Offence Principle," 8 *Legal Theory* 269, 286 (2002). See also Louis B. Schwartz and Dan M. Kahan, "Theft," Joshua Dressler (ed.), *Encyclopedia of Crime and Justice* (New York: Macmillan, 2d. ed. 2002), vol. 4, at 1536 ("[p]roperty security is valued as part of the individual's enjoyment of his belongings and because the community wishes to encourage saving and economic planning, which would be jeopardized if accumulated property could be plundered with impunity").

13. Thanks to Antony Duff for helping with this formulation.

14. Statute of Westminster I, 3 Edw. 1, ch. 15 (1275). See also J. M. Beattie, *Crime and the Courts in England, 1660–1800* (Princeton, NJ: Princeton University Press, 1986) 140.

15. Book Review, 11 *Yale L.J.* 328 (1902); see also Frederick Pollock and Frederick W. Maitland, *The History of English Law* (Cambridge: Cambridge University Press, 1895, rev. 2nd ed. 1968), vol. 2, at 495.

16. For an influential discussion, see Robert Nozick, "Interpersonal Utility Theory," 2 *Social Choice and Welfare* 161 (1985).

17. Jayne W. Barnard, "Allocution for Victims of Economic Crimes," 77 *Notre Dame L. Rev.* 39, 56 (2001).

18. On the controversy over victim impact statements, see Wayne A. Logan, "Through the Past Darkly: A Survey of the Uses and Abuses of Victim Impact Evidence in Capital Trials," 41 *Arizona L. Rev.* 143 (1999).

19. Margaret Jane Radin, "Property and Personhood," 34 *Stanford L. Rev.* 957, 959–960 (1982).

20. *A Maimonides Reader* (Isadore Twersky, ed.) (Springfield, NJ: Berhman, 1972) (*Mishneh Torah,* Book 11) 156.

21. Brent G. Filbert, "Defense of Inconsequential or *De Minimis* Violation in Criminal Prosecution," 68 *A.L.R. 5th* 299.

22. A. T. H. Smith, *Property Offences,* § 2–06, p. 29.

23. Cf. *People v. Meyer*, 75 Cal. 383 (1888) (larceny not committed where defendant removed an overcoat from a department store mannequin and began to walk away with it; since the overcoat was secured to the mannequin by a chain, defendant never had complete control over the disposition and use of the coat).

24. Wayne R. LaFave, *Criminal Law* (Minneapolis: West, 4th ed. 2003) 932 n. 11.

25. For a critique of the appropriation requirement in English law, see Emanuel Melissaris, "The Concept of Appropriation and The Offence of Theft," 70 *Modern L. Rev.* 581 (2007); Alex Steel, "Taking Possession: The Defining Element in Theft," 32 *Melbourne University L. Rev.* 1030 (2008).

26. Model Penal Code § 223.2. As the Code commentary explained, the *actus reus* inquiry is thus now twofold: "whether the actor had control of the property, no matter how he got it, and whether the actor's acquisition or use of the property was authorized." MPC § 223.2, Commentary at 166.

27. (Proposed) Scottish Criminal Code § 77(3)(b).

28. *R. v. Turner* [1971] 2 All ER 441.

29. See Glanville Williams, *Textbook of Criminal Law* (London: Stevens & Sons, 2d ed. 1983) s.33.8; Ormerod and Williams, *Smith's Law of Theft*, at 79.

30. In the unlikely event that Turner actually believed that Brown became the owner of the car when he left it at the garage, Turner could presumably be charged with *attempted* theft of a car, assuming his mistake did not involve a cognizable "legal impossibility."

31. The idea has previously been expressed by Susan W. Brenner, "Is There Such a Thing as 'Virtual Crime?' " 4 *California Criminal L. Rev.* 1, 43 (2001). For an explanation of why theft is not properly understood, from a strict economic perspective, as a zero-sum game, see discussion in Chapter 4.

32. [1984] AC 320, [1983] 3 All ER 288.

33. Oliver Wendell Holmes, *The Common Law* (Mark DeWolfe Howe, ed.) (Cambridge, MA: Harvard University Press, 1963), at 59.

34. Id.

35. Eliakim Katz and Jacob Rosenberg, "Property Rights, Theft, Amnesty, and Efficiency," 15 *European J. Law & Economics* 219 (2003).

36. Simester and Sullivan, "Nature and Rationale of Property Offences," at 174.

37. Id. at 175.

38. Model Penal Code § 3.02, Commentary at 9–10.

39. The history of the necessity defense is a particularly convoluted one. In the famous lifeboat case of *Dudley & Stephens,* 14 Q.B.C. 273, 283 (1884), the court accepted as a given Hale's statement that it was not the law of England that a starving man could be justified in stealing a loaf of bread. Prior to Hale's time (1609–1676), however, English law was apparently more receptive to economic necessity as a defense to theft. See generally Dana Y. Rabin, *Identity, Crime, and Legal Responsibility in Eighteenth-Century England* 86–89 (New York: Palgrave 2004). For an account of how medieval European law dealt with the poverty defense, see Brian Tierney, *Medieval Poor Law: A Sketch of Canonical Theory and Its Application in England* (Berkeley: University of California Press, 1959). Rabbinic law also permits one to commit crimes such as theft in order to preserve life. See *The Babylonian Talmud: Seder Mo'ed: Yoma* 83b (Brooklyn: Soncino Press 1938) (Rabbi Dr. Leo Jung trans).

40. John T. Parry, "The Virtue of Necessity: Reshaping Culpability and the Rule of Law," 36 *Houston L Rev* 397, 403–404 (1999) (noting "anxiety" regularly felt by courts applying the necessity defense).

41. *State v. Tate,* 505 A.2d 941, 946 (N.J. 1986).

42. Cf. Eduardo Moisés Peñalver and Sonia K. Katyal, *Property Outlaws: How Squatters, Pirates, and Protesters Improve the Law of Ownership* (New Haven: Yale University Press, 2010) (detailing ways in which the acts of various kinds of "property outlaws"—trespassers, squatters, Internet pirates, and the like—have led to positive legal innovations).

43. Theft Act 1968, s.1 (requiring "intention of permanently depriving the other of" property); MPC § 223.1 (requiring "purpose to deprive").

44. Canadian Criminal Code § 322(1)(a); Holland, *The Law of Theft,* at 170–172; *La France v. R.* [1975] 2 S.C.R.

45. See, respectively, *Black v. Carmichael,* 1992 SCCR 709; Indian Penal Code (1860) 3.378.

46. Robinson, *Criminal Law of Ancient Rome,* at 25; Kai Ambos, "Is the Development of a Common Substantive Criminal Law for Europe Possible? Some Preliminary Reflections," 12 *Maastricht Journal of European and Comparative Law* 173, 189 (2005).

47. See, e.g., *Maimonides Reader,* at 156. Once again, the rationale is that by engaging in such conduct, one might become accustomed to more serious acts of stealing.

48. Model Penal Code § 223.9 (treated as a misdemeanor form of theft).

49. Theft Act 1968, s. 6 (emphasis added).

50. Model Penal Code § 223.0(1) (emphasis added). See also Model Penal Code § 223.2, Commentary at 174 (citing *State v. Davis,* 38 N.J.L. 176 (N.J. 1875)).

51. A similar point is made in Glanville Williams, "Temporary Appropriation Should be Theft," [1981] *Crim. Rev.* 129. More generally, as Tony Smith has pointed out, nearly all manufactured products are designed for limited use: they wear out or become superseded by new product lines, or go out of fashion. Smith, *Property Offences,* at 191.

52. Nina Mazar et al., "The Dishonesty of Honest People: A Theory of Self-Concept Maintenance," 45 *J. Marketing Research* 633, 633 (2008); Jenn Abelson, "Retailers Crack Down on Serial Returns: Short-Term 'Owners' Costing Firms Billions," *Boston Globe* (Feb. 18 2008), http://www.boston.com/business/articles/2008/02/18/retailers_crack_down_on_serial_returns/?page=full.

53. One exception is the proposed but never adopted Scottish Criminal Code. *A Draft Criminal Code for Scotland with Commentary* (Edinburgh: Scottish Law Commission, 2003), Section 77(2) ("Stealing is appropriating property, without the owner's consent, with the intention of depriving the owner permanently of it *or being reckless as to whether or not the owner is deprived permanently of it.*") (emphasis added).

54. In *State v. Davis,* 38 N.J.L. 176, 187 (1875), a group of Princeton students took a professor's horse and buggy without his permission, drove it recklessly, and abandoned it, leaving it to chance whether the professor would ever get it back. In upholding the conviction, the court held that it was larceny to use another's good "in a reckless, wanton or injurious manner, and then to leave it to mere chance whether the owner ever recovered them or not, and if he recovered them at all would probably recover them in a damaged or altered condition."

55. See generally Alex Steel, "Describing Dishonest Means: The Implications of Seeing Dishonesty as a Course of Conduct or Mental Element," 31 *Adelaide Law Review* 7 (2010).

56. See, e.g., *United States v. Smith-Baltiher,* 424 F.3d 913, 924 (9th Cir. 2005).

57. E.g., *People v. Navarro,* 99 Cal. App. 3d Supp. 1, 10 (Cal. Superior Ct. 1979) ("One does not commit [the offense of theft] by carrying away the chattel of another in the mistaken belief that it is his own, no matter how great may have been the fault leading to this belief, if the belief itself is genuine").

58. Cf. Model Penal Code § 220.3 (criminal mischief defined as purposely, recklessly, or negligently damaging tangible property).

59. Blackstone, *Commentaries,* vol. 4, at *232; J. W. C. Turner, "Larceny and Lucrum," 4 *University of Toronto L.J.* 296 (1941–1942).
60. *Leakey v. Quirke* [1918] N.Z.L.R. 550 (affirming on these facts that the *lucri causa* rule forms no part of New Zealand law).
61. See generally Richard Craswell, "When is a Willful Breach 'Willful'? The Link Between Definitions and Damages," 107 *Michigan L. Rev.* 1501 (2009).
62. If not something even worse. See Emily Kadens, "The Last Bankrupt Hanged: Capital Punishment for Bankruptcy in Eighteenth-Century England," 59 *Duke L.J.* 1229 (2010). On the modern day use of criminal law in the collection of debts, see Lucette Lagnado, "Medical Seizures: Hospitals Try Extreme Measures To Collect Their Overdue Debts," *Wall Street Journal* (October 30, 2003), at A1 (in pursuing debts incurred by poor and uninsured patients, some hospitals use harsh debt-collection technique known as "body attachment," in which insolvent debtors who fail to show up for court hearings are subject to arrest and prison).
63. Efficient breach is the idea that allowing a party to breach the contract and pay damages is sometimes more economically efficient than requiring performance. The *locus classicus* is Robert Birmingham, "Breach of Contract, Damage Measures, and Economic Efficiency," 24 *Rutgers L. Rev.* 273 (1970). See also the Restatement (Second) of Contracts (1981) at Chapter 16. For a critique of the efficient breach theory, see Ian R. Macneil, "Efficient Breach of Contract: Circles in the Sky," 68 *Virginia L. Rev.* 947 (1982).
64. Victor Tadros makes a similar argument in an unpublished manuscript entitled "Wrongs and Crimes" (unpublished manuscript), at 9. For an alternative explanation of why breach of contract is a civil wrong and promissory fraud (at least potentially) a crime, see Monu Bedi, "The Criminal/Civil Divide: An Inter-Common Law Analysis," (March 23, 2011), Stetson University College of Law Research Paper No. 2011–06. Available at SSRN: <http://ssrn.com/abstract=1793421>, at 46 (explaining the distinction based on the fact that contractual duties arise from agreements between the parties, whereas criminal law duties apply to everyone in society regardless of whether they agreed to do anything).
65. Theft Act 1978 s.3(1).
66. Id. at s. 4. Section 223.7(1) of the Model Penal Code contains a somewhat similar provision, though it is limited to theft of services and creates only a presumption that a theft has occurred: "Where compensation for service is ordinarily paid immediately upon the

rendering of such service, as in the case of hotels and restaurants, refusal to pay or absconding without payment or offer to pay gives rise to a presumption that the service was obtained by deception as to intention to pay."

67. [1974] AC 370. The defendant ordered a meal in a restaurant, intending at the time to pay. The meal was served, at which point the defendant changed his mind and decided not to pay. After ten minutes passed, he left the restaurant without paying. In upholding the conviction for obtaining pecuniary advantage by deception under the Theft Act, the House of Lords stated that it was appropriate to look at the defendant's conduct during the whole period he was in the restaurant. By continuing to act as if he would pay for the meal even after he had decided not to, the defendant had committed a fraud.

68. Paul H. Robinson et al., "Making Criminal Codes Functional: A Code of Conduct and a Code of Adjudication," 86 *J. Criminal Law and Criminology* 304, 309 (1996).

69. Id. at 309–310.

70. I previously developed this argument in Stuart P. Green, "Prototype Theory and the Classification of Offenses in a Revised Model Penal Code: A General Approach to the Special Part," 4 *Buffalo Crim. L. Rev.* 301, 337 (2000).

71. Feinberg, *Harmless Wrongdoing.*

72. John Locke, *Second Treatise of Government* (Thomas P. Peardon, ed.) (orig. pub. 1690) (Indianapolis: Bobbs-Merrill, rev. ed. 1952), at § 27. My discussion here was aided by the lucid summary in Justin Hughes, "The Philosophy of Intellectual Property," 77 *Georgetown L.J.* 287 (1988).

73. Locke, *Second Treatise,* at § 33.

74. Id. at § 34.

75. Id.

76. Id.

77. Wendy J. Gordon, "A Property Right in Self-Expression: Equality and Individualism in the Natural Law of Intellectual Property," 102 *Yale L.J.* 1533, 1545–1546 (1993).

78. Gordon, id. at 1545–46 (quoting Warren Quinn, "Actions, Intention, and Consequences: The Doctrine of Double Effect," in *Ethics: Problems and Principles* 178, 190 n.25 (John Martin Fischer and Mark Ravizaa, eds. 1991)). The argument is similar to one made by Dan Kahan in saying that "[e]conomic competition may impoverish a merchant every bit as much as theft. The reason that theft but not competition

is viewed as wrongful . . . is that against the background of social norms theft expresses disrespect for the injured party's moral worth whereas competition (at least ordinarily) does not." Dan M. Kahan, "The Secret Ambition of Deterrence," 113 *Harvard L. Rev.* 413, 420 (1999) (footnote omitted).

79. Jeremy Bentham, *An Introduction to the Principles of Morals and Legislation* (J. H. Burns and H. L. A. Hart, eds. 1970), at 303–304. More recently, Andrew Simester and Bob Sullivan have expressed similar views. "On the Nature and Rational of Property Offences," in *Defining Crimes: Essays on the Special Part of the Criminal Law* (R. A. Duff and Stuart P. Green, eds. 2005), at 168, 170. See also Liam Murphy and Thomas Nagel, *The Myth of Ownership: Taxes and Justice* (New York: Oxford University Press, 2002) (on conventional aspects of property and ownership more generally).

80. David Hume, *Treatise of Human Nature,* book III, part I, section I; see also Jeffrey Evans Stake, "The Property 'Instinct,' " 359 *Phil. Trans. R. Soc. Lond.* B 1763 (2004). To say that the rule against stealing reflects a prelegal norm is different, of course, from saying that the rule "one is under an obligation not to steal" is analytically true, as some have suggested, see P. T. Mackenzie, "The Analyticity of 'Stealing,' " 78 *Mind* 611 (1969); Roger Montague, "Stealing and Tautology," 17 *Philosophical Studies* 46 (1966).

81. Interestingly, there is some confusion about exactly where in the Torah the prohibition on stealing is properly located. *Lo tignov,* which Jews and most Protestants regard as the Eighth Commandment, and Catholics and Lutherans as the Seventh Commandment, is normally translated as "You shall not steal." *Exodus* 20:13; *Deuteronomy* 5:17. But many scholars, including Rashi, have suggested that this commandment is properly understood as prohibiting only the stealing of persons, or what is more familiarly known as kidnapping. See *Etz Hayim* (Philadelphia: Jewish Publication Society, 2001), at 448 (commentary on *Exodus* 20:13). According to this approach, the more general prohibition on stealing is found in the Tenth Commandment, *Exodus* 20:14 ("You shall not covet your neighbor's house . . . or anything that is your neighbor's."); *Deuteronomy* 5:18. More directly on point are the specific Levitical laws concerning duties owed to one's fellowmen: "You shall not steal; you shall not deal deceitfully or falsely with one another." *Leviticus* 19:11. "You shall not falsify measures of length, weight, or capacity. You shall have an honest balance [and] honest weights." *Leviticus* 19:35.

82. Douglas Hay, "Poaching and the Game Laws on Cannock Chase," in *Albion's Fatal Tree* (Douglas Hay, et al. eds, New York: Pantheon, 1975), 207–208. See also Clive Emsley, *Crime and Society in England, 1750–1900* (London: Longman, 2d ed. 1996) 81 ("[Hostility to the [poaching laws] was not confined to a single class and spread across social groups, particularly when the creatures defined by the law as protected were regarded by communities as vermin"). Something similar can be found with respect to the mid-nineteenth century prohibitions on gleaning, see Peter King, *Crime and Law in England, 1750–1840* (Cambridge: Cambridge University Press, 2006) 308–338, and taking water from a tap or pump in the street, see Emsley, at 2.

83. Robert Hughes, *The Fatal Shore: The Epic of Australia's Founding* (New York: Alfred A. Knopf, 1987) 357.

84. Lawrence Kohlberg, "The Development of Children's Orientation Towards a Moral Order: I. Sequence in the Development of Moral Thought," 6 *Vita Humana*, 11, 19 (1963).

85. See, e.g., Estelle Peisach and Mildred Hardeman, "Moral Reasoning in Early Childhood: Lying and Stealing," 142 *J. Genetic Psychology* 107 (1983); Jerome Kagan and Sharon Lamb (eds.), *The Emergence of Morality in Young Children* (Chicago: University of Chicago Press, 1987). See also Ori Friedman and Karen Neary, "First Possession Beyond the Law: Adults' and Young Children's Intuitions about Ownership," 83 *Tulane L. Rev.* 679 (2009) (reviewing research showing that children and adults make inferences about ownership based on the first person known to possess an object); Jeremy A. Blumenthal, " 'To Be Human': A Psychological Perspective on Property Law," 83 *Tulane L. Rev.* 609 (2009).

86. James E. Krier, "Evolutionary Theory and the Origin of Property Rights," 95 *Cornell L. Rev.* 139, 144 (2009).

87. Discussed in Bruce L. Benson, "Enforcement of Private Property Rights in Primitive Societies: Law Without Government," 1 *Journal of Libertarian Studies* 1 (1989). For a useful collection of articles on the evolutionary approach to property law, see Symposium, "The Evolution of Property Rights," 31 *J. Legal Studies* No. 2, Pt. 2 (2002).

88. Lawrence M. Friedman, *Crime and Punishment in American History* (New York: Basic Books, 1993) 108–109.

89. Jeffrey Evans Stake, "The Property 'Instinct,' " 359 *Philosophical Transactions of the Royal Society, Biological Sciences* 1763 (2004). See also Oliver R. Goodenough, "Why Do Good People Steal Intellectual Property?," *The Gruter Institute Working Papers on Law, Economics, and*

Evolutionary Biology: Vol. 4: Article 3, http://www.bepress.com/giwp/defauit/vol4/issl/art3 (2007).

90. See Donald Brown, *Human Universals* (New York: McGraw Hill, 1991) (among institutions and practices that appear in every human society is that of property).

91. Stake, "The Property Instinct," at 1765.

92. Consider the kinds of behavior that people demonstrate with respect to the possession of things. Studies show that people often demand more to give up some good they already possess than they would be willing to pay for the same thing. D. Kahneman and A. Tversky, "Choices, Values, and Frames," 39 *American Psychology* 341 (1984). What one has taken from one's "endowment" has a greater subjective impact than financially equivalent gains. As a result, people tend to be more aggressive in defending objects they already possess than they are in intruding on others' possession. This asymmetry has been referred to as the "endowment effect" or "bourgeois strategy." See Maynard Smith, *Evolution and the Theory of Games* (Cambridge University Press, 1992). See also Owen D. Jones and Sarah F. Brosnan, "Law, Biology, and Property: A New Theory of the Endowment Effect," 49 *William & Mary L. Rev.* 1935 (2008).

93. Cf. Paul H. Robinson et al., "The Origins of Shared Intuitions of Justice," 60 *Vanderbilt L. Rev.* 1633, 1654 (2007) (Core intuitions of justice "probably include the notions that unjustified physical aggression, taking of another's property, and cheating in exchanges are all wrong and should be punished"). I have previously considered the possibility that some aspects of criminal law reflect a "deep structure" or "universal grammar." Stuart P. Green, "The Universal Grammar of Criminal Law," 98 *Michigan L. Rev.* 2104 (2000).

94. CLRC Eighth Report, at 161.

95. See, e.g., Tom H. Clutton-Brock and Geoff A. Parker, "Punishment in Animal Societies," 373 *Nature* 209, 211 (1995) (behavior akin to theft is the target of retribution in animal societies).

96. Jeremy Bentham, *An Introduction to the Principles of Morals and Legislation* (J. H. Burns and H. L. A. Hart, eds. 1970), at 303–304.

97. Id.; Jeremy Bentham, *The Theory of Legislation* (Dobbs Ferry, NY: Oceana Publications, 1975) (orig. pub. 1802) 69.

98. *State v. Bennett,* 246 P.3d 387 (Idaho, 2010).

99. *State v. Sobiek,* 30 Cal.App. 3d 458 (1973).

100. Idaho Code § 18–2402(6).

101. *Bennett,* 246 P.3d at 389.

102. Earlier cases had held that joint owners of property could not steal from each other. See, e.g., *State v. Elsbury*, 175 P.2d 430, 434 (Nev. 1946).

103. *Sobiek*, 30 Cal.App. 3d at 468.

104. Consider, for example, the law concerning theft or fraud by failing to disclose information. Under Section 223(3) of the Model Penal Code, a defendant is liable for theft if she "fails to correct a false impression which . . . the deceiver knows to be influencing another *to whom he stands in a fiduciary or confidential relationship.*" MPC § 223.3(4) (emphasis added). Similarly, under Section 3 of the Fraud Act 2006, a defendant commits fraud if, among other things, he "dishonestly fails to disclose to another person information which he is *under a legal duty to disclose*" (emphasis added). See also Glanville Williams, "Mistake in the Law of Theft," 36 *Cambridge L.J.* 62 (1977) (on cases in which a victim owner is induced to transfer property mistakenly to the offender).

105. See Wayne Sandholtz, *Prohibiting Plunder: How Norms Change* (Oxford: Oxford University Press, 2007).

106. Emsley, *Crime and Society in England,* at 82.

107. See data cited in Chapter 4; see also Peñalver and Katyal, *Property Outlaws,* at 38 (noting, anecdotally, an increase in the number of their law students who have become more sympathetic to claims of intellectual property rights).

108. See generally Nicola Lacey, Celia Wells, and Oliver Quick, *Reconstructing Criminal Law: Text and Materials* (Cambridge: Cambridge University Press, 3d ed. 2003), 312–315.

109. David Gray makes a similar point in "Punishment as Suffering," 63 *Vanderbilt L. Rev.* 1619, 1662 (2010).

110. Cf. Laura Bathurst, "Theft as 'Involuntary Gifting' among the Tacana of Northern Bolivia," 7 *Tipití: Journal of the Society for the Anthropology of Lowland South America* 181 (2009) (among the Tacana, indigenous peoples of remote Northern Bolivia, an egalitarian ethic and strong "sharing obligations" are enforced by theft-like "involuntary gifting," in which property is redistributed from wealthy to poor).

111. The fact that *D* is not merely without property but is legally barred from owning it avoids the possibility that *D* is in some way to blame for his impoverishment. Nor is it necessary to worry about cases in which *D* voluntarily decides to forgo property ownership, as in a commune. I take it that a legal order that denied *D* property rights in this way would qualify as unjust even if *D*'s basic day-to-day needs were provided for.

112. For a useful discussion, see Carol M. Rose, "The Moral Sense of Property," (2007) 48 *William & Mary L. Rev.* 1897, 1899.

113. Thinking about theft in a society like this may shed light on what Proudhon meant when he made the famous claim that "property is theft." Pierre-Joseph Proudhon, *What Is Property?* (Donald R. Kelley and Bonnie G. Smith, eds.) (Cambridge: Cambridge University Press, 1994) (orig. pub. 1840). At one level, of course, the claim is self-refuting: Obviously, not all property can be theft since the concept of theft presupposes the existence of property. But, presumably, Proudhon was trying to point to the fact that a regime of property rights can be just or unjust. When it is used to oppress, the oppressor is acting "like a thief"—he is stealing what is owed to the oppressed. Cf. Abbie Hoffman, *Steal This Book* (Pirate Editions, 1971) (providing advice on stealing food, shoplifting, and stealing credit cards, among other crimes, and arguing that such conduct is not immoral when committed against an unjust regime).

114. The concepts of *malum prohibitum* and *malum in se* are dealt with at length in Stuart P. Green, "Why It's a Crime to Tear the Tag Off a Mattress: Overcriminalization and the Moral Content of Regulatory Offenses," 46 *Emory LJ.* 1533, 1570–1580 (1997).

115. John Rawls, *A Theory of Justice* (Cambridge, MA: Harvard University Press, 1971) 114–115 ("[I]n contrast with obligations [like those derived in the original position] natural duties have no necessary connection with institutions or social practices; their content is not, in general, defined by the rules of these arrangements. Thus we have a natural duty not to be cruel, and a duty to help another, whether or not we have committed ourselves to these actions. It is no defense or excuse to say that we have made no promise not to be cruel or vindictive. . . . Indeed, a promise not to kill, for example, is normally ludicrously redundant, and the suggestion that it establishes a moral requirement where none already existed is mistaken. . . . A further feature of natural duties is that they hold between persons irrespective of their institutional relationships; they obtain between all as equal moral persons").

116. J. W. Harris, *Property and Justice* (Oxford: Oxford University Press, 1996) 14.

117. Cf. Victor Tadros, "Poverty and Criminal Responsibility" (2009) 43 *Journal of Value Inquiry* 391, 392 (suggesting that a justification rationale in such cases might apply "to people who have less than their fair share of wealth who take goods from people who have more than their fair share of wealth"). Cf. M. C. Dillon, "Why Should Anyone Refrain from Stealing?," 83 *Ethics* 338 (1973) (addressing the

question of how people can be morally bound not to steal in an economically unjust world).

118. An even harder question arises in cases in which an unjustly impoverished offender steals from one who has not unjustly benefited from the system, including victims who are themselves unjustly impoverished. (This supposes, for purposes of discussion, that otherwise impoverished citizens were permitted to own certain limited types of property, or property of very low monetary value.) An argument could be made that, unless a given law of theft is enacted against a background of property laws that treat *D* fairly, the law is simply not binding on *D,* and his stealing would not be wrong. This approach seems inconsistent, however, with the intuition that the impoverished victim has had what few rights he possesses violated, and that it is *D* who is responsible for the violation. For this reason, I am inclined to say that *D* should be viewed as non-culpable only when he steals from those who are in some way complicit in causing his unjust impoverishment. For further discussion, see Stuart P. Green, "Just Deserts in Unjust Societies," in R. A. Duff and Stuart P. Green (eds.) *Philosophical Foundations of Criminal Law* (Oxford: Oxford University Press, 2011), at 352–376.

119. A fifth term that often characterized the difference between lawful and unlawful appropriations of property was "trespass." As described in Chapter 1, the earliest common law theft offenses, robbery and larceny, required that an owner have goods in his possession— typically, on his person or in his home or place of business—and that these be taken from him without his consent. It was this physical taking without the owner's permission that was said to constitute a trespass and therefore larceny. Thus, if the offender wrongfully converted property already in his possession, he did not take it from anyone else's possession and so could not be guilty of larceny. For example, one who sold property to another and then failed to deliver it could not be guilty of larceny. Nor would it be larceny for a repairman, who properly received an item to be repaired, if he later carried it off with intent to steal.

120. E.g., *Connecticut v. Huot,* 365 A.2d 1144, 1147 (Conn. 1976).

121. On why consent tends to appear primarily as an affirmative defense rather than as an offense element, see Stuart P. Green, "Consent and the Grammar of Theft Law," 28 *Cardozo Law Review* 2505, 2519–2521 (2007).

122. [1972] A.C. 626.

123. [1984] A.C 320.

124. [2001] 2 A.C. 241.

125. Peter Westen, *The Logic of Consent* (Farnham, Surrey: Ashgate, 2004), at 4.

126. Westen, at 180.

127. Hobbs Act, 18 U.S.C. § 1951(b)(2) (emphasis added).

128. *Smith v. United States,* 291 F.2d 220 (9th Cir. 1961); Schwartz and Kahan, "Theft," at 1559.

129. Model Penal Code § 232.2.

130. StGB § 242(1).

131. Model Penal Code § 223.2, Commentary at 166.

132. Larceny Act 1916, 6 & 7 Geo. 5, c. 50, §1(1) ("A person steals who, without the consent of the owner, fraudulently and without a claim of right made in good faith, takes and carries away anything capable of being stolen with intent, at the time of such taking, permanently to deprive the owner thereof"); Canadian Criminal Code § 322(1) ("[e]very one commits theft who fraudulently and without colour of right takes, or fraudulently and without colour of right converts to his use or to the use of another person, anything, whether animate or inanimate, with intent . . . (a) to deprive, temporarily or absolutely, the owner of it"); Queensland (Australia) Criminal Code § 155.(1)(a) (person "steals" if he "fraudulently takes the property or converts the property to the use of the person or anyone else"); French Penal Code Art. 311–1 ("*le vol est la soustraction frauduleuse de la chose d'autrui*"). There are also narrower contexts in which *fraudulently* refers specifically to the mental element necessary in some jurisdictions to commit embezzlement or larceny by a bailee. See, respectively, LaFave, (4th ed.) at 954 (describing law of embezzlement in some U.S. jurisdictions), and C. R. Williams and M. S. Weinberg, *Property Offences* (Sydney: The Law Book Co., 2d ed. 1986) 204–205 (describing law of larceny by bailee in Australian state of New South Wales).

133. Winifred H. Holland, *The Law of Theft and Related Offences* (Scarborough, Ontario: Carswell, 1998), at 182.

134. Id. at 177–178.

135. See *R. v. Pace,* 3 C.C.C. 348, 364 (1964) (Canada) and *R. v. Brais,* 7 C.C.C. (2d) 301 (B.C.C.A. 1972) (Canada), respectively.

136. J. T. Atrens, "The Mental Element in Theft," 3 *University of British Columbia L.Rev.* 112, 131 (1968).

137. *Cabbage, R. & R.* 292 (1815), cited in J. T. Lowe, "The Fraudulent Intent in Larceny," *Crim. L. Rev.* 78, 79 (1956); Atrens, "The Mental Element in Theft," at 131–132 (criticizing this view).

138. J. C. Smith, "The Fraudulent Intent in Larceny: Another View," *Crim. L.Rev.* 238, 240 (1956). The argument was stronger, Smith argued, where the defendant had the present ability to repay the money taken and therefore imposed no risk on the owner's property.

139. 2 C.C.C. 189 (Ont. C.A.) (1965) (Canada). Canadian courts have not, however, been consistent in accepting the "prank" defense. See, e.g., *Bogner v. The Queen,* [1975] 33 C.R.N.X. 349 (Que. C.A.) (taking of rocking chair from porch of hotel, though a "joke," was sufficient to establish theft).

140. *Oxford English Dictionary,* "Fraud."

141. Model Criminal Code Officers Committee of the Standing Committee of Attorneys-General, *Chapter 3: Theft, Fraud, Bribery and Related Offences Report*; Law Reform Commission of Canada, Report on Theft and Fraud, No. 12 (1979), at 28. In addition, many Canadian courts, in interpreting the term "fraudulently" under Canadian law, have looked to English cases interpreting the term "dishonestly."

142. Holland, *The Law of Theft,* at 183.

143. See, e.g., Nina Mazar and Dan Ariely, "Dishonesty in Everyday Life and its Policy Implications," 25 *J. Public Policy & Marketing* 1 (2006); On Amir, Dan Ariely and Nina Mazar, "The Dishonesty of Honest People: A Theory of Self-Concept Maintenance," 45 *J. Marketing Research* 633 (2008).

144. Theft Act 1968, s. 2(1)(a).

145. Theft Act 1968, s. 2(1)(b).

146. A. T. H. Smith, *Property Offences,* at 253.

147. Theft Act 1968, s. 2(1)(c). Chapter 3 will deal with failure to return lost property cases.

148. See, e.g., D. W. Elliott, "Dishonesty in the Theft Act: A Dispensable Concept," *Crim. L. Rev.* 395 (1982); P. Glazebrook, "Revising the Theft Acts," 52 Camb. L.J. 191, 193 (1993); Edward Griew, "Dishonesty: The Objections to Feely and Ghosh," *Crim. L. Rev.* 341 (1985); A. Halpin, "The Test for Dishonesty [1996] *Crim. L R.* 283; Alex Steel, "An Appropriate Test for Dishonesty?," 24 *Crim. L.J.* 46 (2000); C. R. Williams, "The Shifting Meaning of Dishonesty," 23 *Crim. L.J.* 275 (1999); Glanville Williams, "The Standard of Honesty," *New L.J.* (1983). Most of this criticism has gone to the question of how exactly to instruct the jury on the meaning of *dishonesty* and on the danger that different juries will reach inconsistent verdicts. Such procedural questions are not the concern here. In any event, it is somewhat ironic that *dishonesty* has been criticized on these grounds, given that its supposed advantage over its predecessor *fraudulently* was

that it would be easier for juries to understand. CLRC Eighth Report at 139.

149. [1973] Q.B. 530.

150. Id.

151. *Ghosh* [1982] Q.B. 1053.

152. The elaboration on *Ghosh's* hypothetical comes from J. C. Smith, *The Law of Theft*, at 74.

153. *Ghosh*, at 1064.

154. *Oxford English Dictionary*, "Dishonesty."

155. This was different from Biblical law, which used *gezel* exclusively in its more familiar sense of taking without consent. Menachem Elon, *Jewish Law: History, Sources, Principles* (Bernard Auerbach and Melvin J. Sykes, trans., Philadelphia: Jewish Publication Society, 1994), vol. 1, at 218.

156. Elon, id.

157. Maimonides, *The Code of Maimonides: Book XI (The Book of Torts)* (Hyman Klein, tr. 1954), at 1 S3 (emphasis added). For an even more radical theory of stealing that occurs in Jewish law, see Joseph Telushkin, *A Code of Jewish Ethics—II: Love Your Neighbor as Yourself* (New York: Bell Tower, 2009), at 160 (suggesting that person who refuses to give money to charity has committed theft).

158. See, e.g., Jeffrie G. Murphy, "Indian Casinos and the Morality of Gambling," in *Character, Liberty, and Law* (Dordrecht: Kluwer, 1998) 167. Maimonides's suggestion that gambling is immoral because one "gets something for nothing" does not seem to be a particularly promising start since such a view would seem to lead to the obviously problematic view that it is immoral as well to accept gifts.

159. E.g., *State v. Parsons*, 87 P. 399 (Wash. 1906).

160. See *Nichols v. State*, 32 N.W. 543 (Wis. 1887) (defendant gained entry while being concealed in a box).

161. Perkins and Boyce, *Criminal Law*, at 249.

162. Blackstone, *Commentaries* vol. 4, *227.

163. As for how such cases should be prosecuted in practice, consider again the case of the lawyer who converts his client's funds to his own use. I would say that such a defendant should be punished for the more serious of two offenses, embezzlement or false pretenses, but not both. It would be unjust to punish the defendant for both offenses since he committed only a single theft. Similarly, the defendant who commits burglary through breach of trust should be prosecuted for burglary (the more serious offense). On the other hand, the defendant who commits theft by both housebreaking and

violence (for example, by obtaining entry to a house by pointing a gun at the homeowner's head) should be prosecuted either for (1) theft by housebreaking and the separate offense of assault, or (2) robbery and the separate offense of criminal trespass, since both assault and criminal trespass are free-standing crimes. To punish the defendant for both robbery and burglary, however, would be to punish him twice for a single theft.

164. Nicolai V. Gogol, "The Overcoat," in *The Overcoat and Other Tales of Good and Evil* (David Magarshack, trans.) (New York: Norton, 1957) 257.

165. Cf. MPC Art. 222 with *Harris v. Commonwealth,* 477 S.E.2d 3 (Va. App. 1996), *aff'd en banc,* 484 S.E.2d 170 (1997).

166. Cf. Brendan O'Flaherty and Rajiv Sethi, "Why Have Robberies Become Less Frequent but More Violent?," 25 *J. Law, Economics & Organization* 518 (2009) (conceptualizing robbery as involving separate elements of acquisition and violence).

167. See H. Mitchell Caldwell and Jennifer Allison, "Counting Victims and Multiplying Counts: Business Robbery, Faux Victims, and Draconian Punishment," 46 *Idaho L. Rev.* 647 (2010).

168. 3 Co. Inst. *68 (quoted in Perkins and Boyce, *Criminal Law,* at 344).

169. E.g., Model Penal Code § 213.1.

170. See Eric Hobsbawm, *Bandits* (New York: New Press, rev. ed. 2000).

171. Model Penal Code § 222.1, Commentary at 98. On the sociology of robbery, see Richard T. Wright and Scott H. Decker, *Armed Robbers in Action: Stickups and Street Culture* (Boston: Northeastern University Press, 1997).

172. Discussed in Stuart P. Green, "Note to O. J.: Call the Dream Team," *Boston Globe* (Sept. 18, 2007). In November 2008, Simpson was convicted of numerous counts of robbery and kidnapping. Steve Freis, "O. J. Simpson Convicted of Robbery and Kidnapping," *N.Y. Times* (Oct. 4, 2008), http://www.nytimes.com/2008/10/04 /world/americas/04iht-simpson.1.16687098.html?_r=1&scp=1&sq= o.j.%20simpson%20convicted%20robbery&st=cse.

173. For cases holding that it is robbery to use force to recover goods that one owns, see *Edwards v. State,* 181 N.W.2d 383 (Wis. 1970); *State v. Ortiz,* 305 A.2d 800 (N.J. Super. 1973).

174. For cases holding that the proper charge is assault, see *R. v. Robinson* [1977] Crim. L.R.173; *People v. Gailegos,* 274 P.2d 608 (Colo. 1954); *Barton v. State,* 227 S.W. 317 (Tex. 1921); *R. v. Hennings,* 176 Eng. Rep. 462 (1864). See generally Rick Libman, *The Law of Robbery*

(Toronto: Carswell, 1999), at 265–286 (giving numerous examples of the defense of color of right in robbery).

175. *Gali v. State of Israel* [1986] Israel Sup. Ct. 40(4) 169 (applying Jewish law).

176. *State v. Sanchez*, 430 P.2d 781 (N.M. 1967).

177. Andrew Ashworth, "Robbery Re-assessed" [2002] *Crim. L. Rev.* 851. Yet there are cases holding that even a thief who snatches money or a purse from the victim's hand should not generally be regarded as having committed robbery, assuming that no resistance is encountered. *People v. Patton*, 389 N.E.2d 1174 (Ill. 1979). But if the victim's grasp was sufficiently firm that the original snatch was unsuccessful and the thief did not gain possession until after a struggle, then the offense is robbery. Perkins and Boyce, *Criminal Law*, at 347; *Bauer v. State*, 43 P.2d 203 (Ariz.1935).

178. *Principles of Criminal Law* (Oxford: Oxford University Press, 4th ed. 2003), at 391.

179. Id.

180. MPC § 222.1 (second degree felony). If the infliction or attempted infliction is purposeful, then it is treated as a first degree felony.

181. MPC § 223.2; MPC, Comments to Section 222.1, at 108.

182. E.g., N.Y. Penal Law Arts. 160.05 (third degree robbery is forcible stealing), 160.10 (second degree robbery is forcible stealing causing physical injury or involving the display of what appears to be a weapon), 160.15 (third degree robbery is forcible stealing causing serious physical injury or involving a deadly weapon); La. Rev. Stat. Arts. 14:64 (armed robbery), 14:64.1 (first degree robbery), 14:64.4 (second degree robbery), 14:65 (simple robbery), 14:65.1 (purse snatching).

183. This dynamic is discussed in greater detail in Stuart P. Green, "Consent and the Grammar of Theft Law," 28 *Cardozo L. Rev.* 2505, 2515–2516 (2007).

184. This usage I recommend is somewhat different from how the terms are used in both the United States and England. In the former, the term *extortion* typically is used to refer to threats to do both lawful and lawful acts unless *D* is paid, while the term *blackmail* is reserved specifically for cases in which the conduct threatened is the revelation of embarrassing information about *V*. In England, the term *extortion* is reserved for abuse of public office similar to soliciting or accepting a bribe. (It is also sometimes used in this sense in the United States.) *Blackmail*, in turn, is used more broadly to refer to cases in which a person, "with a view to gain for himself or another or

with intent to cause loss to another . . . makes any unwarranted demand with menaces." Theft Act 1968, c. 60, § 21. This latter kind of blackmail is broader than informational blackmail in that it (1) encompasses both demands for money and demands for something other than money and (2) is broad enough to encompass threats of a very wide range of conduct, both lawful and unlawful. A threatened course of conduct will be viewed as a violation of the Theft Act's blackmail provision only if it is deemed an "improper" means of reinforcing a demand. While it is clear that no act known by the defendant to be *unlawful* can be deemed proper, what is less clear under English law is when, if ever, threats to do what is *lawful* will be regarded as improper, and therefore extortionate. Thus, English blackmail law reflects an ambiguity similar to that seen under American extortion law.

185. This thereby gives rise to what is known as the blackmail paradox, the idea that while it is not a crime either to threaten to expose true but damaging information or to demand money as part of a business transaction, it is a crime if the two acts are combined. Having written about the paradox elsewhere, however, I will not do so again here. Green, *Lying, Cheating, and Stealing,* at 216–234; Stuart P. Green, "Taking it to the Streets," 89 *Texas Law Review.* See also 61-67 (2011), *http://www.texaslrev.com/seealso/vol/89/responses/green.*

186. Model Penal Code § 223.4.

187. Theft Act 1968 s. 21.

188. See generally Note, "A Rationale of the Law of Aggravated Theft," 54 *Columbia L. Rev.* 84 (1954).

189. A complex and contested body of scholarship considers exactly how to define the relevant baseline from which it can be determined whether *Y* will be made better off or worse off and whether coercion should be viewed as an essentially empirical concept (in which the question of whether *D* has coerced *V* can be answered based on facts alone, without reference to moral concepts), or whether instead it should be understood as an essentially normative concept (in which the question of whether *D* has coerced *V* cannot be answered without reference to moral judgments, such as whether *D* had a right to treat *V* in such manner). Because I have discussed these issues elsewhere, see Green, *Lying, Cheating, and Stealing,* at 93–96, and because their resolution is not essential for present purposes, I will not deal with them further here.

190. Joshua Dressler, *Understanding Criminal Law* (Newark: Lexis, 4th ed. 2006) 410.

191. Theft Act 1968 s. 9; Model Penal Code § 221.1. It is worth noting that, under the MPC, a "person may not be convicted for both burglary and for the offense which it was his purpose to commit after the burglarious entry," MPC § 221.1(3).

192. Model Penal Code § 221.0.

193. Theft Act 1968, s 9. For a recent study of burglary sentencing in England, see Sentencing Advisory Panel, *Consultation Paper on Sentencing for Burglary in a Dwelling* (2009), http://www.sentencing -guidelines.gov.uk/docs/Consultation%20paper%20on% 20sentencing%20for%20burglary%20in%20a%20dwelling.pdf.

194. For studies of the socio-psychology of burglary, see Richard T. Wright and Scott H. Decker, *Burglars on the Job: Streetlife and Residential Break-ins* (Boston: Northeastern University Press, 1994); Mike Maguire, in collaboration with Trevor Bennett, *Burglary in a Dwelling: The Offence, the Offender, and the Victim* (London: Heinemann, 1982); R. I. Mawby, *Burglary* (Cullompton, UK: Willan Pub., 2001).

195. See Gerald Gordon, *The Criminal Law of Scotland* (Michael Christie (ed.)), vol. 2, 57 (Edinburgh: W. Green, 3d ed. 2001).

196. See Stuart P. Green, "Castles and Carjackers: Proportionality and the Use of Deadly Force in Defense of Dwellings and Vehicles," 1999 *University of Illinois L. Rev.* 1, 28–29.

197. See R. A. Duff, "Harms and Wrongs," 5 *Buffalo Criminal L. Rev.* 13, 22–24 (2001).

198. John M. MacDonald, *Burglary and Theft* (Springfield, IL: Charles C. Thomas, 1980), 135. For further discussion of the effect of burglary on victims, see Roger Tarling and Tonia Davison, *Victims of Burglary: A Review of the Literature* (2000), p 6, http://www.victimsupport.org. uk/vs_england_wales/about_us/publications/burglary_in_britain _report.pdf.

199. Dressler, *Understanding Criminal Law,* at 592.

200. Model Penal Code § 223.

201. Theft Act 1968 s.1.

202. By this, I mean to exclude cases of larceny by trick, as developed in *Pear's Case.*

203. See Model Penal Code § 223.1, Commentary at 128. See also Alex Steel, "The Harms and Wrongs of Stealing: The Harm Principle and Dishonesty in Theft," 31 *University of New South Wales L.J.* 712, 726 (2008).

204. LaFave, *Criminal Law,* at 996 n. 1.

205. Fletcher, *Rethinking Criminal Law,* at 80.

206. *Oxford English Dictionary,* "Furtive."

207. *Oxford English Dictionary*, "Stealth."

208. As Sissela Bok has put it, "[g]iven both the legitimacy of some control over secrecy and openness, and the dangers this control carries for all involved, there can be no presumption either for or against secrecy in general. Secrecy differs in this respect from lying, promise-breaking, violence, and other practices for which the burden of proof rests on those who would defend them. Conversely, secrecy differs from truthfulness, friendship, and other practices carrying a favorable presumption." Sissela Bok, *Secrets: On the Ethics of Concealment and Revelation* (New York: Pantheon Books, 1982), at 26–27.

209. Dressler, *Understanding Criminal Law*, at 562–563.

210. For a detailed socio-psychological study of embezzlement, see Donald R. Cressey, *Other People's Money* (New York: Free Press, 1953).

211. The subject of disloyalty is dealt with in more detail in Green, *Lying, Cheating, and Stealing*, at 98–106.

212. William Shakespeare, *Henry the Fourth, Part I*, IV.ii.14–16.

213. Similar is the famous case of *Bazeley*, 2 Leach 835, 168 Eng. Rep. 517, 563 (1799) (bank teller took money given him by customer for benefit of his employer and converted it to his own use). On the history of embezzlement, see John Styles, "Embezzlement, Industry and the Law in England, 1500–1800," in Maxine Berg, Pat Hudson, and Michael Sonenscher (eds.), *Manufacture in Town and Country Before the Factory* (Cambridge: Cambridge University Press, 1983), 173–210.

214. Hisham Ramadan, "Larceny Offenses in Islamic Law," 2006 *Michigan State L. Rev.* 1609, 1617.

215. *Anon. v. State of Israel*, 35 (4) PD 438 (1981) (Alon, J.), quoted in "Theft and Robbery," in *Jewish Virtual Library*, http://www.jewishvirtuallibrary .org/jsource/judaica/ejud_0002_0019_0_19785.html.

216. See, e.g., Cal. Penal Code § 463; Hawaii Rev. Stat. 111. Comp. Stat. Ann. § § 720 ILCS 5/42–1, 5/42–2; La. Stat. Ann. § 14:62; Miss. Code. Ann. § 97–17–65; N.C. Gen. Stat. § 14–288.6; S.C. Code Ann. § 16–7–10.

217. See Stuart P. Green, "Looting, Law, and Lawlessness," 81 *Tulane L. Rev.* 1129, 1137–1138, 1140–1142 (2007).

218. The argument offered here is developed in much greater detail in Green, id. As in the case of robbery, there is a question about how looting should be classified. On the one hand, it might reasonably be grouped along with offenses against the public order, such as breach of the peace, riot, disorderly conduct, and vagrancy. On the other hand, to the extent that it is viewed as yet another theft offense, it is properly classified as an offense against property.

219. See Havidán Rodríguez et al., "Rising to the Challenges of a Catastrophe: The Emergent and Prosocial Behavior Following Hurricane Katrina," 604 *Annals American Academy Politics & Social Science* 82 (2006).
220. *Cf.* Kenneth W. Simons, "On Equality, Bias Crimes, and Just Deserts," 91 *J. Crim. L. & Criminology* 237, 247–248 (2000) (offering argument that one who exploits vulnerability can justifiably be considered more culpable than one who does not because such exploitation "often reveals an especially heinous disregard for the humanity of others").
221. E. L.Quarantelli and Russell R. Dynes, "Property Norms and Looting: Their Patterns in Community Crises," 31 *Phylon* 168, 169 (1970) (criticizing this view).
222. Dressler, *Understanding Criminal Law,* at 611–612.
223. The concept is discussed in Green, *Lying, Cheating, and Stealing,* at 76–87.
224. Hershey H. Friedman, "*Geneviat Da'at*: The Prohibition Against Deception in Today's World," http://www.jlaw.com/Articles /geneivatdaat.html. The classic text on the subject is Yosef Caro, *Shulchan Aruch* (Choshen Mishpat, 228:6). It should be noted, however, that the offense of *geneviat da'at* is not a perfect analogy to theft by deception since it includes acts that do not involve the appropriation of property. For example, one may not go to the house of a mourner with a bottle of wine that is only partially full and place it strategically among other bottles in a way that people would assume that the reason the bottle was empty was that people had already drunk from it.
225. Vera Bergelson, "Victims and Perpetrators: An Argument for Comparative Liability in Criminal Law," 8 *Buffalo Crim. L. Rev.* 385, 426 (2005); Bernd Schünemann, "The Role of the Victim Within the Criminal Justice System: A Three-Tiered Concept," 3 *Buffalo Crim. L. Rev.* 33, 39–40 (1999) (citing additional German sources).
226. Joe Nocera, "Madoff Victims, Get Over It," *New York Times Executive Blog* (June 29, 2009), http://executivesuite.blogs.nytimes.com/2009 /06/29/madoff-victims-get-over-it/?scp=1&sq=madoff%20victims %20greed&st=cse
227. Model Penal Code § 223.3.
228. MPC § 224.5.
229. MPC § 224.
230. Obtaining property, obtaining a money transfer, obtaining a pecuniary advantage, procuring the execution of a valuable security,

obtaining services, securing the remission of a liability, inducing a creditor to wait for or to forgo payment, and obtaining an exemption from or abatement of liability. Theft Act 1968 ss. 15, 15A, 15B, 16 ; Theft Act 1978 ss. 1, 2. Despite the inclusion of theft in the Theft Acts, the term *theft* in Britain is often reserved for the unlawful obtaining of property through non-deceptive means.

231. Fraud Act 2006, ss 2, 3, 4, 6, and 7, respectively. For a helpful commentary, see David Ormerod, "The Fraud Act 2006—Criminalizing Lying?," *Criminal L. Rev.* 193 (2007).

232. Ormerod and Williams, *Smith's Law of Theft,* at 152–153.

233. *R. v. Jones* [1704] 91 E.R. 330.

3. THEFT AS A CRIME

1. See Douglas Husak, "Crimes Outside the Core," 39 *Tulsa L. Rev.* 755, 762 (2004).

2. The phrase comes from Frances Allen, "The Morality of Means: Three Problems in Criminal Sanctions," 42 *University of Pittsburgh L. Rev.* 737, 738 (1981).

3. For a discussion of such problems, see, e.g., Henry M. Hart, "The Aims of the Criminal Law," 23 *Law & Contemp. Problems* 404 (1958); Paul H. Robinson, "The Criminal-Civil Distinction and the Utility of Desert," 76 *Boston University L. Rev.* 201 (1996); Carol S. Steiker, "Punishment and Procedure: Punishment Theory and the Criminal-Civil Divide," 85 *Georgetown L.J.* 775 (1997).

4. Glanville Williams, "The Definition of Crime," 8 *Current Legal Problems* 107 (1955).

5. Even here, though, it should be acknowledged that there are ambiguities in light of various hybrid civil/criminal remedies. See generally Kenneth Mann, "Punitive Civil Sanctions: The Middleground Between Criminal and Civil Law," 101 *Yale L.J.* 1795 (1992); Andrew Ashworth and Lucia Zedner, "Defending the Criminal Law: Reflections on the Changing Character of Crime, Procedure, and Sanctions," 2 *Criminal Law and Philosophy* 21 (2008).

6. Richard Price, *Lush Life* (New York: Farrar, Straus and Giroux, 2008) 432.

7. Restatement of Torts, § 222A; *Moore v. Regents of the University of California,* 793 P.2d 479 Cal. 1990).

8. W. Page Keeton et al., *Prosser and Keeton on Torts* (Minneapolis: West, 5th ed. 1984), at 92.

9. Stuart M. Speiser et al., *The American Law of Torts*, vol. 7 (Minneapolis: West, 1990), at 697. See also William L. Prosser, "The Nature of Conversion," 42 *Cornell L. Rev.* 168 (1957).

10. Keeton et al., *Prosser and Keeton on Torts*, at 93.

11. Dan B. Dobbs, *The Law of Torts* (Minneapolis: West, 2000), at 130–132.

12. Keeton, at 91 (citing *Herrick v. Humphrey Hardware Co.*, 103 N.W. 685 (Neb. 1905)).

13. See Courtney W. Franks, Comment, "Analyzing the Urge to Merge: Conversion of Intangible Property and the Merger Doctrine in the Wake of *Kremen v. Cohen*," 42 *Houston L. Rev.* 489 (2005).

14. *Kremen v. Cohen*, 337 F.3d 1024, 1033 (9th Cir. 2003).

15. *Custom Teleconnect, Inc. v. Int'l Tel-Servs., Inc.* 254 F. Supp. 2d 1173, 1182 (D. Nev. 2003).

16. Restatement (Second) of Torts § 217.

17. The classic case is *Fouldes v. Willoughby*, 151 Eng. Rep. 1153 (Exch. 1841). See also Prosser, "The Nature of Conversion," at 172.

18. Patricia L. Bellia, "Defending Cyberproperty," 79 *New York University L. Rev.* 2164, 2166 (2004).

19. Dobbs, *The Law of Torts*, at 1343.

20. Id. at 1343–1344 (citing cases).

21. E.g., Pamela H. Bucy, "Fraud by Fright: White Collar Crime by Health Care Providers?," 67 *North Carolina L. Rev.* 855 (1989). One possible substantive difference between civil and criminal fraud occurs in certain securities law contexts, where criminal fraud is sometimes said to require "willfulness," while civil fraud is said to require the lesser mental state of "scienter." The distinction, however, is a relatively slight one. See Joseph Conahan et al., "Securities Fraud," 40 *American Criminal L. Rev.* 1041, 1049–1051 (2003).

22. 248 U.S. 215 (1918).

23. These are considered in Stuart P. Green, "Plagiarism, Norms, and the Limits of Theft Law: Some Observations on the Use of Criminal Sanctions in Enforcing Intellectual Property Rights," 54 *Hastings L.J.* 204–205.

24. See, e.g., *United States Golf Association v. Arroyo Software Corp.*, 81 Cal. Rptr. 2d 708 (Ct. App. 1st Dist. 1999).

25. Colo Rev. Stat. § 18–4–702 (theft of cable television services); Wash. Code Ann. § 4.24.320 (theft of livestock); Wis. Stat. § 779.02(5) (theft by contractor).

26. E.g. Conn. Gen Stat. § 52–564; Fla. Stat. Ann. § 812.35(6); Minn. Stat. Ann. § 604.14; Tex. Civil Practice & Remedies Code § 134.003.

27. E.g., 21 U.S.C. § 853; Racketeering Influenced and Corrupt Organizations Act (RICO), 18 U.S.C. § 1964; *United States v. Bailey,* 419 F.3d 1208 (11th Cir. 2005) (action for conversion and civil theft against famed criminal defense attorney F. Lee Bailey); see also Jennifer Anglim Kreder, "The Choice between Civil and Criminal Remedies in Stolen Art Litigation," 38 *Vanderbilt J. Transnational Law* 1199 (2005).

28. Cf. Neal Kumar Katyal, "Architecture as Crime Control," 111 *Yale L.J.* 1039 (2002); Ian Ayres and Steven D. Levitt, "Measuring Positive Externalities from Unobservable Victim Precaution: An Empirical Analysis of Lojack," 108 *Q.J. Economics* 43 (1998).

29. Joel Feinberg, *Harm to Others* (New York: Oxford University Press, 1987), at 4.

30. Douglas Husak, *Overcriminalization: The Limits of the Criminal Law* (New York: Oxford University Press, 2008).

31. Id. at 55.

32. Id. at 121.

33. Id. at 132.

34. Stuart P. Green, "Is There Too Much Criminal Law?," 6 *Ohio State J. Criminal L.* 737 (2009).

35. Jonathan Schonsheck, *On Criminalization: An Essay in the Philosophy of the Criminal Law* (Dordrecht: Kluwer Academic Publishers, 1994). As this book was going to press, there also appeared A.P. Simester and Andreas von Hirsch, *Crimes, Harms, and Wrongs: On the Principles of Criminalisation* (Oxford: Hart Publishing, 2011).

36. Joel Feinberg, "The Expressive Function of Punishment," in *Doing and Deserving: Essays in the Theory of Responsibility* (Princeton: Princeton University Press, 1970), 95, 98.

37. See Antony Duff, *Punishment, Communication and Community* (Oxford: Oxford University Press, 2001).

38. See Paul H. Robinson and John M. Darley, "The Utility of Desert," 91 *Northwestern. University L. Rev.* 453, 471 (1997).

39. Immanuel Kant, *The Metaphysics of Morals* (Cambridge: Cambridge University Press, 1996) (Mary Gregor, trans.), at 105 [6:332].

40. Id. at 16 [6:333].

41. Id. For an insightful discussion of this dynamic, see David Gray, "Punishment as Suffering," 63 *Vanderbilt L. Rev.* 1619, 1661–1663 (2010).

42. Husak, *Overcriminalization,* at 14.

43. See, e.g., Marvin Wolfgang et al., *National Survey of Crime Severity* (Washington, D.C.: U.S. Department of Justice—Bureau of Justice Statistics) (1985).

44. Id. at vi–x. The first scenario scored 15.5, while the second scored 7.3.
45. See Model Penal Code § 223.1(2).
46. O. F. Robinson, *The Criminal Law of Ancient Rome* (Baltimore, MD: Johns Hopkins University Press, 1995) 24.
47. Id.
48. See *Jones v. Whalley* [2006] 3 W.L.R. 179 (leaving open the question whether private prosecution is still available in the United Kingdom); see also Stuart P. Green, Note, "Private Challenges to Prosecutorial Inaction: A Model Declaratory Judgment Statute," 97 *Yale Law J.* 488 (1988).
49. Federal Bureau Investigation, U.S. Dept. of Justice, *Crime in the United States: Uniform Crime Reports,* at 6 (2010) http://www2.fbi.gov/ucr /cius2009/offenses/property_crime/larceny-theft.html.
50. David Jacobs, "Inequality and Economic Crime," 66 *Sociology & Soc. Research* 12 (1981); Bill McCarthy and John Hagan, "Homelessness: A Criminogenic Situation," 31 *British J. Criminology* 393 (1991); Steven Stack, "Income Inequality and Property Crime," 22 *Criminology* 229 (1984).
51. Lawrence C. Becker, "Criminal Attempts and the Theory of the Law of Crimes," 3 *Philosophy & Public Affairs* 262, 273 (1974).
52. Id. at 279.
53. Id.
54. Susan Dimock, "Retributivism and Trust," 16 *Law and Philosophy* 37, 44 (1997).
55. Sandra Marshall and R. A. Duff, "Criminalization and Sharing Wrongs," 11 *Canadian J. Law & Jurisprudence* 7, 18 (1998). These views are developed in R. A. Duff, *Punishment, Communication, and Community* (2001) 61. A related argument is made by Grant Lamond, "What is a Crime?," 27 *Oxford J. Legal Studies* 609, 621 (2007) (better way to understand crimes is "not as wrongs *to* the public but as wrongs that the community is *responsible* for punishing").
56. Marshall and Duff, "Criminalization and Sharing Wrongs," at 13.
57. Id. at 18.
58. Id. at 19. But see Vera Bergelson, *Victims, Offenders, and Comparative Responsibility* (Stanford, Cal.: Stanford University Press, 2008) (arguing that the victim's comparative fault is relevant in assessing the defendant's culpability).
59. Marshall and Duff, "Criminalization and Sharing Wrongs," at 21.
60. Cf. Marshall and Duff, "Criminalization and Sharing Wrongs," at 10 (implying that such a position will normally be apparent).
61. See, e.g., 18 U.S.C. § 641 (theft of federal money or property).

62. Federal Bureau Investigation, U.S. Dept. of Justice, *Crime in the United States: Uniform Crime Reports,* at 6 (2010) http://www2.fbi.gov/ucr /cius2009/offenses/property_crime/index.html. *Property crime* is defined to include burglary, larceny-theft, motor vehicle theft, and arson. These numbers do not include the so-called theft of intellectual property, a subject that is dealt with in Chapter 4.

63. FBI, *Uniform Crime Reports,* http://www2.fbi.gov/ucr/cius2009 /offenses/property_crime/larceny-theft.html. The statistics in the United Kingdom are similar. In England and Wales in 2007–2008, 79 percent of police and 73 percent of British Crime Survey (BCS) recorded crimes were property related. C. Kershaw, S. Nicholas, and A. Walker (eds.), *Crime in England and Wales 2007–08: Findings from the British Crime Survey and Police Recorded Crime* (Home Office Statistical Bulletin, July 2008), http://www.homeoffice.gov.uk/rds/pdfs08 /hosb0708.pdf.

64. Id. at Table 1. *Larceny-theft* is defined to include pocket-picking, purse-snatching, shoplifting, theft from motor vehicles (except accessories), motor vehicle accessories, bicycles, from buildings, from coin-operated machines, and "all others."

65. Id. at Table 24.

66. http://www2.fbi.gov/ucr/cius2009/offenses/property_crime/larceny -theft.html. Thefts of motor vehicle parts, accessories, and contents makes up the largest portion of reported larcenies—35.8 percent. Id. at Table 23.

67. On the decline in property values, see, e.g., Steve Gibbons, "The Costs of Urban Property Crime," 114 *Economic Journal* 441 (2004); George E. Tita et al., "Crime and Residential Choice: A Neighborhood Level Analysis of the Impact of Crime on Housing Prices," 22 *J. Quantitative Criminology* 299 (2006). On reduction of life satisfaction, see Mark A. Cohen, "The Effect of Crime on Life Satisfaction," 37 *J. Legal Studies* 325 (2008). On psychological distress, see Fran H. Norris and Krzysztof Kaniasty, "Psychological Distress Following Criminal Victimization in the General Population: Cross-Sectional, Longitudinal, and Prospective Analyses," 62 *J. Consulting & Clinical Psychology* 111 (1994). On the decline of neighborhoods, see Julie Berry Cullen and Steven D. Levitt, "Crime, Urban Flight, and the Consequences for Cities," 81 *Rev. Economics & Statistics* 159 (1999); Martin T. Katzman, "The Contribution of Crime to Urban Decline," 17 *Urban Studies* 277 (1980); Ralph B. Taylor, "The Impact of Crime on Communities," 539 *Annals of the American Academy of Political and Social Science* 28 (1995).

68. Damien Cave, "Nonstop Theft and Bribery Stagger Iraq," *N.Y. Times* (Dec. 2, 2007), http://www.nytimes.com/2007/12/02/world/middleeast/02baghdad.html.

69. Andrew Jacobs, "Rampant Fraud Threat to China's Brisk Assent," *N.Y. Times* (October 7, 2010) http://www.nytimes.com/2010/10/07/world/asia/07fraud.html?pagewanted=1&emc=eta1.

70. By *economically efficient,* I mean simply that resources are optimally allocated to serve each person in a way that will produce the most utility while minimizing waste. Many law and economics scholars would deny that thefts can be efficient given the existence of so-called secondary or indirect costs associated with theft, such as the costs of security and of avoiding victimization. See Fred S. McChesney, "Boxed In: Economists and Benefits from Crime," 13 *Int'l Rev. of Law and Econ.* 225 (1993); Gordon Tullock, "The Welfare Costs of Tariffs, Monopolies, and Theft," 5 *Western Econ. J.* 224 (1967); D. Usher, "Theft as a Paradigm for Departures from Efficiency," 39 *Oxford Economic Papers* 235 (1987). It is the total value of primary and secondary costs that is said to justify a blanket prohibition of theft. However, as Husak points out, this contention is an *ipse dixit*: "it is simply an article of faith that thefts must be inefficient when these secondary costs are included in the calculations." Husak, *Overcriminalization,* at 183. For a sophisticated critique of the inefficiency-of-theft hypothesis from within the perspective of law and economics, see Richard L. Hasen and Richard H. McAdams, "The Surprisingly Complex Case Against Theft," 17 *Int'l Rev. of Law & Economics* 367 (1997). For an interesting discussion of the inefficiency hypothesis in the context of intellectual property, see Jonathan M. Barnett, "What's So Bad About Stealing?," 4 *J. Tort Law* 1, 11–13 (2011).

71. One thinks of cases of self-defense, defense-of-others, military combat, law enforcement, mercy killings, and perhaps some rare political assassinations.

72. Guido Calabresi and A. Douglas Melamed, "Property Rules, Liability Rules, and Inalienability Rules: One View of the Cathedral," 85 *Harvard L. Rev.* 1089, 1126 (1972). Perhaps the first scholar to offer an economic theory of crimes was Gary S. Becker, in "Crime and Punishment: An Economic Approach," 76 *J. Political Economy* 169 (1968). Becker's main focus was on the optimal level of criminal enforcement.

73. Richard Posner, *Economic Analysis of Law* 163–164 (orig. ed. 1973); see also Richard Posner, "Economic Theory of the Criminal Law," 85 *Columbia L. Rev.* 1193 (1985).

74. Stephen P. Garvey, "Punishment as Atonement," 46 *UCLA L. Rev.* 1801, 1832–1833 (1999) (footnotes omitted). For a critical assessment of the law and economics approach to criminal law, see Jules L. Coleman, "Crime, Kickers, and Transaction Structures," in J. Pennock and J. Chapman (eds.), *NOMOS XXVII: Criminal Justice* 313 (New York: New York University Press, 1985).

75. Claire Finkelstein, "The Inefficiency of *Mens Rea*," 88 *California L. Rev.* 895 (2000). See also Husak, *Overcriminalization*, at 180–187.

76. See, e.g., Alon Harel and Uzi Segal, "*Criminal Law* and Behavioral Law and Economics: Observations on the Neglected Role of Uncertainty in Deterring Crime," 1 *American Law* & Economics Rev. 276 (1999).

77. Kenneth D. Tunnel, *Choosing Crime: The Criminal Calculus of Property Offenders* (Chicago: Nelson-Hall Pubs. 1992), at 2, 39, 43–50. For insight into the psychology of professional thieves, see Bruce Jackson, *Outside the Law: A Thief's Primer* (New Brunswick, NJ: Transaction Books, 1972) and Edwin H. Sutherland, *The Professional Thief* (Chicago; University of Chicago Press, 1937).

78. The analysis here is suggested by Robert Cooter and Thomas Ulen, *Law and Economics* (Saddle River, NJ: Prentice Hall, 5th ed. 2008).

79. Thanks to Ken Simons for his help here.

80. See, e.g., Daniel S. Nagin, "Criminal Deterrence Research at the Outset of the Twenty-First Century," 23 *Crime & Justice* 1 (1998).

81. Another approach would be to conduct a "laboratory experiment" to test the deterrent effect of criminal sanctions on the incidence of theft. See William T. Harbaugh, Naci H. Mocan, and Michael S. Visser, "Theft and Deterrence," Working Paper 17059 (May 2011), http://www.neber.org/papers/w17059. In this study, high school and college students were given small amounts of money and various opportunities to steal, as well as variable information regarding the likelihood of being caught and the severity of monetary penalties. They were then asked how much they would steal in a given situation. Given that the stakes were so low and that none of the subjects faced the possibility of being deprived of their liberty regardless of how much they stole, as well as the fact that more than 95 percent of the subjects stole in at least one or more of the imagined circumstances, and that nearly half stole in every one of the thirteen sets of opportunities given, I am skeptical that the results of this study can be viewed as particularly meaningful.

82. See, respectively, Copyright Felony Act, Pub. L. No. 102–561, 106 Stat. 4233 (1992) (codified as amended at 18 U.S.C. § 2319 (1994)); No

Electronic Theft Act of 1997, Pub. L. No. 105–147, 111 Stat. 2678 (amending 17 U.S.C. § 506(a) (1994)); Douglas Hay, "Poaching and the Game Laws on Cannock Chase," in Douglas Hay et al. (eds.), *Albion's Fatal Tree* (New York: Pantheon, 1975), 207–208.

83. See Leon Radzinowicz, *A History of English Criminal Law and its Administration from 1750* (New York: Macmillan, 1948) vol. 1, at 501. Though, as Radzinowicz points out, it is unclear whether what rose was the incidence of pickpocketing itself or instead merely its rate of prosecution and conviction.

84. See generally Darryl K. Brown, "Cost-Benefit Analysis in Criminal Law," 92 *California L. Rev.* 323 (2004).

85. Regarding indirect costs of criminalization, such as stress on families, single parents, stigma, harm to family dynamics, diminished earning potential, increased juvenile delinquency, and increased risk of abuse, see generally Marc Mauer and Meda Chesney-Lind (eds.), *Invisible Punishment: The Collateral Consequences of Mass Imprisonment* (New York: New Press, 2002); John Hagan and Ronit Dinovitzer, "Collateral Consequences of Imprisonment for Children, Communities, and Prisoners," in Michael Tonry and Joan Petersilia (eds.), 26 *Crime and Justice: A Review of Research* 121 (Chicago: University of Chicago Press, 1999).

86. See Nils Jareborg, "Criminalization as Last Resort *(Ultima Ratio),*" 2 *Ohio State J. Crim. L.* 521 (2004).

87. Andrew Ashworth, *Principles of Criminal Law* (Oxford: Oxford University Press, 4th ed. 2003) 66.

88. Cf. Douglas Husak, "The Criminal Law as Last Resort," 24 *Oxford J. Legal Studies* 207, 224–225 (2004) (expanding on this point).

89. Id. at 224.

90. Max L. Veech and Charles R. Moon, "De Minimis Non Curat Lex," 45 *Michigan L. Rev.* 537 (1947).

91. Feinberg, *Harms to Others,* at 189.

92. Id.

93. Ashworth, *Principles of Criminal Law,* at 48.

94. Brent G. Filbert, "Defense of Inconsequential or *De Minimis* Violation in Criminal Prosecution," 68 *A.L.R.* 5th 299, 299 (2006).

95. *Hessel v. O'Hearn,* 977 F.2d 299, 303 (7th Cir. 1992).

96. For a similar argument, see Stanislaw Pomorski, "On Multiculturalism, Concepts of Crime, and the '*De Minimis*' Defense," 1997 *Brigham Young University L. Rev.* 51, 54 (1997).

97. Id. at 78.

98. Model Penal Code § 2.12, Commentary at 403.

99. Id. at 403–404.
100. N.J. Stat. Ann. § 2C:2–11; Haw. Rev. Stat. § 702–236; Pa. Cons. Stat. Ann. tit. 18, § 312; Me. Rev. Stat. Ann. tit. 17A, § 12; Guam Code Ann. tit. 9, § 7.67.
101. *Talmud,* Sanhedrin 57a; *Maimonides Reader,* at 156.
102. *R. v. Li* [1984] 16 C.C.C. (3d) 382 (Ont. H.C.).
103. Statute of Westminster I, 3 Edw. 1, ch. 15 (1275).
104. See Ramadam, "Larceny Offenses in Islamic Law," 2006 *Michigan State L. Rev.* at 1627.
105. Though, for a discussion of how juries deal with cases in which the harm is *de minimis,* see Harry Kalven, Jr. and Hans Zeisel, *The American Jury* (Boston: Little, Brown, 1966) 258–285.
106. 480 A.2d 236 (N.J. Super. 1984). In dismissing the case, the court found that at the time of the offense, the defendant was a full-time student pursuing a degree in electrical engineering, that he had no prior record, that a conviction would seriously damage his ability to find a job in the engineering field, that he had worked his way through college, and that he had already suffered substantial detriment in his personal life from the notoriety of his arrest.
107. 485 A.2d 345 (N.J. Super. 1984).
108. For a New Jersey case holding that the defense did not apply, see *State v. Stern,* 484 A.2d 38 (N.J. Super. 1984) (refusing to apply the defense to a case involving theft of $42.15 through the padding of an expense account).
109. 417 A.2d 712 (Pa. Super. 1980).
110. 504 A.2d 330 (Pa. Super. 1986). See also *Commonwealth v. Matty,* 619 A.2d 1383 (Pa. Super. 1993) (refusing to reverse on *de minimis* grounds a conviction for theft of services in the amount of $32.00 in a case involving a prison warden who used a prison inmate and county funds to install a fan in the home of his secretary's mother).
111. Cf. Andrew von Hirsch, *Past or Future Crimes: Deservedness and Dangerousness in the Sentencing of Criminals* (Manchester: Manchester University Press, 1985) 86 ("Shoplifting is not rendered serious by the large number of people who commit this crime and by the aggregate injury done, for no shoplifter has control over the number of other persons who choose to engage in this conduct.")
112. I have written about the role of reactive emotions in criminal law in Green, *Lying, Cheating, and Stealing,* at 123–124.
113. Saint Augustine, *Confessions* (Henry Chadwick, trans.) (New York: Oxford University Press, 1998), book II, at 33.
114. See Marshall and Duff, "Criminalization and Sharing Wrongs," at 13.

115. See Douglas Husak, "The *De Minimis* 'Defense' to Criminal Liability," in R. A. Duff and Stuart P. Green, *Philosophical Foundations of Criminal Law* (Oxford: Oxford University Press, 2011), 328. I am grateful to Husak for helpful discussions on this topic of concurrent common interest.

116. Id. at 345.

117. Id. at 346.

118. Id. at 345.

119. Tried in jurisdictions with draconian Three Strikes legislation, some repeat offenders who committed relatively minor cases of theft ended up receiving life sentences. See, e.g., *Lockyer v. Andrade,* 538 U.S. 63 (2003) (upholding, against Eighth Amendment challenge, life sentence for habitual offender who shoplifted approximately $150 in videotapes from two different stores).

120. Cf. Douglas Husak, "The *De Minimis* 'Defense' to Criminal Liability," at 69 (considering *de minimis* defense in the context of possession of small amounts of prohibited drugs).

121. Cf. *Raymon v. Alvord Independent School District,* 639 F.2d 257, 257 (5th Cir. 1981) ("[e]ach litigant who improperly seeks federal judicial relief for a petty claim forces other litigants with more serious claims to await a day in court").

122. Feinberg, *Harm to Others,* at 189–190. See also Andrew Inesi, "A Theory of *De Minimis* and a Proposal for Its Application in Copyright," 21 *Berkeley Tech. L.J.* 945, 953 (2006).

123. Arizona Stat. § 13–1805(G); California Penal Code § 490.5; Colorado Crim. Code § 53a–119; Delaware Code Ann., tit. 11, part I, ch. 5, subch. III, subpart D, § 840; District of Columbia Code Div. iv, § 22–3213; Florida Crim. Code § 812.015(8); Georgia Crim. Code § 16–8–14; Hawaii Rev. Stat. div. 5, tit. 37 § 708–833.5; Idaho Crim. Code § 18–4624; Ill. 16A–3; Kansas Crim. Code § 60–3331(g); Maryland Code of Crimes § 3–1301(g); Massachusetts Gen. Laws, part IV, title I, ch. 266, § 30A; Michigan Stat. § 750.356c; Minnesota Crim. Code § 629.366; Mississippi Stat. § 97–23–93; Nebraska Stat. 28–511.01; North Carolina Stat. §14–72(e); New Hampshire Rev. Stat. tit. LXII, ch. 644:17; New Jersey Stat. Ann. 2C:20–11; New Mexico Stat. Ann. § 30–16–20; Pennsylvania Penal Code 3929; Puerto Rico Penal Code ch. 269, subch. I, § 4271c; Rhode Island Gen. Laws § 11–14–20; South Carolina Stat. § 16–13–110; Utah Crim. Code § 76.6–602; Vermont Crim. Code § 2577; West Virginia Stat. § 61–3A–3; Wisconsin Crim. Code § 943.50(4); Wyoming Stat. Ann. § 6–3–404.

124. Arizona Stat. § 13–1805.
125. See, e.g., D.C. Stat. § 22–3213(a). Alternatively, the concealment of property is sometimes taken to create a presumption, or constitute *prima facie* evidence that the defendant intended to steal it. See Alaska Crim. Law § 11.46.220; Arizona Crim. Code § 13–1805(B); Arkansas Stat. § 5–36–102; Connecticut Penal Code § 53a–119(9); Delaware Crim. Code § 840; Indiana Code § 35–43–4–4; Kentucky Rev. Stat., tit. XL, § 433.234; Maine Crim. Code § 361–A; Mississippi Stat. § 97–23.93(2); North Carolina Stat. § 14–72.1(a); New Mexico Crim. Code § 30–16–22; South Carolina Stat. § 16–13–120.
126. E.g. Mass. Gen. Laws Part IV, ch. 266, § 30A.
127. Alaska Stat. § 09.68.110; Ariz. Rev. Stat. § 12–691, 13–1805; Calif. § 490.5(c); Connecticut Gen. Stat. § 52–564a; Delaware Code tit. 10, Part V, ch. 81, § 8143(a)(1); Ill. § 16A–7; Kansas § 60–3331(a); Maryland § 3–1302; Massachusetts Gen. Laws, part III, title II, ch. 231, § 85F _; Michigan § 600.2953; Mississippi Code § 97–23–96; Mo. § 570.087.1(2); Montana § 27–1–718; Nebraska § 26–21–194; Nevada Rev. Stat. tit. 52, § 597.860; New Hampshire Rev. Stat. tit. LV, ch. 544-C:1; New Jersey Stat. Ann. § 2A:61C–1; New Mexico Stat. § 30–16–21; North Carolina Gen. Stat. § 1–538.2; Okla. tit. 21, part VII, ch. 68, § 1731.1; Oregon Rev. Stat. tit. 3, § 30.875; Rhode Island Gen. Laws § 11–41–28; South Dakota Stat. § 22–30A.19.1; Tennessee Code Ann. § 39–14–144; Utah Code Ann. § 78–11–15; Virginia Ann. Code § 8.01–44.4; Washington RCW § 4.24.230(1); West Virginia Stat. Ann. § 1–1–127; Wisconsin Stat. § 943.51(1).
128. Arizona Rev. Stat. § 12–692; California § 490.5(b); Delaware Code tit. 10, Part V, ch. 81, § 8143; Idaho § 48–702; Kansas § 21–3701(b); Missouri Stat. § 570.087.1(3); Nevada Rev. Stat. tit. 52, § 597.870; North Carolina Gen. Stat. § 1–538.2(b); Tennessee Code Ann. § 39–14–144(2); Utah Code Ann. § 78–11–16; Washington RCW § 4.24.230(2); W.V. Stat. Ann. § 1–1–127(b).
129. Alaska § 11.46.230; Arizona § 13–1805(c); Ark. Code § 5–36–116; Cal. § 490.5(f); Colo. § 18–4–407; Conn. Gen. Stat. § 52a–119a(a); Del. §840; Fla. § 812.015(3); Idaho § 48–705; Iowa § 808.12; Kansas § 433.236; Ky. Rev. Stat., tit. XL, § 433.236; Miss. § 97–23–95; Mont. § 7–32–4303; N.C. § 14–72.1(c); Nev. Rev. Stat. tit. 52, § 597–850; R.I. Gen. Laws § 11–41–21; S.D. § 22–30A–19.2; Tenn. § 40–7–116; Utah Code Ann. § 77–7–12; Va. Ann. Code § 8.01–226.9; Vermont § 2576; W.V. Ann. Code § 61–3A–4; Wyo. Stat. Ann. § 6–3–404.
130. Alaska § 15–10–14; Mass. Gen. Laws, part III, title II, ch. 231, § 94B; Mich. Comp. Laws § 600.2917; N.D. § 12–34–14(2); Utah Code

§ 77–7–14. A few states also make it a crime to possess a shoplifting device. Conn. Gen. Stat. § 53a–127f; Fla. § 812.015(7); Mich. § 764.16; Minn. Stat. § 609.521; Mich. § 764.16; Miss. SEC § 97–23–93.1; N.D. § 12.1–23–14(1); N.M. § 30–16–23; Va. Code Ann. § 18.2–105.2; W.V. § 61–3A–4a.

131. For parallel developments in Europe, see Peter Lewisch, "A Case Study on the Legal Regulation of Shoplifting in Austria and the 'Criminal Tourism' from the East," 12 *International Rev. Law & Economics* 439 (1992); W. L. F. Felstiner and A. B. Drew, "Should Some Theft be Decriminalized? A Look at the (West) German Experience," 17 *Judges' Journal* 16 (1978); M. S. Zaki, "Shoplifting—Problem and Criterion of Decriminalization," *Revue de Science Criminelle et de Droit Penal Compare* 521 (Sept. 1977).

132. Dena Cox et al., "When Consumer Behavior Goes Bad: An Investigation of Adolescent Shoplifting," 17 *J. Consumer Research* 149 (1990).

133. See generally Allison Morris, *Women, Crime and Criminal Justice* (Oxford: Blackwell, 1987) 29–31; D. J. I. Murphy, *Customers and Thieves: An Ethnography of Shoplifting* (Aldershot, UK: Gower, 1986); Lloyd W. Klemke, *The Sociology of Shoplifting: Boosters and Snitches Today* (Westport, CT: Praeger, 1992).

134. American Psychiatric Association, *The Diagnostic and Statistical Manual of Mental Disorders* 667 (Arlington, VA: American Psychiatric Assoc., 4th ed. revised, 2000); Therese Krasnovsky and Robert C. Lane, "Shoplifting: A Review of the Literature," 3 *Aggression and Violent Behavior* 219 (1998).

135. National Association for Shoplifting Prevention, *http:// shopliftingprevention.org.* According to one social history, during the nineteenth century, a new form of consumer culture enticed middle-class women not only to shop in department stores, but also to steal. In the interest of concealing this darker side of consumerism, the authorities allowed such women (though not their working-class counterparts) to shoplift and then plead that they were suffering from what was a newly invented incapacitating illness. Elaine S. Abelson, *When Ladies Go-A-Thieving: Middle Class Shoplifters in the Victorian Department Store* (Oxford: Oxford University Press, 1989). As this book was going to press, there appeared another social history of shoplifting: Rachel Shteir, *The Steal: A Cultural History of Shoplifting* (New York: Penguin Press, 2011).

136. On the other hand, as the economy worsened in late 2008 and more people were out of work, the incidence of shoplifting markedly

increased. Ian Urbina and Sean D. Hamill, "As Economy Dips, Arrests for Shoplifting Soar," *N.Y. Times* (Dec. 23, 2008), http://www.nytimes.com/2008/12/23/us/23shoplift.html?emc=eta1.

137. Note, "Shoplifting and the Law of Arrest," 62 *Yale L.J.* 799–800 (1953).

138. Jerry Adler, "The Thrill of Theft," *Newsweek* (Feb. 25, 2002).

139. "Report: Wal-Mart Loosens Shoplifting Policy," *CNNMoney.com,* http://money.cnn.com/2006/07/13/news/companies/walmart _shoplifters/index.htm.

140. See, e.g., National Coalition to Prevent Shoplifting, *Shoplifting and the Law—a Model Code* (Rockville, MD: National Criminal Justice Reference Service, 1980).

141. See, e.g., Ariz. Rev. Stat. §13–1805(C).

142. Corey Kilganon and Jeffrey E. Singer, "Stores' Treatment of Shoplifters Tests Rights," *N.Y. Times* (June 22, 2010), http://www.nytimes.com/2010/06/22/nyregion/22shoplift.html?scp=1&sq= shoplifting&st=cse.

143. One of the interesting side effects of such practices is that employee theft and shoplifting committed against small retail businesses tend to be significantly underreported to the police. See Natalie Taylor, *Reporting of Crime against Small Retail Businesses* (Canberra: Australian Institute of Criminology, 2002).

144. Matt Villano, "Sticky Fingers in the Supply Closet," *N.Y. Times* (April 30, 2006); *2006 Stealing Vault Office Supplies Survey,* http://www.vault.com/pdf-ads/survey-results/Stealing%20Office%20Supplies %20Survey%20Results%20112006.pdf; see also Association of Certified Fraud Examiners, *2006 Report to the Nation on Occupational Fraud and Abuse, <2006 Report to the Nation on Occupational Fraud and Abuse>.*

145. Another problem is theft of proprietary data, such as customer lists, particularly by employees who have recently been "downsized." See Ponemom Institute, *Data Loss Risks During Downsizing* (Feb. 23, 2009), http://www.ponemon.org/local/upload/fckjail/generalcontent/18 /file/Data%20Loss%20Risks%20During%20Downsizing%20 FINAL%201.pdf.

146. *2006 Stealing Vault Office Supplies Survey.* For other explanations of how employees rationalize thefts from employers, see J. Greenberg and K. S. Scott, "Why Do Workers Bite the Hands That Feed Them? Employee Theft as a Social Exchange Process," 18 *Research in Organizational Behavior* 11 (1996); Roy J. Lewicki et al., "Dishonesty as Deviance: A Typology of Workplace Dishonesty and Contributing

Factors," *Research on Negotiation in Organizations,* vol. 6, 53 (Roy J. Lewicki et al., eds., 1997); J. M. Schmidtke, "The Relationship Between Social Norm Consensus, Perceived Similarity, and Observer Reactions to Coworker Theft," 46 *Human Resource Management* 561 (2007).

147. In this context, it is worth noting that the Bible gives field workers the right to eat a small amount of the crop they are working to harvest, while nevertheless protecting the field owner from rapacious workers who would take too much. See *Deuteronomy* 23:26–27 ("When you come [as a worker] into another man's vineyard, you may eat as many grapes as you want, until you are full, but you must not put any in your vessel. When you enter another man's field of standing grain, you may pluck ears with your hand; but you must not put a sickle to your neighbor's grain").

148. See MPC §§ 210(2) & (3); 211.1; Markus D. Dubber, *Criminal Law: Model Penal Code* (New York: Foundation Press, 2002) 182.

149. Fowler V. Harper and Fleming James, Jr., *The Law of Torts,* vol. 1, at 113–115 (1956); William L. Prosser, "The Nature of Conversion," 42 *Cornell L. Rev.* 168, 169 (1957). The word *trover* comes from the French *trouver,* to find.

150. LaFave, *Criminal Law,* at 928–931; Perkins and Boyce, *Criminal Law,* at 308–314.

151. MPC § 223.5.

152. J. C. Smith, The Law of Theft *(London: Butterworths, 8th ed. 1997) § 2-117, at 70–71.*

153. Theft Act 1968, s. 3(1).

154. See Holland, *The Law of Theft,* at 137 (in the context of finding, "a later formation of intent following an innocent acquisition would constitute theft").

155. Tony Honoré, "Are Omissions Less Culpable?" in Peter Cane and Jane Stapleton (eds.), *Essays for Patrick Atiyah* (Oxford: Oxford University Press, 1991) 31, 33–34. For alternative approaches, see Larry Alexander, "Criminal Liability for Omissions: An Inventory of Issues," in Stephen Shute and A. P. Simester (eds.), *Criminal Law Theory: Doctrines of the General Part* (Oxford: Oxford University Press, 2002); Andrew Ashworth, "The Scope of Criminal Liability for Omissions," 105 *Law Quarterly Rev.* 424 (1989); A. P. Simester, "Why Omissions are Special," 1 *Legal Theory* 311 (1995); Glanville Williams, "Criminal Omissions," 107 *Law Quarterly Rev.* 86 (1990).

156. Simon de Bruxelles, "Magistrate Convicted for Giving Wife Rolex He Found in Tesco's," *TimesOnline.com* (Jan. 28, 2005) http://www

.timesonline.co.uk/tol/news/uk/article507375.ece. Similar is the case of the lost iPhone discussed later in the chapter.

157. See Michael J. Broyde and Michael Hecht, "The Return of Lost Property According to Jewish and Common Law: A Comparison," 12 *J. Law & Religion* 225, 235 (1995–1996) ("The exact parameters of the obligation to assist in property return is of some dispute within Jewish law. Most authorities are of the opinion that one who sees lost property and then declines to pick it up has transgressed both the negative prohibition of 'you have no right to withdraw [from returning it]' and the positive commandment of 'you shall give it back to him.'") (citations omitted). The moral obligation to act affirmatively to find the owner of lost property is based on Deuteronomy 22:1–3, which states: "If you see your fellow's ox or sheep gone astray, do not ignore it; you must take it back to him. . . . You shall do the same with his ass; you shall do the same with his garment; and so too shall you do with anything that your fellow loses and you find; you must not remain indifferent."

158. John Kleinig, "Good Samaritanism," 5 *Philosophy & Public Affairs* 382 (1976). For example, Vermont's statute, Vt. Stat. Ann. tit. 12 § 519(a), makes it a crime to fail to give "reasonable assistance" to another person whom one "knows . . . is exposed to grave physical harm," if such aid "can be rendered without danger or peril" to the bystander.

159. I leave to the side those cases in which the found property is itself vital to a person's physical well-being, as where a defendant finds another's vial of insulin, takes possession of it, and fails to look for its owner.

160. Perhaps this asymmetry reflects the "endowment effect" or "bourgeois strategy" inherent in our attitudes towards property described in Chapter 2, to the effect that people tend to be more aggressive in defending objects they already have in their possession than they are in intruding on others' possession. See Owen D. Jones and Sarah F. Brosnan, "Law, Biology, and Property: A New Theory of the Endowment Effect," 49 *William & Mary L. Rev.* 1935 (2008).

161. The seminal piece is J. O. Urmson, "Saints and Heroes," in *Essays in Moral Philosophy,* A. Melden (ed.) (Seattle: University of Washington Press, 1958). For a helpful taxonomy of morally significant actions, see Heidi Hurd, "Duties Beyond the Call of Duty," 6 *Annual Review of Law and Ethics* 1 (1998) (taxonomy includes actions that are required, actions that are forbidden, actions that are praiseworthy but not required [supererogatory], actions that are blameworthy but not forbidden [suberogatory], actions that are supererogatory if

performed and suberogatory if omitted, and amoral or morally neutral actions).

162. Richard G. Jones, "Cabdriver Thanked for Returning a Stradivarius," *N.Y. Times* (May 7, 2008), http://www.nytimes.com/2008/05/07 /nyregion/07violin.html?scp=3&sq=stradivarius&st=nyt.

163. E.g., N.Y. Pers. Prop. L. §§ 251–58.

164. Against this it might be argued that the relevant question is not how one would feel if one lost one's watch and had the finder return it, but rather how one would feel if one lost one's watch and knew that its finder was *failing* to return it. If this is right, it suggests an interesting asymmetry in our reactive emotions that calls for further inquiry.

165. Mark D. West, "Losers: Recovering Lost Property in Japan and the United States," 37 *Law and Society Review* 369 (2003).

166. Saul Levmore, "Waiting for Rescue: An Essay on the Evolution and Incentive Structure of the Law of Affirmative Obligations," 72 *Virginia L. Rev.* 879 (1986).

167. Model Penal Code § 223.5.

168. Theft Act s. 39(1). Cf. Emanuel Melissaris, "The Concept of Appropriation and the Offence of Theft," 70 *Modern L. Rev.* 581, 590–591 (2007) (arguing that property left with an offender for safekeeping is not appropriated by the offender unless and until he "replace[s] the owner in [a] special proprietary relationship with the thing. . . . His attitude towards the [left property] is that of its owner, he behaves as if the [property] were *his*").

169. Were Rowlett to withdraw the funds and spend them, I assume that he would be unambiguously guilty of theft, since he would have knowingly appropriated funds belonging to another with the intent to deprive the other of them permanently. Cf. *R. v. Shadrokh-Cigari* [1988] Crim. L.R. 465.

170. See, e.g., R. H. Helmholz, "Equitable Division and the Law of Finders," 52 *Fordham L. Rev.* 313 (1983); R. H. Helmholz, "Wrongful Possession of Chattels: Hornbook Law and Case Law," 80 *Northwestern University L. Rev.* 1221 (1987); William Landes and Richard Posner, "Salvors, Finders, Good Samaritans, and Other Rescuers: An Economic Study of Law and Altruism," 7 *J. Legal* Stud. 83 (1978); Jennifer S. Moorman, "Finders Weepers, Losers Weepers? Benjamin v. Lindner Aviation, Inc.," 82 *Iowa L. Rev.* 717 (1997); John V. Orth, "What's Wrong with the Law of Finders and How to Fix It," 4 *Green Bag* 2d 391 (2001); Richard A. Posner, "Savigny, Holmes, and the Law and Economics of Possession," 86 *Virginia L. Rev.* 535 (2000).

171. Julian Barnes, "Kitty Zipper," *The New Yorker* (Sept. 29, 1997), 78.

172. For another example of the difficulty in determining when property should properly labeled abandoned, see *Williams v. Phillips,* 41 Crim. App. Rep. 5 (1957) (upholding theft conviction of "dustmen" who helped themselves to trash left on curb by householder for trash collection by local authority; court reasoned that refuse remained property belonging to the householder until collected, whereupon property passed to the local authority); see generally Robin Hickey, "Stealing Abandoned Goods: Possessory Title in Proceedings for Theft," 26 *Legal Studies* 584 (2006).

173. "Can You Keep Ship-Wrecked Goods?," *BBC News,* http://news.bbc .co.uk/1/hi/magazine/6287047.stm.

174. "Police Crack Down on Scavengers," *BBC News,* http://news.bbc .co.uk/2/hi/uk_news/england/6290887.stm.

175. Joseph William Singer, *Introduction to Property* (New York: Aspen, 2d ed. 2005), at 803; Leeanna Izuel, Comment, "Property Owners' Constructive Possession of Treasure Trove: Rethinking the Finders Keepers Rule," 38 *UCLA L. Rev.* 1659 (1991).

176. La. Civ. Code § 3420.

177. Singer, *Introduction to Property,* at 803.

178. Id.

179. See, e.g., *Rex v. Pierce,* 6 Cox Crim. Cas. 117 (1852). The distinction between lost and mislaid property is even more significant in Jewish law. See Broyde and Hecht, "The Return of Lost Property According to Jewish and Common Law." While a person is compelled to act affirmatively when he encounters lost property, he is in fact prohibited from picking up mislaid property, the rationale being that if property is placed in a particular place that is relatively secure, the easiest way to ensure that the object is returned to its owner is to do nothing: the owner will return to retrieve possession.

180. Perkins and Boyce, *Criminal Law,* at 311, make a similar point.

181. The predominant term in the United States is *receiving,* in England *handling,* and in Canada *possessing.* I shall use all three terms interchangeably, except where specifically noted.

182. The text in this section borrows from Stuart P. Green, "Thieving and Receiving: Overcriminalizing the Possession of Stolen Property," 14 *New Criminal Law Review* 35 (2011).

183. 3 & 4 Wm. & M., c.9, § 4 (1692).

184. Larceny Act, 7 & 8 Geo. IV, c. 29, § 54 (1827).

185. MPC Article 233 (treating receiving as interchangeable, for purposes of proof, with, and subject to same penalty as, theft by unlawful

taking, theft by deception, theft by extortion, and theft by failing to return lost or misdelivered property).

186. Under Canadian law, theft of property worth more than $5,000 is subject to a term not exceeding ten years, and theft of property worth less than that is subject to a term not exceeding two years. Criminal Code of Canada §§ 322, 334. The same penalty scheme applies, *mutatis mutandi,* to possession of stolen property. Id. at §§ 354–355. See also Holland, *The Law of Theft,* at 285–297.

187. The maximum penalty for handling is fourteen years, Theft Act 1968, s. 22, while the maximum penalty for theft is seven years, s. 7. For an explanation of why the scheme works this way, see below note 236.

188. 80 Eng. Rep. 4 (1602).

189. Slander could also be committed by attributing to the plaintiff a loathsome or communicable disease, a matter inconsistent with the proper conduct of one's business, or unchastity (in the case of a woman). See Fowler V. Harper et al., *Harper, James, and Gray on Torts,* § 5.10–13, at 376–387 (New York: Aspen) (discussing four categories of slander actionable per se).

190. *Dawson,* 80 Eng. Rep. 4.

191. See generally Wayne T. Logan, "Criminal Law Sanctuaries," 38 *Harvard Civil Rights-Civil Liberties L. Rev.* 321 (2003).

192. 3 & 4 Wm. & M., c. 9, § 4 (1692). One problem, however, was that an offender could not be convicted of being an accessory to handling unless the principal had already been convicted. 5 Anne c. 31.

193. LaFave, *Criminal Law,* at 985; Larceny (England) Act, 7 & 8 Geo. IV, c. 29, § 54 (1827). The history and policies surrounding the offense of receiving stolen property are considered in detail in Jerome Hall, *Theft, Law, and Society,* ch.5 (2d ed. 1952).

194. Bruce P. Smith, "The Presumption of Innocence and the English Law of Theft, 1750–1850," 23 *Law & History Rev.* 133, 142 (2005).

195. Id.

196. Id. at 158.

197. G. Robert Blakey and Michael Goldsmith, "Criminal Redistribution of Stolen Property: The Need for Law Reform," 74 *Michigan L. Rev.* 1511, 1512 (1976).

198. See generally Gerald Howson, *Thief-Taker General: Jonathan Wild and the Emergence of Crime and Corruption as a Way of Life in Eighteenth-Century England* (Piscataway, NJ: Transaction Publishers, 1985; orig. publ. 1970); Hall, *Theft, Law, and Society,* at 73–76.

199. E.g., *Coates v. State,* 229 N.E. 2d 640 (Ind. 1967) (where charge was receiving but evidence was that defendant had committed theft, case was unproved); *Seymour* [1951] 1 All E.R. 1006 (C.C.A.).

200. MPC § 223.1(1). Another related development in twentieth-century law that deserves mention here is the proliferation of money laundering laws. As Peter Alldridge has explained: "Offences of handling have the obvious similarity to offences of laundering in that they are offences of disposal of unlawfully acquired property. There is a substantial overlap between handling and laundering offences and there have been suggestions that the laundering offences are little but an updated version of handling. In many ways the panic surrounding laundering now has echoes of that surrounding Wild and the other thief-takers in the eighteenth century." Peter Aldridge, *Money Laundering Law: Forfeiture, Confiscation, Civil Recovery, Criminal Laundering and Taxation of the Proceeds of Crime* (Oxford: Hart Publishing, 2003) 210.

201. There is an exception if "the property is received, retained, or disposed with purpose to restore it to the owner."

202. Model Penal Code § 223.6.

203. English Theft Act 1968 s. 22(1).

204. Canadian Criminal Code § 354.

205. Under Canadian law, only theft of property worth more than $5,000 is indictable as a felony, id. at § 334(a), and only possession of property obtained by means of a felony constitutes criminal possession, § 354(1)(a).

206. Interestingly, *belief* is not a *mens rea* term that is even recognized by the general part of the MPC, see § 2.02(2).

207. Victor Tadros, "Wrongdoing and Motivation," in *Philosophical Foundations of Criminal Law* (R. A. Duff and Stuart P. Green, eds., 2011) 206, 210.

208. Id. at 211.

209. Theft Act 1968 s. 22(1) (emphasis added).

210. MPC § 223.2(1) (emphasis added).

211. MPC Commentary, § 223.6, at 232.

212. See MPC Commentary, § 223.2, at 163–64.

213. Cf. David Ormerod, "The Fraud Act 2006—Criminalising Lying," *Crim. L. Rev.* [2007] 193, 206 (noting that "in theft there must actually be a transfer").

214. *Maimonides Reader: Mishneh Torah, Book 11: Torts* 156–157 (Isadore Twersky ed.) (Springfield, NJ: Berhman House, 1972).

215. Marilyn Walsh and Duncan Chappel, "Operational Parameters of the Stolen Property System," 2 *J. Criminal Justice* 113, 126 (1974).

216. A. T. H. Smith, *Property Offences* (London: Sweet & Maxwell, 1994), at 944 (citing *Battams*, 1 Cr. App. R.(S) 15, 16 (1979)).

217. The extent to which even this is true will vary depending in part on the type of good stolen: some goods, such as personal electronics, jewelry, and automobiles, are said to be "hotter" than others. See Ronald V. Clarke, *Hot Products: Understanding, Anticipating and Reducing Demand for Stolen Goods,* Police Research Series Paper 112 (London: Home Office, 1999), http://rds.homeoffice.gov.uk/rds /prgpdfs/fprs112.pdf.

218. The term *proxy crimes* is used by, among others, Larry Alexander and Kim Ferzan, with Stephen Morse, *Crime and Culpability: A Theory of Criminal Law* (Cambridge: Cambridge University Press, 2009).

219. See, e.g., Husak, *Overcriminalization,* at 44–45; Andrew Ashworth and Lucia Zedner, "Just Prevention: Preventive Justice and the Limits of the Criminal Law," in R. A. Duff and Stuart P. Green (eds.), *Philosophical Foundations of Criminal Law* (Oxford: Oxford University Press, 2011) 279; Markus Dirk Dubber, "Policing Possession: The War on Crime and the End of Criminal Law," 91 *J. Crim. L. & Criminology* 829 (2002); Markus Dirk Dubber, "The Possession Paradigm: The Special Part and the Police Power Model of the Criminal Process," in R. A. Duff and Stuart P. Green (eds.), *Defining Crimes: Essays on the Special Part of the Criminal Law* (Oxford: Oxford University Press, 2005) 91; George Fletcher, *Rethinking Criminal Law* (Boston: Little, Brown, 1978) 197–202.

220. See Sanford H. Kadish, "Complicity, Cause and Blame: A Study in the Interpretation of Doctrine," 73 *California L. Rev.* 323, 343 (1985).

221. Cf. Perkins and Boyce, *Criminal Law,* at 394 (referring to cases in which the receiver "induces misguided youths to steal and sometimes even teaches them the 'tricks of the trade.'"). On the question, more generally, whether an actor who commits the actual crime and the one who aids and abets in her act should be regarded as equally culpable, see Green, *Lying, Cheating, and Stealing,* at 209.

222. See R. D. Hursh, Annotation, "Thief as Accomplice of One Charged with Receiving Stolen Property, or Vice Versa, Within Rule Requiring Corroboration or Cautionary Instruction," 53 *A.L.R.2d* 817 (1957).

223. The case is discussed further in Stuart P. Green, "iPhone, Gizmodo, and Moral Clarity about Crime," *Christian Science Monitor* (May 4, 2010), http://www.csmonitor.com/Commentary/Opinion/2010 /0504/iPhone-Gizmodo-and-moral-clarity-about-crime.

224. Greg Sandoval et al., "The People Involved in Sale of Lost iPhone Revealed," *CNet News* (April 29, 2010), http://news.cnet.com/8301 –13579_3–20003782–37.html.

225. Christopher Kutz, "Causeless Complicity," 1 *Criminal Law & Philosophy* 289 (2007). Kutz considers the case of the Department of Justice attorneys who wrote legal memoranda offering a rationale under which detainees suspected of terrorism could be deprived of their right under international law to be free from torture and other forms of abuse, and asks whether the lawyers could be held liable as accomplices to those who actually carried out the torture. In some cases, the memoranda were apparently written in advance of the acts of torture; in other cases, the acts of torture came first and the memoranda were written later, as a means to justify conduct that had already occurred. In the first sort of case, the basis for complicity is straightforward: the lawyers' memoranda arguably encouraged the commission of the acts. The question here, though, is whether the memo writers were morally complicit in the second sort of case as well.

226. Id. at 304.

227. I assume that, on this point, similar reasoning informs Jewish law, which prohibits charitable organizations from accepting contributions from convicted criminals, those under indictment, or those who are known to be involved in criminal enterprises. See Joseph Telushkin, *A Code of Jewish Ethics—II: Love Your Neighbor as Yourself* (New York: Bell Tower, 2009), at 230.

228. Kutz himself is unusual in his willingness to push the idea of criminal complicity well beyond what I assume most criminal law scholars would be willing to endorse. See, e.g., Michael S. Moore, *Causation and Responsibility: An Essay in Law, Morals, and Metaphysics* (Oxford: Oxford University Press, 2009) 299–323; Joshua Dressler, "Reassessing the Theoretical Understandings of Accomplice Liability: New Solutions to an Old Problem," 37 *Hastings L.J.* 91 (1985); Markus Dubber, "Criminalizing Complicity: A Comparative Analysis," 5 *J. International Crim. Justice* 977 (2007); John Gardner, "Complicity and Causality," 1 *Criminal Law & Philosophy* 127 (2007); Robert Weisberg, "Reappraising Complicity," 4 *Buffalo Crim. L. Rev.* 217 (2000).

229. Megan O'Toole, "Ballad of a Bike Dealer," *National Post* (Dec. 16, 2009).

230. As noted, under the Theft Act, the maximum penalty for handling stolen property (fourteen years—Theft Act 1968, s. 22) is greater than the maximum penalty for theft (seven years—id. at s.7). From

this, one might assume that the Theft Act regards handling as the greater wrong. In fact, the real rationale is somewhat more complicated. According to the Criminal Law Revision Committee Report, there might be cases in which a court is called upon to sentence an offender who receives property obtained in a robbery, rather than merely a theft. Because the penalty for robbery is higher than that for theft (indeed, the maximum penalty for robbery is life in prison, Theft Act 1968, s.8), the Committee apparently felt that a court should have the option of imposing a higher penalty for receiving, if only in such cases. Criminal Law Revision Committee, Eighth Report: *Theft and Related Offences,* Cmnd. 2977 (1967), ¶143, at 69.

231. Cf. N.Y. McKinney's Penal Law § 263.11, § 263.16 with N.Y. McKinney's Penal Law § 263.10. A similar distinction is made under federal law. Cf. 18 U.S.C. § 2251(e) (punishment for producing child pornography is fifteen to thirty years) with 18 U.S.C § 2252(b) (punishment for possessing child pornography is five to twenty years). For an argument that the distinction between production and possession should be made even sharper, see Carissa Byrne Hessick, "Disentangling Child Pornography from Child Sex Abuse," 88 *Washington University L. Rev.* 853 (2011). Similarly, possession of 2,880 mgs. of methadone is considered a class A-II felony (meriting, for first time offenders, a prison term of between three and ten years—N.Y. McKinney's Penal Law § 220.18) while the *sale* of the same amount of the drug is considered a more serious class A-I felony (meriting for first time offenders a prison term of between eight and twenty years—N.Y. McKinney's Penal Law § 220.43). For sentencing provisions, see McKinney's Penal Law § 70.71(2)(b)(i)–(ii). Indeed, most states deem possession of drug paraphernalia a misdemeanor and sale a felony. Lawrence O. Gostin and Zita Lazzarini, "Prevention of HIV/AIDS among Injection Drug Users: The Theory and Science of Public Health and Criminal Justice Approaches to Disease Prevention," 46 *Emory L.J.* 587, 626 n.85 (1997). It should be noted, however, that a distinction could be made between drug possession and stolen property possession in that drug possession is prohibited primarily to prevent future use of drugs rather than to punish their production. On the other hand, I take it that the criminalization of drug use itself is much more controversial than the criminalization of both theft and the production of child pornography. Cf. Peter Alldridge, "Dealing with Drug Dealing," in A. P. Simester and A. T. H. Smith (eds.), *Harm and Culpability* 239, 253 (Oxford: Oxford University

Press, 1996) (mentioning the analogy between drug possession and receiving stolen property)

232. Cf. Racketeer Influenced and Corrupt Organizations Act, 18 U.S.C. § 1961(5) (defining pattern of racketeering activity as requiring at least two acts of racketeering within a ten year period).

233. This is essentially the approach taken in Spain and France. Under the Spanish Criminal Code, when the value of property received is relatively small, the only acts of receiving that are criminalized are those that are "habitual." See Spanish Criminal Code Art. 299. (My thanks to Iñigo Ortíz de Urbina Gimeno for bringing this provision to my attention.) Under the French Criminal Code, habitual receiving is punished by ten years in prison, Art. 321–2, whereas nonhabitual receiving is punished by a term of five years, Art. 321–1.

234. Green, *Lying, Cheating, and Stealing.*

235. Perkins and Boyce, *Criminal Law,* at 363; see also Note, "Whatever Happened to *Durland?* Mail Fraud, RICO, and Justifiable Reliance," 68 *Notre Dame L. Rev.* 333 (1992).

236. 97 E.R. 746 (1761). See also *R. v. Ward,* 92 Eng. Rep. 451 (K.B. 1726) (expanding scope of provision to false endorsement on an unsealed private document).

237. Id.

238. 5 Eliz. 1, c. 14 (1562).

239. 30 Geo. II., c.24, § 1 (1757).

240. *Russ. & R.C.C.* 461 (1821) ("The pretense must relate to past events. Any representation or assurance in relation to a future transaction, may be a promise or a covenant or warranty, but cannot amount to a statutory false promise.")

241. Id. at 463.

242. E.g., *Commonwealth v. Drew,* 36 Mass. 179 (1837).

243. One of the leading cases is *Hameyer v. State,* 29 N.W. 2d 458 (Neb. 1947).

244. Model Penal Code § 223.3.

245. Ian Ayres and Gregory Klass, *Insincere Promises: The Law of Misrepresented Intent* (New Haven: Yale University Press, 2005), 175.

246. Fraud Act 2006 § 2(3).

247. See Robert Birmingham, "Breach of Contract, Damage Measures, and Economic Efficiency," 24 *Rutgers L. Rev.* 273, 284 (1970) ("Repudiation of obligations should be encouraged where the promisor is able to profit from his default after placing his promisee in as good a position as he would have occupied had performance

been rendered"); see also Charles Goetz and Robert Scott, "Liquidated Damages, Penalties, and the Just Compensation Principle: A Theory of Efficient Breach," 77 *Columbia L. Rev.* 554 (1977).

248. 157 F.2d 697 (D.C. Cir. 1946).

249. Ayres and Klass, *Insincere Promises,* at 184.

250. For a real-life example, consider the case of Lawrence Salander, a once-prominent New York art dealer who pleaded guilty to, among other acts, selling paintings he did not own and selling fractional shares in a painting that added up to more than 100 percent. See James Barron, "Art Dealer Pleads Guilty in $120 Million Fraud Case," *N.Y. Times* (March 18, 2010), http://www.nytimes.com/2010/03/19 /nyregion/19salander.html?scp=2&sq=lawrence%20b%20 salander&st=cse.

251. David Firestone and Robert D. McFadden, "Scores of Bodies Strewn at Site of Crematory," *N.Y. Times* (Feb. 17, 2002), at A1.

252. Ayres and Klass, *Insincere Promises,* at 21.

253. The example is also from Ayers and Klass, *Insincere Promises,* at 184.

254. Id. at 171.

255. N.Y. Penal Law § 155.05(2)(d) (also quoted in Ayres and Klass, *Insincere Promises,* at p. 185) (emphasis added).

256. Model Penal Code § 224.5.

257. Perkins and Boyce, *Criminal Law,* at 384.

258. MPC § 224.5.

259. 434 U.S. 357 (1978).

260. Ayres and Klass, *Insincere Promises,* at 190.

261. Described in Creola Johnson, "Payday Loans: Shrewd Business or Predatory Lending?," 87 *Minnesota L. Rev.* 1 (2002); Richard J. Thomas, Note, "Rolling Over Borrowers: Preventing Excessive Refinancing and Other Necessary Changes in the Payday Loan Industry," 48 *William. & Mary L. Rev.* 2401 (2007).

262. Thomas, "Rolling Over Borrowers," at 2408.

263. Id. at 2417 (quoting Johnson, "Payday Loans," at 130).

264. The term *Theft by Extortion* is redundant because the term *extortion* itself refers to a kind of theft. A more appropriate name for the offense would be Theft by Coercion. Such a label would also parallel Theft by Deception, the name of the offense that precedes it in the MPC.

265. MPC § 223.4. The provision further provides an affirmative defense to prosecution based on paragraphs (2), (3) or (4) that the property obtained by threat of accusation, exposure, lawsuit, or other invocation of official action was honestly claimed as restitution or

indemnification for harm done in the circumstances to which such accusation, exposure, lawsuit or other official action relates or as compensation for property or lawful services.

266. MPC § 223.1(1). In England, there is no offense known as extortion. Rather, under Section 21 of the Theft Act 1968, a person is guilty of blackmail if, "with a view to gain for himself or with intent to cause loss to another, he makes any unwarranted demand with menaces." Theft Act 1968, c.60, s.21 (UK). Under the Theft Act, blackmail is conceptually distinct from, and subject to a higher penalty than, theft (a maximum of fourteen years versus seven years). In my view, the English provision suffers from the same problem of overbreadth discussed in the text.

267. Cf. Theft Act 1968 § 21(1) (maximum penalty for blackmail is fourteen years) with § 7 (maximum penalty for theft is seven years.

268. MPC § 223.4.

269. Many of these cases are discussed in Green, *Lying, Cheating, and Stealing*, at 224–234.

270. Id.

4. PROPERTY IN THEFT LAW

1. For a useful discussion of theft of several forms of property not dealt with in this chapter, including money and debts, choses in action, and trusts and liens, see Alex Steel, "Problematic and Unnecessary? Issues with the Use of the Theft Offence to Protect Intangible Property," 30 *Sydney L. Rev.* 575 (2008).

2. Computer Crime and Intellectual Property Section, U.S. Department of Justice, *Prosecuting Intellectual Property Crime* 1 (3d ed. 2006), available at http://www.cybercrime.gov/ipmanual/ipma2006.pdf; Stephen Siwak, *Engines of Growth: Economic Contributions of the U.S. Intellectual Property Industries* http://www.nbcuni.com/About_NBC _Universal/Intellectual_Property/pdf/Engines_of_Growth.pdf

3. International Intellectual Property Alliance, *Copyright Industries in the U.S. Economy* (2006), available at http://www.ifpi.org/content/ library/20070130-report.pdf; Lauren E. Abolsky, Note, "Operation Blackbeard: Is Government Prioritization Enough to Deter Intellectual Property Criminals?," 14 *Fordham Intellectual Property, Media, & Entertainment L.J.* 578, 586 (2004).

4. John R. Grimm et al., "Intellectual Property Crimes," 47 *American Criminal Law Review* 741 (2010).

5. See Abbie Hoffman, *Steal This Book* (New York: Pirate Editions, 1971). See also Murad Ahmed, "Book-stealing: Want to Buy a Hot Read?," *The Times* (Feb. 6, 2009), http://entertainment.timesonline .co.uk/tol/arts_and_entertainment/books/article5670983.ece (an estimated 100 million books are stolen from bookshops in the United Kingdom annually).

6. See, e.g., Aaron M. Bailey, Comment, "A Nation of Felons? Napster, The NET Act, and the Criminal Prosecution of File-Sharing," 50 *American University L. Rev.* 473, 482 n.53 (2000); Jonathan M. Barnett, "What's So Bad About Stealing?," 4 *J. Tort Law* 1 (2011); Oliver R. Goodenough and Gregory Decker, "Why Do Good People Steal Intellectual Property?," in Michael Freeman and Oliver Goodenough (eds.), *Law, Mind, and Brain* (Burlington, VT: Ashgate, 2009) 345; Mohsen Manesh, "The Immorality of Theft, the Amorality of Infringement," 2006 *Stanford Technology L. Rev.* 5; Alexander Peukert, "Why Do 'Good People' Disregard Copyright on the Internet?," forthcoming in Christophe Geiger (ed.), *Criminal Enforcement: A Blessing or a Curse for Intellectual Property* (Cheltenham: Edward Elgar, forthcoming 2011); Tom R. Tyler, "Compliance With Intellectual Property Laws: A Psychological Perspective," 29 *New York University J. International Law & Policy* 219, 219–220 (Fall 1996–Winter 1997)

7. Pamela Samuelson, "Information as Property: Do *Ruckelshaus* and *Carpenter* Signal a Changing Direction in Intellectual Property Law?," 38 *Catholic University L. Rev.* 365, 370 (1989).

8. Id.

9. Contrast Michael J. Hostetler, Note, "Intangible Property under the Federal Mail Fraud Statute and the Takings Clause: A Case Study," 50 *Duke L.J.* 589 (2000) (arguing for uniform definition of property across legal categories).

10. See *Ruckelshaus v. Monsanto*, 467 U.S. 986, 1000 (1984) (holding that research data submitted to federal agency documenting the safety of the submitter's product should be considered property within the meaning of the Fifth Amendment's Takings Clause; submitter was therefore entitled to just compensation); See also Thomas W. Merrill, "The Landscape of Constitutional Property," 86 *Virginia L. Rev.* 885 (2000).

11. See *Cleveland v. United States*, 531 U.S. 12 (2000) (holding that state video poker machine licenses do not constitute property for purposes of federal mail fraud statute because interest state has in such licenses is primarily regulatory, rather than economic, and

mail fraud statute is intended to protect economic rather than regulatory interests).

12. A. T. H. Smith, *Property Offences*, at 54.

13. For example, in *Grand Upright Music Ltd. v. Warner Bros. Records, Inc.*, 780 F. Supp. 182, 182 (S.D.N.Y. 1991), a case involving a hip-hop artist who had sampled copyrighted music, the court, in referring the case to the U.S. Attorney for possible criminal prosecution, went so far as to invoke the commandment, "Thou Shalt Not Steal."

14. E.g., Elisabeth Landes and Richard A. Posner, "The Economics of the Baby Shortage," 7 *J. Leg. Stud.* 323 (1978).

15. E.g., Margaret Jane Radin, *Contested Commodities: The Trouble with Trade in Sex, Children, Body Parts, and Other Things* 154–163 (Cambridge, MA: Harvard University Press, 2001); Debra Satz, *Why Some Things Should Not be for Sale: The Moral Limits of Markets* (New York: Oxford University Press, 2010).

16. Niva Elkin-Koren and Neil Weinstock Netanel (eds), *The Commodification of Information* (The Hague: Kluwer, 2002); Wendy J. Gordon and Sam Postbrief, "On Commodifying Intangibles," 10 *Yale J. Law & Humanities* 135 (1998).

17. MPC Commentary to § 223.2, at 167.

18. For a helpful summary, see Lawrence B. Solum, "Legal Theory Lexicon: Public and Private Goods," *Legal Theory Blog* (Sept. 27, 2009), http://lsolum.typepad.com/legaltheory/2009/09/legal-theory-lexicon-public-and-private-goods.html. See also Roger P. Merges, Peter S. Menell, and Mark A. Lemley, *Intellectual Property in the New Technological Age* (Boston: Wolters Kluwer, rev. 4th ed. 2007), at 2; Robert Cooter and Thomas Ulen, *Law and Economics* (Saddle River, NJ: Prentice Hall, 5th ed. 2008).

19. Joseph E. Stiglitz, "Knowledge as a Global Public Good," in Inge Kaul, Isabelle Grunberg, and Marc A. Stern (eds.), *Global Public Goods: International Cooperation in the 21st Century* (New York: Oxford University Press, 1999), at 308, 309–310.

20. "Excludability," *Wikipedia*, http://en.wikipedia.org/wiki/Excludability

21. The *locus classicus* is Paul A. Samuelson, "The Pure Theory of Public Expenditure," 36 *Review of Economics and Statistics* 387 (1954). See also William M. Landes and Richard A. Posner, "An Economic Analysis of Copyright Law," 18 *J. Legal Studies* 325, 326 (1999).

22. Samuelson, "The Pure Theory of Public Expenditure." See also Richard Cornes and Todd Sandler, *The Theory of Externalities, Public Goods and Club Goods* (New York: Cambridge University Press, 1986).

23. The *locus classicus is* Garrett Hardin, "The Tragedy of the Commons," 162 *Science* 1243 (1968).

24. The *locus classicus* is James M. Buchanan, "An Economic Theory of Clubs," 32 *Economica* 1 (1965). See also Cornes and Sandler, *The Theory of Externalities,* at 33–34.

25. See Solum, "Legal Theory Lexicon 029: Public and Private Goods," *Legal Theory Blog* (March 28, 2004), http://legal-theory -lexicon-029-public-and.html. Another intriguing way to think about the economic status of intellectual property is in terms of what Henry Smith has called the "semicommons." See Henry Smith, "Governing the Tele-Semicommons," 22 *Yale J. Regulation* 289 (2005); Henry Smith, "Intellectual Property as Property: Delineating Entitlements in Information," 116 *Yale L.J.* 1742 (2007). The classic example given is of medieval open fields in which farmers had private property in strips of land for purposes of growing grain but were obligated to open these strips and, together with other farmers, form one large grazing commons during periods right after the harvest and fallow seasons. This is an example of a property regime that mixes elements of private and common property.

26. On the concept of zero-sumness, see generally Morton D. Davis, *Game Theory: A Nontechnical Introduction* (Mineola, NY: Dover Publications, 1997) 11–23. I say theft is a zero-sum transaction only in the common sense, rather than strictly economic, meaning of the term because theft sometimes imposes costs on victims and societies that exceed the value of the property stolen, and in such cases, is more properly spoken of as a "negative-sum game."

27. See discussion and sources cited in Stuart P. Green, *Lying, Cheating, and Stealing,* at 246 and n.14. I have suggested that it is reasonable, however, to think of the evasion of government fees, licenses, permits, and special assessments as a form of theft.

28. Cf. *Warshaw v. Eastman Kodak Co.,* 252 S.E.2d 182 (Ga. App. 1979) (denying suit to recover property alleged to be obscene).

29. 139 N.E. 562 (N.Y. 1923).

30. 41 Stat. 315, tit. 2, § 25.

31. *Otis,* 139 N.E. at 562.

32. Id. at 563.

33. Model Penal Code § 223.0(7). For a recent English case involving theft of illegal drugs, see *R. v. Smith* [2011] EWCA Crim 66, discussed in A. T. H. Smith, "Can Proscribed Drugs be the Subject of Theft?," 70 *Cambridge L.J.* 289 (2011).

34. *Rex v. Wilkins,* 1 Leach CL 520, 168 Eng. Rep. 362 (1789); *Rex v. Beboning,* 17 Ont. L. 23 (1908); J. A. Bock, "Stolen Money or Property as Subject of Larceny or Robbery," 89 *A.L.R. 2d* 1435; L. S. Rogers, "Gambling or Lottery Paraphernalia as Subject of Larceny, Burglary, or Robbery," 51 *A.L.R.2d* 1396. Jerome Hall suggests otherwise, see Hall, *Theft, Law and Society,* at 102–103, but, on examination, none of the cases he cites actually supports the view that stealing contraband or proceeds of illegal gambling does not constitute theft.

35. For a sociological study of the problem, see Bruce A. Jacobs, *Robbing Drug Dealers: Violence beyond the Law* (New York: Aldine, 2000).

36. Richard Wagner, *Das Rheingold,* Scene 2. Jewish law follows a similar rule. A thief who steals from a rightful owner must pay *kefel,* a form of double compensation. One who steals from another thief has no such heightened liability; he must pay only simple restitution. See Moses Jung, *The Jewish Law of Theft* (Philadelphia: Dropsie College, 1929) 107–108.

37. See, e.g., 1779 N.C. Sess. Laws ch. 142, § 2 (making theft of slave a capital offense). See also Robinson, *The Criminal Law of Ancient Rome,* at 32–35 (regarding stealing of slaves in Roman law). Indeed, it is has sometimes been suggested that Emancipation constituted a serious "disruption" of slave owners' property rights. Carol M. Rose, "Property and Expropriation: Themes and Variations in American Law," 2000 *Utah L. Rev.* 1, 24–28 (2000).

38. Robinson, *The Criminal Law of Ancient Rome,* at 34–35. Curiously, the offense of *plagium*—stealing a child under the age of puberty—continues to be viewed as an aggravated form of theft in Scotland today. Gordon, *The Criminal Law of Scotland,* at 478.

39. See generally Kevin Bales, *Disposable People: New Slavery in the Global Economy* (Berkeley: University of California Press, rev. ed. 2004).

40. See, e.g., Ying Chan, "Cook Tells of New York Kidnapping Nightmare," *South China Morning Post* (Oct. 11, 1993), at 20 (describing cases in which Chinese immigrants, brought to the United States by "people smugglers," have been abducted by rival gangs and held for ransom). Thanks to Ko-Lin Chin for bringing this case to my attention.

41. Rohan Hardcastle, *Law and the Human Body: Property Rights, Ownership and Control* (Oxford: Hart Publishing, 2007) 64.

42. Alan Feuer, "Dentist Pleads Guilty to Stealing and Selling Body Parts," *N.Y. Times* (March 19, 2008), http://www.nytimes.com

/2008/03/19/nyregion/thecity/19bones.html?_r=1&scp=1&sq=
mastromarino&st=cse

43. Mary Dodge and Gilbert Geis, *Stealing Dreams: A Fertility Clinic Scandal* (Boston: Northeastern University Press, 2004); See also Judith D. Fischer, "Misappropriation of Human Eggs and Embryos and the Tort of Conversion: A Relational View," 32 *Loyola Los Angeles L. Rev.* 381 (1999).

44. *Moore v. Regents of the University of California,* 793 P.2d 479 (Cal. 1990). For a somewhat similar case, involving Henrietta Lacks, the unwitting donor of cancerous cells that gave rise to an "immortal" cell line used in generations of important medical research, see Rebecca Skloot, *The Immortal Life of Henrietta Lacks* (New York: Random House, 2010).

45. See, e.g., National Organ Transplant Act of 1984, Pub. L. No. 98–507, 99 Stat. 2339 (1984) (codified as amended in scattered sections of 42 U.S.C.); Human Tissue Act 2004 (U.K.) s.32.

46. A. T. H. Smith, *Property Offences,* at 46–47.

47. N.Y. Public Health Law § 4216. See also Model Penal Code § 250.10 (making it a crime to "treat[] a corpse in a way that [one] knows would outrage ordinary family sensibilities"); John S. Herbrand, "Validity, Construction, and Application of Statutes Making it a Criminal Offense to Mistreat or Wrongfully Dispose of Dead Body," 81 *A.L.R.3d* 1071.

48. See J. A. Bryant, "Construction and Application of Graverobbing Statutes," 53 *A.L.R.* 701. For a discussion of the posthumous harms caused by corpse desecration, see Joel Feinberg, *Offense to Others* (New York: Oxford University Press, 1985) 56. For a compelling novelistic treatment of grave robbery, see Hannah Tinti, *The Good Thief* (New York: Dial Press, 2008).

49. Corpses have generally been viewed as at most a form of quasi-property, over which family members retain a limited array of rights, including the right to possess the body for purposes of burial, exclude others, and decide how it should ultimately be disposed of. Radhika Rao, "Property, Privacy, and the Human Body," 80 *Boston University L. Rev.* 359, 383 (2000). See also Norman Cantor, *After We Die: The Life and Times of the Human Cadaver* (Washington, D.C.: Georgetown University Press, 2010) 47–48; Jonathan Herring, "Giving, Selling and Sharing Bodies," in Andrew Bainham et al. (eds.), *Body Lore and Laws* (Oxford: Hart, 2002), 43.

50. *Doodeward v. Spence* [1908] 6 CLR 406.

51. *R. v. Kelly* [1999] QB 621.

52. Lyria Bennett Moses, "The Applicability of Property Law in New Contexts: From Cells to Cyberspace," 30 *Sydney L. Rev.* 639, 642 (2008).

53. Cal. Penal Code § 367g.

54. For a similar conclusion with respect to the "theft" of DNA, see Elizabeth E. Joh, "DNA Theft: Recognizing the Crime of Nonconsensual Genetic Collection and Testing," 91 *Boston University L. Rev.* 665 (2011).

55. See, e.g., James Boyle, *Shamans, Software and Spleens: Law and the Construction of the Information Society* (Cambridge, Mass: Harvard University Press, 1997); Maxwell J. Melman, "Moore v. Regents of the University of California," in Gerald Korngold and Andrew P. Morris (eds.), *Property Stories* (New York: Foundation Press, 2004); Roxanne Mykitiuk, "Fragmenting the Body," 2 *Australian Feminist L.J.* 63, 77 (1994).

56. 13 B.C.L.R. (2d) 273 (1987).

57. The discussion in this paragraph comes from Stuart P. Green, "Consent and the Grammar of Theft Law," 28 *Cardozo L. Rev.* 2505 (2007).

58. See, e.g., *Boro v. Superior Court,* 210 Cal. Rptr. 122 (Cal. Ct. App. 1985).

59. See, e.g., *State v. Ely,* 194 N.W. 988 (Wash. 1921).

60. See generally Joel Feinberg, *Harm to Self* (New York: Oxford University Press, 1986) 292–293.

61. On such questions, see Peter de Marneffe, *Liberalism and Prostitution* (Oxford: Oxford University Press, 2010); Michelle Madden Dempsey, "Sex Trafficking and Criminalization: In Defense of Feminist Abolitionism," 158 *University of Pennsylvania L. Rev.* 1729 (2010).

62. I am grateful to Annalise Acorn for her help with these points.

63. See generally Hall, *Theft, Law and Society,* at 83.

64. See *Mullaly v. People,* 41 Sickels 365 (1881) (citing Coke).

65. MPC § 223.0(6); A. T. H. Smith, *Property Offences,* at 71 (interpreting Theft Act 1968 § 4(4)).

66. See, e.g., Gary L Francione, *Animals, Property, and the Law* (Philadelphia: Temple University Press, 1995).

67. I recognize that, in the view of some theorists, in a society which truly respected animal rights, humans would no longer be bringing domesticated animals into existence in the first place. See id. In such a world, the incidence of such abductions would eventually disappear.

68. So as to avoid even the appearance that I might have engaged in self-plagiarism, I need to acknowledge that the discussion here borrows from Stuart P. Green, "Plagiarism, Norms, and the Limits of

Theft Law: Some Observations on the Use of Criminal Sanctions in Enforcing Intellectual Property Rights," 54 *Hastings L.J.* 167 (2002).

69. Leo Katz, *Ill-Gotten Gains: Evasion, Blackmail, Fraud, and Kindred Puzzles of the Law* 197–201 (Chicago: University of Chicago Press, 1996).

70. *Cf.* Howard P. Tuckman and Jack Leahey, "What Is an Article Worth?," 83 *J. Political Economy* 951, 951–952 (1975).

71. I have thus changed my mind since last writing about the issue. See Green, "Plagiarism, Norms, and the Limits of Theft Law," at 220. In my earlier work, I offered two examples of when we might say that credit for authorship should be regarded as a form of property for purposes of theft law. The first is when a politician or corporate executive pays a ghostwriter to write a speech. I argued that the executive is typically buying not just the ghostwriter's creative efforts, but also the right to claim the speech as her own. Thus, if the ghostwriter were to tell people that it was actually *his* work that the executive was representing as her own, that would be a kind of theft. The second example involved a firm that held a competition offering a cash prize to the employee who developed the best new design for a widget. If *X* developed a prize-winning idea that *Y* stole and submitted as his own, *X* would be deprived of the credit for the idea and, indirectly, the prize to which he was entitled.

I have since reconsidered, however. Perhaps we can say in both of these cases that credit for authorship should be regarded as property for purposes of theft law. But neither case actually involves what is commonly thought of as plagiarism. In both cases, the market value of the credit claimed comes from some independent source. In the normal case of plagiarism, the plagiarist simply claims credit to which he is not entitled, and that credit has no separate market value that would make it property. Accordingly, I would maintain that, at least in the vast majority of cases, plagiarism should not be regarded as theft.

72. For more on this point, see Green, "Plagiarism, Norms, and the Limits of the Theft Law," at 228–35.

73. 18 U.S.C. § 704.

74. 18 U.S.C. § 704(b), (c), (d).

75. Given a split among the lower courts, the issue will presumably have to be resolved by the Supreme Court. Cf. *United States v. Alvarez*, 617 F.3d 1198 (9th Cir. 2010) (holding statute unconstitutional under the First Amendment) with *United States v. Perelman*, 737 F.Supp. 2d 1221

(D. Nev. 2010) (upholding statute) and *United States v. Robins,* 59 F. Supp. 2d 815 (W.D. Va. 2011) (upholding statute).

76. 32 C.F.R. § 578.4.

77. "Medal of Honor," *Wikipedia,* http://en.wikipedia.org/wiki/Medal _of_honor.

78. For a recent case in Australia, see "Fake War Veteran Sent to Jail," smh.com.au (Dec. 22, 2010), http://m.smh.com.au/national/fake -war-veteran-sent-to-jail-20101221–194gh.html (elderly man who had never served in the military claimed for twenty-two years to be World War II veteran and received $464,000 in undeserved pension and disability payments).

79. See, e.g., 151 Cong. Rec. S12684–01.

80. Robert Vito, "Florida Man Wears Medal Without Honor," *CNN.com* (Dec. 4, 1996), http://www.cnn.com/US/9612/04/medal.without .honor/.

81. "Homer vs. Lisa and the 8th Commandment," *The Simpsons* (Fox television broadcast, Feb. 7, 1991). My summary is indebted to Wikipedia, "Homer vs. Lisa and the 8th Commandment," http:// en.wikipedia.org/wiki/Homer_vs._Lisa_and_the_8th_Commandment.

82. The story of Prometheus's theft appears in Hesiod's version rather than Aeschylus's. According to Hesiod, the humans originally had fire, but Zeus, in anger for a trick played on him by Prometheus, hid it from them. Prometheus then stole it back and gave it to humans once again. See Hesiod, *Theogony* (M.L. West, trans.) (New York: Oxford University Press, reissued 2009). Matt Groenig named the father of his television family after his own father, Homer Groenig, who in turn may have been named for the epic poet who, along with Hesiod, is one of the two earliest Greek poets whose work has survived.

83. CLRC Eighth Report at 5. Cmnd 2977, *Theft and Related Offences,* para. 85.

84. Theft Act 1968 s.13.

85. Model Penal Code § 223.0(6).

86. See, e.g., 47 U.S.C. § 553 (unauthorized reception of cable service); 47 U.S.C. § 605 (unauthorized use of communications); Wisconsin Rev. Stat. § 943.47 (theft of satellite cable programming); Kansas Rev. Stat. § 21–3704 (theft of, inter alia, telephone and cable television service); Wash. Rev. Stat. § 9A.56.262 (theft of telecommunications services). For Canadian and English provisions, see the discussion in Holland, *The Law of Theft,* at 82–85 and A. T. H.

Smith, *Property Offences,* ch. 12, respectively. The French provision can be found in *Code Pénal* Art. 311.2 ("Dishonest appropriation of energy to the prejudice of another person is assimilated to theft").

87. I am grateful to Christine Bator, Ari Chivukula, Todd Morrison, and J. C. Spender for helping me understand the technologies described herein.

88. My account here borrows from "Cable Television," *Wikipedia,* http://en.wikipedia.org/wiki/Cable_television; "How Cable Television Works," *HowStuffWorks,* http://www.howstuffworks.com /cable-tv.htm.

89. Paul Davidson, "Power Theft Surges in Bad Times," *USA Today* (March 17, 2009), http://www.usatoday.com/printedition /news/20090317/1apowertheft17_st.art.htm?csp=23&RM _Exclude=aol.

90. See, respectively, 17 U.S.C. § 504(a) [Copyright Act]; 15 U.S.C. § 1117(a) [Lanham Act § 35(a)]; 35 U.S.C. § 284 [Patent Act]; see also Melville B. Nimmer and David Nimmer, *Nimmer on Copyright* (Newark: LexisNexis, 2008); J. Thomas McCarthy, *McCarthy on Trademarks and Unfair Competition,* vol. 5, § 30:58–62 (Minneapolis: West, 4th ed. 1998–2011); Richard Cauley, *Winning the Patent Damages Case: A Litigator's Guide to Economic Models and Other Damages Strategies* (New York: Oxford University Press, 2d ed. 2011).

91. My account here borrows from Wanda Marie Thibodeaux, "How Cable Television Works," *ehow.com,* http://www.ehow.com/how-does _4914663_how-cable-television-works.html. See also Andrew Russell, Comment, "Placeshifting, the Slingbox, and Cable Theft Statutes: Will Slingbox Use Land You in Prison?," 81 *Temple L. Rev.* 1239 (2008).

92. See generally Benjamin Kern, "Whacking, Joyriding and War-Driving: Roaming Use of Wi-Fi and the Law," 21 *Santa Clara Computer & High Tech L.J.* 101, 104 (2004); Ned Snow, "Accessing the Internet through the Neighbor's Wireless Internet Connection: Physical Trespass in Virtual Reality," 84 *Nebraska L. Rev.* 1226 (2006); Grant J. Guillot, Comment, "Trespassing through Cyberspace: Should Wireless Piggybacking Constitute a Crime or Tort Under Louisiana Law?," 69 *Louisiana L. Rev.* 389 (2009).

93. Guillot, "Trespassing through Cyperspace," at 400.

94. Id. at 400–401.

95. I put to the side cases in which users access a Wi-Fi network for the purpose of causing malicious damage, such as spreading a

virus or misappropriating trade secrets or personal identity information.

96. Cf. Snow, "Accessing the Internet through the Neighbor's Wireless Internet Connection," at 1255–1260 (considering and ultimately rejecting this argument).

97. Michael Marriott, "Hey Neighbor, Stop Piggybacking on My Wireless," *N.Y. Times* (March 5, 2006), http://www.nytimes.com/2006/03/05 /technology/05wireless.html.

98. A. T. H. Smith, *Property Offences,* at 4.

99. 270 F.2d 274 (9th Cir. 1959).

100. Model Penal Code § 223.7.

101. Id. § 223.7.

102. Id. § 223.1(1).

103. Fraud Act 2006 § 11.

104. Id. § 11(3)(b).

105. Theft Act 1978 s. 1(1) (repealed).

106. "Difference in Goods and Services," *Scribd.com,* http://www.scribd .com/doc/17342628/Difference-in-Goods-and-Services -wwwmanagementsourceblogspotcom.

107. "Goods and services," *Wikipedia,* http://en.wikipedia.org/wiki /Goods_and_services.

108. An analogous issue arises under Article 2 of the Uniform Commercial Code, which applies to "transactions in goods," but not transactions in services. Thus, in deciding whether the warranty provisions of the article should apply, courts have had to decide whether, for example, a blood transfusion qualified as a good or service. See, e.g., *Perlmutter v. Beth David Hospital,* 123 N.E.2d 792 (N.Y. 1954) (holding that blood transfusion is a service rather than a good and therefore not subject to the warranty provisions of Article 2). Trademark law also distinguishes between trademarks (for goods) and service marks (for services). 15 U.S.C. § 1127.

109. Cf. Susan W. Brenner, "Is There Such a Thing as 'Virtual Crime?'," 4 *California Criminal L. Rev.* 1, 43 (2001) (describing theft of services as involving a zero-sum game).

110. The term they use is *theft of time,* see Laureen Snider, "Theft of Time: Disciplining Through Science and Law," 40 *Osgoode Hall L.J.* 89, 90 n.2 (2002) (critical of the term), which is clearly inaccurate. If the employee is stealing anything when she gets paid for a job she never intended to perform, it is her employer's money.

111. See, respectively, 17 U.S.C. § 504(a) [Copyright Act]; 15 U.S.C. § 1117(a) [Lanham Act § 35(a)]; 35 U.S.C. § 284 [Patent Act].

112. See Geraldine Szott Moohr, "Federal Criminal Fraud and the Development of Intangible Property Rights in Information," 2000 *University of Illinois L. Rev.* 683, 687.
113. A. T. H. Smith, *Property Offences*, at 45.
114. Id. at 51 *et seq.* See also Hall, *Theft, Law and Society*, at 100.
115. Council Draft No. 4 (March 4, 1953), at b.
116. Model Penal Code § 223.0(6).
117. Theft Act 1968 s.4. The provision also made clear that land and things attached to it cannot be stolen except in certain circumstances of violating a trust, that plants cannot be stolen unless done for commercial purposes, and that wild animals cannot be stolen unless they have been reduced to possession. Id.
118. Canadian Criminal Code § 322(1).
119. One basic distinction is between "original creative work" (which is potentially copyrightable) and "mere facts" (which are not). See *Feist Publications, Inc. v. Rural Telephone Service Co.*, 499 U.S. 340 (1991) (holding that "white pages" telephone directory containing alphabetical listing of names, addresses, and telephone numbers was not protected by copyright law).
120. See, e.g., Luciano Floridi, *The Philosophy of Information* (Oxford: Oxford University Press, 2011).
121. Private plaintiffs have also sought to use the law of misappropriation, as articulated in the Supreme Court's decision in *International News Service v. Associated Press*, 248 U.S. 215 (1918), discussed in Chapter 3.
122. 484 U.S. 19 (1987).
123. Id. at 25.
124. 825 P.2d 758 (Wyo. 1992).
125. To the same effect is *Collins v. State*, 946 P.2d 1055, 1183 (Nev. 1997) (secret passwords to secure storage units obtained in course of burglary held to constitute property for purpose of larceny statute).
126. 591 P.2d 1036 (Colo. 1979) (en banc).
127. 68 Crim. App. Rep. 183 (1979).
128. Id. at 185–186.
129. Id. at 186.
130. [1988] 1 S.C.R. 963. For commentary written as the case was making its way to the Canadian Supreme Court, see Ernest Weinreb, "Information and Property," 38 *University of Toronto Law Journal* 117 (1988); R. Grant Hammond, "Theft of Information," 100 *Law Quarterly Rev.* 252 (1984).
131. Ms. at ¶ 21.

132. Id. at ¶ 24.
133. Id. at ¶ 35.
134. Id. at ¶ 32.
135. Cf. *Reno v. Condon,* 528 U.S. 141, 148 (2000) (finding that information on driver's license constitutes "thing in interstate commerce" and that Congress therefore had constitutional authority to regulate sale of personal information obtained through state departments of motor vehicles).
136. Susan Brenner has made the same point in various publications. Susan W. Brenner, *Law in an Era of Smart Technology* (New York: Oxford University Press, 2007) 179; Susan W. Brenner, "Is There Such a Thing as 'Virtual Crime?,' " 4 *California Crim. L. Rev.* 1, *47 (2001) (theft of information does not satisfy zero-sum paradigm); Susan W. Brenner, "Law in an Era of Pervasive Technology," 15 *Widener L.J.* 667, 782 (2006). See also Deborah Fisch Nigri, "Theft of Information and the Concept of Property in the Information Age," in J. W. Harris, *Property Problems from Genes to Pension Funds* (London: Kluwer, 1997) 55 (making similar point).
137. Scottish Criminal Code (proposed) § 77(3)(b) (emphasis added).
138. The court in *Stewart* recognized the possibility that the taking of confidential information might effectively deprive its owner of its use, but, for reasons that are not at all clear, it regarded such cases as "far-fetched" and "fanciful." *Stewart,* at ¶ 36.
139. Respectively, S. A. Cole and Henry Pontell, "Don't Be Low Hanging Fruit: Identity Theft as Moral Panic," in Torin Monahan (ed.), *Surveillance and Security* (London: Routledge, 2006), 125; Sean Hoar, "Identity Theft: The Crime of the New Millenium," 80 *Oregon L. Rev.* 1423 (2001).
140. Javelin Strategy & Research, *2010 Identity Fraud Survey Report* (Pleasanton, CA: 2010). See also Federal Trade Commission, *Identity Theft Survey Report 2006* (Washington, DC: Nov. 2007), http://www.ftc.gov/os/2007/11/SynovateFinalReportIDTheft2006.pdf. For a critique of attempts to quantify identity theft and a proposal that better data be collected from lending institutions, see Chris Jay Hoofnagle, "Identity Theft: Making the Known Unknowns Known, 21 *Harvard J. L.Tech.* 97 (2007).
141. The history of the concept is reviewed in Megan M. McNally, "Trial by Circumstance: Is Identity Theft a Modern-Day Moral Panic?," (Ph.D. Dissertation, Rutgers University Department of Criminal Justice, May 2008) 24–42.

142. See generally Graeme R. Newman and Megan M. McNally, "Identity Theft Literature Review," research report submitted to U.S. Department of Justice (Jan. 7, 2005), at 63 *et seq* & Appendix 3.

143. 18 U.S.C. § 1028(a)(7). See also 18 U.S.C. § 1028 (fraud in connection with identity documents), 18 U.S.C. § 1029 (fraud in connection with access devices such as credit cards), and 42 U.S.C. § 408(a)(7) (fraud in connection with the misuse of Social Security numbers).

144. See generally Peter Grabosky, Russell G. Smith, and Gillian Dempsey, *Electronic Theft: Unlawful Acquisition in Cyberspace* (Cambridge: Cambridge University Press, 2001) 157 *et seq*; Megan M. McNally and Graeme R. Newman (eds.), *Perspectives on Identity Theft* (Monsey, NY: Crime Prevention Studies, vol. 23, 2008). See also *The President's Identity Theft Task Force Report* (September 2008), http://www.idtheft.gov/reports/StrategicPlan.pdf.

145. Some exceptions are Lindsay Farmer, "The Metamorphoses of Theft" (unpublished manuscript); Lynn M. LoPucki, "Human Identification Theory and the Identity Theft Problem," 80 *Texas L. Rev.* 89 (2001); Alex Steel, "The True Identity of Australian Identity Theft Offences: A Measured Response or an Unjustified Status Offence?," 33 *University of New South Wales L.J.* 503 (2010).

146. There are also cases in which the offender obtains or possesses information about another's identity but never actually uses it to commit a fraud or other criminal act. For reasons that I have not been able to discern, some authors reserve the use of the term *identity theft* for the act of obtaining the information itself and use the term *identity fraud* to refer to the use of such information to obtain a benefit. See, e.g., Max Anhoury, "Understanding the Difference between Identity Theft and Identity Fraud," *IO.Blog* (Dec. 8, 2009), http://blog.iovation.com/2009/12/08/identity-theft-and-identity-fraud/.

147. Consider the case of a man named Karl Hackett, who assumed the identity of his flatmate, Lee Simm, after Simm committed suicide. For fifteen years, Hackett was able to escape his criminal record by living as Simm. In 1999, Hackett (using the name Simm) decided to "kill off" his former self for good by claiming that he had died in a train crash. At this point he was caught. Emily Finch, "What a Tangled Web We Weave: Identity Theft and the Internet," in Y. Jewkes (ed.), *Dot.cons: Crime, Deviance, and Identity on the Internet* (Collompton, England: Willan, 2003) 86. For a fictional account of a man who kills his victim and then assumes his identity, see Patricia Highsmith, *The*

Talented Mr. Ripley (New York: Coward-McCann, 1955), made into the 1999 film directed by Anthony Minghella.

148. "The Decline of the English Burglary," *The Economist* (May 27, 2004), http://www.economist.com/node/2709203?story_id=2709203.

149. Cf. Pennington, Krishnamurthi, Reidy, and Stephan, "A Precise Model for Identity Theft Statutes," 46 *Crim. L. Bulletin* 5 (proposing elaborate statutory scheme that includes "identity embezzlement").

150. Newman and McNally, "Identity Theft Literature Review," at 43–44.

151. Id. at 13.

152. See, e.g., James Verini, "The Great Cyber-Heist," *New York Times Magazine* (Nov. 14, 2010), http://www.nytimes.com/2010/11/14/magazine/14Hacker-t.html?_r=1&ref=magazine (describing case of identity thief Albert Gonzalez, who was part of cyber-crime gang that stole personal information on millions of credit card accounts).

153. The phrase is borrowed from Michiko Kakutani, "A Stolen Identity in 'Talk Talk' by T. C. Boyle," *N.Y. Times* (July 4, 2006), http://www.nytimes.com/2006/07/04/books/04kaku.html.

154. T. C. Boyle, *Talk Talk* (New York: Penguin, 2006) 69. For additional, real-life, chilling stories of the impact identity theft has on its victims, see Frank W. Abagnale, *Stealing Your Life: The Ultimate Identity Theft Prevention Plan* (New York: Broadway, 2007).

155. *Pennsylvania Coal v. Mahon*, 260 U.S. 393, 415 (1922). Thanks to Ken Simons for his thoughts here.

156. Alice Haemmerli, "Whose Who? The Case for a Kantian Right of Publicity," 49 *Duke L.J.* 383 (1999).

157. 18 U.S.C. § 912.

158. E.g. *Alvarado v. People*, 132 P.3d 1205 (Colo. 2006), interpreting Colo. Rev. Stat. § 18–5–113.

159. *Oxford English Dictionary*, "Piracy." See also Christina Mulligan and Brian Patrick Quinn, "Who Are You Calling a Pirate? Shaping Public Discourse in the Intellectual Property Debates" (October 22, 2010), Brandeis University Department of English Eighth Annual Graduate Conference, 2010, available at SSRN: http://ssrn.com/abstract=1695461; Matthew K. Dames, "The Framing of 'Piracy': Etymology, Lobbying & Policy" (April 21, 2009). Available at SSRN: http://ssrn.com/abstract=1392914.

160. Eric Holder, Remarks at Press Conference Announcing the Intellectual Property Rights Initiative (July 23, 1999), http://www.justice.gov/criminal/cybercrime/dagipini.htm.

161. Quoted in Lauren E. Abolsky, Note, "Operation Blackbeard: Is Government Prioritization Enough to Deter Intellectual Property

Criminals?," 14 *Fordham Intellectual Property, Media & Entertainment L.J.*
567, 599 (2004). See also Statement of U.S. Customs Commissioner
Robert C. Bonner, quoted in press release, United States Department
of Justice, "Warez Leader Sentenced to 46 Months" (May 17, 2002),
http://www.justice.gov/criminal/cybercrime/sankusSent.htm (noting
that "Star Wars Episode 2 opened in theaters only yesterday. But
because of software pirates . . . it likely opened on the Internet weeks
ago. This is stealing, plain and simple, and those engaged in the theft
of intellectual property deserve to be prosecuted and punished").

162. See generally Geoffrey Neri, Note, "Sticky Fingers or Sticky Norms?
Unauthorized Music Downloading and Unsettled Social Norms," 93
Georgetown L.J. 733, 745–754 (2005).

163. U.S. Department of Commerce, Information Infrastructure Task
Force, Intellectual Property and the National Infrastructure: The
Report of the Working Group Report on Intellectual Property Rights
(1995), at 205, http://www.uspto.gov/web/offices/com/doc/ipnii/.
For criticism, see, e.g., Jessica Litman, *Digital Copyright: Protecting
Intellectual Property on the Internet* (Amherst, NY: Prometheus Books,
2001) 96.

164. U.S. Department of Justice, Rules in Cyberspace, http://www.justice
.gov/criminal/cybercrime/rules/rules.htm.

165. See, e.g., Executive Office of the President, "2010 Joint Strategic Plan
on Intellectual Property Enforcement," http://www.whitehouse.
gov/sites/default/files/omb/assets/intellectualproperty/
intellectualproperty_strategic_plan.pdf (repeating language of *theft*
to refer to intellectual property infringement).

166. U.S. Department of Justice, Bureau of Justice Statistics, *Intellectual
Property Theft, 2002*, http://bjs.ojp.usdoj.gov/index.
cfm?ty=pbdetail&iid=998.

167. Described in Jessica Reyman, *The Rhetoric of Intellectual Property* (New
York: Routledge, 2010).

168. Described in Patricia Louise Loughlan, " 'You Wouldn't Steal a Car':
Intellectual Property and the Language of Theft," 29 *European
Intellectual Property Review* 401 (2007).

169. See *A&M Records, Inc. v. Napster, Inc.*, 239 F.3d 1004 (9th Cir. 2001),
and *Metro-Goldwyn-Mayer Studios, Inc. v. Grokster, Ltd.*, 259 F. Supp. 2d
1029 (C.D. Cal. 2000). The MPAA's co-plaintiff in the suit was the
Recording Industry Association of America (RIAA). More recently,
MusicUnited, a Web site largely supported by the RIAA, has compared illegal downloading to both "shoplifting" and "stealing
something—say, a picture or a piece of clothing—from a friend's

house." "Who Really Cares?," *MusicUnited.org*, http://www
.musicunited.org/1_whocares.aspx.

170. Quoted in "Film and Music Industries File Suit Against Scour.
com,"*MI2N.com* (July 20, 2000), http://www.mi2n.com/press.
php3?press_nb=10489.

171. Pub. L. No. 105–147; 111 Stat. 2678, codified in various sections of 17
and 18 U.S.C.

172. 18 U.S.C. § 1832(a).

173. Pub. L. No. 110–403, 122 Stat. 4256, codified in scattered sections of
15 U.S.C. See Grace Pyun, Legislative Update, "The 2008 PRO-IP
Act: The Inadequacy of the Property Paradigm in Criminal Intellectual
Property Law and its Effect on Prosecutorial Boundaries," 19 *DePaul
J. Art, Technology & Intellectual Property Law* 355, 379–380 (2009)
(quoting statements of Representative Marsha Blackburn ["These
industries are suffering from rampant theft of their intellectual
property online"] and Senator Patrick Leahy ["Intellectual property
is the lifeblood of our economy, and protecting that property from
theft . . . is important."]).

174. "Copynorms" outside the United States sometimes differ signifi-
cantly. See, e.g., William P. Alford, *To Steal a Book Is an Elegant Offense:
Intellectual Property Law in Chinese Civilization* (Stanford: Stanford
University Press, 1995).

175. Pew Internet & American Life Project, *Music Downloading, File-sharing
and Copyright* (2003), available at http://www.pewinternet.org
/˜/media//Files/Reports/2003/PIP_Copyright_Memo.pdf; Pew
Internet & American Life Project, *The State of Music Downloading
and File-sharing Online* (2004), available at http://www.pewtrusts.
org/uploadedFiles/wwwpewtrustsorg/Reports/Society_and_the
_Internet/pew_internet_download_042504.pdf; Pew Internet &
American Life Project, *Music and Video Downloading* (2005), available
at http://www.pewinternet.org/Reports/2005/Music-and-Video
-Downloading.aspx. Older data regarding how the public views the
morality of illegal copying and downloading are summarized in
Moohr, "The Crime of Copyright Infringement," at 767–768.

176. Younger persons were especially unlikely to be concerned about
copyright. Seventy-two percent of online Americans aged eighteen to
twenty-nine say they do not care whether the music they download
onto their computers is copyrighted. Asked who they thought should
be regarded as "responsible for the pirating of music and movie files,"
53 percent said it was the firms that own and operate file-sharing
networks. Only 18 percent said it was individual file traders, and 12

percent said that both companies and individuals should shoulder responsibility. Pew Internet & American Life Project, *Music Downloading, File-sharing and Copyright.*

177. Geraldine Szott Moohr, "Defining Overcriminalization Through Cost-Benefit Analysis: The Example of Criminal Copyright Laws," 54 *American University L. Rev.* 783, 808 (2005).

178. G. Stephen Taylor and J. P. Shim, "A Comparative Examination of Attitudes Toward Software Piracy Among Business Professors and Executives," 46 *Human Relations* 419, 421 (1993).

179. Yuval Feldman and Janice Nadler, "The Law and Norms of File Sharing," 43 *San Diego L.Rev.* 578, 582 (2006) (citing brief filed by industry in Supreme Court *Grokster* case).

180. Stephen E. Siwek, Institute for Policy Innovation, "The True Cost of Copyright Industry Piracy to the U.S. Economy" (Oct. 2007), available at http://www.ipi.org/IPI/IPIPublications.nsf/PublicationLookupFull TextPDF/02DA0B4B44F2AE9286257369005ACB57/$File /CopyrightPiracy.pdf?OpenElement.

181. Pew Internet & American Life Project, *Music and Video Downloading* (2005).

182. On the relationship between increased difficulty of infringement and increased availability of legal alternatives, see Eduardo Moisés Peñalver and Sonia K. Katyal, *Property Outlaws: How Squatters, Pirates, and Protesters Improve the Law of Ownership* (New Haven: Yale University Press, 2010), at 208–226.

183. E.g., Stephen L. Carter, "Does it Matter Whether Intellectual Property is Property?," 68 *Chicago-Kent L. Rev.* 715 (1993); Richard Epstein, "Liberty versus Property? Cracks in the Foundations of Copyright Law," 42 *San Diego L. Rev.* 1 (2005); Mark A. Lemley, "Property, Intellectual Property, and Free Riding," 83 *Texas L. Rev.* 1031 (2005).

184. Steven Penney, "Crime, Copyright, and the Digital Age," in Law Commission of Canada, *What is Crime?* (Vancouver: University of British Columbia Press, 2004) 61, 67.

185. Landes & Posner, "Economic Analysis of Copyright Law," at 326.

186. Moohr, "Economic Espionage Act," at 143.

187. Penney, "Crime, Copyright, and the Digital Age," at 66.

188. U.S. Constitution, Art. I, § 8, cl. 8.

189. Peñalver and Katyal, *Property Outlaws*, at 39.

190. See, e.g., Ann Bartow, "Arresting Technology: An Essay," 1 *Buffalo Intellectual Property L.J.* 95 (2001).

191. For a helpful discussion, see Brian M. Hoffstadt, "Dispossession, Intellectual Property, and the Sin of Theoretical Homogeneity," 80 *Southern California L. Rev.* 909, 939–40 (2007).
192. See Steel, "Problematic and Unnecessary," at 599 (recommending similar approach).
193. E.g., Miguel Helft, "Twins' Facebook Fight Rages On," *New York Times* (Dec. 30, 2010), http://www.nytimes.com/2010/12/31/business /31twins.html?_r=1&scp=3&sq=zuckerberg&st=cse.
194. See complaint in *Connectu, Inc. v. Facebook, Inc.* (D. Mass., filed March 28, 2007), http://dockets.justia.com/docket/massachusetts/madce /1:2007cv10593/108516/.
195. 17 U.S.C. § 102(a).
196. Copyright Act, 17 U.S.C. § 102. Regarding copyrighting of yoga asanas and tattoos, respectively, see *Open Source Yoga Unity v. Choudhury,* 2005 WL 756558 (N.D.Cal., 2005); Noam Cohen, "On Tyson's Face, It's Art. On Film, a Legal Issue," *N.Y. Times* (May 20, 2011), http://www.nytimes.com/2011/05/21/business/media/21tattoo .html?ref=tattoos.
197. Id. at 102(b). See also *Feist Publications, Inc. v. Rural Telephone Services Co.,* 499 U.S. 340 (1996).
198. 17 U.S.C. § 107.
199. 17 U.S.C. § 302(a).
200. Roger E. Schechter and John R. Thomas, *Intellectual Property: The Law of Copyrights, Patents and Trademarks* (St. Paul: West, 2003) 168.
201. 17 U.S.C. § 506(a)(2). Infringement of the first kind was not treated as a crime until enactment of the No Electronic Theft Act, Pub. L. No. 105–147, 111 Stat. 2678 (1997). The NET Act overruled the decision in *United States v. LaMacchia,* 871 F. Supp. 536 (D. Mass. 1994) (defendant did not violate criminal provisions of Copyright Act because, despite causing copyright holders of software programs more than $1 million in damages, he never benefitted financially from infringement). For helpful scholarly commentary, see Lydia Pallas Loren, "Digitization, Commmodification, Criminalization: The Evolution of Criminal Copyright Infringement and the Importance of the Willfulness Requirement," 77 *Washington University L.Q.* 835 (1999); Geraldine Szott Moohr, "The Crime of Copyright Infringement: An Inquiry Based on Morality, Harm, and Criminal Theory," 83 *Boston University L. Rev.* 731 (2003); Geraldine Szott Moohr, "Defining Overcriminalization Through Cost-Benefit Analysis: The Example of Criminal Copyright Laws," 54 *American*

University L. Rev. 783 (2005); Penney, "Crime, Copyright, and the Digital Age."

202. I previously dealt with the preemption question in Green, "Plagiarism, Norms, and the Limits of the Theft Law," at 224–227 (suggesting that there is a good argument that federal copyright law would preempt a state law prosecution for theft).

203. E.g., Cheng Lim Saw, "The Case of Criminalising Primary Infringements of Copyright—Perspectives from Singapore," 18 *International J. Law & Information Technology* 95 (2010) ("it is this author's thesis that drawing parallels with the law of theft—at least from the conceptual/moral dimension—is . . . worthwhile in the attempt to justify the criminalisation of non-commercial infringements of copyright on a 'significant' scale").

204. 473 U.S. 207 (1985); 18 U.S.C. § 2314.

205. 473 U.S. at 216–217 (citations omitted).

206. See *Rank Film Distributors Ltd. v. Video Information Centre*, [1982] AC 380, 443 (Lord Wilberforce) ("[i]nfringement of copyright is not theft"). Gerry Moohr also believes that the "equat[ion] of infringement with theft" is unjustified, in part because it "fails to acknowledge that the rights provided by copyright law are limited in significant ways." Moohr, "Crime of Copyright Infringement," at 766.

207. Thanks to Reid Weisbord for helping me think through this paragraph.

208. To be fair, the Court's decision in *Dowling* did refer to this point, if only in passing. See *Dowling*, 473 U.S. at 217 (infringer "does not assume physical control over the copyright; nor does he wholly deprive its owner of its use").

209. Under *Princeton University Press v. Michigan Document Services, Inc.*, 99 F.3d 1381 (6th Cir. 1996) (en banc), this would clearly not constitute fair use.

210. See William M. Landes and Richard A. Posner, "An Economic Analysis of Copyright Law," 18 *J. Legal Studies* 325, 326 (1999).

211. This seems to be the understanding of at least some Jewish jurists as well. See Neil W. Netanel and David Nimmer, "Is Copyright Property? The Debate in Jewish Law," 12 *Theoretical Inquiries in Law* 217, 235–236 (2011) ("[E]ven if we accept that copyright is property under Jewish law, the violation of that right is not necessarily 'stealing.' . . . [A] couple of leading proponents of the copyright-is-property school conclude that unlicensed copying is actually an unlawful *use* of that property for the copyist's benefit, not an unlawful *conversion* of property. According to this view, unlicensed copying is actionable

under the Jewish law of unjust enrichment *(ze neheneh ve-ze haser)*, not theft *(gezel).*") (citations omitted).

212. Cf. the discussion of aggregate harms in Joel Feinberg, *Harm to Others* 193–198, 225–232 (New York: Oxford University Press, 1984).

213. 35 U.S.C. § 101 *et seq.* Schechter and Thomas, *Intellectual Property*, at 2–3.

214. Schechter and Thomas, at 282.

215. 35 U.S.C. § 154. For patents filed prior to June 8, 1995, the term of patent is either twenty years from the earliest claimed filing date or seventeen years from the issue date, whichever is longer.

216. 35 U.S.C. § 271(a).

217. See Noel Mendez, Comment, "Patent Infringers, Come Out with Your Hands Up!: Should the United States Criminalize Patent Infringement?," 6 *Buffalo Intellectual Property L.J.* 34, 63 (2008).

218. See Michael H. Davis, "Patent Politics," 56 *South Carolina L. Rev.* 337, 345 n.31 ("At times, ordinary patent infringement is characterized as theft").

219. Schechter and Thomas, *Intellectual Property*, at 461. As such, patent holders arguably have the greatest power to exclude infringers in that neither reverse engineering nor independent invention makes the use of patented technology permitted. Irina D. Manta, "The Puzzle of Criminal Sanctions for Intellectual Property Infringement," 24 *Harvard J. Law & Technology* 469 (2011).

220. John R. Allison and Mark A. Lemley, "Empirical Evidence on the Validity of Litigated Patents," 26 *AIPLA Q.J.* 185, 205 (1988).

221. Manta, "The Puzzle of Criminal Sanctions for Intellectual Property Infringement."

222. Direct infringement occurs where the infringer directly employs the patented invention itself. Indirect infringement occurs where the infringer encourages another person to infringe a patent. Stephen M. McJohn, *Intellectual Property* (New York: Aspen, 2d ed. 2006) 219.

223. 853 F.2d 1557 (9th Cir. 1988).

224. The facts and procedural history are described in *Kearns v. Chrysler Corp.*, 32 F.3d 1541 (Fed. Cir. 1994). See also John Seabrook, "A Flash of Genius," *The New Yorker* (Jan. 11, 1993).

225. Though it should be noted that, in the actual case, the infringement was found to be nonwillful.

226. See generally Schechter and Thomas, *Intellectual Property*, at 540; 17 U.S.C. § 1051.

227. The federal law of trademark is laid out in 15 U.S.C. § 1052 (purpose is to identify and distinguish goods and services), § 1053 (service marks), § 1059 (term of mark and renewal), § 1127 (goods).

228. 15 U.S.C. § 1114.

229. Peñalver and Katyal, *Property Outlaws,* at 41.

230. 18 U.S.C. § 2320.

231. Schechter and Thomas, *Intellectual Property,* at 677; David J. Goldstone and Peter J. Toren, "The Criminalization of Trademark Counterfeiting," 31 *Connecticut L. Rev.* 1 (1998).

232. See, e.g., Fred S. McChesney, "Deception, Trademark Infringement and the Lanham Act: A Property-Rights Reconciliation," 78 *Virginia L. Rev.* 49, 54 (1992) ("Trademark infringement . . . is essentially theft. Rather than negotiate for a license to use the trademark, the guilty defendant has simply taken it."); Pyun, "Legislative Update," at 379; John Grimm et al., "Intellectual Property Crimes," 47 *American Criminal L. Rev.* 741, 757 n.124 (2010).

233. 710 F.2d 1480 (11th Cir. 1983), *cert. denied,* 465 U.S. 1102 (1984).

234. Cf. Landes and Posner, "Trademark Law: An Economic Perspective," 30 *J. Law & Economics* 265, 274 (1987) (a "trademark is not a public good; it has social value only when used to mark a single brand").

235. Thomas J. McCarthy, *McCarthy on Trademarks and Unfair Competition,* § 12.1 (Eagan, MN: Thomson/West, 4th ed. 2007).

236. *Bimbo Bakeries USA, Inc. v. Botticella,* 613 F.3d 102 (3d Cir. 2010); William Neuman, "A Man with Muffin Secrets, but No Job with Them," *N.Y. Times* (Aug. 6, 2010), http://www.nytimes.com/2010/08 /07/business/07muffin.html?scp=1&sq=english%20muffins&st=cse.

237. Restatement (Third) of Unfair Competition § 39.

238. Schechter and Thomas, *Intellectual Property,* at 531.

239. Trade secret cases of this sort resemble other "disloyalty crimes," such as accepting a bribe and trading on inside information obtained from the firm where one works, discussed in Green, *Lying, Cheating, and Stealing,* at 98–106, 203–205, 237–238.

240. Schechter and Thomas, *Intellectual Property,* at 533.

241. Restatement (Third) of Unfair Competition § 39 (1995); Uniform Trade Secrets Act § § 1–12, 14 U.L.A. 433 (1985); Restatement of Torts § § 757–759 (1939).

242. Economic Espionage Act of 1996, 18 U.S.C. § § 1831–1839. For commentary, see Geraldine Szott Moohr, "The Problematic Role of Criminal Law in Regulating Use of Information: The Case of the Economic Espionage Act," 80 *North Carolina L. Rev.* 853 (2002); James H. A. Pooley, Mark A. Lemley, and Peter J. Toren, "Understanding the Economic Espionage Act of 1996," 5 *Texas Intellectual Property L.J.* 177 (1997); Peter J. G. Toren, "The Prosecution of Trade Secrets Thefts Under Federal Law," 22 *Pepperdine L. Rev.* 59 (1994). Many

states also have criminal theft of trade secrets laws. See Eli Lederman, "Criminal Liability for Breach of Confidential Commercial Information," 38 *Emory L.J.* 921 (1989).

243. Moohr, "Problematic Role of Criminal Law in Regulating Use of Information," at 886–887.

244. Id. at 888–890.

245. See Pamela Samuelson, "Principles for Resolving Conflicts Between Trade Secrets and the First Amendment," 58 *Hastings L.J.* 777, 805–807 (2007).

246. See Robert G. Bone, "A New Look at Trade Secrets Law: Doctrine in Search of Justification," 86 *California L. Rev.* 241 (1998).

247. James W. Hill, "Trade Secrets, Unjust Enrichment, and the Classification of Obligations," 4 *Virginia J. Law & Technology* 2 (1999).

248. 467 U.S. 986, 1003 (1984) (noting that treating trade secrets as property "is consonant with a notion of 'property' that extends beyond land and tangible goods"). See also Richard A. Epstein, "The Constitutional Protection of Trade Secrets under the Takings Clause," 71 *University of Chicago L. Rev.* 57 (2004); Charles Tait Graves, "Trade Secrets as Property: Theory and Consequences," 15 *J. Intellectual Property L.* 39 (2007); Samuelson, "Principles for Resolving Conflicts between Trade Secrets and the First Amendment."

249. 18 U.S.C. § 1832.

250. Moohr, "Problematic Role of Criminal Law in Regulating Use of Information," at 894.

251. See Joshua Fairfield, "Virtual Property," 85 *Boston University Law Review* 1047, 1049–1050 (2005).

252. See, e.g., Lawrence Lessig, *Code and Other Law of Cyberspace* (New York: Basic Books, 1999) 122–141.

253. Fairfield, "Virtual Property," at 1049.

254. Id. at 1050–1051; Andrea Vanina Arias, Comment, "Life, Liberty, and the Pursuit of Swords and Armor: Regulating the Theft of Virtual Goods," 57 *Emory L.J.* 1301 (2008).

255. 337 F.3d 1024 (9th Cir. 2003).

256. Id. at 1030.

257. For what is apparently the first criminal conviction in a case of domain name theft, see Mary Pat Gallagher, "Internet Domain Name Theft Conviction May Be First in U.S." *New Jersey Law Journal* (Dec. 14, 2010) http://www.law.com/jsp/nj/PubArticleNJ.jsp?id=120247619659 4&slreturn=1&hbxlogin=1 (defendant pled guilty to stealing domain name *www.p2p.com* by hacking into account files on Web site domain

name registrar GoDaddy and altering the registration information to transfer ownership of the domain to himself).

258. "Stephen M. Cohen," *Wikipedia,* http://en.wikipedia.org/wiki /Stephen_M._Cohen.

259. E.g., *Playboy Enterprises, Inc. v. Chuckleberry Publishing, Inc.,* 687 F.2d 563 (2d Cir. 1982) (trademark infringement suit).

260. Arias, "Life, Liberty, and the Pursuit of Swords and Armor," at 1302. Thanks to Matt Grayson for helping me understand the workings of MMORPGS.

261. Allen Chein, Note, "A Practical Look at Virtual Property," 80 *St. John's L. Rev.* 1059, 1067 (2006).

262. Arias, "Life, Liberty, and the Pursuit of Swords and Armor," at 1302. See also Edward Castronova, "Virtual Worlds: A First-Hand Account of Markets and Society on the Cyberian Frontier," (CESifo Working Paper No. 618, Dec. 2001), available at http://papers.ssrn.com/sol3 /papers.cfm?abstract_id=294828 (documenting virtual economy of Sony's *Everquest* MMORPG).

263. Arias, "Life, Liberty, and the Pursuit of Virtual Swords," at 1307. See also John William Nelson, "The Virtual Property Problem: What Property Rights in Virtual Resources Might Look Like, How They Might Work, and Why They are a Bad Idea," 41 *McGeorge L. Rev.* 281, 297–303 (2010) (describing different modes of virtual theft).

264. Arias, "Life, Liberty, and the Pursuit of Virtual Swords," at 1307.

265. Silvia Spring, "Virtual Thievery," *Newsweek* (Dec. 11, 2006), http:// www.newsweek.com/2006/12/10/games-virtual-thievery.html.

266. See, e.g., Earnest Cavalli, "Police Refuse to Aid in Virtual Theft Case," *Wired* (Feb. 4, 2008), http://www.wired.com/gamelife/2008 /02/police-refuse-t/.

267. See Fairfield, "Virtual Property," at 1085–1088 (describing criminal proceedings in China and South Korea); Murad Ahmed, "Real-World Arrest for Man who Stole RuneScape Virtual Characters, *The Times* (Nov. 30, 2009) (arrest in England); Arias, "Life, Liberty, and the Pursuit of Virtual Swords," at 1343–1344 (arrests in Taiwan and the Netherlands).

268. See F. Gregory Lastowka and Dan Hunter, "The Law of the Virtual Worlds," 92 *California L. Rev.* 1, 31 (2004).

269. See Susan W. Brenner, "Fantasy Crimes: The Role of Criminal Law in Virtual Worlds," 11 *Vanderbilt J. Entertainment & Technology L.* 1, 72–73 (2008).

270. Cf. Dan M. Kahan, "Gentle Nudges Vs. Hard Shoves: Solving the Sticky Norms Problem" (2000) 67 *University of Chicago L. Rev.* 607

(referring to the problem of prevailing social norms that have not yet caught up to legislation).

271. Peñalver and Katyal, *Property Outlaws,* at 42.

272. Marshall and Duff, "Criminalization and Sharing Wrongs," at 13.

CONCLUSION

1. For further discussion of this point, see Stuart P. Green, "Prototype Theory and the Classification of Offenses in a Revised Model Penal Code: A General Approach to the Special Part," 4 *Buffalo Crim. L. Rev.* 301, 337 (2000).

2. Quoting Ashworth, *Principles of Criminal Law,* at 89–90.

3. See Pennington et al., "A Precise Model for Identity Theft Statutes," 46 *Crim. L. Bulletin* 5.

Index

Abagnale, Frank, 130
abandoned property, 87, 143, 177–79
academic culture, 222
Alldridge, Peter, 341n200
American Law Institute, 20–21
animals, theft of, 14, 113, 219–20
animus furandi, 17, 52, 84. *See also
mens rea*
Anthony of Padua, theft of
relic of, 35
anti-vivisectionists, theft by, 158
appropriation: as element of theft,
22, 38, 78–81; irreversibility of,
80–81. *See also* misappropriation
Argentine Criminal Code, 42
Ashworth, Andrew, 53, 119–20, 155,
158, 161
asportation, 9, 78, 187, 235
Assange, Julian, 239–40
assault, 87, 103–5, 119, 141–43, 169
Augustine (theft of pears), 163, 166
Auschwitz, theft of *Arbeit Macht Frei*
sign at, 35
Australia, theft law in, 39–40, 45,
86, 109
Australian Model Law Officers
Committee, 39
Austria, theft law in, 42

*Avia Group International, Inc. v. L.A.
Gear California, Inc.,* 258
Ayres, Ian, 196–99

bad check, passing, 58–64, 116,
129–30, 143, 148, 198–200
bandits, as heroes, 118
Becker, Lawrence, 145
Bennett, Dale, 20
Bennett, State v., 100
Bentham, Jeremy, 95, 99
Biblical law against stealing, 96,
308n81, 336n147
bicycles, theft of, x, 57–64, 76, 149,
191, 203
The Bicycle Thief (Vittorio De Sica),
76, 149
Black Act, 11, 15
blackmail, 12, 13, 50–51, 58–63, 116,
120; paradox, 319n185. *See also*
extortion
Blackstone, William, 230
blameworthiness. *See* retributivism
Blockburger v. United States, 51
"Body Stealing" law (New York),
215–16
Bok, Sissela, 321n208
Booker, Cory, 174